Deep Learning with PyTorch Step-by-Step: A Beginner's Guide

Volume III—Sequences & NLP

Daniel Voigt Godoy

Version 1.1.1

Deep Learning with PyTorch Step-by-Step: A Beginner's Guide

Volume III—Sequences & NLP

by Daniel Voigt Godoy

May 2021: First Edition

Revision History for the First Edition:

- 2021-05-18: v1.0
- 2021-12-15: v1.1
- 2022-02-12: v1.1.1

For more information, please send an email to contact @ dvgodoy.com

"*What I cannot create, I do not understand.*"

Richard P. Feynman

Table of Contents

Preface

If you're reading this, I probably don't need to tell you that deep learning is amazing and PyTorch is cool, right?

But I will tell you, briefly, how this series of books came to be. In 2016, I started teaching a class on machine learning with Apache Spark and, a couple of years later, another class on the fundamentals of machine learning.

At some point, I tried to find a blog post that would visually explain, in a clear and concise manner, the concepts behind binary cross-entropy so that I could show it to my students. Since I could not find any that fit my purpose, I decided to write one myself. Although I thought of it as a fairly basic topic, it turned out to be my most popular blog post[1]! My readers have welcomed the simple, straightforward, and conversational way I explained the topic.

Then, in 2019, I used the same approach for writing another blog post: "Understanding PyTorch with an example: a step-by-step tutorial."[2] Once again, I was amazed by the reaction from the readers!

It was their positive feedback that motivated me to write this series of books to help beginners start their journey into deep learning and PyTorch.

In the first volume, I cover the basics of gradient descent, the fundamentals of PyTorch, training linear and logistic regressions, evaluation metrics, and more. If you have absolutely no experience with PyTorch, this is your starting point.

The second volume is mostly focused on computer vision: deeper models and activation functions, convolutional neural networks, initialization schemes, schedulers, and transfer learning. If your goal is to learn about deep learning models for computer vision, and you're already comfortable training simple models in PyTorch, the second volume is the right one for you.

Then, this third volume focuses on all things sequence: recurrent neural networks and their variations, sequence-to-sequence models, attention, self-attention, and the Transformer architecture. The very last chapter of this volume is a crash course on natural language processing: from the basics of word tokenization all the way up to fine-tuning large models (BERT and GPT-2) using the HuggingFace library. This volume is more demanding than the other two, and you're going to enjoy it more if you already have a solid understanding of deep learning models.

These books are meant to be read in order, and, although they *can* be read independently, I strongly recommend you read them as the one, long book I originally wrote :-)

I hope you enjoy reading this series as much as I enjoyed writing it.

[1] https://bit.ly/2UW5iTg

[2] https://bit.ly/2TpzwxR

Acknowledgements

First and foremost, I'd like to thank YOU, my reader, for making this book possible. If it weren't for the amazing feedback I got from the thousands of readers of my blog post about PyTorch, I would have never mustered the strength to start *and finish* such a major undertaking as writing a 1,000-page book series!

I'd like to thank my good friends Jesús Martínez-Blanco (who managed to read absolutely *everything* that I wrote), Jakub Cieslik, Hannah Berscheid, Mihail Vieru, Ramona Theresa Steck, Mehdi Belayet Lincon, and António Góis for helping me out and dedicating a good chunk of their time to reading, proofing, and suggesting improvements to my drafts. I'm forever grateful for your support! I'd also like to thank my friend José Luis Lopez Pino for the initial push I needed to actually *start* writing this book.

Many thanks to my friends José Quesada and David Anderson for taking me as a student at the Data Science Retreat in 2015 and, later on, for inviting me to be a teacher there. That was the starting point of my career both as a data scientist and as teacher.

I'd also like to thank the PyTorch developers for developing such an amazing framework, and the teams from Leanpub and Towards Data Science for making it incredibly easy for content creators like me to share their work with the community.

Finally, I'd like to thank my wife, Jerusa, for always being supportive throughout the entire writing of this series of books, and for taking the time to read *every* single page in it :-)

About the Author

Daniel is a data scientist, developer, writer, and teacher. He has been teaching machine learning and distributed computing technologies at Data Science Retreat, the longest-running Berlin-based bootcamp, since 2016, helping more than 150 students advance their careers.

Daniel is also the main contributor of two Python packages: HandySpark[3] and DeepReplay.[4]

His professional background includes 20 years of experience working for companies in several industries: banking, government, fintech, retail, and mobility.

[3] https://github.com/dvgodoy/handyspark

[4] https://github.com/dvgodoy/deepreplay

Frequently Asked Questions (FAQ)

Why PyTorch?

First, coding in PyTorch is **fun** :-) Really, there is something to it that makes it very enjoyable to write code in. Some say it is because it is very **pythonic**, or maybe there is something else, who knows? I hope that, by the end of this book, you feel like that too!

Second, maybe there are even some *unexpected benefits* to your health—check Andrej Karpathy's tweet[5] about it!

Jokes aside, PyTorch is the **fastest-growing**[6] framework for developing deep learning models and it has a **huge ecosystem**.[7] That is, there are many *tools* and *libraries* developed on top of PyTorch. It is the **preferred framework**[8] in academia already and is making its way in the industry.

Several companies are already powered by PyTorch;[9] to name a few:

- **Facebook**: The company is the original developer of PyTorch, released in October 2016.
- **Tesla**: Watch Andrej Karpathy (AI director at Tesla) speak about "*how Tesla is using PyTorch to develop full self-driving capabilities for its vehicles.*"[10]
- **OpenAI**: In January 2020, OpenAI decided to standardize its deep learning framework on PyTorch.[11]
- **fastai**: fastai is a library[12] built on top of PyTorch to simplify model training and is used in its "*Practical Deep Learning for Coders*"[13] course. The fastai library is deeply connected to PyTorch and "*you can't become really proficient at using fastai if you don't know PyTorch well, too.*"
- **Uber**: The company is a significant contributor to PyTorch's ecosystem, having developed libraries like Pyro[14] (probabilistic programming) and Horovod[15] (a distributed training framework).
- **Airbnb**: PyTorch sits at the core of the company's dialog assistant for customer service.[16]

This series of books **aims to get you started with PyTorch** while giving you a **solid understanding of how it works**.

Why This Book?

If you're looking for a book where you can learn about deep learning and PyTorch without having to spend hours deciphering cryptic text and code, and one that's easy and enjoyable to read, this is it :-)

First, this is **not** a typical book: most tutorials *start* with some nice and pretty, but complex, task to illustrate how to use PyTorch. It may seem cool, but I believe it **distracts** you from the **main goal**: learning **how PyTorch works**. In this book, I present a **structured**, **incremental**, and **from-first-principles** approach to learn PyTorch.

Second, this is **not** a **formal book** in any way: I am writing this book **as if I were having a conversation with you**, the reader. I will ask you **questions** (and give you answers shortly afterward), and I will also make (silly) **jokes**.

My job here is to make you **understand** the topic, so I will **avoid fancy mathematical notation** as much as possible and **spell it out in plain English**.

In this third book of the *Deep Learning with PyTorch Step-by-Step* series, I will **guide** you through the **development** of many models in PyTorch, showing you why PyTorch makes it much **easier** and more **intuitive** to build models in Python: *recurrent neural networks*, *attention*, *Transformers*, *embeddings*, and much, much more.

We will build, **step-by-step**, not only the models themselves but also your **understanding** as I show you both the **reasoning** behind the code and **how to avoid** some **common pitfalls** and **errors** along the way.

There is yet another advantage of **focusing on the basics**: this book is likely to have a **longer shelf life**. It is fairly common for technical books, especially those focusing on cutting-edge technology, to become outdated quickly. Hopefully, this is not going to be the case here, since the **underlying mechanics are not changing and neither are the concepts**. It is expected that some syntax changes over time, but I do not see backward compatibility-breaking changes coming anytime soon.

One more thing: If you hadn't noticed already, I **really** like to make use of **visual cues**, that is, **bold** and *italic* highlights. I firmly believe this helps the reader to **grasp** the **key ideas** I am trying to convey in a sentence more easily. You can find more on that in the section "**How to Read This Book.**"

Who Should Read This Book?

I wrote this book for **beginners in general**—not only PyTorch beginners. Every now and then, I will spend some time explaining some **fundamental concepts** that I believe are **essential** to have a proper **understanding of what's going on in the code**.

The best example is **gradient descent**, covered in the first volume, which most people are familiar with at some level. Maybe you know its general idea, perhaps you've seen it in Andrew Ng's Machine Learning course, or maybe you've even **computed some partial derivatives yourself**!

In real life, the **mechanics** of gradient descent will be **handled automatically by PyTorch** (uh, spoiler alert!). But, I will walk you through it anyway, because lots of **elements in the code**, as well as **choices of hyper-parameters** (learning rate, mini-batch size, etc.), can be much more easily understood if you know **where they come from**.

Maybe you already know some of these concepts well: If this is the case, you can simply *skip* them, since I've made these explanations as *independent* as possible from the rest of the content.

But **I want to make sure everyone is on the same page**, so, if you have just heard about a given concept or if you are unsure if you have entirely understood it, these explanations are for you.

What Do I Need to Know?

This is a book for beginners, so I am assuming as **little prior knowledge** as possible; as mentioned in the previous section, I will take the time to explain fundamental concepts whenever needed.

That being said, this is what I expect from you, the reader:

- to be able to code in **Python** (if you are familiar with object-oriented programming [OOP], even better)
- to be able to work with PyData stack (**numpy**, **matplotlib**, and **pandas**) and **Jupyter notebooks**
- to be familiar with some basic concepts used in **machine learning**, like:
  - supervised learning: regression and classification
  - loss functions for regression and classification (mean squared error, cross-entropy, etc.)
  - training-validation-test split
  - underfitting and overfitting (bias-variance trade-off)
- to have read Volumes I and II, or to have a solid understanding of deep learning models and PyTorch

Even so, I am still briefly touching on **some** of these topics, but I need to draw a line somewhere; otherwise, this book would be gigantic!

How to Read This Book

Since this book is a **beginner's guide**, it is meant to be read **sequentially**, as ideas and concepts are progressively built. The same holds true for the **code** inside the book—you should be able to *reproduce* all outputs, provided you execute the chunks of code in the same order as they are introduced.

This book is **visually** different than other books: As I've mentioned already in the "**Why This Book?**" section, I **really** like to make use of **visual cues**. Although this is not, *strictly speaking*, a **convention**, this is how you can interpret those cues:

- I use **bold** to highlight what I believe to be the **most relevant words** in a sentence or paragraph, while *italicized* words are considered *important* too (not important enough to be bold, though)
- *Variables*, *coefficients*, and *parameters* in general, are *italicized*
- `Classes` and `methods` are written in a `monospaced` font

- Every **code cell** is followed by *another* cell showing the corresponding **outputs** (if any)
- **All code** presented in the book is available at its **official repository** on GitHub:

https://github.com/dvgodoy/PyTorchStepByStep

Code cells with **titles** are an important piece of the workflow:

Title Goes Here

```
# Whatever is being done here is going to impact OTHER code
# cells. Besides, most cells have COMMENTS explaining what
# is happening
x = [1., 2., 3.]
print(x)
```

If there is any output to the code cell, titled or not, there *will* be another code cell depicting the corresponding **output** so you can *check* if you successfully reproduced it or not.

Output

```
[1.0, 2.0, 3.0]
```

Some code cells **do not** have titles—running them does not affect the workflow:

```
# Those cells illustrate HOW TO CODE something, but they are
# NOT part of the main workflow
dummy = ['a', 'b', 'c']
print(dummy[::-1])
```

But even these cells have their outputs shown!

Output

```
['c', 'b', 'a']
```

I use asides to communicate a variety of things, according to the corresponding icon:

WARNING

Potential **problems** or things to **look out** for.

TIP

Key aspects I really want you to **remember**.

INFORMATION

Important information to **pay attention** to.

IMPORTANT

Really important information to **pay attention** to.

TECHNICAL

Technical aspects of **parameterization** or **inner workings of algorithms**.

QUESTION AND ANSWER

Asking myself **questions** (pretending to be you, the reader) and answering them, either in the same block or shortly after.

DISCUSSION

Really brief discussion on a concept or topic.

LATER

Important topics that will be covered in more detail later.

SILLY

Jokes, puns, memes, quotes from movies.

What's Next?

It's time to **set up** an environment for your learning journey using the **Setup Guide**.

[5] https://bit.ly/2MQoYRo

[6] https://bit.ly/37uZgLB

[7] https://pytorch.org/ecosystem/

[8] https://bit.ly/2MTN0Lh

[9] https://bit.ly/2UFHFve

[10] https://bit.ly/2XXJkyo

[11] https://openai.com/blog/openai-pytorch/

[12] https://docs.fast.ai/

[13] https://course.fast.ai/

[14] http://pyro.ai/

[15] https://github.com/horovod/horovod

[16] https://bit.ly/30CPhm5

Setup Guide

Official Repository

This book's official repository is available on GitHub:

https://github.com/dvgodoy/PyTorchStepByStep

It contains **one Jupyter notebook** for every **chapter** in this book. Each notebook contains **all the code shown** in its corresponding chapter, and you should be able to **run its cells in sequence** to get the **same outputs**, as shown in the book. I strongly believe that being able to **reproduce the results** brings **confidence** to the reader.

Even though I did my best to ensure the **reproducibility** of the results, you may **still** find some minor differences in your outputs (especially during model training). Unfortunately, completely reproducible results are not guaranteed across PyTorch releases, and results may not be reproducible between CPU and GPU executions, even when using identical seeds.[17]

Environment

There are **three options** for you to run the Jupyter notebooks:

- Google Colab (*https://colab.research.google.com*)
- Binder (*https://mybinder.org*)
- Local Installation

Let's briefly explore the **pros** and **cons** of each of these options.

Google Colab

Google Colab "*allows you to write and execute Python in your browser, with zero configuration required, free access to GPUs and easy sharing.*"[18].

You can easily **load notebooks directly from GitHub** using Colab's special URL (*https://colab.research.google.com/github/*). Just type in the GitHub's user or organization (like mine, `dvgodoy`), and it will show you a list of all its public repositories (like this book's, `PyTorchStepByStep`).

After choosing a repository, it will list the available notebooks and corresponding links to open them in a new browser tab.

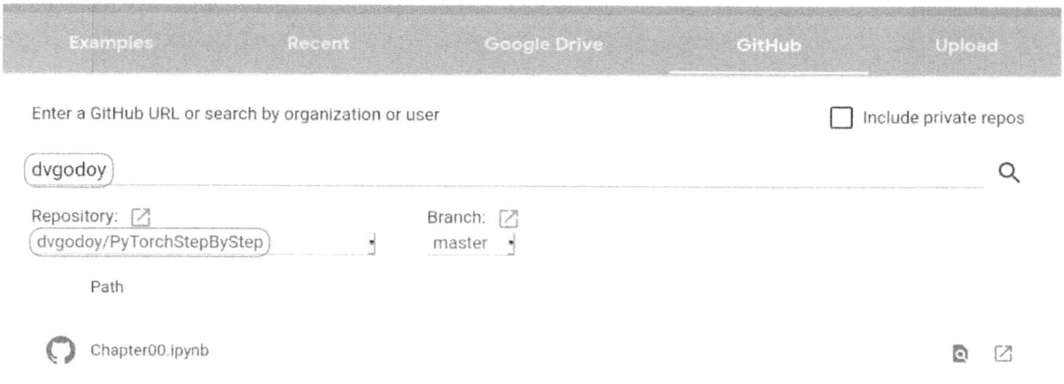

Figure S.1 - Google Colab's special URL

You also get access to a **GPU**, which is very useful to train deep learning models **faster**. More important, if you **make changes** to the notebook, Google Colab will **keep them**. The whole setup is very convenient; the only **cons** I can think of are:

- You need to be **logged in** to a Google account.
- You need to (re)install Python packages that are not part of Google Colab's default configuration.

Binder

Binder "*allows you to create custom computing environments that can be shared and used by many remote users.*"[19]

You can also **load notebooks directly from GitHub**, but the process is slightly different. Binder will create something like a *virtual machine* (technically, it is a container, but let's leave it at that), clone the repository, and start Jupyter. This allows you to have access to **Jupyter's home page** in your browser, just like you would if you were running it locally, but everything is running in a JupyterHub server on their end.

Just go to Binder's site (*https://mybinder.org/*) and type in the URL to the GitHub repository you want to explore (for instance, `https://github.com/dvgodoy/PyTorchStepByStep`) and click on **Launch**. It will take a couple of minutes to build the image and open Jupyter's home page.

You can also **launch Binder** for this book's repository directly using the following link: *https://mybinder.org/v2/gh/dvgodoy/PyTorchStepByStep/master*.

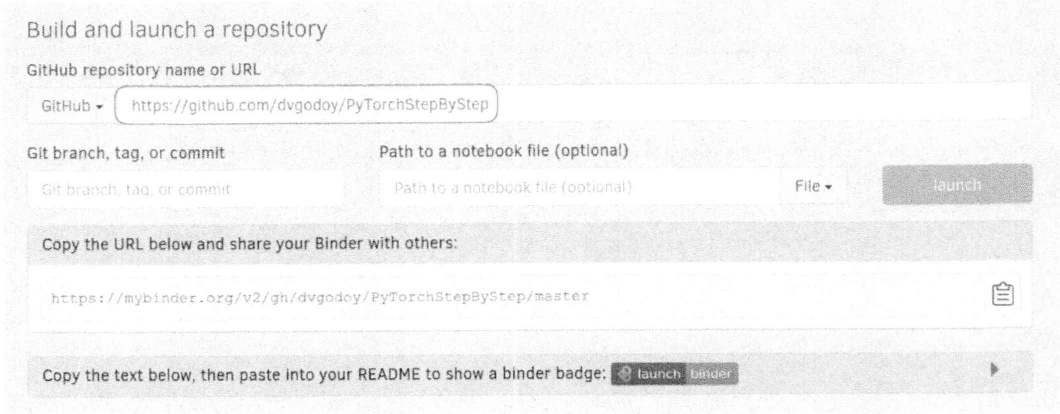

Figure S.2 - Binder's page

Binder is very convenient since it **does not require a prior setup** of any kind. Any Python packages needed to successfully run the environment are likely installed during launch (if provided by the author of the repository).

On the other hand, it may **take time** to start, and it **does not keep your changes** after your session expires (so, make sure you **download** any notebooks you modify).

Local Installation

This option will give you more **flexibility**, but it will require **more effort to set up**. I encourage you to try setting up your own environment. It may seem daunting at first, but you can surely accomplish it by following **seven easy steps**:

Checklist

- [ ] 1. Install **Anaconda**.
- [ ] 2. Create and activate a **virtual environment**.
- [ ] 3. Install **PyTorch** package.
- [ ] 4. Install **TensorBoard** package.
- [ ] 5. Install **GraphViz** software and **TorchViz** package **(optional)**.
- [ ] 6. Install **git** and **clone** the repository.
- [ ] 7. Start **Jupyter** notebook.

1. Anaconda

If you don't have **Anaconda's Individual Edition**[20] installed yet, this would be a good time to do it. It is a convenient way to start since it contains most of the Python libraries a data scientist will ever need to develop and train models.

Please follow the **installation instructions** for your OS:

- Windows (*https://docs.anaconda.com/anaconda/install/windows/*)
- macOS (*https://docs.anaconda.com/anaconda/install/mac-os/*)
- Linux (*https://docs.anaconda.com/anaconda/install/linux/*)

Make sure you choose **Python 3.X** version since Python 2 was discontinued in January 2020.

After installing Anaconda, it is time to create an **environment**.

2. Conda (Virtual) Environments

Virtual environments are a convenient way to isolate Python installations associated with different projects.

"What is an environment?"

It is pretty much a **replication of Python itself and some (or all) of its libraries**, so, effectively, you'll end up with multiple Python installations on your computer.

"Why can't I just use one single Python installation for everything?"

With so many independently developed Python **libraries**, each having many different **versions** and each version having various **dependencies** (on other libraries), **things can get out of hand** real quick.

It is beyond the scope of this guide to debate these issues, but take my word for it (or Google it!)—you'll benefit a great deal if you pick up the habit of **creating a different environment for every project you start working on**.

"How do I create an environment?"

First, you need to choose a **name** for your environment :-) Let's call ours `pytorchbook` (or anything else you find easy to remember). Then, you need to open a **terminal** (in Ubuntu) or **Anaconda Prompt** (in Windows or macOS) and type the following command:

```
$ conda create -n pytorchbook anaconda
```

The command above creates a Conda environment named `pytorchbook` and includes **all Anaconda packages** in it (time to get a coffee, it will take a while...). If you want to learn more about creating and using Conda environments, please check Anaconda's "Managing Environments"[21] user guide.

Did it finish creating the environment? Good! It is time to **activate it**, meaning, making **that Python installation** the one to be used now. In the same terminal (or Anaconda prompt), just type:

```
$ conda activate pytorchbook
```

Your prompt should look like this (if you're using Linux):

```
(pytorchbook)$
```

or like this (if you're using Windows):

```
(pytorchbook)C:\>
```

Done! You are using a **brand new Conda environment** now. You'll need to **activate it** every time you open a new terminal, or, if you're a Windows or macOS user, you can open the corresponding Anaconda prompt (it will show up as **Anaconda Prompt (pytorchbook)**, in our case), which will have it activated from the start.

IMPORTANT: From now on, I am assuming you'll activate the `pytorchbook` environment every time you open a terminal or Anaconda prompt. Further installation steps **must** be executed inside the environment.

3. PyTorch

PyTorch is the coolest **deep learning framework**, just in case you skipped the introduction.

It is "*an open source machine learning framework that accelerates the path from research prototyping to production deployment.*"[22] Sounds good, right? Well, I probably don't have to convince you at this point :-)

It is time to install the star of the show :-) We can go straight to the **Start Locally** (*https://pytorch.org/get-started/locally/*) section of PyTorch's website, and it will automatically select the options that best suit your local environment, and it will show you the **command to run**.

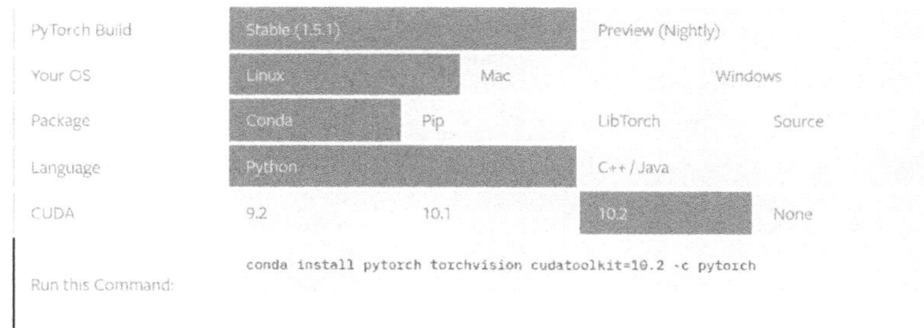
START LOCALLY
Select your preferences and run the install command. Stable represents the most currently tested and supported version of PyTorch. This should be suitable for many users. Preview is available if you want the latest, not fully tested and supported, 1.5 builds that are generated nightly. Please ensure that you have met the prerequisites below (e.g., numpy), depending on your package manager. Anaconda is our recommended package manager since it installs all dependencies. You can also install previous versions of PyTorch. Note that LibTorch is only available for C++.
PyTorch Build
Stable (1.5.1)
Preview (Nightly)
Your OS
Linux
Mac
Windows
Package
Conda
Pip
LibTorch
Source
Language
Python
C++ / Java
CUDA
9.2
10.1
10.2
None
Run this Command:
conda install pytorch torchvision cudatoolkit=10.2 -c pytorch

Figure S.3 - PyTorch's Start Locally page

Some of these options are given:

- PyTorch Build: Always select a **Stable** version.
- Package: I am assuming you're using **Conda**.
- Language: Obviously, **Python**.

So, two options remain: **Your OS** and **CUDA**.

"*What is CUDA?*" you ask.

Using GPU / CUDA

CUDA "*is a parallel computing platform and programming model developed by NVIDIA for general computing on graphical processing units (GPUs).*"[23]

If you have a **GPU** in your computer (likely a *GeForce* graphics card), you can leverage its power to train deep learning models **much faster** than using a CPU. In this case, you should choose a PyTorch installation that includes CUDA support.

This is not enough, though: If you haven't done so yet, you need to install up-to-date drivers, the CUDA Toolkit, and the CUDA Deep Neural Network library (cuDNN). Unfortunately, more detailed installation instructions for CUDA are outside the scope of this book.

The **advantage** of using a GPU is that it allows you to **iterate faster** and **experiment with more-complex models and a more extensive range of hyper-parameters**.

In my case, I use **Linux**, and I have a **GPU** with CUDA version 10.2 installed. So I would run the following command in the **terminal** (after activating the environment):

```
(pytorchbook)$ conda install pytorch torchvision\
cudatoolkit=10.2 -c pytorch
```

Using CPU

If you **do not** have a **GPU**, you should choose **None** for CUDA.

"*Would I be able to run the code* ***without*** *a GPU?*" you ask.

Sure! The code and the examples in this book were designed to allow **all readers** to follow them promptly. Some examples may demand a bit more computing power, but we are talking about a **couple of minutes** in a CPU, not hours. If you do not have a GPU, **don't worry**! Besides, you can always use Google Colab if you need to use a GPU for a while!

If I had a **Windows** computer, and **no GPU**, I would have to run the following command in the **Anaconda prompt (pytorchbook)**:

```
(pytorchbook) C:\> conda install pytorch torchvision cpuonly\
 -c pytorch
```

Installing CUDA

CUDA: Installing drivers for a GeForce graphics card, NVIDIA's cuDNN, and CUDA Toolkit can be challenging and is highly dependent on which model you own and which OS you use.

For installing GeForce's drivers, go to GeForce's website (*https://www.geforce.com/drivers*), select your OS and the model of your graphics card, and follow the installation instructions.

For installing NVIDIA's CUDA Deep Neural Network library (cuDNN), you need to register at *https://developer.nvidia.com/cudnn*.

For installing CUDA Toolkit (*https://developer.nvidia.com/cuda-toolkit*), please follow instructions for your OS and choose a local installer or executable file.

macOS: If you're a macOS user, please beware that PyTorch's binaries **DO NOT** support **CUDA**, meaning you'll need to install PyTorch **from source** if you want to use your GPU. This is a somewhat **complicated** process (as described in *https://github.com/pytorch/pytorch#from-source*), so, if you don't feel like doing it, you can choose to proceed **without CUDA**, and you'll still be able to execute the code in this book promptly.

4. TensorBoard

TensorBoard is TensorFlow's **visualization toolkit**, and "*provides the visualization and tooling needed for machine learning experimentation.*"[24]

TensorBoard is a powerful tool, and we can use it even if we are developing models in PyTorch. Luckily, you don't need to install the whole TensorFlow to get it; you can easily **install TensorBoard alone** using **Conda**. You just need to run this command in your **terminal** or **Anaconda prompt** (again, after activating the environment):

```
(pytorchbook)$ conda install -c conda-forge tensorboard
```

5. GraphViz and Torchviz (optional)

This step is optional, mostly because the installation of GraphViz can sometimes be *challenging* (especially on Windows). If for any reason you do not succeed in installing it correctly, or if you decide to skip this installation step, you will still be **able to execute the code in this series of books** (except for a couple of cells that generate images of a model's structure in the "Dynamic Computation Graph" section of Chapter 1 in Volume I).

GraphViz is an open source graph visualization software. It is "*a way of representing structural information as diagrams of abstract graphs and networks.*"[25]

We need to install GraphViz to use **TorchViz**, a neat package that allows us to visualize a model's structure. Please check the **installation instructions** for your OS at *https://www.graphviz.org/download/*.

If you are using Windows, please use the **GraphViz's Windows Package** installer at *https://graphviz.gitlab.io/_pages/Download/windows/graphviz-2.38.msi*.

You also need to add GraphViz to the PATH (environment variable) in Windows. Most likely, you can find the GraphViz executable file at `C:\ProgramFiles(x86)\Graphviz2.38\bin`. Once you find it, you need to set or change the PATH accordingly, adding GraphViz's location to it.

For more details on how to do that, please refer to "How to Add to Windows PATH Environment Variable."[26]

For additional information, you can also check the "How to Install Graphviz Software"[27] guide.

After installing GraphViz, you can install the **torchviz**[28] package. This package is **not** part of Anaconda Distribution Repository[29] and is only available at **PyPI**[30], the Python Package Index, so we need to `pip install` it.

Once again, open a **terminal** or **Anaconda prompt** and run this command (just once more: after activating the environment):

```
(pytorchbook)$ pip install torchviz
```

To check your GraphViz / TorchViz installation, you can try the Python code below:

```
(pytorchbook)$ python

Python 3.7.5 (default, Oct 25 2019, 15:51:11)
[GCC 7.3.0] :: Anaconda, Inc. on linux
Type "help", "copyright", "credits" or "license" for more
information.
>>> import torch
>>> from torchviz import make_dot
>>> v = torch.tensor(1.0, requires_grad=True)
>>> make_dot(v)
```

If everything is **working correctly**, you should see something like this:

Output

```
<graphviz.dot.Digraph object at 0x7ff540c56f50>
```

If you get an **error** of any kind (the one below is pretty common), it means there is still some kind of **installation issue** with GraphViz.

Output

```
ExecutableNotFound: failed to execute ['dot', '-Tsvg'], make
sure the Graphviz executables are on your systems' PATH
```

6. Git

It is *way* beyond this guide's scope to introduce you to version control and its most popular tool: `git`. If you are familiar with it already, great, you can skip this section altogether!

Otherwise, I'd recommend you to learn more about it; it will **definitely** be useful for you later down the line. In the meantime, I will show you the bare minimum so you can use `git` to **clone the repository** containing all code used in this book and get your **own, local copy** of it to modify and experiment with as you please. First, you need to install it. So, head to its downloads page (*https://git-scm.com/downloads*) and follow instructions for your OS. Once the installation is complete, please open a **new terminal** or **Anaconda prompt** (it's OK to close the previous one). In the new terminal or Anaconda prompt, you should be able to **run `git` commands**.

To clone this book's repository, you only need to run:

```
(pytorchbook)$ git clone https://github.com/dvgodoy/\
PyTorchStepByStep.git
```

The command above will create a `PyTorchStepByStep` folder that contains a local copy of everything available on GitHub's repository.

conda install vs pip install

Although they may seem equivalent at first sight, you should **prefer `conda install`** over `pip install` when working with Anaconda and its virtual environments.

This is because `conda install` is sensitive to the active virtual environment: The package will be installed only for that environment. If you use `pip install`, and `pip` itself is not installed in the active environment, it will fall back to the **global `pip`**, and you definitely **do not** want that.

Why not? Remember the problem with **dependencies** I mentioned in the virtual environment section? That's why! The `conda` installer assumes it handles all packages that are part of its repository and keeps track of the complicated network of dependencies among them (to learn more about this, check the "Install with Conda"[31] article).

To learn more about the differences between `conda` and `pip`, read "Understanding Conda and Pip."[32]

As a rule, first try to `conda install` a given package and, only if it does not exist there, fall back to `pip install`, as we did with `torchviz`.

7. Jupyter

After cloning the repository, navigate to the `PyTorchStepByStep` folder and, **once inside it, start Jupyter** on your terminal or Anaconda prompt:

```
(pytorchbook)$ jupyter notebook
```

This will open your browser, and you will see **Jupyter's home page** containing the repository's notebooks and code.

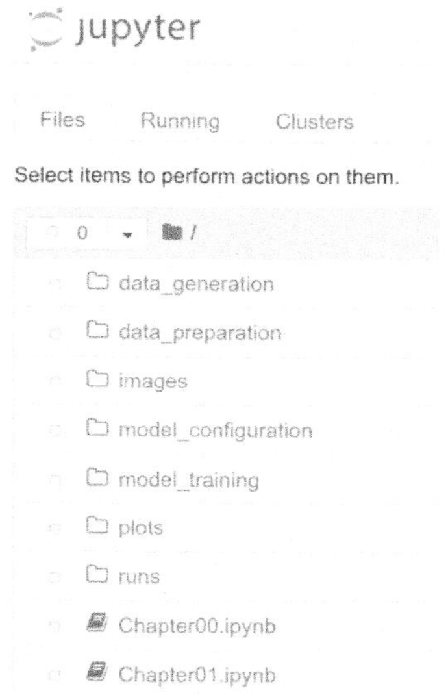

Figure S.4 - Running Jupyter

Moving On

Regardless of which of the three environments you chose, now you are ready to move on and tackle the development of your first PyTorch model, **step-by-step**!

[17] https://pytorch.org/docs/stable/notes/randomness.html

[18] https://colab.research.google.com/notebooks/intro.ipynb

[19] https://mybinder.readthedocs.io/en/latest/

[20] https://www.anaconda.com/products/individual

[21] https://bit.ly/2MVk0CM

[22] https://pytorch.org/

[23] https://developer.nvidia.com/cuda-zone

[24] https://www.tensorflow.org/tensorboard

[25] https://www.graphviz.org/

[26] https://bit.ly/3fIwYA5

[27] https://bit.ly/30Ayct3

[28] https://github.com/szagoruyko/pytorchviz

[29] https://docs.anaconda.com/anaconda/packages/pkg-docs/

[30] https://pypi.org/

[31] https://bit.ly/37onBTt

[32] https://bit.ly/2AAh8J5

The StepByStep Class

Spoilers

In this chapter, we will:

- define a **class** to handle **model training**
- implement the **constructor** method
- understand the difference between **public**, **protected**, and **private** methods of a class
- **integrate the code** developed in the first volume into the `StepByStep` class
- **instantiate** our class and use it to run a **classy** pipeline

This chapter is an adaptation of **Chapter 2.1** from **Volume I**.

If you have already read **Volume I—Fundamentals** of ***Deep Learning with PyTorch Step-by-Step***, you can either choose to skip this chapter altogether or use it as a review of the model training part.

Jupyter Notebook

The Jupyter notebook corresponding to this chapter[33] is part of the official ***Deep Learning with PyTorch Step-by-Step*** repository on GitHub. You can also run it directly in **Google Colab**[34].

If you're using a *local installation*, open your terminal or Anaconda prompt and navigate to the `PyTorchStepByStep` folder you cloned from GitHub. Then, *activate* the `pytorchbook` environment and run `jupyter notebook`:

```
$ conda activate pytorchbook

(pytorchbook)$ jupyter notebook
```

If you're using Jupyter's default settings, `http://localhost:8888/notebooks/Chapter02.1.ipynb` should open Chapter 2.1's notebook. If not, just click on `Chapter02.1.ipynb` on your Jupyter's home page.

Imports

For the sake of organization, all libraries needed throughout the code used in any given chapter are imported at its very beginning. For this chapter, we'll need the following imports:

```
import numpy as np
import datetime

import torch
import torch.optim as optim
import torch.nn as nn
import torch.functional as F
from torch.utils.data import DataLoader, TensorDataset, random_split
from torch.utils.tensorboard import SummaryWriter

import matplotlib.pyplot as plt
%matplotlib inline
plt.style.use('fivethirtyeight')
```

Going Classy

Our training pipeline is going to be divided into **three steps**: *data preparation, model configuration*, and *model training*. The `StepByStep` class was designed to handle most aspects related to the **model training** part, namely, computing gradients, updating parameters, mini-batch handling, etc. In this chapter, we'll build this class from scratch, so we can use it for training our models later on, allowing us to focus on the models themselves.

I am assuming you have a *working knowledge* of **object-oriented programming (OOP)** in order to benefit the most from this chapter. If that's not the case, now is the time to follow tutorials like Real Python's "Object-Oriented Programming (OOP) in Python 3"[35] and "Supercharge Your Classes With Python super()."[36]

The Class

Let's start by defining our class with a rather unoriginal name: `StepByStep`. We're starting it from scratch: Either we don't specify a parent class, or we inherit it from the fundamental `object` class. I personally prefer the latter, so our class definition looks like this:

```
# A completely empty (and useless) class
class StepByStep(object):
    pass
```

Boring, right? Let's make it more interesting.

The Constructor

"From where do we start building a class?"

That would be the **constructor**, the `__init__(self)` method that we've already seen a couple of times when handling both **model** and **dataset** classes in Volume I.

The constructor **defines the parts that make up the class**. These parts are the **attributes** of the class. Typical attributes include:

- **arguments** provided by the user
- **placeholders** for other objects that are not available at the moment of creation (pretty much like *delayed* arguments)
- **variables** we may want to keep track of
- **functions** that are dynamically built using some of the arguments and **higher-order functions**

Let's see how each of these applies to our problem.

Arguments

Let's start with the **arguments**, the part that **needs to be specified by the user**. We know that the training loop stays the same, regardless of which **optimizer**, **loss**, or even **model** we're using.

So, these **three** elements, **optimizer**, **loss**, and **model**, will be our main **arguments**. The user **needs** to specify these; we can't figure them out on our own.

But there is one more piece of information needed: the **device** to be used for training the model. Instead of asking the user to supply it, we'll *automatically check* if there is a GPU available and fall back to a CPU if there isn't. But we still want to give the user a chance to use a different device (whatever the reason may be); thus, we add a very simple method (conveniently named **to()**) that allows the user to specify a device.

Our constructor (`__init__()`) method will initially look like this:

```
class StepByStep(object):
    def __init__(self, model, loss_fn, optimizer):
        # Here we define the attributes of our class
        # We start by storing the arguments as attributes
        # to use later
        self.model = model
        self.loss_fn = loss_fn
        self.optimizer = optimizer
        self.device = 'cuda' if torch.cuda.is_available() else 'cpu'
        # Let's send the model to the specified device right away
        self.model.to(self.device)

    def to(self, device):
        # This method allows the user to specify a different device
        # It sets the corresponding attribute (to be used later in
        # the mini-batches) and sends the model to the device
        try:
            self.device = device
            self.model.to(self.device)
        except RuntimeError:
            self.device = ('cuda' if torch.cuda.is_available()
                           else 'cpu')
            print(f"Couldn't send it to {device}, \
                    sending it to {self.device} instead.")
            self.model.to(self.device)
```

Placeholders

Next, let's tackle the **placeholders** or *delayed arguments*. We expect the user to **eventually** provide **some** of these, as they are *not necessarily required*. There are another three elements that fall into that category: **train and validation data loaders** and a **summary writer** to interface with TensorBoard.

We need to append the following code to the constructor method above (I am not reproducing the rest of the method here for the sake of simplicity; in the Jupyter notebook you'll find the full code):

```
        # These attributes are defined here, but since they are
        # not available at the moment of creation, we keep them None
        self.train_loader = None
        self.val_loader = None
        self.writer = None
```

The **train data loader** is obviously required. How could we possibly train a model without it?

*"Why don't we make the train data loader an **argument** then?"*

Conceptually speaking, the data loader (and the dataset it contains) is **not** part of the model. It is the **input** we use to train the model. Since we **can** specify a model without it, it shouldn't be made an argument of our class.

In other words, our `StepByStep` class is **defined by a particular combination of arguments** (model, loss function, and optimizer), which can then be used to perform model training on any (compatible) dataset.

The **validation data loader** is not required (although it is recommended), and the **summary writer** is definitely optional.

The class should implement **methods** to allow the user to supply those at a later time (both methods should be placed *inside* the `StepByStep` class, after the constructor method):

```
    def set_loaders(self, train_loader, val_loader=None):
        # This method allows the user to define which train_loader
        # (and val_loader, optionally) to use
        # Both loaders are then assigned to attributes of the class
        # So they can be referred to later
        self.train_loader = train_loader
        self.val_loader = val_loader

    def set_tensorboard(self, name, folder='runs'):
        # This method allows the user to create a SummaryWriter to
        # interface with TensorBoard
        suffix = datetime.datetime.now().strftime('%Y%m%d%H%M%S')
        self.writer = SummaryWriter(f'{folder}/{name}_{suffix}')
```

"*Why do we need to specify a default value to the* `val_loader`*? Its placeholder value is already* `None`."

Since the validation loader is **optional**, setting a **default value** for a particular argument in the method's definition frees the user from having to provide that argument when calling the method. The best default value, in our case, is the same value we chose when specifying the placeholder for the validation loader: `None`.

Variables

Then, there are **variables** we may want to keep track of. Typical examples are the **number of epochs**, and the training and validation **losses**. These variables are likely to be computed and updated internally by the class.

We need to **append the following code to the constructor** method (like we did with the placeholders):

```
        # These attributes are going to be computed internally
        self.losses = []
        self.val_losses = []
        self.total_epochs = 0
```

"*Can't we just set these variables whenever we use them for the first time?*"

Yes, we could, and we would probably get away with it just fine since our class is quite simple. As classes grow more complex, though, it may lead to problems. So, it is **best practice** to **define all attributes of a class in the constructor method**.

Functions

For convenience, sometimes it is useful to create **attributes** that are **functions**, which will be called somewhere else inside the class. In our case, we can create both `train_step_fn()` and `val_step_fn()` attributes using two higher-order functions, `_make_train_step_fn()` and `_make_val_step_fn()`, respectively. Both of them use a model, a loss function, and an optimizer as arguments, and all of those are already known attributes of our `StepByStep` class at construction time.

Step Methods

```
def _make_train_step_fn(self):
    # This method does not need ARGS... it can use directly
    # the attributes: self.model, self.loss_fn and self.optimizer

    # Builds function that performs a step in the train loop
    def perform_train_step_fn(x, y):
        # Sets model to TRAIN mode
        self.model.train()

        # Step 1 - Computes model's predicted output - forward pass
        yhat = self.model(x)
        # Step 2 - Computes the loss
        loss = self.loss_fn(yhat, y)
        # Step 3 - Computes gradients for "b" and "w" parameters
        loss.backward()
        # Step 4 - Updates parameters using gradients and the
        # learning rate
        self.optimizer.step()
        self.optimizer.zero_grad()

        # Returns the loss
        return loss.item()

    # Returns the function that will be called inside the train loop
    return perform_train_step_fn

def _make_val_step_fn(self):
```

```
    # Builds function that performs a step in the validation loop
    def perform_val_step_fn(x, y):
        # Sets model to EVAL mode
        self.model.eval()

        # Step 1 - Computes model's predicted output - forward pass
        yhat = self.model(x)
        # Step 2 - Computes the loss
        loss = self.loss_fn(yhat, y)
        # There is no need to compute Steps 3 and 4,
        # since we don't update parameters during evaluation
        return loss.item()

    return perform_val_step_fn
```

The code below will be the last addition to our constructor method (once again, as we did with the placeholders):

```
        # Creates the train_step function for our model,
        # loss function and optimizer
        # Note: there are NO ARGS there! It makes use of the class
        # attributes directly
        self.train_step_fn = self._make_train_step_fn()
        # Creates the val_step function for our model and loss
        self.val_step_fn = self._make_val_step_fn()
```

If you have patched together the pieces of code above, your code should look like this:

StepByStep Class

```
class StepByStep(object):
    def __init__(self, model, loss_fn, optimizer):
        # Here we define the attributes of our class
        # We start by storing the arguments as attributes
        # to use them later
        self.model = model
        self.loss_fn = loss_fn
        self.optimizer = optimizer
        self.device = 'cuda' if torch.cuda.is_available() else 'cpu'
        # Let's send the model to the specified device right away
```

```
        self.model.to(self.device)

        # These attributes are defined here, but since they are
        # not available at the moment of creation, we keep them None
        self.train_loader = None
        self.val_loader = None
        self.writer = None

        # These attributes are going to be computed internally
        self.losses = []
        self.val_losses = []
        self.total_epochs = 0

        # Creates the train_step function for our model,
        # loss function and optimizer
        # Note: there are NO ARGS there! It makes use of the class
        # attributes directly
        self.train_step_fn = self._make_train_step_fn()
        # Creates the val_step function for our model and loss
        self.val_step_fn = self._make_val_step_fn()

    def to(self, device):
        # This method allows the user to specify a different device
        # It sets the corresponding attribute (to be used later in
        # the mini-batches) and sends the model to the device
        try:
            self.device = device
            self.model.to(self.device)
        except RuntimeError:
            self.device = ('cuda' if torch.cuda.is_available()
                           else 'cpu')
            print(f"Couldn't send it to {device}, \
                    sending it to {self.device} instead.")
            self.model.to(self.device)

    def set_loaders(self, train_loader, val_loader=None):
        # This method allows the user to define which train_loader
        # (and val_loader, optionally) to use
        # Both loaders are then assigned to attributes of the class
        # So they can be referred to later
        self.train_loader = train_loader
        self.val_loader = val_loader
```

```
    def set_tensorboard(self, name, folder='runs'):
        # This method allows the user to create a SummaryWriter to
        # interface with TensorBoard
        suffix = datetime.datetime.now().strftime('%Y%m%d%H%M%S')
        self.writer = SummaryWriter(f'{folder}/{name}_{suffix}')
```

"Why do these methods have an underscore as a prefix? How is this different than the double underscore in the `__init__()` *method?"*

Methods, _methods, and __methods

Some programming languages, like Java, have three kinds of methods: public, protected, and private. **Public methods** are the kind you're most familiar with: They can be **called by the user**.

Protected methods, on the other hand, **shouldn't** be called by the user—they are supposed to be called either **internally** or by the **child class** (the child class can call a protected method from its parent class).

Finally, **private methods** are supposed to be called **exclusively internally**. They should be invisible even to a child class.

These rules are strictly enforced in Java, but **Python** takes a more relaxed approach: **All methods are public**, meaning you can call whatever method you want. But you can **suggest** the appropriate usage by **prefixing the method name** with a **single underscore** (for **protected methods**) or a **double underscore** (for **private methods**). This way, the user is aware of the programmer's intention.

In our example, both `_make_train_step_fn()` and `_make_val_step_fn()` are defined as **protected methods**. I expect users **not to call them directly**, but if someone decides to define a class that inherits from `StepByStep`, they **should feel entitled** to do so.

setattr

The `setattr` function sets the value of the specified attribute of a given object. But **methods** are also **attributes**, so we can use this function to "attach" a method to an existing class and to all its existing instances in one go!

Yes, this is a hack! No, you should not use it in your regular code! Using `setattr` to build a class by appending methods to it incrementally serves educational purposes only.

To illustrate how it works and why it may be dangerous, I will show you a little example. Let's create a simple `Dog` class, which takes only the dog's name as argument:

```
class Dog(object):
    def __init__(self, name):
        self.name = name
```

Next, let's **instantiate** our class; that is, we are *creating* a dog. Let's call it Rex. Its name is going to be stored in the `name` attribute:

```
rex = Dog('Rex')
print(rex.name)
```

Output

```
Rex
```

Then, let's create a `bark()` function that takes an **instance of `Dog`** as argument:

```
def bark(dog):
    print('{} barks: "Woof!"'.format(dog.name))
```

Sure enough, we can call this function to make Rex bark:

```
bark(rex)
```

Output

```
Rex barks: "Woof!"
```

But that's **not** what we want. We want our dogs to be able to bark out of the box! So we will use `setattr` to give dogs the ability to bark. There is **one thing we need to change**, though, and that's the function's argument. Since we want the bark function to be a method of the `Dog` class itself, the **argument** needs to be the **method's own instance**: `self`.

```
def bark(self):
    print('{} barks: "Woof!"'.format(self.name))

setattr(Dog, 'bark', bark)
```

Does it work? Let's create a new dog:

```
fido = Dog('Fido')
fido.bark()
```

Output

```
Fido barks: "Woof!"
```

Of course it works! Not only new dogs can bark now, but **all dogs can bark**:

```
rex.bark()
```

Output

```
Rex barks: "Woof!"
```

See? We effectively **modified the underlying `Dog` class** and **all its instances** at once! It looks very cool, sure. And it can wreak havoc too!

In order to make the **additions** to our code **visually simpler**; that is, without having to *replicate the full class* every time I introduce a new method, I am resorting to something that **shouldn't be used in regular circumstances**: `setattr`.[37]

```
# ATTENTION! Using SETATTR for educational purposes only :-)
setattr(StepByStep, '_make_train_step_fn', _make_train_step_fn)
setattr(StepByStep, '_make_val_step_fn', _make_val_step_fn)
```

Using `setattr` is a **hack**, I can't stress this enough! **Please don't use `setattr` in your regular code**.

Instead of creating an attribute or method directly in the class, as we've been doing so far, it is possible to use `setattr` to create them dynamically. In our `StepByStep` class, the last two lines of code created two methods in the class, each having the same name of the function used to create the method.

OK, but there are still some parts missing in order to perform model training. Let's keep adding more methods.

Training Methods

The next method we need to add corresponds to the **mini-batch loop**, and it needs a **data loader** and a **step function**. We actually have both of them as attributes: `self.train_loader` and `self.train_step_fn`, for training; `self.val_loader` and `self.val_step_fn`, for validation. The only thing this method needs to know is if it is handling training or validation data. The code should look like this:

Mini-Batch

```
1 def _mini_batch(self, validation=False):
2     # The mini-batch can be used with both loaders
3     # The argument `validation` defines which loader and
4     # corresponding step function are going to be used
5     if validation:
6         data_loader = self.val_loader
7         step_fn = self.val_step_fn
8     else:
9         data_loader = self.train_loader
10        step_fn = self.train_step_fn
11
12    if data_loader is None:
13        return None
14
15    # Once the data loader and step function are set, this is the
16    # same mini-batch loop we had before
17    mini_batch_losses = []
18    for x_batch, y_batch in data_loader:
19        x_batch = x_batch.to(self.device)
20        y_batch = y_batch.to(self.device)
21
22        mini_batch_loss = step_fn(x_batch, y_batch)
23        mini_batch_losses.append(mini_batch_loss)
24
25    loss = np.mean(mini_batch_losses)
26
27    return loss
28
29 setattr(StepByStep, '_mini_batch', _mini_batch)
```

Moreover, if the user decides **not** to provide a validation loader, it will retain its initial None value from the constructor method. If that's the case, we don't have a corresponding loss to compute, and it returns None instead (line 13 in the snippet above).

What's left to do? The **training loop**, of course! It will take a **number of epochs** and a **random seed** as arguments.

Moreover, we need to ensure the **reproducibility of the training loop**. In Volume I, we have already set up seeds to ensure the reproducibility of the *random split* (data preparation) and the *model initialization* (model configuration). So, in order to gain flexibility without compromising reproducibility, we need to set yet another random seed.

We're building a method to take care of seed-setting only, following PyTorch's guidelines on reproducibility[38]:

Seeds

```
def set_seed(self, seed=42):
    torch.backends.cudnn.deterministic = True
    torch.backends.cudnn.benchmark = False
    torch.manual_seed(seed)
    np.random.seed(seed)
    random.seed(seed)
    try:
        self.train_loader.sampler.generator.manual_seed(seed)
    except AttributeError:
        pass

setattr(StepByStep, 'set_seed', set_seed)
```

It is also time to use the variables we defined as attributes in the constructor method: `self.total_epochs`, `self.losses`, and `self.val_losses`. All of them are being updated inside the training loop.

```
def train(self, n_epochs, seed=42):
    # To ensure reproducibility of the training process
    self.set_seed(seed)

    for epoch in range(n_epochs):
        # Keeps track of the number of epochs
        # by updating the corresponding attribute
        self.total_epochs += 1

        # inner loop
        # Performs training using mini-batches
        loss = self._mini_batch(validation=False)
        self.losses.append(loss)

        # VALIDATION
        # no gradients in validation!
        with torch.no_grad():
            # Performs evaluation using mini-batches
            val_loss = self._mini_batch(validation=True)
            self.val_losses.append(val_loss)

        # If a SummaryWriter has been set...
        if self.writer:
            scalars = {'training': loss}
            if val_loss is not None:
                scalars.update({'validation': val_loss})
            # Records both losses for each epoch under tag "loss"
            self.writer.add_scalars(main_tag='loss',
                                    tag_scalar_dict=scalars,
                                    global_step=epoch)

    if self.writer:
        # Flushes the writer
        self.writer.flush()

setattr(StepByStep, 'train', train)
```

Did you notice this function **does not return anything**? It doesn't need to! Instead of returning values, it simply updates several class attributes: `self.losses`, `self.val_losses`, and `self.total_epochs`.

The current state of development of our `StepByStep` class already allows us to train a model fully. Now, let's give our class the ability to save and load models as well.

Saving and Loading Models

The methods for saving and loading checkpoints should look like this:

Saving

```
def save_checkpoint(self, filename):
    # Builds dictionary with all elements for resuming training
    checkpoint = {
        'epoch': self.total_epochs,
        'model_state_dict': self.model.state_dict(),
        'optimizer_state_dict': self.optimizer.state_dict(),
        'loss': self.losses,
        'val_loss': self.val_losses
    }
    torch.save(checkpoint, filename)

setattr(StepByStep, 'save_checkpoint', save_checkpoint)
```

Loading

```
def load_checkpoint(self, filename):
    # Loads dictionary
    checkpoint = torch.load(filename)

    # Restore state for model and optimizer
    self.model.load_state_dict(checkpoint['model_state_dict'])
    self.optimizer.load_state_dict(
        checkpoint['optimizer_state_dict']
    )
    self.total_epochs = checkpoint['epoch']
    self.losses = checkpoint['loss']
    self.val_losses = checkpoint['val_loss']

    self.model.train() # always use TRAIN for resuming training

setattr(StepByStep, 'load_checkpoint', load_checkpoint)
```

Notice that the model is set to **training mode** after loading the checkpoint.

What about making predictions? To make it easier for the user to make predictions for any new data points, we will be handling all the *Numpy* to PyTorch back and forth conversion inside the function.

Making Predictions

```
def predict(self, x):
    # Set it to evaluation mode for predictions
    self.model.eval()
    # Take a Numpy input and make it a float tensor
    x_tensor = torch.as_tensor(x).float()
    # Send input to device and use model for prediction
    y_hat_tensor = self.model(x_tensor.to(self.device))
    # Set it back to train mode
    self.model.train()
    # Detach it, bring it to CPU and back to Numpy
    return y_hat_tensor.detach().cpu().numpy()

setattr(StepByStep, 'predict', predict)
```

First, we set the model to **evaluation mode**, as it is required in order to make predictions. Then, we convert the `x` argument (assumed to be a *Numpy* array) to a float PyTorch tensor, send it to the configured device, and use the model to make a prediction.

Next, we set the model back to **training mode**. The last step includes detaching the tensor containing the predictions and making it a *Numpy* array to be returned to the user.

Visualization Methods

Since we have kept track of both training and validation losses as attributes, let's build a simple plot for them:

Losses

```
def plot_losses(self):
    fig = plt.figure(figsize=(10, 4))
    plt.plot(self.losses, label='Training Loss', c='b')
    if self.val_loader:
        plt.plot(self.val_losses, label='Validation Loss', c='r')
    plt.yscale('log')
    plt.xlabel('Epochs')
    plt.ylabel('Loss')
    plt.legend()
    plt.tight_layout()
    return fig

setattr(StepByStep, 'plot_losses', plot_losses)
```

Finally, if both training loader and TensorBoard were already configured, we can use the former to fetch a single mini-batch and the latter to build the model graph in TensorBoard:

Model Graph

```
def add_graph(self):
    if self.train_loader and self.writer:
        # Fetches a single mini-batch so we can use add_graph
        x_dummy, y_dummy = next(iter(self.train_loader))
        self.writer.add_graph(self.model, x_dummy.to(self.device))

setattr(StepByStep, 'add_graph', add_graph)
```

Methods Added in Volume II

In Volume II, many methods were added to the `StepByStep` class. Moreover, some methods were slightly modified to incorporate techniques covered in Volume II, like learning rate scheduling and gradient clipping.

The following methods are going to be explicitly used in Volume III:

- `count_parameters()`: added in Chapter 4, it uses PyTorch's `numel()` to return the total **num**ber of **el**ements (clever, right?) of all **gradient-requiring tensors**.

StepByStep Method

```
def count_parameters(self):
    return sum(p.numel()
               for p in self.model.parameters()
               if p.requires_grad)

setattr(StepByStep, 'count_parameters', count_parameters)
```

- `loader_apply()`: added in Chapter 5, it **applies a function to each mini-batch**, and **stacks the results** before applying a reducing function such as sum or mean.

StepByStep Method

```
@staticmethod
def loader_apply(loader, func, reduce='sum'):
    results = [func(x, y) for i, (x, y) in enumerate(loader)]
    results = torch.stack(results, axis=0)

    if reduce == 'sum':
        results = results.sum(axis=0)
    elif reduce == 'mean':
        results = results.float().mean(axis=0)

    return results

setattr(StepByStep, 'loader_apply', loader_apply)
```

- `correct()`: added in Chapter 5, it takes features (*x*) and labels (*y*), as returned by a data loader, and takes all necessary steps to produce **two values for each class**: the **number of correct predictions**, and the **number of data points in that class**.

```
def correct(self, x, y, threshold=.5):
    self.model.eval()
    yhat = self.model(x.to(self.device))
    y = y.to(self.device)
    self.model.train()

    # We get the size of the batch and the number of classes
    # (only 1, if it is binary)
    n_samples, n_dims = yhat.shape
    if n_dims > 1:
        # In a multiclass classification, the largest logit
        # always wins, so we don't bother getting probs

        # This is PyTorch's version of argmax, but it
        # returns a tuple: (max value, index of max value)
        _, predicted = torch.max(yhat, 1)
    else:
        n_dims += 1
        # In binary classification, we NEED to check if the
        # last layer is a sigmoid (and then it produces probs)
        if isinstance(self.model, nn.Sequential) and \
           isinstance(self.model[-1], nn.Sigmoid):
            predicted = (yhat > threshold).long()
        # or something else (logits), which we need to convert
        # using a sigmoid
        else:
            predicted = (torch.sigmoid(yhat)>threshold).long()

    # How many samples got classified
    correctly for each class
    result = []
    for c in range(n_dims):
        n_class = (y == c).sum().item()
        n_correct = (predicted[y == c] == c).sum().item()
        result.append((n_correct, n_class))
    return torch.tensor(result)

setattr(StepByStep, 'correct', correct)
```

The Full Code

If you'd like to check what the full code of the class looks like, you can see it `https://github.com/dvgodoy/PyTorchStepByStep/blob/master/stepbystep/v4.py` or in the Jupyter notebook of this chapter.

We are **classy** now, so let's build a **classy pipeline** too!

Classy Pipeline

Our pipeline is composed of of three steps: **data preparation**, **model configuration**, and **model training**. The last step, model training, was already integrated into our `StepByStep` class. Let's take a look at the other two steps but, first, let's generate our synthetic data and use it to build a `TensorDataset`.

Data Generation

```
true_b = 1
true_w = 2
N = 100

# Data Generation
np.random.seed(42)
x = np.random.rand(N, 1)
y = true_b + true_w * x + (.1 * np.random.randn(N, 1))
```

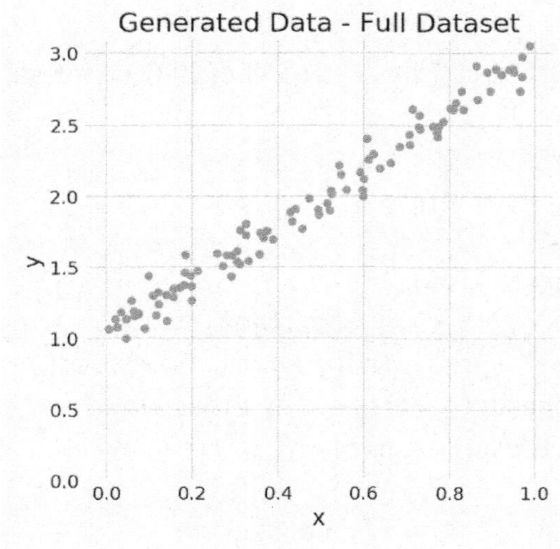

Figure SBS.1 - Full dataset

The first part of the pipeline is the **data preparation**.

Data Preparation

```
torch.manual_seed(13)
# Builds tensors from Numpy arrays BEFORE split
x_tensor = torch.as_tensor(x).float()
y_tensor = torch.as_tensor(y).float()
# Builds dataset containing ALL data points
dataset = TensorDataset(x_tensor, y_tensor)

# Performs the split
ratio = .8
n_total = len(dataset)
n_train = int(n_total * ratio)
n_val = n_total - n_train
train_data, val_data = random_split(dataset, [n_train, n_val])

# Builds a loader of each set
train_loader = DataLoader(
    dataset=train_data, batch_size=16, shuffle=True
)
val_loader = DataLoader(dataset=val_data, batch_size=16)
```

Next in line is the **model configuration**. We need to define the elements that should be passed as **arguments** to our `StepByStep` class: **model**, **loss function**, and **optimizer**. Notice that we do not need to send the model to the device at this point since this is going to be handled by our class' constructor.

Model Configuration

```
# Sets learning rate - this is "eta" ~ the "n"-like Greek letter
lr = 0.1

torch.manual_seed(42)
# Now we can create a model
model = nn.Sequential(nn.Linear(1, 1))

# Defines an SGD optimizer to update the parameters
# (now retrieved directly from the model)
optimizer = optim.SGD(model.parameters(), lr=lr)

# Defines an MSE loss function
loss_fn = nn.MSELoss(reduction='mean')
```

Let's inspect the randomly initialized parameters of our model:

```
print(model.state_dict())
```

Output

```
OrderedDict([('0.weight', tensor([[0.7645]])),
             ('0.bias', tensor([0.8300]))])
```

These are **CPU tensors**, since our model wasn't sent anywhere (yet).

And now the **fun** begins: Let's put our `StepByStep` class to good use and **train our model**.

Model Training

We start by **instantiating** the `StepByStep` class with the corresponding arguments. Next, we set its loaders using the appropriately named method `set_loaders()`. Then, we set up an interface with TensorBoard and name our experiment **classy** (what else could it be?!).

Notebook Cell 2.1.1

```
sbs = StepByStep(model, loss_fn, optimizer)
sbs.set_loaders(train_loader, val_loader)
sbs.set_tensorboard('classy')
```

One important thing to notice is that the `model` attribute of the `sbs` object is **the same object** as the `model` variable created in the model configuration. It is **not a copy**! We can easily verify this:

```
print(sbs.model == model)
print(sbs.model)
```

Output

```
True
Sequential(
  (0): Linear(in_features=1, out_features=1, bias=True)
)
```

As expected, the equality holds. If we print the model itself, we get our simple **one input-one output** model.

Let's **train the model** for 200 epochs now:

Notebook Cell 2.1.2

```
sbs.train(n_epochs=200)
```

Done! It is trained! Really? Really! Let's check it out:

```
print(model.state_dict()) # remember, model == sbs.model
print(sbs.total_epochs)
```

Output

```
OrderedDict([('0.weight', tensor([[1.9414]], device='cuda:0')),
             '0.bias', tensor([1.0233], device='cuda:0'))])
200
```

Our class sent the model to the available device (a GPU, in this case), and now the model's parameters are **GPU tensors**.

Let's take a look at the losses:

```
fig = sbs.plot_losses()
```

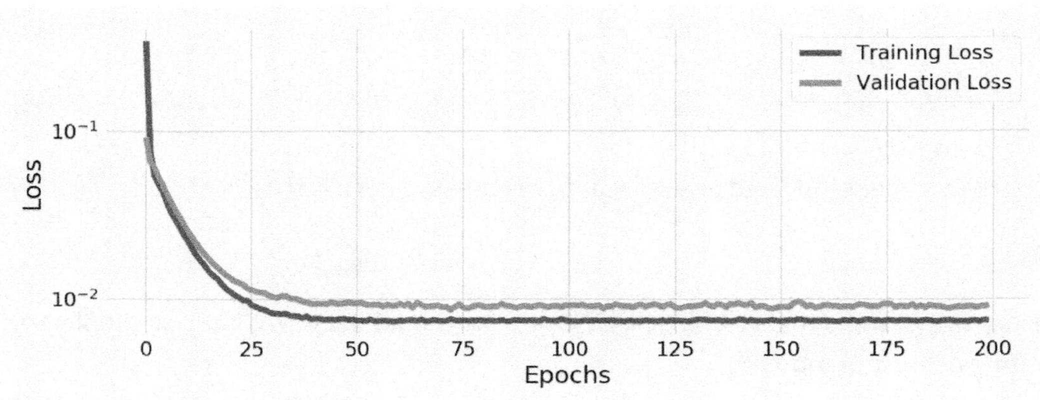

Figure SBS.2 - Losses

Again, no surprises here; what about making predictions for new, never seen before data points?

Making Predictions

Let's make up some data points for our feature **x**, and shape them as a single-column matrix:

```
new_data = np.array([.5, .3, .7]).reshape(-1, 1)
```

Output

```
array([[0.5],
       [0.3],
       [0.7]])
```

Since the *Numpy* array to PyTorch tensor conversion is already handled by the `predict()` method, we can call the method right away, passing the array as its argument:

```
predictions = sbs.predict(new_data)
predictions
```

Output

```
array([[1.9939734],
       [1.6056864],
       [2.3822603]], dtype=float32)
```

And now we have predictions! Easy, right?

What if, instead of making predictions, we wanted to **checkpoint** the model to resume training later?

Checkpointing

That's a no-brainer—the `save_checkpoint()` method handles the state dictionaries for us and saves them to a file:

Notebook Cell 2.1.3

```
sbs.save_checkpoint('model_checkpoint.pth')
```

Resuming Training

First, we need to **set the stage**, loading the data and configuring the model, before actually loading the model. We can do this by simply running the same **model configuration** as before:

Run - Model Configuration V4

```
%run -i model_configuration/v4.py
```

Let's double-check that we do have an **untrained model**:

```
print(model.state_dict())
```

Output

```
OrderedDict([('0.weight', tensor([[0.7645]], device='cuda:0')),
             ('0.bias', tensor([0.8300], device='cuda:0'))])
```

Good, same as before! Besides, the model configuration has created the **three elements** we need to pass as **arguments** to **instantiate** our `StepByStep` class:

Notebook Cell 2.1.4

```
new_sbs = StepByStep(model, loss_fn, optimizer)
```

Next, let's **load the trained model** back using the `load_checkpoint()` method and then inspect the model's weights:

Notebook Cell 2.1.5

```
new_sbs.load_checkpoint('model_checkpoint.pth')
print(model.state_dict())
```

Output

```
OrderedDict([('0.weight', tensor([[1.9414]], device='cuda:0')),
             ('0.bias', tensor([1.0233], device='cuda:0'))])
```

Great, these are the weights of our trained model. Let's **train it a bit further**.

But we are still missing one thing ... the data! First, we need to **set the data loader(s)**, and then we can train our model for another, say, 50 epochs.

Notebook Cell 2.1.6

```
new_sbs.set_loaders(train_loader, val_loader)
new_sbs.train(n_epochs=50)
```

Let's take a look at the losses:

```
fig = new_sbs.plot_losses()
```

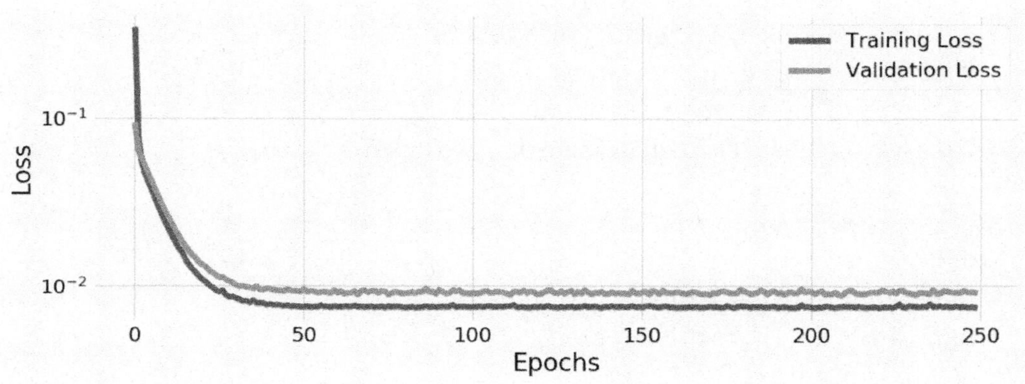

Figure SBS.3 - More losses!

We have loss values over 250 epochs now. The losses for the first 200 epochs were loaded from the checkpoint, and the losses for the last 50 epochs were computed after training was resumed.

If the losses haven't changed, it means the training loss was at a **minimum** already. So, we expect the **weights to remain unchanged**. Let's check it out:

```
print(sbs.model.state_dict())
```

Output

```
OrderedDict([('0.weight', tensor([[1.9414]], device='cuda:0')),
('0.bias', tensor([1.0233], device='cuda:0'))])
```

No changes, indeed.

Putting It All Together

In this chapter, we have developed the `StepByStep` class to more easily train models. We divided our pipeline into three parts, data preparation, model configuration, and model training, and used the newly developed class to make our pipeline **classy** :-)

Data Preparation

```
torch.manual_seed(13)
# Builds tensors from numpy arrays BEFORE split
x_tensor = torch.as_tensor(x).float()
y_tensor = torch.as_tensor(y).float()
# Builds dataset containing ALL data points
dataset = TensorDataset(x_tensor, y_tensor)

# Performs the split
ratio = .8
n_total = len(dataset)
n_train = int(n_total * ratio)
n_val = n_total - n_train
train_data, val_data = random_split(dataset, [n_train, n_val])

# Builds a loader of each set
train_loader = DataLoader(
    dataset=train_data, batch_size=16, shuffle=True
)
val_loader = DataLoader(dataset=val_data, batch_size=16)
```

Model Configuration

```
# Sets learning rate - this is "eta" ~ the "n"-like Greek letter
lr = 0.1

torch.manual_seed(42)
# Now we can create a model
model = nn.Sequential(nn.Linear(1, 1))

# Defines an SGD optimizer to update the parameters
# (now retrieved directly from the model)
optimizer = optim.SGD(model.parameters(), lr=lr)

# Defines an MSE loss function
loss_fn = nn.MSELoss(reduction='mean')
```

Model Training

```
n_epochs = 200

sbs = StepByStep(model, loss_fn, optimizer)
sbs.set_loaders(train_loader, val_loader)
sbs.set_tensorboard('classy')
sbs.train(n_epochs=n_epochs)
```

```
print(model.state_dict())
```

Output

```
OrderedDict([('0.weight', tensor([[1.9414]], device='cuda:0')),
             ('0.bias', tensor([1.0233], device='cuda:0'))])
```

Recap

In this chapter, we've implemented many methods. This is what we've covered:

- defining our `StepByStep` **class**
- understanding the purpose of the **constructor** (`__init__()`) method
- defining the **arguments** of the constructor method
- defining **class' attributes** to store *arguments*, *placeholders*, and *variables* we need to keep track of
- defining **functions as attributes**, using higher-order functions and the class' attributes to build functions that perform training and validation steps
- understanding the **difference** between **public**, **protected**, and **private methods**, and Python's "relaxed" approach to it
- creating methods to set **data loaders** and **TensorBoard** integration
- implementing **training** methods: `_mini_batch()` and `train()`
- implementing **saving and loading** methods: `save_checkpoint()` and `load_checkpoint()`
- implementing a method for **making predictions** that takes care of all boilerplate code regarding *Numpy*-to-PyTorch conversion and back
- implementing methods to **plot losses** and add the **model's graph** to TensorBoard
- **instantiating** our `StepByStep` class and running a **classy** pipeline: configuring the model, loading the data, training the model, making predictions, checkpointing, and resuming training. The whole nine yards!

Congratulations! You have developed a **fully-functioning class** that implements all methods relevant to model training and evaluation. From now on, we'll use it over and over again to tackle different tasks and models.

[33] https://github.com/dvgodoy/PyTorchStepByStep/blob/master/Chapter02.1.ipynb

[34] https://colab.research.google.com/github/dvgodoy/PyTorchStepByStep/blob/master/Chapter02.1.ipynb

[35] https://realpython.com/python3-object-oriented-programming/

[36] https://realpython.com/python-super/

[37] https://www.w3schools.com/python/ref_func_setattr.asp

[38] https://pytorch.org/docs/stable/notes/randomness.html

Chapter 8
Sequences

Spoilers

In this chapter, we will:

- learn about the characteristics of **sequential data** and generate our own
- understand the **inner workings** of **recurrent layers**
- build and train models to perform **classification** of **sequences**
- understand the importance of the **hidden state** as the **representation of a sequence**
- visualize the **journey of a hidden state** from beginning to end of a sequence
- pre-process **variable-length sequences** using **padding** and **packing** techniques, as well as the **collate function**
- learn how **1D convolutions** can be used on sequential data

Jupyter Notebook

The Jupyter notebook corresponding to Chapter 8[39] is part of the official ***Deep Learning with PyTorch Step-by-Step*** repository on GitHub. You can also run it directly in **Google Colab**[40].

If you're using a *local installation*, open your terminal or Anaconda prompt and navigate to the `PyTorchStepByStep` folder you cloned from GitHub. Then, *activate* the `pytorchbook` environment and run `jupyter notebook`:

```
$ conda activate pytorchbook

(pytorchbook)$ jupyter notebook
```

If you're using Jupyter's default settings, `http://localhost:8888/notebooks/Chapter08.ipynb` should open Chapter 8's notebook. If not, just click on `Chapter08.ipynb` in your Jupyter's home page.

Imports

For the sake of organization, all libraries needed throughout the code used in any given chapter are imported at its very beginning. For this chapter, we'll need the following imports:

```
import numpy as np

import torch
import torch.optim as optim
import torch.nn as nn
import torch.nn.functional as F
from torch.utils.data import DataLoader, Dataset, random_split, \
    TensorDataset
from torch.nn.utils import rnn as rnn_utils

from data_generation.square_sequences import generate_sequences
from stepbystep.v4 import StepByStep
```

Sequences

In this third volume of the series, we'll dive into a new kind of input: **sequences**! So far, each data point has been considered in and of itself; that is, each data point has had a label to call its own. An image of a hand was classified as "*rock*," "*paper*," or "*scissors*" based on its pixel values alone, without paying any attention to other images' pixel values. This **won't** be the case anymore.

In sequence problems, an **ordered sequence of data points shares a single label**—emphasis on **being ordered**.

*"Why is **ordered** so important?"*

If the data points **aren't ordered**, even if they share a single label, they are **not a sequence**, but rather a **collection** of data points.

Let's think of a slightly contrived example: greyscale images with *shuffled* pixels. Each pixel has a single value, but **a pixel alone doesn't have a label**. It is the **collection of shuffled pixels**, the shuffled image, that **has a label**: a duck, a dog, or a cat (labeled before shuffling the pixels, of course).

Before shuffling, the pixels were **ordered**; that is, they *had an underlying two-dimensional structure*. This structure can be exploited by the convolutional neural networks: The kernel moving around the image looks at a pixel in the center and all its neighbors in both dimensions, height and width.

If the underlying structure has a **single dimension**, though, that's a **sequence**. This particular structure can be exploited by **recurrent neural networks** and their many variants, as well as by **1D convolutional neural networks**, which constitute the subject of this chapter.

There are two main types of **sequence problems**: **time series** and **natural language processing (NLP)**. We'll start by generating a synthetic dataset and then use it to illustrate the **inner workings** of **recurrent neural networks**, **encoder-decoder** models, **attention mechanisms**, and even **Transformers**! Only then will we get to the natural language processing part.

I chose to follow this *sequence* of topics because I find it much easier to develop intuition (and to produce meaningful visualizations) while working with a two-dimensional dataset, as opposed to 100-dimensional word embeddings.

Data Generation

Our data points are **two-dimensional**, so they can be visualized as an image, and **ordered**, so they are a **sequence**. We'll be **drawing squares**! Each square, as depicted in the figure below, has **four corners** (duh!), with each corner assigned a **letter** and a **color**. The bottom-left corner is **A** and **gray**, the bottom-right one is **D** and **red**, and so on.

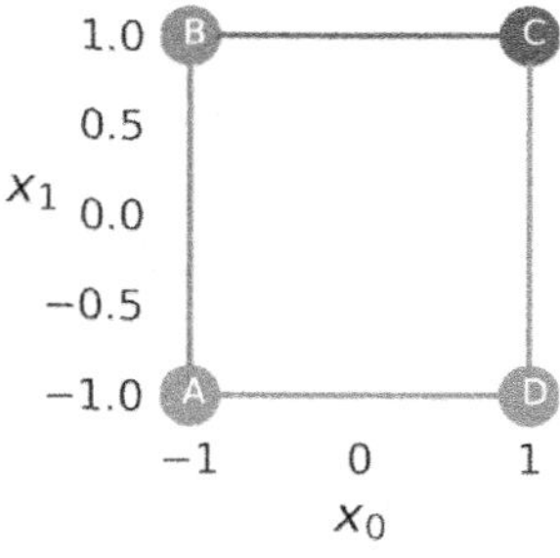

Figure 8.1 - Our colored square

The **coordinates** (x_0, x_1) of the four corners are our **data points**. The "*perfect*" square has the coordinates depicted in the figure above: `A=(-1, -1)`, `B=(-1, 1)`, `C=(1, 1)`, and `D=(1,-1)`. Sure enough, we'll generate a dataset full of **noisy squares**, each having its corners *around* these perfect coordinates.

Now, we need to give each **sequence of data points (corners)** a **label**. Assuming you can draw a square **starting at any corner**, and draw it **without lifting your pencil** at any time, you can choose to draw it **clockwise** or **counterclockwise**. These are our labels.

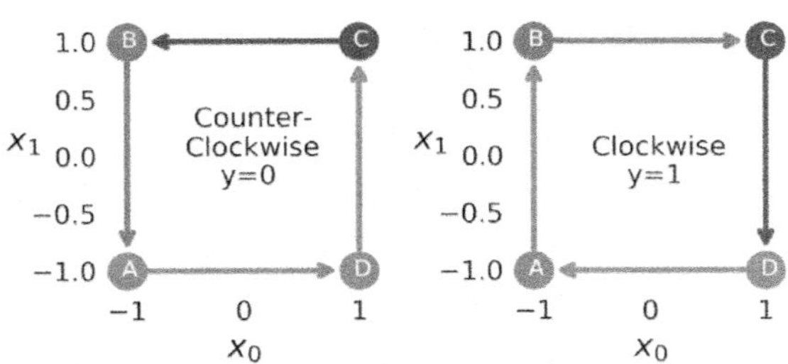

Figure 8.2 - Drawing directions

Since there are four corners to start from, and there are two directions to follow, there are effectively eight possible sequences.

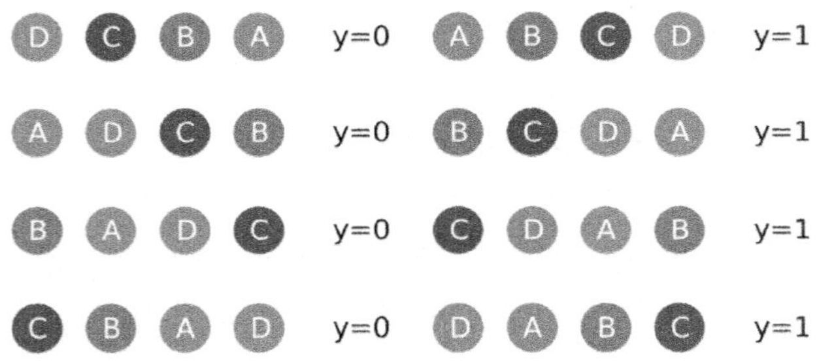

Figure 8.3 - Possible sequences of corners

Our task is to **classify the sequence** of corners: **Is it drawn in a clockwise direction**? A familiar binary classification problem!

Let's generate 128 random noisy squares:

Data Generation

```
points, directions = generate_sequences(n=128, seed=13)
```

And then let's visualize the first ten squares:

```
fig = plot_data(points, directions)
```

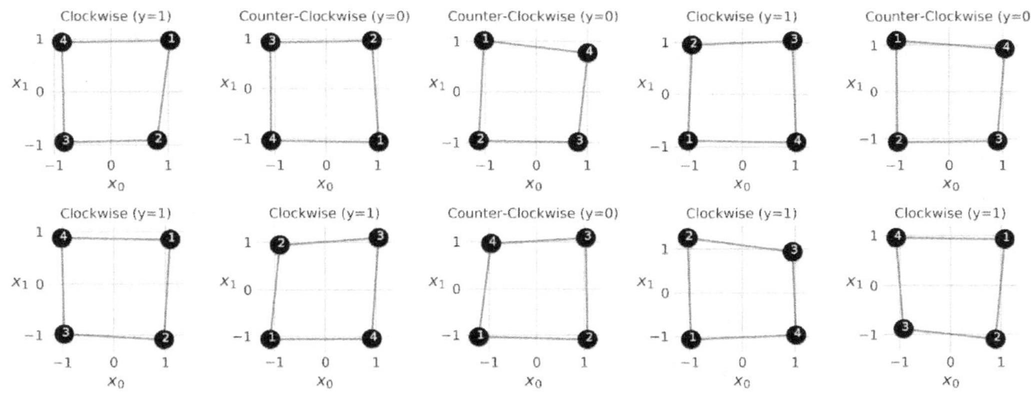

Figure 8.4 - Sequence dataset

The corners show the **order** in which they were drawn. In the first square, the drawing **started at the top-right corner** (corresponding to the *blue C* corner) and followed a **clockwise direction** (corresponding to the *CDAB* sequence).

In the next chapter, we'll use **the first two corners** to predict the **other two**, so the model will need to learn **not only the direction but also the coordinates**. We'll build a **sequence-to-sequence** model that uses one sequence to predict another.

For now, we're sticking to **classifying the direction**, given all **four data points** of a given square. But, first, we need to introduce...

Recurrent Neural Networks (RNNs)

Recurrent neural networks are perfectly suited for **sequence** problems since they take advantage of the **underlying structure** of the data, namely, the **order of the data points**. We'll see in great detail **how the data points**, sequentially presented to a recurrent neural network, **modify the RNN's internal (hidden) state**, which will ultimately be a **representation of the full sequence**.

SPOILER ALERT: Recurrent neural networks are all about **producing a hidden state that best represents a sequence**.

*"But what **is** a hidden state anyway?"*

Excellent question! A hidden state is simply a **vector**. The size of the vector is up to you. Really. You need to specify the number of **hidden dimensions**, which means specifying the size of the vector that represents a hidden state. Let's create a **two-dimensional hidden state** just for kicks:

```
hidden_state = torch.zeros(2)
hidden_state
```

Output

```
tensor([0., 0.])
```

That's actually a fine example of an **initial hidden state**, as we'll see shortly. But, before diving deep into the journey of a hidden state through an RNN, let's take a look at its top-level representation:

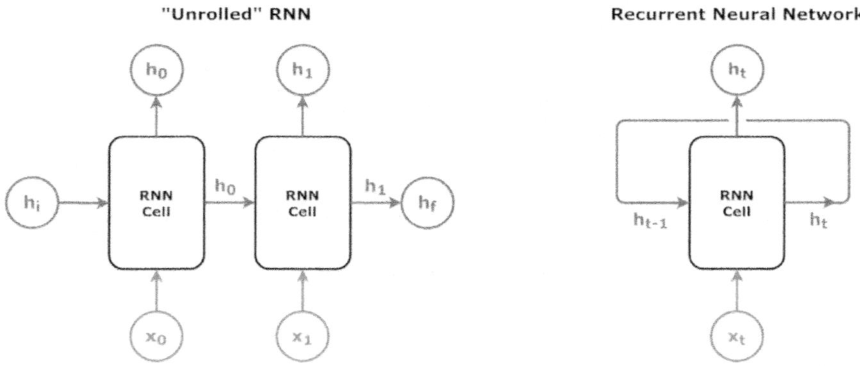

Figure 8.5 - Top-level representation of an RNN

If you've ever seen figures representing RNNs, you've probably bumped into one of the two versions depicted above: "*unrolled*" or not. Let's start with the **unrolled** one: It shows a **sequence of two data points** being fed to an RNN. We can describe the flow of information inside an RNN in **five easy steps**:

1. There is an **initial hidden state** (h_i) that represents the **state of the empty sequence** and is usually **initialized with zeros** (like the one we created above).
2. An RNN cell takes **two inputs**: the **hidden state** representing the state of the

sequence *so far*, and **a data point from the sequence** (like the coordinates of one of the corners from a given square).

3. The two inputs are used to **produce a new hidden state** (h_0 for the first data point), representing the **updated state of the sequence** now that a new point was presented to it.
4. The new hidden state is **both** the **output of the current step** and **one of the inputs of the next step**.
5. If there is **yet another data point in the sequence**, it goes back to **Step #2**; if not, the **last hidden state** (h_1 in the figure above) is also the **final hidden state** (h_f) of the whole RNN.

Since the **final hidden state** is a representation of the **full sequence**, that's what we're going to use as **features** for our **classifier**.

In a way, that's not so different from the way we used CNNs in Volume II: There, we'd run the pixels through multiple convolutional blocks (convolutional layer + activation + pooling) and flatten them into a vector at the end to use as features for a classifier.

Here, we run a sequence of data points through RNN cells and use the final hidden state (also a vector) as features for a classifier.

There is a **fundamental difference** between CNNs and RNNs, though: While there are several **different convolutional layers**, each learning its own filters, the **RNN cell is one and the same.** In this sense, the "*unrolled*" representation is misleading: It definitely *looks like* each input is being fed to a different RNN cell, but that's *not* the case.

There is only **one cell**, which will learn a particular set of weights and biases, and which will **transform the inputs exactly the same way in every step of the sequence**. Don't worry if this doesn't completely make sense to you just yet; I promise it will become more clear soon, especially in the "Journey of a Hidden State" section.

RNN Cell

Let's take a look at some of the *internals* of an RNN cell:

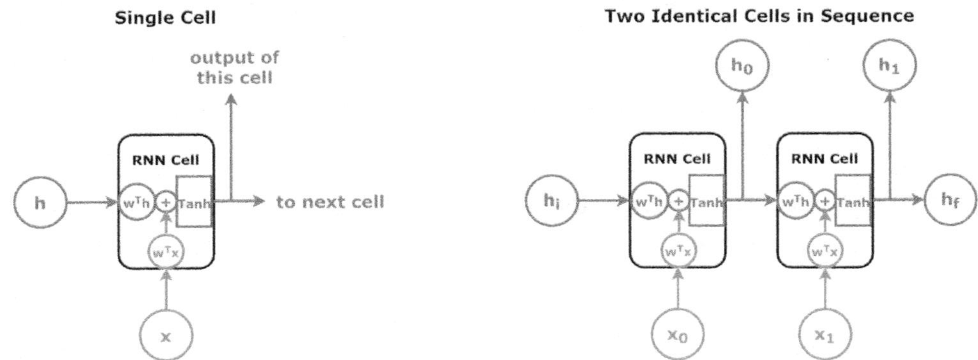

Figure 8.6 - Internals of an RNN cell

On the left, we have a **single RNN cell**. It has **three main components**:

- A **linear layer** to transform the **hidden state** (in blue)
- A **linear layer** to transform the **data point from the sequence** (in red)
- An **activation function**, usually the hyperbolic tangent (TanH), which is applied to the **sum of both transformed inputs**

We can also represent them as equations:

$$
\begin{aligned}
\text{RNN}: \quad t_h &= W_{hh} \quad h_{t-1} + b_{hh} \\
t_x &= W_{ih} \quad x_t + b_{ih} \\
h_t &= \tanh \quad (t_h + t_x)
\end{aligned}
$$

Equation 8.1 - RNN

I chose to split the equation into smaller colored parts to highlight the fact that these are simple linear layers producing both a **transformed hidden state** (t_h) and a **transformed data point** (t_x). The updated hidden (h_t) state is both the output of this particular cell and one of the inputs of the "*next*" cell.

But there is **no other cell**, really; it is just the **same cell over and over again**, as depicted on the right side of the figure above. So, in the second step of the sequence, the updated hidden state will run through the **very same linear layer** the initial hidden state ran through. The same goes for the second data point.

Considering this, the **not "*unrolled*"** ("*rolled*" doesn't sound right!) representation is a better characterization of the internal structure of an RNN.

Let's dive **deeper** into the internals of an RNN cell and look at it at the **neuron level**:

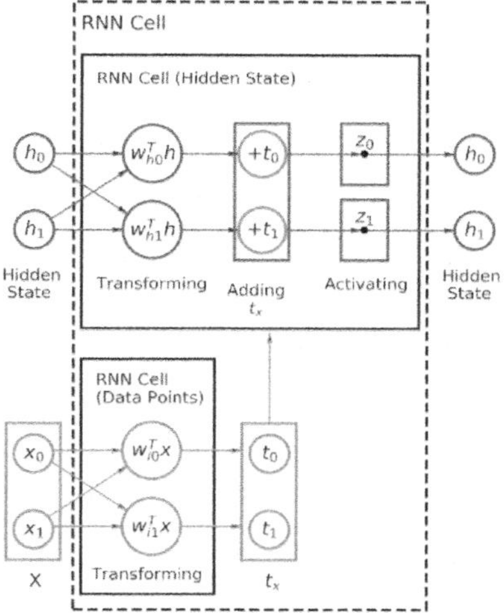

Figure 8.7 - RNN cell at neuron level

Since one can choose the number of hidden dimensions, I chose **two dimensions**, simply because I want to be able to easily **visualize the results**. Hence, **two blue neurons** are transforming the hidden state.

The number of **red neurons** transforming the data point will **necessarily** be the **same** as the chosen **number of hidden dimensions** since both transformed outputs need to be added together. But this **doesn't mean** the **data points** must have the **same number of dimensions**.

Coincidentally, our data points have **two coordinates**, but even if we had 25 dimensions, these 25 features would **still** be mapped into **two dimensions** by the two red neurons.

The only operation left is the activation function, most likely the hyperbolic tangent, which will produce the updated hidden state.

"Why hyperbolic tangent? Isn't ReLU a better activation function?"

The hyperbolic tangent has a "*competitive advantage*" here since it maps the feature space to clearly defined boundaries: the interval (-1, 1). This guarantees that, at every step of the sequence, the **hidden state is always within these boundaries**. Given that we have **only one linear layer with which to transform the hidden state**, regardless of which step of the sequence it is being used in, it is definitely convenient to have its values within a predictable range. We'll get back to this in the "Journey of a Hidden State" section.

Now, let's see how an RNN cell works in code. We'll create one using PyTorch's own `nn.RNNCell` and **disassemble** it into its components to manually reproduce all the steps involved in **updating the hidden state**. To create a cell, we need to tell it the `input_size` (number of features in our data points) and the `hidden_size` (the size of the vector representing the hidden state). It is also possible to tell it not to add biases, and to use a ReLU instead of TanH, but we're sticking to the defaults.

```
n_features = 2
hidden_dim = 2

torch.manual_seed(19)
rnn_cell = nn.RNNCell(input_size=n_features, hidden_size=hidden_dim)
rnn_state = rnn_cell.state_dict()
rnn_state
```

Output

```
OrderedDict([('weight_ih', tensor([[ 0.6627, -0.4245],
                       [ 0.5373,  0.2294]])),
             ('weight_hh', tensor([[-0.4015, -0.5385],
                       [-0.1956, -0.6835]])),
             ('bias_ih', tensor([0.4954, 0.6533])),
             ('bias_hh', tensor([-0.3565, -0.2904]))])
```

The `weight_ih` and `bias_ih` (`i` stands for inputs—the data) tensors correspond to the **red neurons** in Figure 8.7. The `weight_hh` and `bias_hh` (`h` stands for hidden) tensors, to the **blue neurons**. We can use these weights to create **two linear layers**:

```
linear_input = nn.Linear(n_features, hidden_dim)
linear_hidden = nn.Linear(hidden_dim, hidden_dim)

with torch.no_grad():
    linear_input.weight = nn.Parameter(rnn_state['weight_ih'])
    linear_input.bias = nn.Parameter(rnn_state['bias_ih'])
    linear_hidden.weight = nn.Parameter(rnn_state['weight_hh'])
    linear_hidden.bias = nn.Parameter(rnn_state['bias_hh'])
```

Now, let's work our way through the mechanics of the RNN cell! It all starts with the **initial hidden state** representing the **empty sequence**:

```
initial_hidden = torch.zeros(1, hidden_dim)
initial_hidden
```

Output

```
tensor([[0., 0.]])
```

Then, we use the **two blue neurons**, the `linear_hidden` layer, to **transform the hidden state**:

```
th = linear_hidden(initial_hidden)
th
```

Output

```
tensor([[-0.3565, -0.2904]], grad_fn=<AddmmBackward>)
```

Cool! Now, let's take look at a **sequence of data points** from our dataset:

```
X = torch.as_tensor(points[0]).float()
X
```

Output

```
tensor([[ 1.0349,  0.9661],
        [ 0.8055, -0.9169],
        [-0.8251, -0.9499],
        [-0.8670,  0.9342]])
```

As expected, four data points, two coordinates each. The first data point, [1.0349, 0.9661], corresponding to the top-right corner of the square, is going to be transformed by the `linear_input` layers (the **two red neurons**):

```
tx = linear_input(X[0:1])
tx
```

Output

```
tensor([[0.7712, 1.4310]], grad_fn=<AddmmBackward>)
```

There we go: We got both t_x and t_h. Let's add them together:

```
adding = th + tx
adding
```

Output

```
tensor([[0.4146, 1.1405]], grad_fn=<AddBackward0>)
```

The **effect of adding t_x is similar to the effect of adding the bias**: It is effectively **translating** the transformed hidden state to the right (by 0.7712) and up (by 1.4310).

Finally, the hyperbolic tangent activation function "compresses" the feature space back into the (-1, 1) interval:

```
torch.tanh(adding)
```

Output

```
tensor([[0.3924, 0.8146]], grad_fn=<TanhBackward>)
```

That's the **updated hidden state**!

Now, let's take a quick sanity check, feeding the same input to the original RNN cell:

```
rnn_cell(X[0:1])
```

Output

```
tensor([[0.3924, 0.8146]], grad_fn=<TanhBackward>)
```

Great, the values match.

We can also **visualize** this sequence of operations, assuming that every hidden space "*lives*" in a feature space delimited by the boundaries given by the hyperbolic tangent. So, the initial hidden state (0, 0) sits at the center of this feature space, depicted in the left-most plot in the figure below:

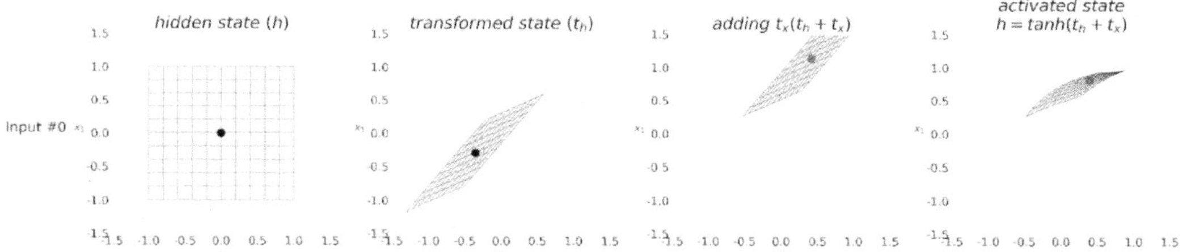

Figure 8.8 - Evolution of the hidden state

The **transformed hidden state** (the output of `linear_hidden()`) is depicted in the second plot: It went through an **affine transformation**. The point in the center corresponds to t_h. In the third plot, we can see the effect of **adding t_x** (the output of `linear_input()`): The whole feature space was **translated** to the right and up. And then, in the right most plot, the **hyperbolic tangent** works its magic and brings the whole feature space **back to the (-1, 1) range**. That was the **first step** in the journey of a hidden state. We'll do it once again, using the full sequence, after training a model.

I guess it is time to feed the **full sequence** to the RNN cell, right? You may be tempted to do it like this:

```
# WRONG!
rnn_cell(X)
```

Output

```
tensor([[ 0.3924,  0.8146],
        [ 0.7864,  0.5266],
        [-0.0047, -0.2897],
        [-0.6817,  0.1109]], grad_fn=<TanhBackward>)
```

This is **wrong**! Remember, the RNN cell has **two inputs**: one hidden state and one data point.

"Where is the hidden state then?"

That's exactly the problem! If not provided, it defaults to the zeros corresponding to the initial hidden state. So, the call above is **not** processing **four steps of a sequence**, but rather processing the **first step of what it is assuming to be four sequences**.

To effectively use the RNN cell in a sequence, we need to **loop over the data points** and **provide the updated hidden state at each step**:

```
hidden = torch.zeros(1, hidden_dim)
for i in range(X.shape[0]):
    out = rnn_cell(X[i:i+1], hidden)
    print(out)
    hidden = out
```

Output

```
tensor([[0.3924, 0.8146]], grad_fn=<TanhBackward>)
tensor([[ 0.4347, -0.0481]], grad_fn=<TanhBackward>)
tensor([[-0.1521, -0.3367]], grad_fn=<TanhBackward>)
tensor([[-0.5297,  0.3551]], grad_fn=<TanhBackward>)
```

Now we're talking! The last hidden state, (-0.5297, 0.3551), is the representation of the full sequence.

Figure 8.9 depicts what the loop above looks like at the neuron level. In it, you can easily see what I call "*the journey of a hidden state*": It is **transformed**, **translated** (adding the input), and **activated** many times over. Moreover, you can also see that the **data points are independently transformed**—the model will learn the best way to transform them. We'll get back to this after training a model.

At this point, you may be thinking:

"Looping over the data points in a sequence?! That looks like a lot of work!"

And you're absolutely right! Instead of an RNN cell, we can use a full-fledged…

RNN Layer

The `nn.RNN` layer takes care of the hidden state handling for us, no matter how long the input sequence is. This is the layer we'll actually be using in the model. We've been through the inner workings of its cells, but the full-fledged RNN offers **many more options** (stacked and / or bidirectional layers, for instance) and **one tricky thing regarding the shapes of inputs and outputs** (yes, shapes are a kinda *recurrent* problem—pun intended!).

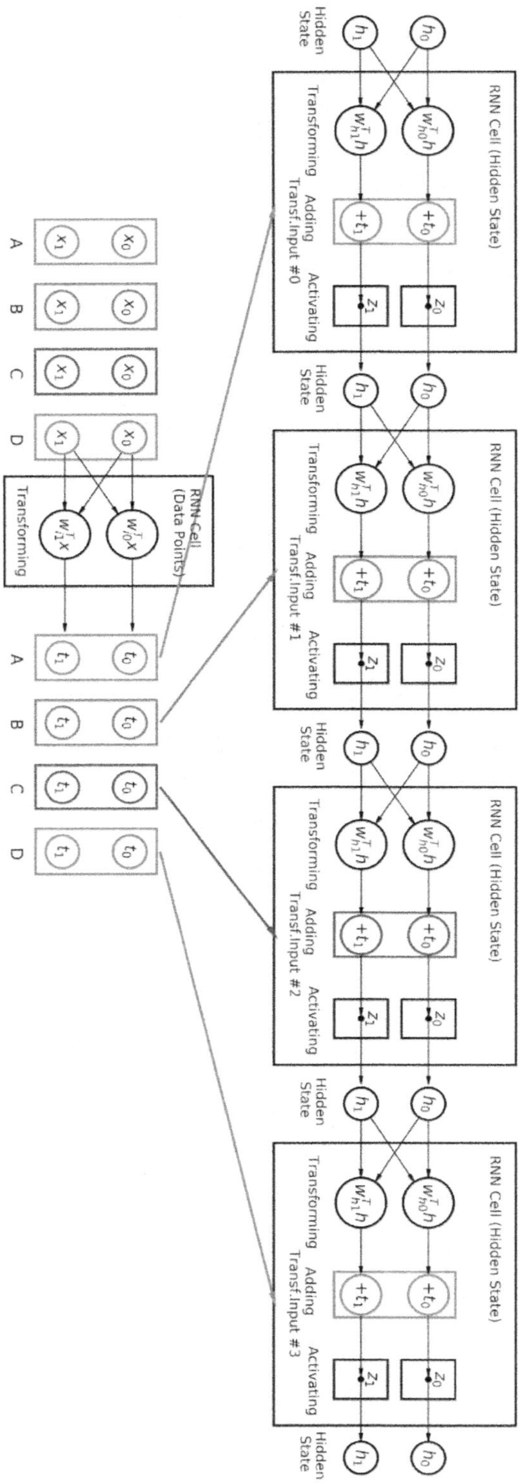

Figure 8.9 - Multiple cells in sequence

Let's take a look at the RNN's arguments:

- `input_size`: It is the number of features in each data point of the sequence.
- `hidden_size`: It is the number of hidden dimensions you want to use.
- `bias`: Just like any other layer, it includes the bias in the equations.
- `nonlinearity`: By default, it uses the hyperbolic tangent, but you can change it to ReLU if you want.

The four arguments above are exactly the same as those in the RNN cell. So, we can easily create a full-fledged RNN like that:

```
n_features = 2
hidden_dim = 2

torch.manual_seed(19)
rnn = nn.RNN(input_size=n_features, hidden_size=hidden_dim)
rnn.state_dict()
```

Output

```
OrderedDict([('weight_ih_l0', tensor([[ 0.6627, -0.4245],
                      [ 0.5373,  0.2294]])),
             ('weight_hh_l0', tensor([[-0.4015, -0.5385],
                      [-0.1956, -0.6835]])),
             ('bias_ih_l0', tensor([0.4954, 0.6533])),
             ('bias_hh_l0', tensor([-0.3565, -0.2904]))])
```

Since the seed is exactly the same, you'll notice that the **weights** and **biases** have **exactly the same values** as our former RNN cell. The only difference is in the **parameters' names**: Now they all have an `_l0` suffix to indicate they belong to the **first "*layer.*"**

*"What do you mean by **layer**? Isn't the RNN itself a layer?"*

Yes, the RNN itself can be a layer in our model. But it may have its **own internal layers**! You can configure those with the following four extra arguments:

- `num_layers`: The RNN we've been using so far has *one* layer (the default value), but if you use **more than one**, you'll be creating a **stacked RNN**, which we'll see in its own section.

- `bidirectional`: So far, our RNNs have been handling sequences in the **left-to-right direction** (the default), but if you set this argument to `True`, you'll be creating a **bidirectional RNN**, which we'll also see in its own section.
- `dropout`: This introduces an RNN's **own dropout layer between its internal layers**, so it only makes sense if you're using a **stacked RNN**.

And I saved the best (actually, the worst) for last:

- `batch_first`: The documentation says, "*if* `True`, *then the input and output tensors are provided as (batch, seq, feature),*" which makes you think that you only need to set it to `True` and it will turn everything into your nice and familiar tensors where different batches are concatenated together as its first dimension—and you'd be sorely mistaken.

"*Why? What's wrong with that?*"

The problem is, you need to read the documentation very literally: **Only** the input and output tensors are going to be batch first; **the hidden state will never be batch first**. This behavior *may* bring complications you need to be aware of.

Shapes

Before going through an example, let's take a look at the expected inputs and outputs of our RNN:

- Inputs:
  - The **input tensor** containing the **sequence** you want to run through the RNN:
    - The default shape is **sequence-first**; that is, **(sequence length, batch size, number of features)**, which we're abbreviating to **(L, N, F)**.
    - But if you choose `batch_first`, it will *flip* the first two dimensions, and then it will expect an **(N, L, F)** shape, which is what you're likely getting from a data loader.
    - By the way, the input can also be a **packed sequence**—we'll get back to that in a later section.

- The **initial hidden state**, which defaults to zeros if not provided:
  - A simple RNN will have a hidden state tensor with shape **(1, N, H)**.
  - A stacked RNN (more on that in the next section) will have a hidden state tensor with shape **(number of stacked layers, N, H)**.
  - A bidirectional RNN (more on that later) will have a hidden state tensor with shape **(2*number of stacked layers, N, H)**.

- Outputs:
  - The **output tensor** contains the **hidden states** corresponding to the outputs of its RNN cells for **all steps in the sequence**:
    - A simple RNN will have an output tensor with shape **(L, N, H)**.
    - A bidirectional RNN (more on that later) will have an output tensor with shape **(L, N, 2*H)**.
    - If you choose `batch_first`, it will *flip* the first two dimensions and then produce outputs with shape **(N, L, H)**.
  - The **final hidden state** corresponding to the representation of the full sequence and its shape follows the same rules as the initial hidden state.

Let's illustrate the differences between shapes by creating a "*batch*" containing **three sequences**, each having **four data points** (corners), with each data point having **two coordinates**. Its shape is **(3, 4, 2)**, and it is an example of a *batch-first* tensor **(N, L, F)**, like a mini-batch you'd get from a data loader:

```
batch = torch.as_tensor(points[:3]).float()
batch.shape
```

Output

```
torch.Size([3, 4, 2])
```

Since RNNs use **sequence-first** by default, we *could* explicitly change the shape of the batch using `permute()` to *flip* the first two dimensions:

```
permuted_batch = batch.permute(1, 0, 2)
permuted_batch.shape
```

Output

```
torch.Size([4, 3, 2])
```

Now the data is in an "*RNN-friendly*" shape, and we can run it through a regular RNN to get two *sequence-first* tensors back:

```
torch.manual_seed(19)
rnn = nn.RNN(input_size=n_features, hidden_size=hidden_dim)
out, final_hidden = rnn(permuted_batch)
out.shape, final_hidden.shape
```

Output

```
(torch.Size([4, 3, 2]), torch.Size([1, 3, 2]))
```

For simple RNNs, the **last element of the output IS the final hidden state**!

```
(out[-1] == final_hidden).all()
```

Output

```
tensor(True)
```

Once we're done with the RNN, we can turn the data **back to our familiar batch-first shape**:

```
batch_hidden = final_hidden.permute(1, 0, 2)
batch.shape
```

Output

```
torch.Size([3, 1, 2])
```

That seems like a lot of work, though. Alternatively, we could set the RNN's `batch_first` argument to `True` so we can use the batch above without any modifications:

```
torch.manual_seed(19)
rnn_batch_first = nn.RNN(input_size=n_features,
                         hidden_size=hidden_dim,
                         batch_first=True)
out, final_hidden = rnn_batch_first(batch)
out.shape, final_hidden.shape
```

Output

```
(torch.Size([3, 4, 2]), torch.Size([1, 3, 2]))
```

But then you get these **two distinct shapes as a result**: *batch-first* (N, L, H) for the output and *sequence-first* (1, N, H) for the final hidden state.

On the one hand, this can lead to confusion. On the other hand, most of the time we **won't** be handling the hidden state, and we'll handle the **batch-first output** instead. So, we can stick with **batch-first** for now and, when it comes the time we *have* to handle the hidden state, I will highlight the difference in shapes once again.

In a nutshell, the **RNN's default behavior** is to handle tensors having the shape **(L, N, H)** for hidden states and **(L, N, F)** for sequences of data points. Datasets and **data loaders**, unless customized otherwise, will produce **data points** in the shape **(N, L, F)**.

To address this difference, we'll be using the **`batch_first`** argument to turn both **inputs and outputs** into this **familiar batch-first shape**.

Stacked RNN

First, take **one RNN** and feed it a **sequence of data points**. Next, take **another RNN** and feed it the **sequence of outputs produced by the first RNN**. There you go—you have a **stacked RNN** where each of the RNNs is considered a "*layer*" of the stacked one. The figure below depicts a stacked RNN with two "*layers*."

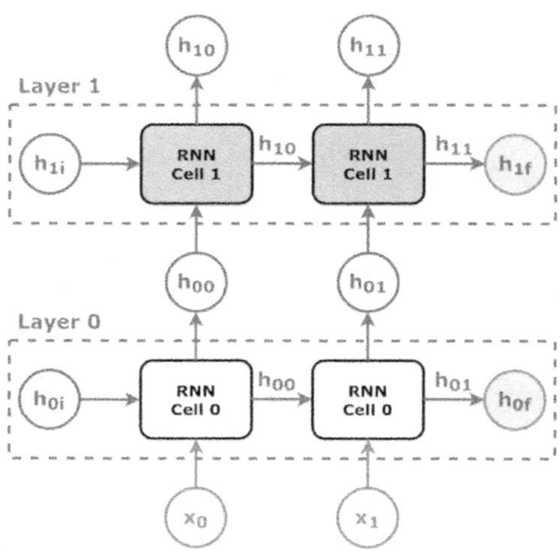

Figure 8.10 - Stacked RNN with two layers

"Two layers only? It doesn't seem much..."

It may not seem like it, but a two-layer stacked RNN is already computationally expensive, since not only does one cell depend on the previous one, but also one "*layer*" depends on the other.

Each "*layer*" starts with its own initial hidden state and produces **its own final hidden state**. The **output of the stacked RNN**—that is, the hidden states at each step of the sequence—are **the hidden states of the top-most layer**.

Let's create a stacked RNN with two layers:

```
torch.manual_seed(19)
rnn_stacked = nn.RNN(input_size=2, hidden_size=2,
                     num_layers=2, batch_first=True)
state = rnn_stacked.state_dict()
state
```

Output

```
OrderedDict([('weight_ih_l0', tensor([[ 0.6627, -0.4245],
                         [ 0.5373,  0.2294]])),
             ('weight_hh_l0', tensor([[-0.4015, -0.5385],
                         [-0.1956, -0.6835]])),
             ('bias_ih_l0', tensor([0.4954, 0.6533])),
             ('bias_hh_l0', tensor([-0.3565, -0.2904])),
             ('weight_ih_l1', tensor([[-0.6701, -0.5811],
                         [-0.0170, -0.5856]])),
             ('weight_hh_l1', tensor([[ 0.1159, -0.6978],
                         [ 0.3241, -0.0983]])),
             ('bias_ih_l1', tensor([-0.3163, -0.2153])),
             ('bias_hh_l1', tensor([ 0.0722, -0.3242]))])
```

From the RNN's state dictionary, we can see it has **two groups** of weights and biases, one for each layer, with each layer indicated by its corresponding suffix (`_l0` and `_l1`).

Now, let's create **two simple RNNs** and use the weights and biases above to set their weights accordingly. Each RNN will behave as one of the layers of the stacked one:

```
rnn_layer0 = nn.RNN(input_size=2, hidden_size=2, batch_first=True)
rnn_layer1 = nn.RNN(input_size=2, hidden_size=2, batch_first=True)

rnn_layer0.load_state_dict(dict(list(state.items())[:4]))
rnn_layer1.load_state_dict(dict([(k[:-1]+'0', v)
                                 for k, v in
                                 list(state.items())[4:]]))
```

Output

```
<All keys matched successfully>
```

Now, let's make **a batch containing one sequence** from our synthetic dataset (thus having shape `(N=1, L=4, F=2)`):

```
x = torch.as_tensor(points[0:1]).float()
```

The RNN representing the first layer takes the sequence of data points as usual:

```
out0, h0 = rnn_layer0(x)
```

It produces the expected two outputs: a sequence of hidden states (`out0`) and the final hidden state (`h0`) for this layer.

Next, it uses the **sequence of hidden states as inputs for the next layer**:

```
out1, h1 = rnn_layer1(out0)
```

The second layer produces the expected two outputs again: another sequence of hidden states (`out1`) and the final hidden state (`h1`) for this layer.

The **overall output of the stacked RNN** must have two elements as well:

- A **sequence of hidden states**, produced by the **last layer** (`out1`).
- The **concatenation** of **final hidden states** of **all layers**.

```
out1, torch.cat([h0, h1])
```

Output

```
(tensor([[[-0.7533, -0.7711],
          [-0.0566, -0.5960],
          [ 0.4324, -0.2908],
          [ 0.1563, -0.5152]]], grad_fn=<TransposeBackward1>),
 tensor([[[-0.5297,  0.3551]],

         [[ 0.1563, -0.5152]]], grad_fn=<CatBackward>))
```

Done! We've replicated the inner workings of a stacked RNN using two simple RNNs. You can double-check the results by feeding the sequence of data points to the actual stacked RNN itself:

```
out, hidden = rnn_stacked(x)
out, hidden
```

And you'll get exactly the same results.

For **stacked** RNNs, the **last element of the output is the final hidden state of the LAST LAYER**! But, since we're using a `batch_first` layer, we need to *permute* the hidden state's dimensions to *batch-first* as well:

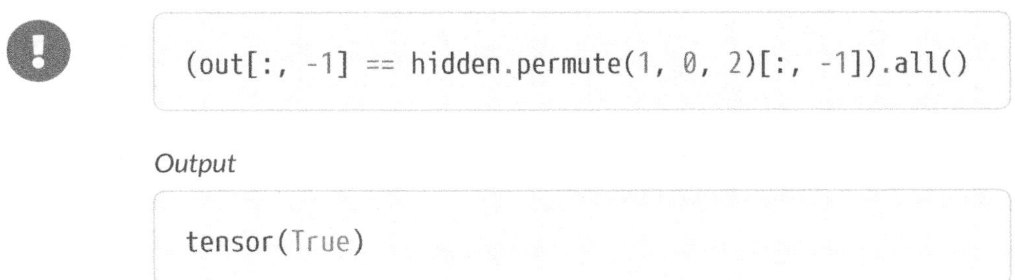

```
(out[:, -1] == hidden.permute(1, 0, 2)[:, -1]).all()
```

Output

```
tensor(True)
```

Bidirectional RNN

First, take **one RNN** and feed it a **sequence of data points**. Next, take **another RNN** and feed it the **sequence of data points in reversed order**. There you go—you've got a **bidirectional RNN** where each of the RNNs is considered a "*direction.*" The figure below depicts a bidirectional RNN.

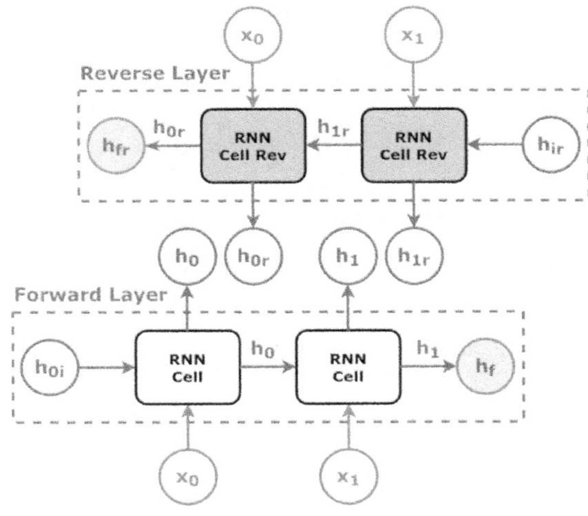

Figure 8.11 - Bidirectional RNN

Each "*layer*" starts with its own initial hidden state and produces **its own final hidden state.** But, unlike the stacked version, it **keeps both sequences of hidden states** produced at each step. Moreover, it also **reverses** the sequence of hidden states produced by the reverse layer to make both sequences match (h_0 with h_{0r}, h_1 with h_{1r}, and so on).

"Why would you need a bidirectional RNN?"

The **reverse layer** allows the network to look at "*future*" information in a given sequence, thus better describing the **context** in which the elements of the sequence exist. This is particularly important in natural language processing tasks, where the role of a given word sometimes may only be ascertained by the word that *follows* it. These relationships would never be captured by a unidirectional RNN.

Let's create a bidirectional RNN:

```
torch.manual_seed(19)
rnn_bidirect = nn.RNN(input_size=2, hidden_size=2,
                      bidirectional=True, batch_first=True)
state = rnn_bidirect.state_dict()
state
```

Output

```
OrderedDict([('weight_ih_l0', tensor([[ 0.6627, -0.4245],
                      [ 0.5373,  0.2294]])),
             ('weight_hh_l0', tensor([[-0.4015, -0.5385],
                      [-0.1956, -0.6835]])),
             ('bias_ih_l0', tensor([0.4954, 0.6533])),
             ('bias_hh_l0', tensor([-0.3565, -0.2904])),
             ('weight_ih_l0_reverse', tensor([[-0.6701, -0.5811],
                      [-0.0170, -0.5856]])),
             ('weight_hh_l0_reverse', tensor([[ 0.1159, -0.6978],
                      [ 0.3241, -0.0983]])),
             ('bias_ih_l0_reverse', tensor([-0.3163, -0.2153])),
             ('bias_hh_l0_reverse', tensor([ 0.0722, -0.3242]))])
```

From its state dictionary, we can see it has **two groups** of weights and biases, one for each layer, with each layer indicated by its corresponding suffix (`_l0` and _l0_reverse).

Once again, let's create **two simple RNNs**, and then use the weights and biases above to set their weights accordingly. Each RNN will behave as one of the layers from the bidirectional one:

```
rnn_forward = nn.RNN(input_size=2, hidden_size=2, batch_first=True)
rnn_reverse = nn.RNN(input_size=2, hidden_size=2, batch_first=True)

rnn_forward.load_state_dict(dict(list(state.items())[:4]))
rnn_reverse.load_state_dict(dict([(k[:-8], v)
                                  for k, v in
                                  list(state.items())[4:]]))
```

Output

```
<All keys matched successfully>
```

We'll be using the same single-sequence batch from before, but we also need it **in reverse**. We can use PyTorch's `flip()` to reverse the dimension corresponding to the sequence (L):

```
x_rev = torch.flip(x, dims=[1]) #N, L, F
x_rev
```

Output

```
tensor([[[-0.8670,  0.9342],
         [-0.8251, -0.9499],
         [ 0.8055, -0.9169],
         [ 1.0349,  0.9661]]])
```

Since there is **no dependency** between the two layers, we just need to feed each layer its corresponding sequence (regular and reversed) and remember to **reverse back** the **sequence of hidden states**.

```
out, h = rnn_forward(x)
out_rev, h_rev = rnn_reverse(x_rev)
out_rev_back = torch.flip(out_rev, dims=[1])
```

The **overall output of the bidirectional RNN** must have two elements as well:

- A **concatenation** side-by-side of **both sequences of hidden states** (`out` and `out_rev_back`).
- The **concatenation** of the **final hidden states** of **both layers**.

```
torch.cat([out, out_rev_back], dim=2), torch.cat([h, h_rev])
```

Output

```
(tensor([[[ 0.3924,  0.8146, -0.9355, -0.8353],
          [ 0.4347, -0.0481, -0.1766,  0.2596],
          [-0.1521, -0.3367,  0.8829,  0.0425],
          [-0.5297,  0.3551, -0.2032, -0.7901]]], grad_fn
=<CatBackward>),
 tensor([[[-0.5297,  0.3551]],

         [[-0.9355, -0.8353]]], grad_fn=<CatBackward>))
```

Done! We've replicated the inner workings of a bidirectional RNN using two simple RNNs. You can double-check the results by feeding the sequence of data points to the actual bidirectional RNN:

```
out, hidden = rnn_bidirect(x)
```

And, once again, you'll get the very same results.

For **bidirectional** RNNs, the **last element of the output ISN'T the final hidden state**! Once again, since we're using a batch_first layer, we need to *permute* the hidden state's dimensions to *batch-first* as well:

```
out[:, -1] == hidden.permute(1, 0, 2).view(1, -1)
```

Output

```
tensor([[ True,  True, False, False]])
```

Bidirectional RNNs are **different** because the **final hidden state** corresponds to the **last element in the sequence** for the **forward layer** and to the **first element in the sequence** for the **reverse layer**. The **output**, on the other hand, is **aligned to sequence**, hence the difference.

Square Model

It is finally time to build a **model** to classify the direction in which the square was drawn: clockwise or counterclockwise. Let's put into practice what we've learned so far and use a **simple RNN** to obtain the **final hidden state** that **represents the full sequence** and use it to train a **classifier layer**, which is, once again, the same as a **logistic regression**.

"*There can be only one ... hidden state.*"

Connor MacLeod

Data Generation

If you hadn't noticed yet, we only have a *training set*. But, since our data is synthetic anyway, let's simply **generate new data**, which, by definition, wasn't seen by the model and therefore qualifies as validation or test data (just make sure to pick a different seed for the generation):

Data Generation

```
test_points, test_directions = generate_sequences(seed=19)
```

Data Preparation

There is nothing special about it: typical data preparation using a tensor dataset and data loaders that will yield batches of sequences with shape (N=16, L=4, F=2).

Data Preparation

```
train_data = TensorDataset(
    torch.as_tensor(points).float(),
    torch.as_tensor(directions).view(-1, 1).float()
)
test_data = TensorDataset(
    torch.as_tensor(test_points).float(),
    torch.as_tensor(test_directions).view(-1, 1).float()
)
train_loader = DataLoader(
    train_data, batch_size=16, shuffle=True
)
test_loader = DataLoader(test_data, batch_size=16)
```

Model Configuration

The main structure behind the `SquareModel` is fairly simple: a simple **RNN layer** followed by a **linear layer** that works as a classifier producing logits. Then, in the `forward()` method, the linear layer takes the **last output** of the recurrent layer as its input.

Model Configuration

```
class SquareModel(nn.Module):
    def __init__(self, n_features, hidden_dim, n_outputs):
        super(SquareModel, self).__init__()
        self.hidden_dim = hidden_dim
        self.n_features = n_features
        self.n_outputs = n_outputs
        self.hidden = None
        # Simple RNN
        self.basic_rnn = nn.RNN(self.n_features,
                                self.hidden_dim,
                                batch_first=True)
        # Classifier to produce as many logits as outputs
        self.classifier = nn.Linear(self.hidden_dim,
                                    self.n_outputs)

    def forward(self, X):
        # X is batch first (N, L, F)
        # output is (N, L, H)
        # final hidden state is (1, N, H)
        batch_first_output, self.hidden = self.basic_rnn(X)

        # only last item in sequence (N, 1, H)
        last_output = batch_first_output[:, -1]
        # classifier will output (N, 1, n_outputs)
        out = self.classifier(last_output)

        # final output is (N, n_outputs)
        return out.view(-1, self.n_outputs)
```

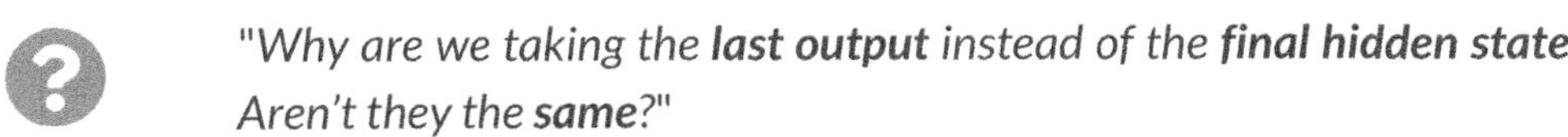

*"Why are we taking the **last output** instead of the **final hidden state**? Aren't they the **same**?"*

They are the same in most cases, yes, but they **are different** if you're using **bidirectional RNNs**. By using the **last output**, we're ensuring that the code will work for all sorts of RNNs: simple, stacked, *and* bidirectional. Besides, we want to *avoid* handling the hidden state anyway, because it's always in *sequence-first* shape.

In the next chapter, we'll be using the **full output**, that is, the **full sequence of hidden states**, for encoder-decoder models.

Next, we create an instance of the model, the corresponding loss function for a binary classification problem, and an optimizer:

Model Configuration

```
torch.manual_seed(21)
model = SquareModel(n_features=2, hidden_dim=2, n_outputs=1)
loss = nn.BCEWithLogitsLoss()
optimizer = optim.Adam(model.parameters(), lr=0.01)
```

Model Training

Then, we train our `SquareModel` over 100 epochs, as usual, visualize the losses, and evaluate its accuracy on the test data:

Model Training

```
sbs_rnn = StepByStep(model, loss, optimizer)
sbs_rnn.set_loaders(train_loader, test_loader)
sbs_rnn.train(100)
```

```
fig = sbs_rnn.plot_losses()
```

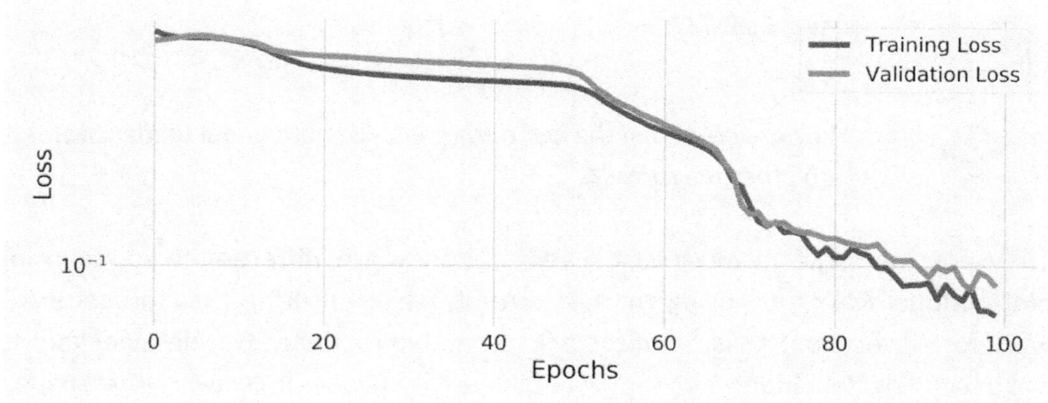

Figure 8.12 - Losses—`SquareModel`

```
StepByStep.loader_apply(test_loader, sbs_rnn.correct)
```

Output

```
tensor([[50, 53],
        [75, 75]])
```

Our simple model hit 97.65% accuracy on the test data. Very good, but, then again, this is a toy dataset.

Now, for the *fun* part :-)

Visualizing the Model

In this section, we're going to thoroughly explore **how** the model managed to successfully classify the sequences. We'll see the following:

- How the model **transforms the inputs**.
- How the **classifier separates the final hidden states**.
- What the **sequence of hidden states** looks like.
- The **journey of a hidden state** through *every* **transformation**, **translation**, and **activation**.

Buckle up!

Transformed Inputs

While the hidden state is sequentially transformed, we've already seen (in Figure 8.9) that the **data points are independently transformed**; that is, every data point (corner) goes through **the same affine transformation**. This means we can simply use the parameters `weights_ih_l0` and `bias_ih_l0` learned by our model to see what's happening to the inputs (data points) before they are added up to the transformed hidden state:

```
state = model.basic_rnn.state_dict()
state['weight_ih_l0'], state['bias_ih_l0']
```

Output

```
(tensor([[-0.5873, -2.5140],
         [-1.6189, -0.4233]], device='cuda:0'),
 tensor([0.8272, 0.9219], device='cuda:0'))
```

"What does it look like?"

Let's visualize the transformed "*perfect*" square.

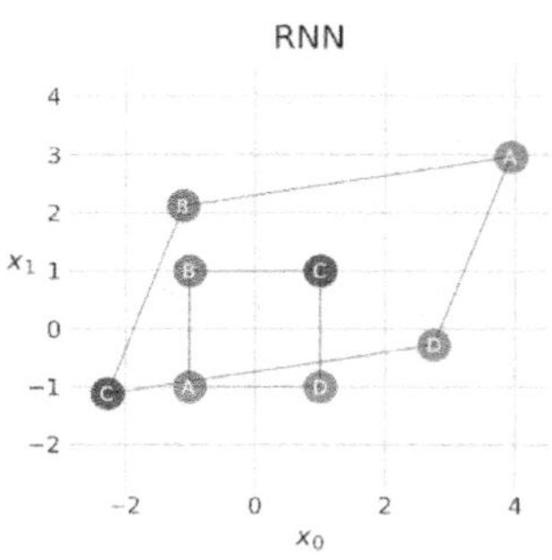

Figure 8.13 - Transformed inputs (corners)

Our `SquareModel` learned that it needs to **scale**, **shear**, **flip**, and **translate** the inputs (corners) at every step before adding each of them to the transformed hidden state.

Hidden States

Remember, there are eight possible sequences (Figure 8.3) since it is possible to start at any of the four corners, and move in either direction. Each corner was assigned a **color** (as in the figure above), and since **clockwise** is the **positive class**, it is represented by a "+" sign.

If we use the "*perfect*" square as input to our trained model, that's what the **final hidden states** look like for each of the eight sequences.

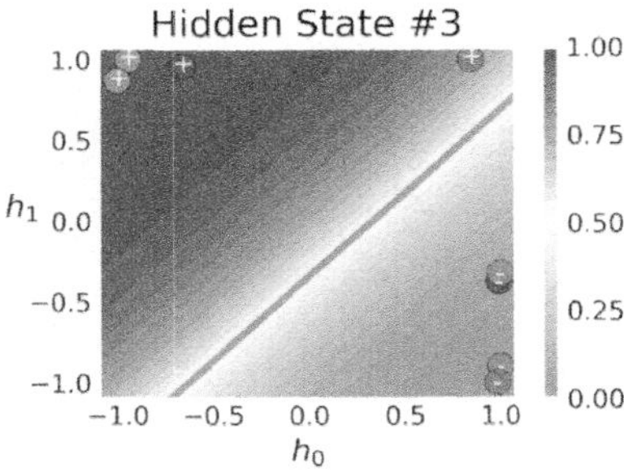

Figure 8.14 - Final hidden states for eight sequences of the "perfect" square

For **clockwise** movement, the final hidden states are situated in the upper-left region, while **counterclockwise** movement brings the final hidden states to the lower-right corner. The decision boundary, as expected from a logistic regression, is a straight line. The point closest to the decision boundary—that is, the one the model is less confident about—corresponds to the sequence starting at the *B corner* (green) and moving clockwise (+).

"What about the ***other hidden states*** *for the* ***actual sequences****?"*

Let's visualize them as well. In the figure below, **clockwise** sequences are represented by **blue points** and **counterclockwise** sequences, by **red points.**

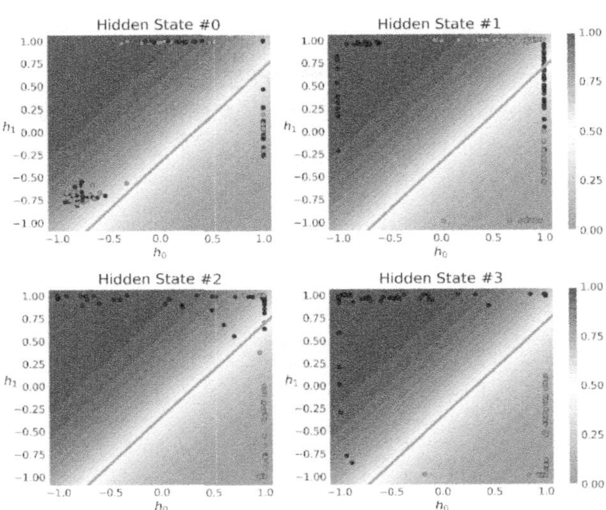

Figure 8.15 - Sequence of hidden states

We can see that the model already achieves *some separation* after "*seeing*" **two data points (corners)**, corresponding to "Hidden State #1." After "*seeing*" the third corner, most of the sequences are already correctly classified, and, after observing all corners, it gets every *noisy square* right.

*"Can we pick **one sequence** and observe its **hidden state** from its initial to its final values?"*

Sure we can!

The Journey of a Hidden State

Let's use the **ABCD** sequence of the "*perfect*" square for this. The initial hidden state is (0, 0) by default, and it is colored black. Every time a new data point (corner) is going to be used in the computation, the affected hidden state is colored accordingly (gray, green, blue, and red, in order).

The figure below **tracks the progress of the hidden state** over **every operation performed inside the RNN**.

The **first column** has the hidden state that's an **input** for the RNN cell at a given step; the **second column** has the **transformed hidden state**; the **third**, the **translated hidden state** (by adding the transformed input); and the **last**, the **activated hidden state**.

There are **four rows**, one for each data point (corner) in our sequence. The initial hidden state of each row is the activated state of the previous row, so it starts at the initial hidden state of the whole sequence (0, 0) and, after processing the gray, green, blue, and red corners, ends at the final hidden state, the red dot close to (-1, 1) in the last plot.

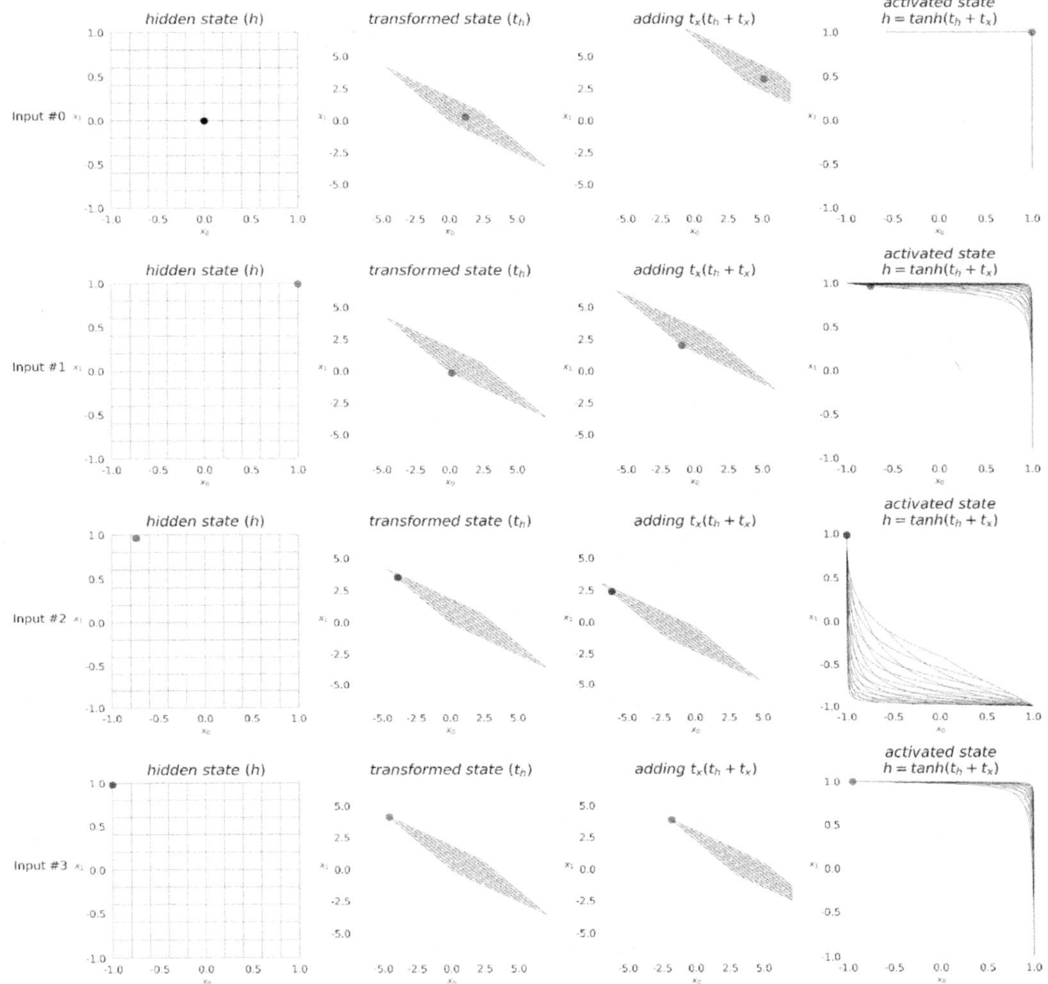

Figure 8.16 - Transforming the hidden state

If we **connect all the hidden states' positions** throughout the whole sequence and **color the path** following the assigned colors for each corner, we get to visualize everything in a single plot in the end.

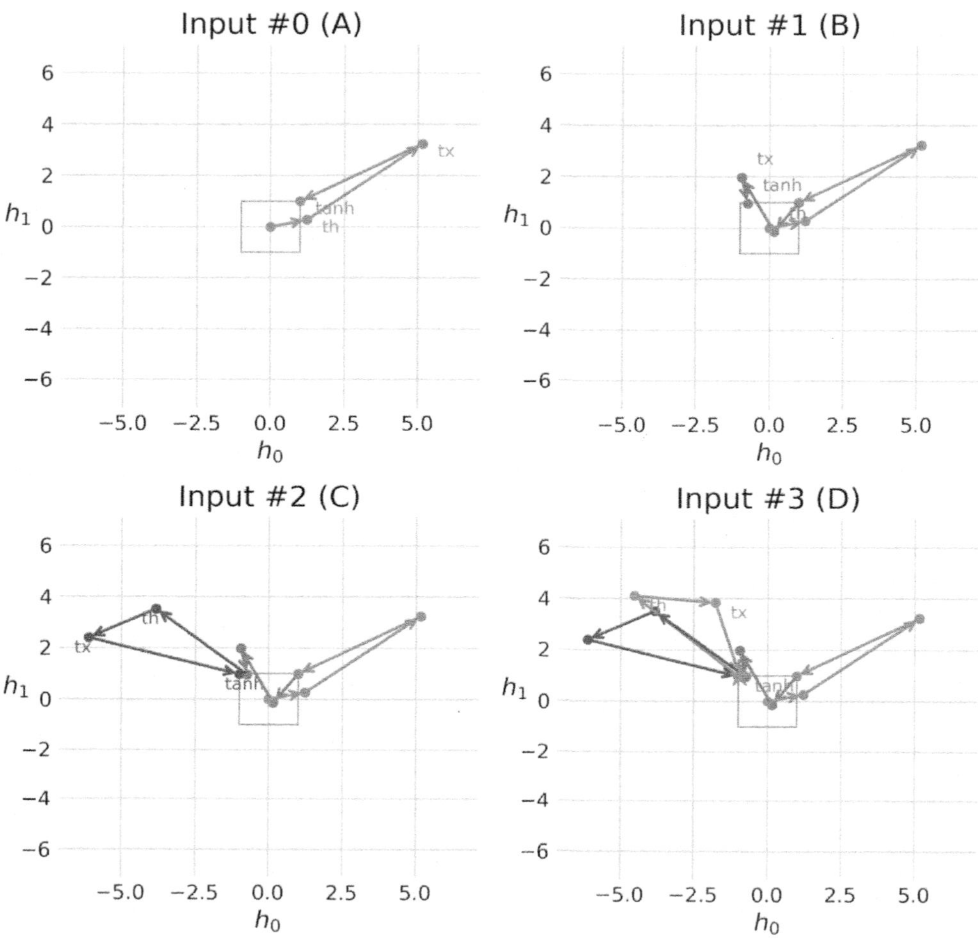

Figure 8.17 - The path of the hidden state

The red square at the center shows the [-1, 1] bound given by the hyperbolic-tangent activation. Every hidden state (the last point of a given color [corner]) will be inside or at the edge of the red square. The final position is depicted by a star.

Can We Do Better?

There are a couple of questions I'd like to raise:

- What if the **previous hidden state contains more information** than the **newly computed one**?
- What if **the data point adds more information** than the **previous hidden state** had?

Since the RNN cell has both of them (t_h and t_x) on the same footing and **simply adds them up**, there is no way to address the two questions above. To do so, we would need something different, like...

Gated Recurrent Units (GRUs)

Gated recurrent units, or GRUs for short, provide the answer to those two questions! Let's see how they do it by tackling one problem at a time. What if, instead of simply computing a **new hidden state** and going with it, we tried a **weighted average** of both hidden states, **old and new**?

$$h_{\text{new}} = \tanh(t_h + t_x)$$
$$h' = h_{\text{new}} * (1 - z) + h_{\text{old}} * z$$

Equation 8.2 - Weighted average of old and new hidden states

The new **parameter *z*** controls **how much weight** the GRU should give to the **old hidden state**. OK, the first question has been addressed, and we can recover the typical RNN behavior simply by **setting *z* to zero**.

Now, what if, instead of computing the new hidden state by simply **adding up t_h and t_x**, we tried **scaling t_h** first?

$$h_{\text{new}} = n = \tanh(r * t_h + t_x)$$

Equation 8.3 - Scaling the old hidden state

The new **parameter *r*** controls **how much we keep** from the **old hidden state** before adding the transformed input. For **low values of *r***, the **relative importance of the data point is increased**, thus addressing the second question. Moreover, we can recover the typical RNN behavior simply by **setting *r* to one**. The new hidden state is called **candidate hidden state** (***n***).

Next, we can **combine these two changes** into a single expression:

$$h' = \tanh(r * t_h + t_x) * (1 - z) + h * z$$

Equation 8.4 - Hidden state, the GRU way

And we've (re)**invented the gated recurrent unit** cell on our own :-)

By the way, the two new parameters **r** and **z** are called **gates**—respectively, **reset** and **update** gates. Both of them must produce values **between zero and one**, thus allowing **only a fraction of the original values** to go through.

Every gate **produces a vector of values** (each value between zero and one) with a **size** corresponding to the **number of hidden dimensions**. For **two** hidden dimensions, a gate may have values like **[0.52, 0.87]** for example.

Since gates produce vectors, operations involving them are **element-wise multiplications.**

GRU Cell

If we place both expressions next to one another, we can more easily see that the **RNN is a special case of the GRU** (for *r*=1 and *z*=0):

$$
\begin{aligned}
\text{RNN}: h' &= \tanh(t_h + t_x) \\
\text{GRU}: h' &= \underbrace{\underbrace{\tanh(r * t_{hn} + t_{xn})}_{n} * (1 - z) + h * z}_{\text{weighted average of } n \text{ and } h}
\end{aligned}
$$

Equation 8.5 - RNN vs GRU

*"OK, I see it; but where do **r** and **z** come from?"*

Well, this is a deep learning book, so the **only right answer** to "*Where does **something** come from*" is, a **neural network**! Just kidding ... or am I? Actually, we'll train **both gates** using a structure that is **pretty much an RNN cell**, except for the fact that it uses a **sigmoid** activation function:

$$
\begin{aligned}
r(\text{eset gate}) &= \sigma(t_{hr} + t_{xr}) \\
z(\text{update gate}) &= \sigma(t_{hz} + t_{xz}) \\
n &= \tanh(r * t_{hn} + t_{xn})
\end{aligned}
$$

Equation 8.6 - Gates (r and z) and candidate hidden state (n)

Every **gate** worthy of its name will use a **sigmoid activation function** to produce gate-compatible values **between zero and one**.

Moreover, since all components of a GRU (*n*, *r*, and *z*) share a similar structure, it should be no surprise that its corresponding transformations (t_h and t_x) are also similarly computed:

$$
\begin{aligned}
r \text{ (hidden)} & : t_{hr} & = & \; W_{hr} & h & \; + & b_{hr} \\
r \text{ (input)} & : t_{xr} & = & \; W_{ir} & x & \; + & b_{ir} \\
z \text{ (hidden)} & : t_{hz} & = & \; W_{hz} & h & \; + & b_{hz} \\
z \text{ (input)} & : t_{xz} & = & \; W_{iz} & x & \; + & b_{iz} \\
n \text{ (hidden)} & : t_{hn} & = & \; W_{hn} & h & \; + & b_{hn} \\
n \text{ (input)} & : t_{xn} & = & \; W_{in} & x & \; + & b_{in}
\end{aligned}
$$

Equation 8.7 - Transformations of a GRU

See? They all follow the same logic! Actually, let's *literally* **see** how all these components are connected in the following diagram.

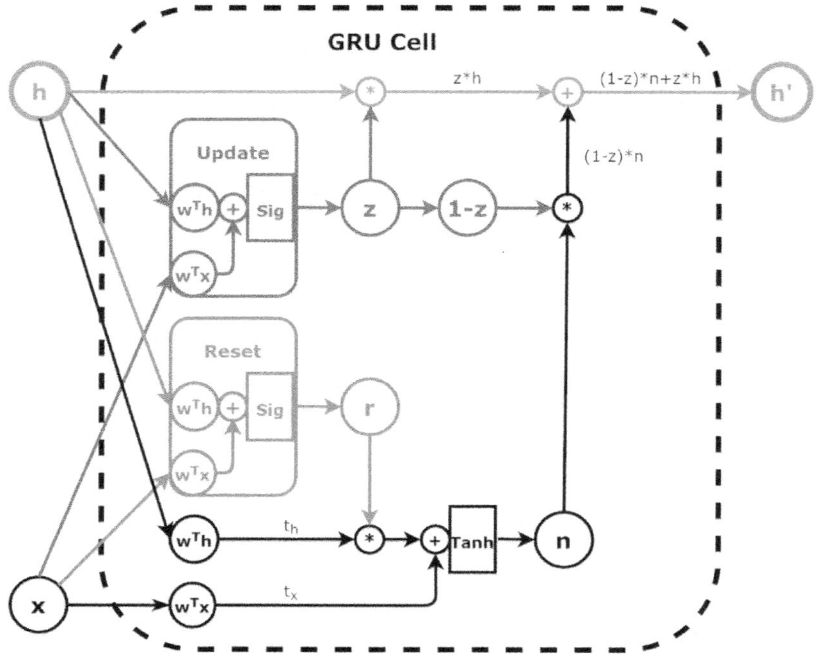

Figure 8.18 - Internals of a GRU cell

The gates are following the same color convention I used in the equations: **red** for the **reset gate** (*r*) and **blue** for the **update gate** (*z*). The path of the **(new) candidate hidden state** (*n*) is drawn in **black** and joins the **(old) hidden state** (*h*), drawn in **gray**, to produce the **actual new hidden state** (*h'*).

To really understand the flow of information inside the GRU cell, I suggest you try these exercises:

- First, learn to look *past* (or literally ignore) the **internals of the gates**: both *r* and *z* are simply **values between zero and one** (for each hidden dimension).
- Pretend ***r*=1**; can you see that the **resulting *n*** is equivalent to the output of a **simple RNN**?
- Keep ***r*=1**, and now pretend ***z*=0**; can you see that the **new hidden state *h'*** is equivalent to the output of a **simple RNN**?
- Now pretend ***z*=1**; can you see that the **new hidden state *h'*** is simply a **copy of the old hidden state** (in other words, the data [x] does not have any effect)?
- If you **decrease *r* all the way to zero**, the **resulting *n*** is **less and less influenced** by the **old hidden state**.
- If you **decrease *z* all the way to zero**, the **new hidden state *h'*** is **closer and closer** to ***n***.

- For **r=0** and **z=0**, the cell becomes equivalent to a **linear layer** followed by a **TanH** activation function (in other words, the old hidden state [*h*] does not have any effect).

Now, let's see how a GRU cell works in code. We'll create one using PyTorch's own `nn.GRUCell` and **disassemble** it into its components to manually reproduce all the steps involved in **updating the hidden state**. To create a cell, we need to tell it the `input_size` (number of features in our data points) and the `hidden_size` (the size of the vector representing the hidden state), exactly the same as in the RNN cell. The nonlinearity is fixed, though, as the hyperbolic tangent.

```
n_features = 2
hidden_dim = 2

torch.manual_seed(17)
gru_cell = nn.GRUCell(input_size=n_features, hidden_size=hidden_dim)
gru_state = gru_cell.state_dict()
gru_state
```

Output

```
OrderedDict([('weight_ih', tensor([[-0.0930,  0.0497],
                                   [ 0.4670, -0.5319],
                                   [-0.6656,  0.0699],
                                   [-0.1662,  0.0654],
                                   [-0.0449, -0.6828],
                                   [-0.6769, -0.1889]])),
             ('weight_hh', tensor([[-0.4167, -0.4352],
                                   [-0.2060, -0.3989],
                                   [-0.7070, -0.5083],
                                   [ 0.1418,  0.0930],
                                   [-0.5729, -0.5700],
                                   [-0.1818, -0.6691]])),
             ('bias_ih',
              tensor([-0.4316,  0.4019,  0.1222, -0.4647, -0.5578,
0.4493])),
             ('bias_hh',
              tensor([-0.6800,  0.4422, -0.3559, -0.0279,  0.6553,
0.2918]))])
```

*"Wait! There is something definitely **weird** with these shapes..."*

Yeah, you're right! Instead of returning **separate weights** for each of the GRU cell's components (*r*, *z*, and *n*), the `state_dict()` returns the **concatenated weights and biases**.

```
Wx, bx = gru_state['weight_ih'], gru_state['bias_ih']
Wh, bh = gru_state['weight_hh'], gru_state['bias_hh']

print(Wx.shape, Wh.shape)
print(bx.shape, bh.shape)
```

Output

```
torch.Size([6, 2]) torch.Size([6, 2])
torch.Size([6]) torch.Size([6])
```

The shape is **(3*hidden_dim, n_features)** for `weight_ih`, **(3*hidden_dim, hidden_dim)** for `weight_hh`, and simply **(3*hidden_dim)** for both biases.

For `Wx` and `bx` in the state dictionary above, we can split the values like this:

$$
\begin{aligned}
W_{xr} &= \begin{cases} -0.0930, & 0.0497, \\ 0.4670, & -0.5319, \end{cases} \\
W_{xz} &= \begin{cases} -0.6656, & 0.0699, \\ -0.1662, & 0.0654, \end{cases} \\
W_{xn} &= \begin{cases} -0.0449, & -0.6828, \\ -0.6769, & -0.1889 \end{cases}
\end{aligned}
$$

$$
\underbrace{-0.4316, 0.4019}_{b_{xr}}, \underbrace{0.1222, -0.4647}_{b_{xz}}, \underbrace{-0.5578, 0.4493}_{b_{xn}}
$$

Equation 8.8 - Splitting tensors into their r, z, and n components

In code, we can use `split()` to get tensors for each of the components:

```
Wxr, Wxz, Wxn = Wx.split(hidden_dim, dim=0)
bxr, bxz, bxn = bx.split(hidden_dim, dim=0)

Whr, Whz, Whn = Wh.split(hidden_dim, dim=0)
bhr, bhz, bhn = bh.split(hidden_dim, dim=0)

Wxr, bxr
```

Output

```
(tensor([[-0.0930,  0.0497],
         [ 0.4670, -0.5319]]), tensor([-0.4316,  0.4019]))
```

Next, let's use the weights and biases to create the corresponding linear layers:

```
def linear_layers(Wx, bx, Wh, bh):
    hidden_dim, n_features = Wx.size()
    lin_input = nn.Linear(n_features, hidden_dim)
    lin_input.load_state_dict({'weight': Wx, 'bias': bx})
    lin_hidden = nn.Linear(hidden_dim, hidden_dim)
    lin_hidden.load_state_dict({'weight': Wh, 'bias': bh})
    return lin_hidden, lin_input

# reset gate - red
r_hidden, r_input = linear_layers(Wxr, bxr, Whr, bhr)
# update gate - blue
z_hidden, z_input = linear_layers(Wxz, bxz, Whz, bhz)
# candidate state - black
n_hidden, n_input = linear_layers(Wxn, bxn, Whn, bhn)
```

Then, let's use these layers to create functions that replicate **both gates (*r* and *z*)** and the **candidate hidden state (*n*)**:

```
def reset_gate(h, x):
    thr = r_hidden(h)
    txr = r_input(x)
    r = torch.sigmoid(thr + txr)
    return r  # red

def update_gate(h, x):
    thz = z_hidden(h)
    txz = z_input(x)
    z = torch.sigmoid(thz + txz)
    return z  # blue

def candidate_n(h, x, r):
    thn = n_hidden(h)
    txn = n_input(x)
    n = torch.tanh(r * thn + txn)
    return n  # black
```

Cool—all the transformations and activations are handled by the functions above. This means we can replicate the mechanics of a GRU cell at its component level (*r*, *z*, and *n*). We also need an **initial hidden state** and the **first data point (corner)** of a sequence:

```
initial_hidden = torch.zeros(1, hidden_dim)
X = torch.as_tensor(points[0]).float()
first_corner = X[0:1]
```

We use both values to get the output from the **reset gate (*r*)**:

```
r = reset_gate(initial_hidden, first_corner)
r
```

Output

```
tensor([[0.2387, 0.6928]], grad_fn=<SigmoidBackward>)
```

Let's pause for a moment here. First, the reset gate **returns a tensor of size two** because we have **two hidden dimensions**. Second, the **two values may be different** (duh, I know!). What does it mean?

The **reset gate** may **scale each hidden dimension independently**. It can completely suppress the values from one of the hidden dimensions while letting the other pass unchallenged. In geometrical terms, this means that the **hidden space may shrink in one direction while stretching in the other**. We'll visualize it shortly in the journey of a (gated) hidden state.

The reset gate is an input for the **candidate hidden state (*n*)**:

```
n = candidate_n(initial_hidden, first_corner, r)
n
```

Output

```
tensor([[-0.8032, -0.2275]], grad_fn=<TanhBackward>)
```

That *would* be the end of it, and that would be the new hidden state if it wasn't for the **update gate (*z*)**:

```
z = update_gate(initial_hidden, first_corner)
z
```

Output

```
tensor([[0.2984, 0.3540]], grad_fn=<SigmoidBackward>)
```

Another short pause here—the update gate is telling us to keep **29.84% of the first** and **35.40% of the second dimensions of the initial hidden state**. The remaining **70.16%** and **64.6%**, respectively, are coming from the **candidate hidden state (*n*)**. So, the **new hidden state (`h_prime`)** is computed accordingly:

```
h_prime = n*(1-z) + initial_hidden*z
h_prime
```

Output

```
tensor([[-0.5635, -0.1470]], grad_fn=<AddBackward0>)
```

Now, let's take a quick sanity check, feeding the same input to the original GRU cell:

```
gru_cell(first_corner)
```

Output

```
tensor([[-0.5635, -0.1470]], grad_fn=<AddBackward0>)
```

Perfect match!

But, then again, you're likely not inclined to loop over the sequence yourself while using a GRU cell, right? You probably want to use a full-fledged…

GRU Layer

The `nn.GRU` layer takes care of the hidden state handling for us, no matter how long the input sequence is. We've been through this once with the RNN layer. The arguments, inputs, and outputs are **almost** exactly the same for both of them, except for **one small difference**: You **cannot** choose a different activation function anymore. That's it.

And yes, you can create **stacked GRUs** and **bidirectional GRUs** as well. The logic doesn't change a bit—the only difference is that you'll be using a **fancier GRU cell** instead of the basic RNN cell.

So, let's go straight to **creating a model** using a gated recurring unit.

Square Model II — The Quickening

This model is pretty much the same as the original "Square Model," except for **one difference**: Its recurrent neural network is not a plain RNN anymore, but a GRU. Everything else stays exactly the same.

Model Configuration

```
class SquareModelGRU(nn.Module):
    def __init__(self, n_features, hidden_dim, n_outputs):
        super(SquareModelGRU, self).__init__()
        self.hidden_dim = hidden_dim
        self.n_features = n_features
        self.n_outputs = n_outputs
        self.hidden = None
        # Simple GRU
        self.basic_rnn = nn.GRU(self.n_features,
                                self.hidden_dim,
                                batch_first=True)          ①
        # Classifier to produce as many logits as outputs
        self.classifier = nn.Linear(self.hidden_dim,
                                    self.n_outputs)

    def forward(self, X):
        # X is batch first (N, L, F)
        # output is (N, L, H)
        # final hidden state is (1, N, H)
        batch_first_output, self.hidden = self.basic_rnn(X)

        # only last item in sequence (N, 1, H)
        last_output = batch_first_output[:, -1]
        # classifier will output (N, 1, n_outputs)
        out = self.classifier(last_output)

        # final output is (N, n_outputs)
        return out.view(-1, self.n_outputs)
```

① The ONLY change in the code: from `nn.RNN` to `nn.GRU`

We'll be using the same data loaders again, so we're going directly to the model configuration and training.

Model Configuration & Training

Model Configuration

```
torch.manual_seed(21)
model = SquareModelGRU(n_features=2, hidden_dim=2, n_outputs=1)
loss = nn.BCEWithLogitsLoss()
optimizer = optim.Adam(model.parameters(), lr=0.01)
```

Model Training

```
sbs_gru = StepByStep(model, loss, optimizer)
sbs_gru.set_loaders(train_loader, test_loader)
sbs_gru.train(100)
```

```
fig = sbs_gru.plot_losses()
```

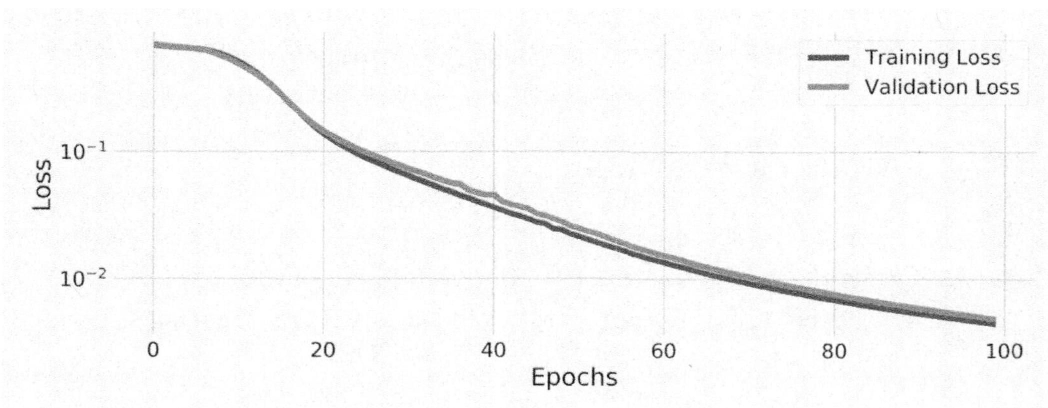

Figure 8.19 - Losses—`SquareModelGRU`

Cool—the loss decreased **much quicker** now, and all it takes is switching from RNN to GRU.

"*The sensation you feel is the* ***quickening***."

Ramirez

```
StepByStep.loader_apply(test_loader, sbs_gru.correct)
```

Output

```
tensor([[53, 53],
        [75, 75]])
```

That's 100% accuracy! Let's try to **visualize** the effect of the GRU architecture on the classification of the hidden states.

Visualizing the Model

Hidden States

Once again, if we use the "*perfect*" square as the input to our newly trained model, we get the following **final hidden states** for each of the eight sequences (plotted sided-by-side with the previous model for easier comparison):

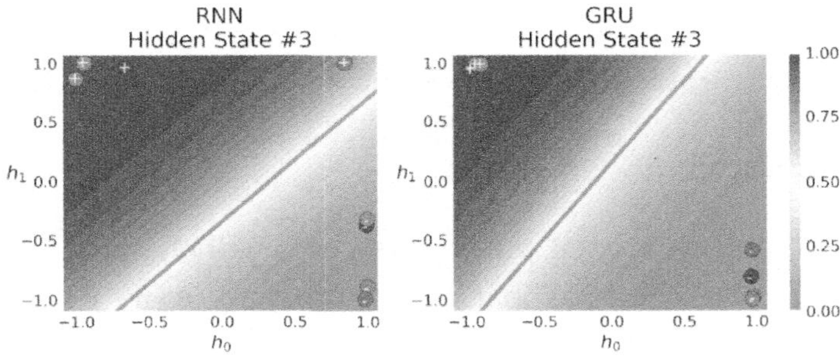

Figure 8.20 - Final hidden states for eight sequences of the "perfect" square

The GRU model achieves a **better separation** of the sequences than its RNN counterpart. What about the actual sequences?

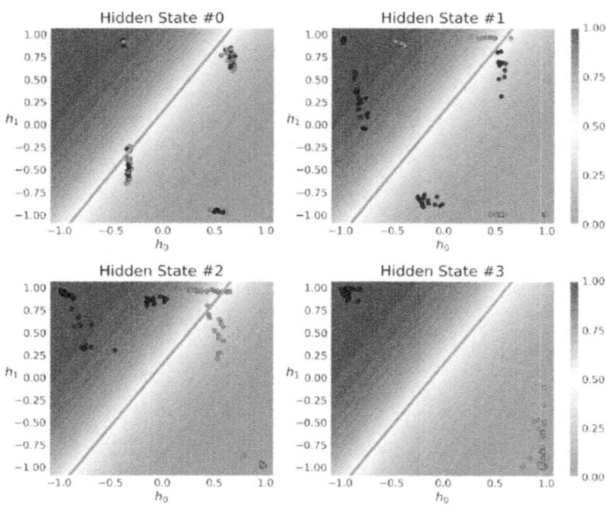

Figure 8.21 - Sequence of hidden states

Like the RNN, the GRU achieves increasingly better separation as it sees more data points. It is interesting to notice that there are **four distinct groups** of sequences, each corresponding to a **starting corner**.

The Journey of a Gated Hidden State

Once again, we're going to track the **journey** of a hidden state using the **ABCD** sequence of the "*perfect*" square. The initial hidden state is `(0, 0)` by default, and it is colored black. Every time a new data point (corner) is going to be used in the computation, the affected hidden state is colored accordingly (gray, green, blue, and red, in order).

Figure 8.22 **tracks the progress of the hidden state** over **every operation performed inside the GRU**.

The **first column** has the hidden state that's an **input** for the GRU cell at a given step; the **third**, **sixth**, and **last** columns correspond to the new operations performed by the GRU. The **third** column shows the **gated hidden state**; the **sixth**, the **gated (candidate) hidden state**; and the **last**, the **weighted average of old and candidate hidden states**.

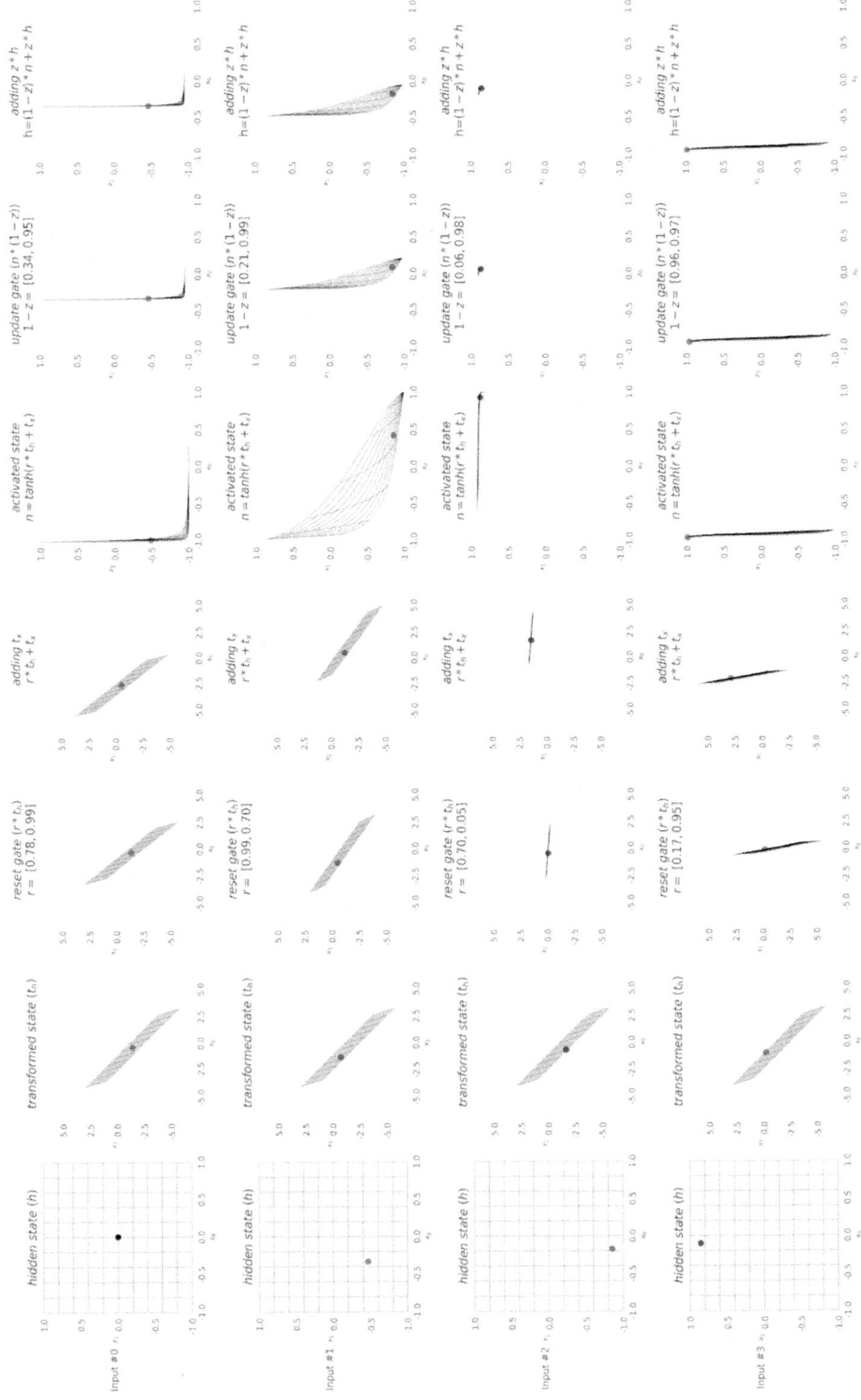

Figure 8.22 - Transforming the hidden state

I'd like to draw your attention to the **third column** in particular: It clearly shows the **effect of a gate**, the reset gate in this case, over the **feature space**. Since a gate has a **distinct value for each dimension**, each dimension will **shrink differently** (it can *only* shrink because values are always between zero and one). In the **third row**, for example, the first dimension gets multiplied by 0.70, while the second dimension gets multiplied by only 0.05, making the resulting feature space *really* small.

Can We Do Better?

The gated recurrent unit is definitely an improvement over the regular RNN, but there are a couple of points I'd like to raise:

- Using the reset gate **inside** the hyperbolic tangent seems "*weird*" (not a scientific argument at all, I know).
- The **best thing** about the **hidden state** is that it is **bounded** by the hyperbolic tangent—it guarantees the next cell will get the hidden state in the same range.
- The **worst thing** about the **hidden state** is that it is **bounded** by the hyperbolic tangent—it constrains the values the hidden state can take and, along with them, the corresponding **gradients**.
- Since we **cannot have the cake** and **eat it too** when it comes to the **hidden state being bounded**, what is preventing us from **using two hidden states in the same cell**?

Yes, let's try that—two hidden states are surely better than one, right?

By the way—I know that GRUs were invented a long time *AFTER* the development of LSTMs, but I've decided to present them in order of increasing complexity. Please don't take the "*story*" I'm telling too literally—it is just a way to facilitate learning.

Long Short-Term Memory (LSTM)

Long short-term memory, or LSTM for short, uses **two states** instead of one. Besides the regular **hidden state (*h*)**, which is **bounded** by the hyperbolic tangent, as usual, it introduces a second **cell state (*c*)** as well, which is **unbounded**.

So, let's work through the points raised in the last section. First, let's keep it simple and use a **regular RNN** to generate a **candidate hidden state (*g*)**:

$$g = \tanh(t_{hg} + t_{xg})$$

Equation 8.9 - LSTM—candidate hidden state

Then, let's turn our attention to the **cell state (*c*)**. What about computing the **new cell state (*c'*)** using a **weighted sum** of the **old cell state** and the **candidate hidden state (*g*)**?

$$c' = g * i + c * f$$

Equation 8.10 - LSTM—new cell state

*"What about **i** and **f**? What are they?"*

They are **gates**, of course: the **input (*i*)** gate and the **forget (*f*)** gate. Now, we're only missing the **new hidden state (*h'*)**. If the **cell state** is unbounded, what about making it **bounded** again?

$$h' = \tanh(c') * o$$

Equation 8.11 - LSTM—new hidden state

Can you *guess* what that **o** is? It is **yet another gate**, the **output (*o*)** gate.

The **cell state** corresponds to the **long-term memory**, while the **hidden state** corresponds to the **short-term memory**.

That's it; we've (re)**invented the long short-term memory** cell on our own!

LSTM Cell

If we place the three expressions next to each other, we can more easily see the differences between them:

$$
\begin{aligned}
\text{RNN}: h' &= \tanh(t_h + t_x) \\
\text{GRU}: h' &= \tanh(r * t_{hn} + t_{xn}) \quad * (1 - z) \quad + h * z \\
\text{LSTM}: c' &= \underbrace{\tanh(t_{hg} + t_{xg})}_{g} \quad * i \quad + c * f \\
h' &= \tanh(c') \quad * o
\end{aligned}
$$

Equation 8.12 - RNN vs GRU vs LSTM

They are not *that* different, to be honest. Sure, the complexity is growing a bit, but it all boils down to finding different ways of **adding up hidden states**, both **old and new**, using **gates**.

The gates themselves always follow the same structure:

$$
\begin{aligned}
i(\text{nput gate}) &= \sigma(t_{hi} + t_{xi}) \\
f(\text{orget gate}) &= \sigma(t_{hf} + t_{xf}) \\
o(\text{utput gate}) &= \sigma(t_{ho} + t_{xo}) \\
g &= \tanh(t_{hg} + t_{xg})
\end{aligned}
$$

Equation 8.13 - LSTM's gates

And the transformations used inside the gates and cells **also** follow the same structure:

$$
\begin{aligned}
i\ (\text{hidden}): t_{hi} &= W_{hi} \quad h + \quad b_{hi} \\
i\ (\text{input}): t_{xi} &= W_{ii} \quad x + \quad b_{ii} \\
f\ (\text{hidden}): t_{hf} &= W_{hf} \quad h + \quad b_{hf} \\
f\ (\text{input}): t_{xf} &= W_{if} \quad x + \quad b_{if} \\
g\ (\text{hidden}): t_{hg} &= W_{hg} \quad h + \quad b_{hg} \\
g\ (\text{input}): t_{xg} &= W_{ig} \quad x + \quad b_{ig} \\
o\ (\text{hidden}): t_{ho} &= W_{ho} \quad h + \quad b_{ho} \\
o\ (\text{input}): t_{xo} &= W_{io} \quad x + \quad b_{io}
\end{aligned}
$$

Equation 8.14 - Gates' internal transformations

Now, let's **visualize** the internals of the LSTM cell.

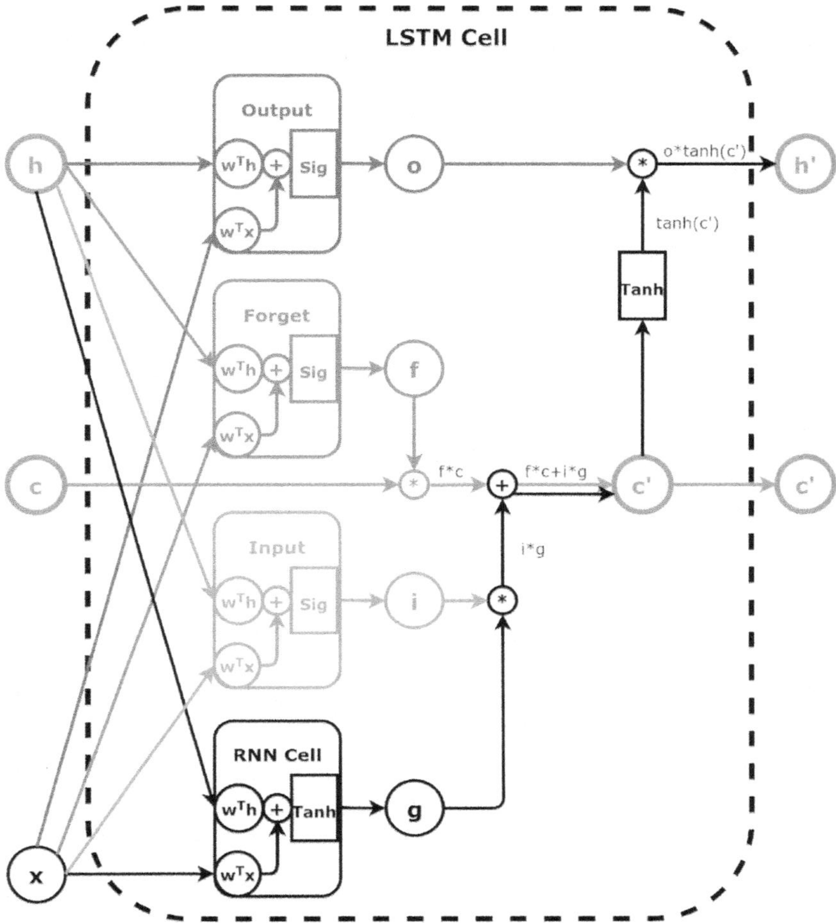

Figure 8.23 - Internals of an LSTM cell

The gates follow the same color convention I used in the equations: **red** for the **forget gate** (*f*), **blue** for the **output gate** (*o*), and **green** for the **input gate (*i*)**. The path of the **(new) candidate hidden state** (*g*) is drawn in **black** and joins the **(old) cell state** (*c*), drawn in **gray**, to produce **both** the **new cell state (*c'*)** and the **actual new hidden state** (*h'*).

To really understand the flow of information inside the LSTM cell, I suggest you try these exercises:

- First, learn to look *past* (or literally ignore) the **internals of the gates**: ***o***, ***f***, and ***i*** are simply **values between zero and one** (for each dimension).
- Pretend ***i*=1** and ***f*=0**—can you see that the **new cell state *c'*** is equivalent to the output of a **simple RNN**?

- Pretend ***i*=0** and ***f*=1**—can you see that the **new cell state *c'*** is simply a **copy of the old cell state** (in other words, the data [x] does not have any effect)?
- If you **decrease** *o* **all the way to zero**, the **new hidden state *h'*** is going to be **zero** as well.

There is **yet another** important **difference** between the two states, hidden and cell: The **cell state** is computed using **two multiplications and one addition only**. No hyperbolic tangent!

"So what? What's wrong with the TanH?"

There is nothing wrong with it, but its **gradients get very small very fast**. This can result in a problem of **vanishing gradients** for longer sequences. But the **cell state does not suffer from this issue**: It is like a "*highway for gradients,*" if you will :-) We're not getting into details about gradient computation in LSTMs, though.

Now, let's see how an LSTM cell works in code. We'll create one using PyTorch's own `nn.LSTMCell` and **disassemble** it into its components to manually reproduce all the steps involved in **updating the hidden state**. To create a cell, we need to tell it the `input_size` (number of features in our data points) and the `hidden_size` (the size of the vector representing the hidden state), exactly the same as in the other two cells. The nonlinearity is, once again, fixed as the hyperbolic tangent.

```
n_features = 2
hidden_dim = 2

torch.manual_seed(17)
lstm_cell = nn.LSTMCell(input_size=n_features,
                        hidden_size=hidden_dim)
lstm_state = lstm_cell.state_dict()
lstm_state
```

Output

```
OrderedDict([('weight_ih', tensor([[-0.0930,  0.0497],
                                    [ 0.4670, -0.5319],
                                    [-0.6656,  0.0699],
                                    [-0.1662,  0.0654],
                                    [-0.0449, -0.6828],
                                    [-0.6769, -0.1889],
                                    [-0.4167, -0.4352],
                                    [-0.2060, -0.3989]])),
             ('weight_hh', tensor([[-0.7070, -0.5083],
                                    [ 0.1418,  0.0930],
                                    [-0.5729, -0.5700],
                                    [-0.1818, -0.6691],
                                    [-0.4316,  0.4019],
                                    [ 0.1222, -0.4647],
                                    [-0.5578,  0.4493],
                                    [-0.6800,  0.4422]])),
             ('bias_ih',
              tensor([-0.3559, -0.0279,  0.6553,  0.2918,  0.4007,
0.3262, -0.0778, -0.3002])),
             ('bias_hh',
              tensor([-0.3991, -0.3200,  0.3483, -0.2604, -0.1582,
0.5558,  0.5761, -0.3919]))])
```

Guess what? We get the same weird shapes again, but this time there are **four** components instead of **three**. You already know the drill: Split the weights and biases using `split()` and create linear layers using the `linear_layers()` function.

```
Wx, bx = lstm_state['weight_ih'], lstm_state['bias_ih']
Wh, bh = lstm_state['weight_hh'], lstm_state['bias_hh']

# Split weights and biases for data points
Wxi, Wxf, Wxg, Wxo = Wx.split(hidden_dim, dim=0)
bxi, bxf, bxg, bxo = bx.split(hidden_dim, dim=0)
# Split weights and biases for hidden state
Whi, Whf, Whg, Who = Wh.split(hidden_dim, dim=0)
bhi, bhf, bhg, bho = bh.split(hidden_dim, dim=0)

# Creates linear layers for the components
# input gate - green
i_hidden, i_input = linear_layers(Wxi, bxi, Whi, bhi)
# forget gate - red
f_hidden, f_input = linear_layers(Wxf, bxf, Whf, bhf)
 # output gate - blue
o_hidden, o_input = linear_layers(Wxo, bxo, Who, bho)
```

*"Wait! Isn't there a component missing? You mentioned **four** of them; where are the linear layers for **g**?"*

Good catch! It turns out we **don't need** linear layers for ***g*** because it is an **RNN cell** on its own! We can simply use `load_state_dict()` to create the corresponding cell:

```
g_cell = nn.RNNCell(n_features, hidden_dim) # black
g_cell.load_state_dict({'weight_ih': Wxg, 'bias_ih': bxg,
                        'weight_hh': Whg, 'bias_hh': bhg})
```

Output

```
<All keys matched successfully>
```

That was easy, right? Since the other components are **gates**, we need to create functions for them:

```
def forget_gate(h, x):
    thf = f_hidden(h)
    txf = f_input(x)
    f = torch.sigmoid(thf + txf)
    return f  # red

def output_gate(h, x):
    tho = o_hidden(h)
    txo = o_input(x)
    o = torch.sigmoid(tho + txo)
    return o  # blue

def input_gate(h, x):
    thi = i_hidden(h)
    txi = i_input(x)
    i = torch.sigmoid(thi + txi)
    return i  # green
```

It is all set—we can replicate the mechanics of an LSTM cell at its component level (*f*, *o*, *i*, and *g*) now. We also need an **initial hidden state**, an **initial cell state**, and the **first data point (corner)** of a sequence:

```
initial_hidden = torch.zeros(1, hidden_dim)
initial_cell = torch.zeros(1, hidden_dim)

X = torch.as_tensor(points[0]).float()
first_corner = X[0:1]
```

Then, we start by computing the **gated input** using both the RNN cell (*g*) and its corresponding gate (*i*):

```
g = g_cell(first_corner)
i = input_gate(initial_hidden, first_corner)
gated_input = g * i
gated_input
```

Output

```
tensor([[-0.1340, -0.0004]], grad_fn=<MulBackward0>)
```

Next, we compute the **gated cell state** using the **old cell state** (*c*) and its corresponding gate, the forget (*f*) gate:

```
f = forget_gate(initial_hidden, first_corner)
gated_cell = initial_cell * f
gated_cell
```

Output

```
tensor([[0., 0.]], grad_fn=<MulBackward0>)
```

Well, that's kinda boring—since the old cell state is the **initial cell state** for the first data point in a sequence, gated or not, it will be a bunch of zeros.

The new, updated **cell state** (*c'*) is simply the **sum** of both the **gated input** and the **gated cell state**:

```
c_prime = gated_cell + gated_input
c_prime
```

Output

```
tensor([[-0.1340, -0.0004]], grad_fn=<AddBackward0>)
```

The only thing missing is "*converting*" the cell state to a **new hidden state** (*h'*) using the hyperbolic tangent and the output (*o*) gate:

```
o = output_gate(initial_hidden, first_corner)
h_prime = o * torch.tanh(c_prime)
h_prime
```

Output

```
tensor([[-5.4936e-02, -8.3816e-05]], grad_fn=<MulBackward0>)
```

The LSTM cell must return **both states**, hidden and cell, in that order, as a tuple:

```
(h_prime, c_prime)
```

Output

```
(tensor([[-5.4936e-02, -8.3816e-05]], grad_fn=<MulBackward0>),
 tensor([[-0.1340, -0.0004]], grad_fn=<AddBackward0>))
```

That's it! Wasn't that bad, right? The formulation of the LSTM may seem scary at first sight, especially if you bump into a huge sequence of equations using *all weights and biases* at once, but it *doesn't have to be that way*.

Finally, let's take a quick sanity check, feeding the same input to the original LSTM cell:

```
lstm_cell(first_corner)
```

Output

```
(tensor([[-5.4936e-02, -8.3816e-05]], grad_fn=<MulBackward0>),
 tensor([[-0.1340, -0.0004]], grad_fn=<AddBackward0>))
```

And we're done with cells. I guess you know what comes next…

LSTM Layer

The `nn.LSTM` layer takes care of the hidden and cell states handling for us, no matter how long the input sequence is. We've been through this once with the RNN layer and then again with the GRU layer. The arguments, inputs, and outputs of the LSTM are **almost** exactly the same as those for the GRU, except for the fact that, as you already know, **LSTMs return two states (hidden and cell) with the same shape** instead of one. By the way, you can create **stacked LSTMs** and **bidirectional LSTMs** too.

So, let's go straight to **creating a model** using a long short-term memory.

Square Model III — The Sorcerer

This model is pretty much the same as the original "Square Model," except for **two differences**: Its recurrent neural network is not a plain RNN anymore, but an LSTM, and it produces two states as output instead of one. Everything else stays exactly the same.

Model Configuration

```
class SquareModelLSTM(nn.Module):
    def __init__(self, n_features, hidden_dim, n_outputs):
        super(SquareModelLSTM, self).__init__()
        self.hidden_dim = hidden_dim
        self.n_features = n_features
        self.n_outputs = n_outputs
        self.hidden = None
        self.cell = None                                        ②
        # Simple LSTM
        self.basic_rnn = nn.LSTM(self.n_features,
                                 self.hidden_dim,
                                 batch_first=True)              ①
        # Classifier to produce as many logits as outputs
        self.classifier = nn.Linear(self.hidden_dim,
                                    self.n_outputs)

    def forward(self, X):
        # X is batch first (N, L, F)
        # output is (N, L, H)
        # final hidden state is (1, N, H)
        # final cell state is (1, N, H)
        batch_first_output, (self.hidden, self.cell) = \
                                            self.basic_rnn(X) ②

        # only last item in sequence (N, 1, H)
        last_output = batch_first_output[:, -1]
        # classifier will output (N, 1, n_outputs)
        out = self.classifier(last_output)
        # final output is (N, n_outputs)
        return out.view(-1, self.n_outputs)
```

① First change: from RNN to LSTM

② Second change: including the **cell state** as output

Model Configuration & Training

Model Configuration

```
torch.manual_seed(21)
model = SquareModelLSTM(n_features=2, hidden_dim=2, n_outputs=1)
loss = nn.BCEWithLogitsLoss()
optimizer = optim.Adam(model.parameters(), lr=0.01)
```

Model Training

```
sbs_lstm = StepByStep(model, loss, optimizer)
sbs_lstm.set_loaders(train_loader, test_loader)
sbs_lstm.train(100)
```

```
fig = sbs_lstm.plot_losses()
```

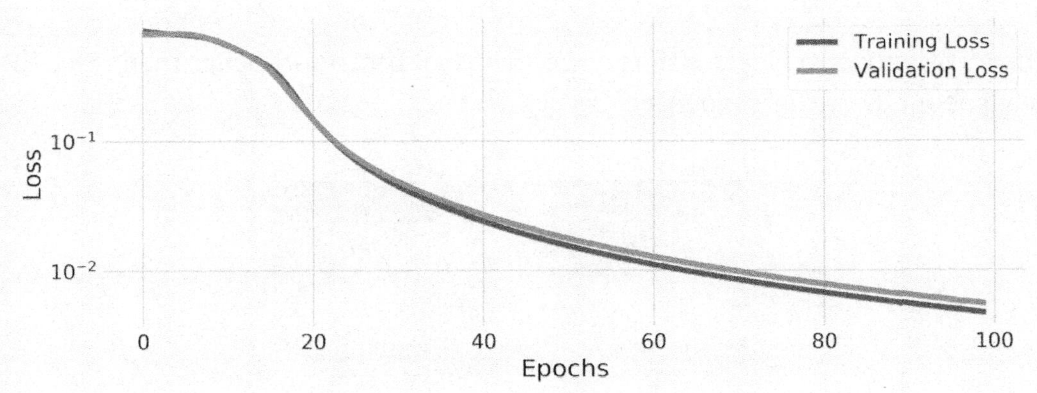

Figure 8.24 - Losses—`SquareModelLSTM`

```
StepByStep.loader_apply(test_loader, sbs_lstm.correct)
```

Output

```
tensor([[53, 53],
        [75, 75]])
```

And that's 100% accuracy again!

Visualizing the Hidden States

Once again, if we use the "*perfect*" square as the input to our latest trained model, we get the following **final hidden states** for each of the eight sequences (plotted side-by-side with the previous models for easier comparison):

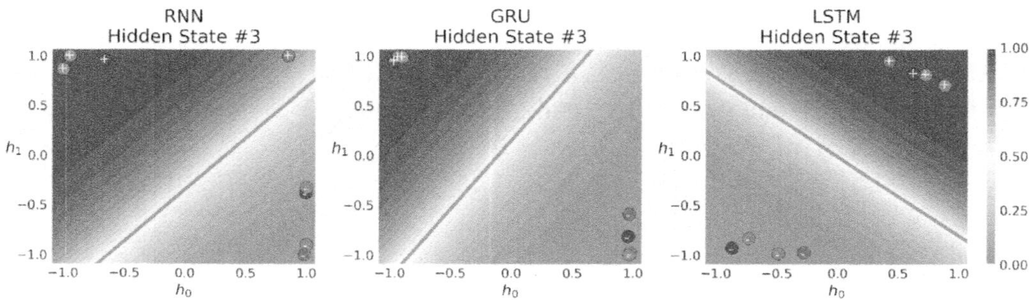

Figure 8.25 - Final hidden states for eight sequences of the "perfect" square

The LSTM model achieves a difference that's *not necessarily better* than the GRU. What about the actual sequences?

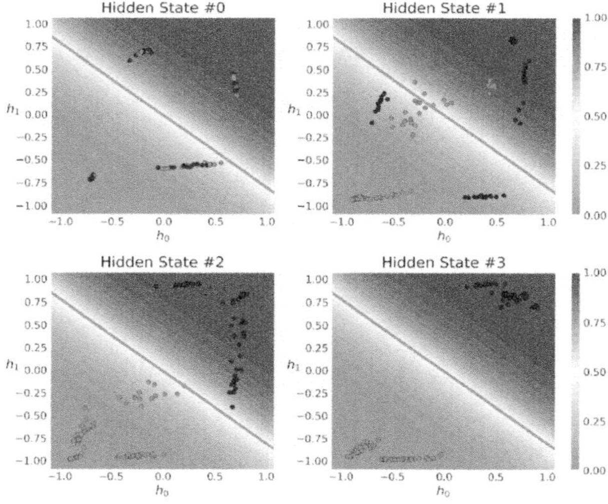

Figure 8.26 - Sequence of hidden states

Like the GRU, the LSTM presents **four distinct groups** of sequences corresponding to the different starting corners. Moreover, it is able to classify most sequences correctly after seeing **only three** points.

Variable-Length Sequences

So far, we've been working with full, regular sequences of four data points each, and that's nice. But what do you do if you get **variable-length sequences**, like the ones below:

```
x0 = points[0]       # 4 data points
x1 = points[1][2:]   # 2 data points
x2 = points[2][1:]   # 3 data points

x0.shape, x1.shape, x2.shape
```

Output

```
((4, 2), (2, 2), (3, 2))
```

The answer: You **pad** them!

*"Could you please remind me again what **padding** is?"*

Sure! Padding means **stuffing with zeros**.

Padding in Computer Vision

Padding an image simply means **adding zeros around it**. An image is worth a thousand words in this case.

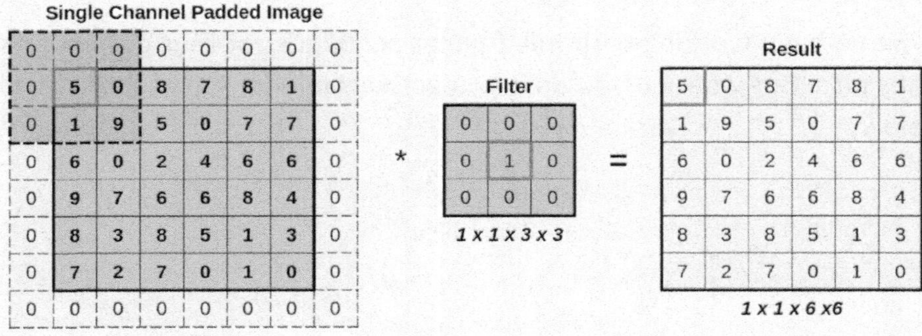

By adding columns and rows of zeros around it, we **expand the input image** such that the gray region **starts centered in the actual top-left corner** of the input image. This simple trick can be used to **preserve the original size** of the image.

Padding

Now, we'll **stuff sequences with zeros** so they all have **matching sizes**. Simple enough, right?

*"OK, it is simple, but **why** are we doing it?"*

We need to pad the sequences because we **cannot create a tensor** out of a list of **elements with different sizes**:

```
all_seqs = [s0, s1, s2]
torch.as_tensor(all_seqs)
```

Output

```
---------------------------------------------------------------------------
ValueError                                Traceback (most recent call last)
<ipython-input-154-9b17f363443c> in <module>
----> 1 torch.as_tensor([x0, x1, x2])

ValueError: expected sequence of length 4 at dim 1 (got 2)
```

We can use PyTorch's `nn.utils.rnn.pad_sequence()` to perform the padding for us. It takes as arguments a **list of sequences**, a **padding value** (default is zero), and the option to make the result **batch-first**. Let's give it a try:

```
seq_tensors = [torch.as_tensor(seq).float() for seq in all_seqs]
padded = rnn_utils.pad_sequence(seq_tensors, batch_first=True)
padded
```

Output

```
tensor([[[ 1.0349,  0.9661],
         [ 0.8055, -0.9169],
         [-0.8251, -0.9499],
         [-0.8670,  0.9342]],

        [[-1.0911,  0.9254],
         [-1.0771, -1.0414],
         [ 0.0000,  0.0000],
         [ 0.0000,  0.0000]],

        [[-1.1247, -0.9683],
         [ 0.8182, -0.9944],
         [ 1.0081,  0.7680],
         [ 0.0000,  0.0000]]])
```

Both the second and the third sequences were shorter than the first, so they got **padded** accordingly to **match the length of the longest sequence**.

Now we can proceed as usual and feed the **padded sequences** to an RNN and look at the results:

```
torch.manual_seed(11)
rnn = nn.RNN(2, 2, batch_first=True)
```

```
output_padded, hidden_padded = rnn(padded)
output_padded
```

Output

```
tensor([[[-0.6388,  0.8505],
         [-0.4215,  0.8979],
         [ 0.3792,  0.3432],
         [ 0.3161, -0.1675]],

        [[ 0.2911, -0.1811],
         [ 0.3051,  0.7055],
         [ 0.0052,  0.5819],
         [-0.0642,  0.6012]],

        [[ 0.3385,  0.5927],
         [-0.3875,  0.9422],
         [-0.4832,  0.6595],
         [-0.1007,  0.5349]]], grad_fn=<PermuteBackward>)
```

Since the sequences were padded to **four data points** each, we got **four hidden states** for each sequence as output.

*"How come the **hidden states** for the **padded points** are **different** from the hidden state of the **last real data point**?"*

Even though each padded point is just a bunch of zeros, it doesn't mean it won't change the hidden state. The hidden state itself gets transformed, and, even if the padded point is full of zeros, its corresponding transformation may include a bias term that gets added nonetheless. This isn't *necessarily* a problem, but, if you don't like padded points modifying your hidden state, you can prevent that by **packing the sequence** instead.

Before moving on to packed sequences, though, let's just check the (permuted, batch-first) final hidden state:

```
hidden_padded.permute(1, 0, 2)
```

Output

```
tensor([[[ 0.3161, -0.1675]],

        [[-0.0642,  0.6012]],

        [[-0.1007,  0.5349]]], grad_fn=<PermuteBackward>)
```

Packing

Packing works like a **concatenation** of sequences: Instead of padding them to have equal-length elements, it **lines the sequences up**, one after the other, and **keeps track of the lengths**, so it knows **the indices corresponding to the start of each sequence**.

Let's work through an example using PyTorch's `nn.utils.rnn.pack_sequence()`. First, it takes a **list of tensors** as input. If your list **is not sorted by decreasing sequence length**, you'll need to set its `enforce_sorted` argument to `False`.

Sorting the sequences by their lengths is **only** necessary if you're planning on **exporting your model** using the **ONNX** format, which allows you to import the model in different frameworks.

```
packed = rnn_utils.pack_sequence(seq_tensors, enforce_sorted=False)
packed
```

Output

```
PackedSequence(data=tensor([[ 1.0349,  0.9661],
        [-1.1247, -0.9683],
        [-1.0911,  0.9254],
        [ 0.8055, -0.9169],
        [ 0.8182, -0.9944],
        [-1.0771, -1.0414],
        [-0.8251, -0.9499],
        [ 1.0081,  0.7680],
        [-0.8670,  0.9342]]), batch_sizes=tensor([3, 3, 2, 1]),
sorted_indices=tensor([0, 2, 1]), unsorted_indices=tensor([0, 2,
1]))
```

The output is a bit *cryptic*, to say the least. Let's decipher it, piece by piece, starting with the `unsorted_indices_tensor`. Even though we didn't sort the list ourselves, PyTorch did it internally, and it found that the **longest sequence** is the **first** (four data points, index 0), followed by the third (three data points, index 2), and then by the shortest one (two data points, index 1).

Once the sequences are listed in order of decreasing length, like in Figure 8.27, the **number of sequences** that are **at least *t* steps long** (corresponding to the number of columns in the figure below) is given by the `batch_sizes` attribute:

Sequence	Length	unsorted indices tensor	1st	2nd	3rd	4th
s0	4	0	#0	#3	#6	#8
s2	3	2	#1	#4	#7	
s1	2	1	#2	#5		
		batch_sizes	3	3	2	1

Figure 8.27 - Packing sequences

For example, the `batch_size` for the **third** column is **two** because **two sequences** have **at least three data points**. Then, it goes through the data points in the same

column-wise fashion, from top to bottom, and from left to right, to assign the data points to the corresponding **indices** in the data tensor.

Finally, it uses these indices to **assemble the `data` tensor**:

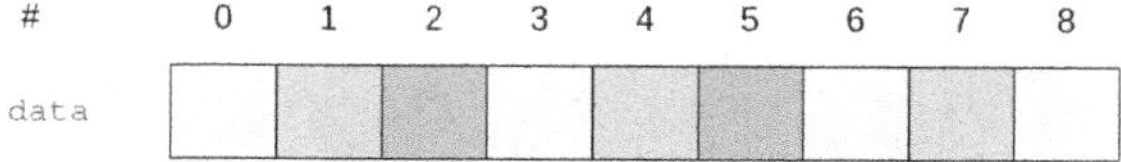

Figure 8.28 - Packed data points

Thus, to retrieve the values of the original sequences, we need to slice the `data` tensor accordingly. For example, we can retrieve the first sequence from the `data` tensor by reading the values from its corresponding indices: 0, 3, 6, and 8.

```
(packed.data[[0, 3, 6, 8]] == seq_tensors[0]).all()
```

Output

```
tensor(True)
```

Once the sequence is properly **packed**, we can feed it directly to an RNN:

```
output_packed, hidden_packed = rnn(packed)
output_packed, hidden_packed
```

Output

```
(PackedSequence(data=tensor([[-0.6388,  0.8505],
        [ 0.3385,  0.5927],
        [ 0.2911, -0.1811],
        [-0.4215,  0.8979],
        [-0.3875,  0.9422],
        [ 0.3051,  0.7055],
        [ 0.3792,  0.3432],
        [-0.4832,  0.6595],
        [ 0.3161, -0.1675]], grad_fn=<CatBackward>), batch_sizes
=tensor([3, 3, 2, 1]), sorted_indices=tensor([0, 2, 1]),
unsorted_indices=tensor([0, 2, 1])),
 tensor([[[ 0.3161, -0.1675],
         [ 0.3051,  0.7055],
         [-0.4832,  0.6595]]], grad_fn=<IndexSelectBackward>))
```

If the **input is packed**, the **output tensor is packed too**, but the **hidden state is not**.

Let's compare both final hidden states, from **padded** and **packed** sequences:

```
hidden_packed == hidden_padded
```

Output

```
tensor([[[ True,  True],
        [False, False],
        [False, False]]])
```

From three sequences, only one matches. Well, this shouldn't be a surprise; after all, we're **packing sequences to avoid updating the hidden state with padded inputs**.

"Cool, so I can use the permuted hidden state, right?"

Well, it depends:

- Yes, if you're using networks that are **not bidirectional**—the final hidden state does match the last output.

- No, if you're using a **bidirectional** network—you're **only** getting the **properly aligned hidden states** in the **last output**, so you'll need to **unpack it**.

To unpack the actual **sequence of hidden states** for the shortest sequence, for example, we *could* get the corresponding indices from the `data` tensor in the packed output:

```
output_packed.data[[2, 5]] # x1 sequence
```

Output

```
tensor([[ 0.2911, -0.1811],
        [ 0.3051,  0.7055]], grad_fn=<IndexBackward>)
```

But that would be *extremely annoying* so, no, you *don't have to.*

Unpacking (to padded)

You can **unpack a sequence** using PyTorch's `nn.utils.rnn.pad_packed_sequence()`. The name does not help, I know; I would rather call it `unpack_sequence_to_padded()` instead. Anyway, we can use it to transform our **packed output** into a **regular, yet padded, output**:

```
output_unpacked, seq_sizes = \
    rnn_utils.pad_packed_sequence(output_packed, batch_first=True)
output_unpacked, seq_sizes
```

Output

```
(tensor([[[-0.6388,  0.8505],
          [-0.4215,  0.8979],
          [ 0.3792,  0.3432],
          [ 0.3161, -0.1675]],

         [[ 0.2911, -0.1811],
          [ 0.3051,  0.7055],
          [ 0.0000,  0.0000],
          [ 0.0000,  0.0000]],

         [[ 0.3385,  0.5927],
          [-0.3875,  0.9422],
          [-0.4832,  0.6595],
          [ 0.0000,  0.0000]]], grad_fn=<IndexSelectBackward>),
 tensor([4, 2, 3]))
```

It returns both the **padded sequences** and the **original sizes**, which will be useful as well.

*"Problem solved then? Can I take the **last output** now?"*

Almost there—if you were to take the last output in the same way we did before, you'd **still get some padded zeros** back:

```
output_unpacked[:, -1]
```

Output

```
tensor([[ 0.3161, -0.1675],
        [ 0.0000,  0.0000],
        [ 0.0000,  0.0000]], grad_fn=<SelectBackward>)
```

So, to **actually get the last output**, we need to use some **fancy indexing** and the information about **original sizes** returned by `pad_packed_sequence()`:

```
seq_idx = torch.arange(seq_sizes.size(0))
output_unpacked[seq_idx, seq_sizes-1]
```

Output

```
tensor([[ 0.3161, -0.1675],
        [ 0.3051,  0.7055],
        [-0.4832,  0.6595]], grad_fn=<IndexBackward>)
```

And we finally have the **last output** for each *packed sequence*, even if we're using a bidirectional network.

Packing (from padded)

You can also convert an *already padded* sequence into a **packed sequence** using PyTorch's `nn.utils.rnn.pack_padded_sequence()`. Since the sequence is already padded, though, we need to compute the **original sizes** ourselves:

```
len_seqs = [len(seq) for seq in all_seqs]
len_seqs
```

Output

```
[4, 2, 3]
```

And then pass them as an argument:

```
packed = rnn_utils.pack_padded_sequence(padded, len_seqs,
                                        enforce_sorted=False,
                                        batch_first=True)

packed
```

Output

```
PackedSequence(data=tensor([[ 1.0349,  0.9661],
        [-1.1247, -0.9683],
        [-1.0911,  0.9254],
        [ 0.8055, -0.9169],
        [ 0.8182, -0.9944],
        [-1.0771, -1.0414],
        [-0.8251, -0.9499],
        [ 1.0081,  0.7680],
        [-0.8670,  0.9342]]), batch_sizes=tensor([3, 3, 2, 1]),
sorted_indices=tensor([0, 2, 1]), unsorted_indices=tensor([0, 2,
1]))
```

Variable-Length Dataset

Let's create a dataset with **variable-length sequences** and train a model using it:

Data Generation

```
var_points, var_directions = generate_sequences(variable_len=True)
var_points[:2]
```

Output

```
[array([[ 1.12636495,  1.1570899 ],
        [ 0.87384513, -1.00750892],
        [-0.9149893 , -1.09150317],
        [-1.0867348 ,  1.07731667]]),
 array([[ 0.92250954, -0.89887678],
        [ 1.0941646 ,  0.92300589]])]
```

Data Preparation

We simply **cannot use a `TensorDataset`**, because we cannot create a tensor out of a list of **elements with different sizes**.

So, we must build a **custom dataset** that **makes a tensor out of each sequence** and, when prompted for a given item, returns the corresponding tensor and associated label:

Data Preparation

```
class CustomDataset(Dataset):
    def __init__(self, x, y):
        self.x = [torch.as_tensor(s).float() for s in x]
        self.y = torch.as_tensor(y).float().view(-1, 1)

    def __getitem__(self, index):
        return (self.x[index], self.y[index])

    def __len__(self):
        return len(self.x)

train_var_data = CustomDataset(var_points, var_directions)
```

But this is *not enough*; if we create a **data loader** for our custom dataset and try to **retrieve a mini-batch** out of it, it will **raise an error**:

```
train_var_loader = DataLoader(
    train_var_data, batch_size=16, shuffle=True
)
next(iter(train_var_loader))
```

Output

```
---------------------------------------------------------------------------
RuntimeError                              Traceback (most recent call last)
<ipython-input-34-596b8081f8d1> in <module>
      1 train_var_loader = DataLoader(train_var_data, batch_size=16,
shuffle=True)
----> 2 next(iter(train_var_loader))
...
RuntimeError: stack expects each tensor to be equal size, but got [
3, 2] at entry 0 and [4, 2] at entry 2
```

It turns out, the data loader is **trying to `stack()` together** the sequences, which, as we know, have **different sizes** and thus **cannot be stacked together**.

We *could* simply **pad** all the sequences and move on with a **`TensorDataset` and regular data loader**. But, in that case, the final hidden states would be affected by the padded data points, as we've already discussed.

We can do *better* than that: We can **pack** our mini-batches using a **collate function**.

Collate Function

The *collate function* takes a **list of tuples** (sampled from a dataset using its `__getitem__()`) and **collates** them **into a batch** that's being returned by the data loader. It gives you the ability to **manipulate the sampled data points** in any way you want to make them into a **mini-batch**.

In our case, we'd like to get all sequences (the first item in every tuple) and *pack them*. Besides, we can get all labels (the second item in every tuple) and make them into a tensor that's in the correct shape for our binary classification task:

Data Preparation

```
def pack_collate(batch):
    X = [item[0] for item in batch]
    y = [item[1] for item in batch]
    X_pack = rnn_utils.pack_sequence(X, enforce_sorted=False)

    return X_pack, torch.as_tensor(y).view(-1, 1)
```

Let's see the function in action by creating a dummy batch of two elements and applying the function to it:

```
# list of tuples returned by the dataset
dummy_batch = [train_var_data[0], train_var_data[1]]
dummy_x, dummy_y = pack_collate(dummy_batch)
dummy_x
```

Output

```
PackedSequence(data=tensor([[ 1.1264,  1.1571],
        [ 0.9225, -0.8989],
        [ 0.8738, -1.0075],
        [ 1.0942,  0.9230],
        [-0.9150, -1.0915],
        [-1.0867,  1.0773]]), batch_sizes=tensor([2, 2, 1, 1]),
sorted_indices=tensor([0, 1]), unsorted_indices=tensor([0, 1]))
```

Two sequences of different sizes go in, one packed sequence comes out. Now we can create a **data loader** that **uses our collate function**:

Data Preparation

```
train_var_loader = DataLoader(train_var_data,
                              batch_size=16,
                              shuffle=True,
                              collate_fn=pack_collate)
x_batch, y_batch = next(iter(train_var_loader))
```

And now every batch coming out of our data loader has a packed sequence.

"Do I have to change the model too?"

Square Model IV — Packed

There are *some* changes we need to make to the model. Let's illustrate them by creating a model that uses a **bidirectional LSTM** and expects **packed sequences as inputs**.

First, since X is a packed sequence now, it means that the **output is packed**, and therefore we need to **unpack it** to a **padded output**.

Once it is unpacked, we can get the **last output** by using the **fancier indexing** (from a couple of pages ago) to get the last (actual) element of the padded sequences. Moreover, using a bidirectional LSTM means that the output for each sequence has an **(N, 1, 2*H)** shape.

```
class SquareModelPacked(nn.Module):
    def __init__(self, n_features, hidden_dim, n_outputs):
        super(SquareModelPacked, self).__init__()
        self.hidden_dim = hidden_dim
        self.n_features = n_features
        self.n_outputs = n_outputs
        self.hidden = None
        self.cell = None
        # Simple LSTM
        self.basic_rnn = nn.LSTM(self.n_features,
                                 self.hidden_dim,
                                 bidirectional=True)
        # Classifier to produce as many logits as outputs
        self.classifier = nn.Linear(2 * self.hidden_dim,
                                    self.n_outputs)          ③

    def forward(self, X):
        # X is a PACKED sequence now
        # final hidden state is (2, N, H) - bidirectional
        # final cell state is (2, N, H) - bidirectional
        rnn_out, (self.hidden, self.cell) = self.basic_rnn(X)
        # unpack the output (N, L, 2*H)
        batch_first_output, seq_sizes = \
            rnn_utils.pad_packed_sequence(rnn_out,
                                          batch_first=True)  ①

        # only last item in sequence (N, 1, 2*H)
        seq_idx = torch.arange(seq_sizes.size(0))
        last_output = batch_first_output[seq_idx, seq_sizes-1]②
        # classifier will output (N, 1, n_outputs)
        out = self.classifier(last_output)

        # final output is (N, n_outputs)
        return out.view(-1, self.n_outputs)
```

① Unpacking the output

② Fancy indexing to retrieve the last output of a padded sequence

③ Two hidden states are concatenated side-by-side in a bidirectional network

Model Configuration & Training

We can use our data loader that outputs packed sequences (`train_var_loader`) to feed our `SquareModelPacked` model and train it in the usual way:

Model Configuration

```
torch.manual_seed(21)
model = SquareModelPacked(n_features=2, hidden_dim=2, n_outputs=1)
loss = nn.BCEWithLogitsLoss()
optimizer = optim.Adam(model.parameters(), lr=0.01)
```

Model Training

```
sbs_packed = StepByStep(model, loss, optimizer)
sbs_packed.set_loaders(train_var_loader)
sbs_packed.train(100)
```

```
fig = sbs_packed.plot_losses()
```

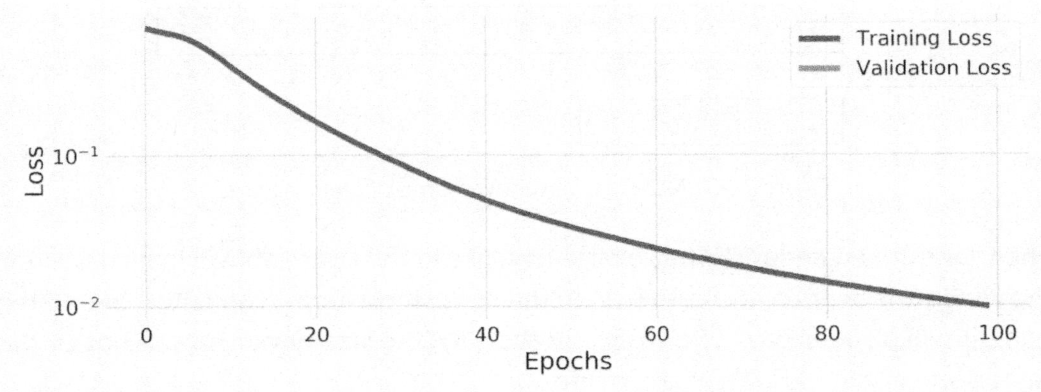

Figure 8.29 - Losses—`SquareModelPacked`

```
StepByStep.loader_apply(train_var_loader, sbs_packed.correct)
```

Output

```
tensor([[66, 66],
        [62, 62]])
```

1D Convolutions

In computer vision, a **convolution** is performed by **repeatedly applying a filter** to a **moving region** over the image. Those are **2D convolutions**, meaning that the **filter was moving in two dimensions**, both along the width (left to right), and the height (top to bottom) of the image.

Guess what **1D convolutions** do? They **move the filter** in **one dimension**, from left to right. The filter works like a **moving window**, performing a **weighted sum of the values in the region it has moved over**. Let's use a sequence of temperature values over thirteen days as an example:

```
temperatures = np.array([5, 11, 15, 6, 5, 3, 3, 0, 0, 3, 4, 2, 1])
```

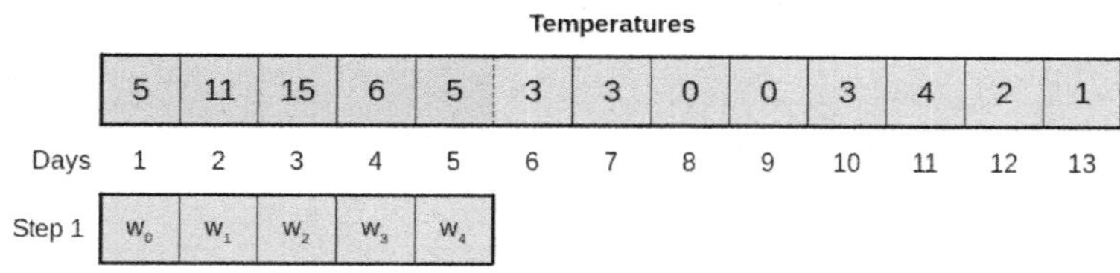

Figure 8.30 - Moving window over series of temperatures

Then, let's use a **window (filter)** of size **five**, like in the figure above. In its first step, the window is over days one to five. In the next step, since it can only move to the right, it will be over days two to six. By the way, the **size of our movement to the right** is, once again, known as the **stride**.

Now, let's assign the same value (0.2) for every **weight** in our **filter** and use PyTorch's `F.conv1d()` to **convolve the filter with our sequence** (don't mind the shape just yet; we'll get back to it in the next section):

```
size = 5
weight = torch.ones(size) * 0.2
F.conv1d(torch.as_tensor(temperatures).float().view(1, 1, -1),
         weight=weight.view(1, 1, -1))
```

Output

```
tensor([[[8.4000, 8.0000, 6.4000, 3.4000, 2.2000,
          1.8000, 2.0000, 1.8000, 2.0000]]])
```

Does it look familiar? That's a **moving average**!

"Does it mean every 1D convolution is a moving average?"

Well, kinda ... in the functional form above, we had to provide the weights, but, as expected, the corresponding **module** (`nn.Conv1d`) will **learn the weights** itself. Since there is no requirement that the weights must add up to one, it won't be a moving average but rather a **moving weighted sum**.

Moreover, it is very unlikely we'll use it over a **single feature** like in the example above. Things get **more interesting** as we include **more features** to be convolved with the **filter**, which brings us to the next topic...

Shapes

For **sequences**, the shape should be **NCL**:

- **N** stands for the **N**umber of sequences (in a mini-batch, for instance)
- **C** stands for the number of **C**hannels (or **filters**) in each element of the sequence
- **L** stands for the **L**ength of each sequence

"Wait, where is the ***number of features*** *in it?"*

Good point! Since 1D convolutions only move along the sequence, **each feature is considered an input channel**. So, you can think of the shape as **NFL** or **N(C/F)L** if you like.

*"Really?! Yet **another** shape for input sequences?"*

Unfortunately, yes. But I've built this small table to help you wrap your head around the different shape conventions while working with sequences as inputs:

	Shape	Use Case
Batch-first	N, L, F	Typical shape; RNNs with `batch_first=True`
RNN-friendly	L, N, F	Default for RNNs (`batch_first=False`)
Sequence-last	N, F, L	Default for 1D convolutions

Having (hopefully) cleared that up, let's use **permute** to get our sequences in the appropriate shape:

```
seqs = torch.as_tensor(points).float() # N, L, F
seqs_length_last = seqs.permute(0, 2, 1)
seqs_length_last.shape # N, F=C, L
```

Output

```
torch.Size([128, 2, 4])
```

Multiple Features or Channels

Our sequences of corners have **two coordinates**; that is, **two features**. These will be considered (input) **channels** as far as the **1D convolution** is concerned, so we create the convolutional layer accordingly:

```
torch.manual_seed(17)
conv_seq = nn.Conv1d(in_channels=2, out_channels=1,
                     kernel_size=2, bias=False)
conv_seq.weight, conv_seq.weight.shape
```

Output

```
(Parameter containing:
 tensor([[[-0.0658,  0.0351],
          [ 0.3302, -0.3761]]], requires_grad=True),
torch.Size([1, 2, 2]))
```

We're using only **one output channel**, so there is only **one filter**, which will produce **one output value** for each region the window moves over. Since the **kernel size** is **two**, each window will move over **two corners**. Any **two corners make an edge** of the square, so there will be **one output for each edge**. This information will be useful for visualizing what the model is actually doing.

Since each channel (feature) will be multiplied, element-wise, by its corresponding weights in the filter, and **all values for all channels are added up** to produce a **single value** anyway, I've chosen to represent the sequence (and the filter) as if it were two-dimensional in the figure below:

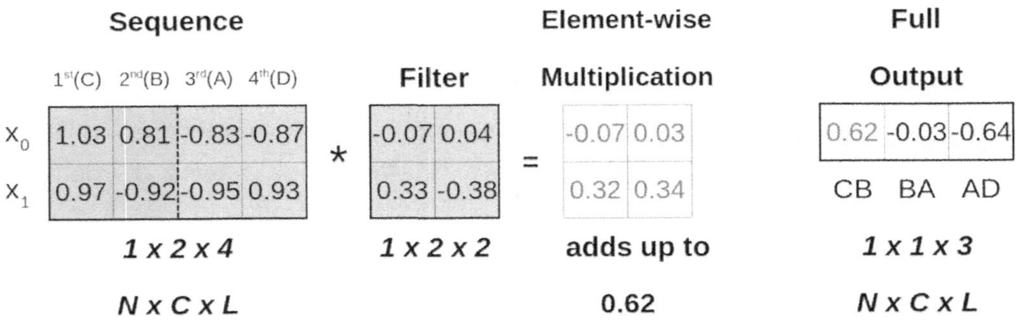

Figure 8.31 - Applying filter over a sequence

Our first sequence corresponds to corners CBAD and, for the first region (in gray, corresponding to the CB edge), it results in an output of 0.6241. Let's use our convolutional layer to get all outputs:

```
conv_seq(seqs_length_last[0:1])
```

Output

```
tensor([[[ 0.6241, -0.0274, -0.6412]]], grad_fn=<SqueezeBackward1>)
```

The resulting **shape** is given by the formula below, where *l* is the *length of the sequence*, *f* is the *filter size*, *p* is the *padding*, and *s* is the *stride*:

$$l_i * f = \frac{(l_i + 2p) - f}{s} + 1$$

Equation 8.15 - Resulting shape

If any of the resulting dimensions are not an integer, they must be **rounded down**.

Dilation

There is yet another operation that can be used with convolutions in any number of dimensions, but that we haven't discussed yet: **dilation**. The general idea is quite simple: Instead of a **contiguous** kernel, it uses a **dilated kernel**. A **dilation of size two**, for instance, means that the kernel uses **every other element** (be it a pixel or a feature value in a sequence).

"Why would I want to do that?"

In a nutshell, the idea is to capture long-term properties of a sequence (like seasonality in a time series, for example) or to integrate information from different scales in an image (local and global context). We're not delving deeper than explaining the mechanism itself, though.

In our example, a **kernel of size two** (so it goes over **two values** in the sequence) with a **dilation of two** (so it **skips every other value** in the sequence) works like this:

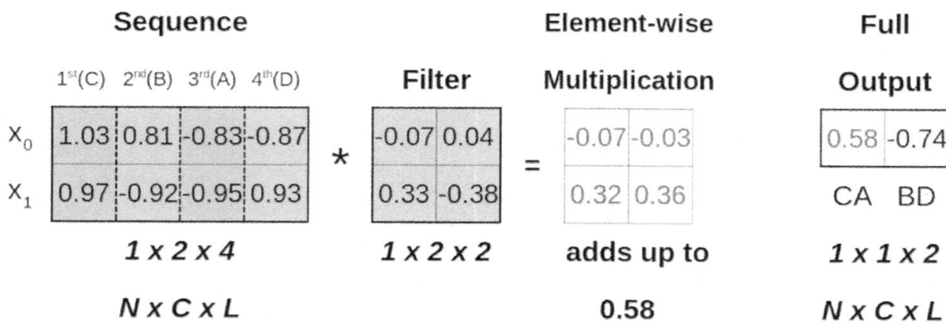

Figure 8.32 - Applying dilated filter over a sequence

The first **dilated region** (in gray) is given by the **first and third** values (corners C and

A), which, when convolved with the filter, will output a value of 0.58. Then, the next **dilated region** will be given by the **second and fourth** values (corners B and D). Now, the convolutional layer has a `dilation` argument as well:

```
torch.manual_seed(17)
conv_dilated = nn.Conv1d(in_channels=2, out_channels=1,
                         kernel_size=2, dilation=2, bias=False)
conv_dilated.weight, conv_dilated.weight.shape
```

Output

```
(Parameter containing:
 tensor([[[-0.0658,  0.0351],
          [ 0.3302, -0.3761]]], requires_grad=True),
torch.Size([1, 2, 2]))
```

If we run our sequence through it, we get the same output as depicted in the figure above.

```
conv_dilated(seqs_length_last[0:1])
```

Output

```
tensor([[[ 0.5793, -0.7376]]], grad_fn=<SqueezeBackward1>)
```

This output is **smaller** than the previous one because the **dilation affects the shape of the output** according to the formula below (*d* stands for *dilation size*):

$$l_i * f = \frac{(l_i + 2p) - d(f - 1) - 1}{s} + 1$$

Equation 8.16 - Resulting shape with dilation

If any of the resulting dimensions are not an integer, they must be **rounded down**.

Data Preparation

The data preparation step is very much like that of the previous models except for the fact that we need to **permute** the dimensions to comply with 1D convolutions' "*sequence-last*" (NFL) shape:

Data Preparation

```
train_data = TensorDataset(
    torch.as_tensor(points).float().permute(0, 2, 1),
    torch.as_tensor(directions).view(-1, 1).float()
)
test_data = TensorDataset(
    torch.as_tensor(test_points).float().permute(0, 2, 1),
    torch.as_tensor(test_directions).view(-1, 1).float()
)
train_loader = DataLoader(
    train_data, batch_size=16, shuffle=True
)
test_loader = DataLoader(test_data, batch_size=16)
```

Model Configuration & Training

The model is quite simple: a single `nn.Conv1d` layer followed by an activation function (ReLU), a flattening layer (which is only *squeezing* the channel dimension out), and a linear layer to combine the outputs (three values for each sequence, as shown in Figure 8.31) into logits for our binary classification.

Model Configuration

```
torch.manual_seed(21)
model = nn.Sequential()
model.add_module('conv1d', nn.Conv1d(in_channels=2,
                                     out_channels=1,
                                     kernel_size=2))
model.add_module('relu', nn.ReLU())
model.add_module('flatten', nn.Flatten())
model.add_module('output', nn.Linear(3, 1))

loss = nn.BCEWithLogitsLoss()
optimizer = optim.Adam(model.parameters(), lr=0.01)
```

Model Training

```
sbs_conv1 = StepByStep(model, loss, optimizer)
sbs_conv1.set_loaders(train_loader, test_loader)
sbs_conv1.train(100)
```

```
fig = sbs_conv1.plot_losses()
```

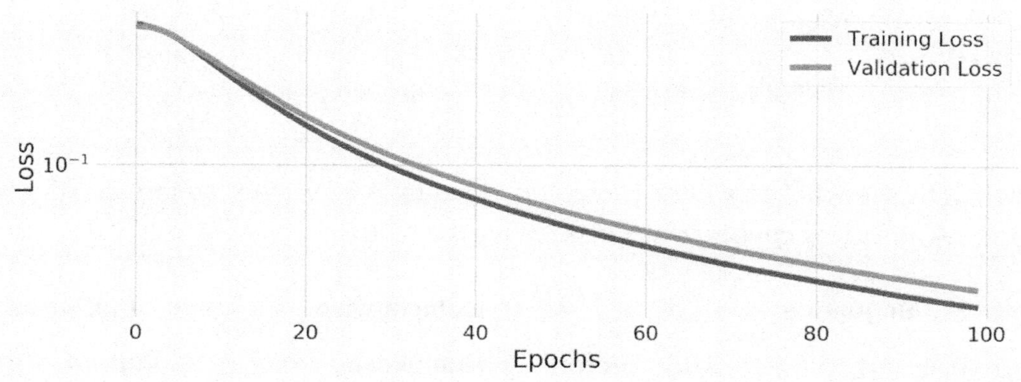

Figure 8.33 - Losses—the edge model

```
StepByStep.loader_apply(test_loader, sbs_conv1.correct)
```

Output

```
tensor([[53, 53],
        [75, 75]])
```

Once again, the model's accuracy is perfect. Maybe you've noticed it was much *faster* to train too. How come this simple model performed so well? Let's try to figure out what it did under the hood...

Visualizing the Model

The key component of our model is the `nn.Conv1d` layer, so let's take a look at its `state_dict()`:

```
model.conv1d.state_dict()
```

Output

```
OrderedDict([('weight', tensor([[[-0.2186,  2.3289],
                         [-2.3765, -0.1814]]], device='cuda:0')),
             ('bias', tensor([-0.5457], device='cuda:0'))])
```

Then, let's see what this filter is doing by feeding it a "*perfect*" square starting at corner **A** and going **counterclockwise** (sequence ADCB):

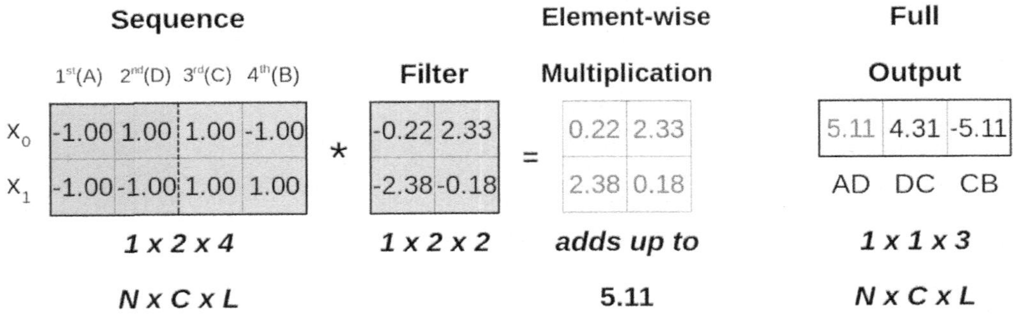

Figure 8.34 - Applying filter over the "perfect" square

The figure above shows us the element-wise multiplication and result for the **first region**, corresponding to the **AD edge** of our square (without including the *bias* value from the convolutional layer). The outputs on the right are the "*edge features*."

We can actually find an expression to compute them as a **weighted sum of the coordinates** for both the **first** (x^{1st}) and the **second** (x^{2nd}) corners included in the region being convolved:

$$\text{edge feature} = -0.22\ x_0^{1\text{st}} - 2.38\ x_1^{1\text{st}} + 2.33\ x_0^{2\text{nd}} - 0.18\ x_1^{2\text{nd}} - 0.5457$$

Equation 8.17 - Equation for "edge feature"

From the expression above, and given that the coordinates' values are close to one (in absolute value), the only way for the **edge feature** to have a **positive value** is for

x^{1st}_1 and x^{2nd}_0 to be approximately -1 and 1, respectively. This is the case for **two edges** only, **AD** and **DC**:

$$\overline{\text{AD}}\ or\ \overline{\text{DC}} \implies x_1^{\text{1st}} \approx -1 \text{ and } x_0^{\text{2nd}} \approx 1 \implies \text{edge feature} > 0$$

Equation 8.18 - Detected edges

Every other edge will return a **negative value** and thus be clipped at **zero** by the ReLU activation function. Our model learned to **choose two edges with the same direction** to perform the classification.

*"Why **two** edges? Shouldn't a **single** edge suffice?"*

It *should* if our sequences actually **had four edges** ... but they **don't**. We *do* have **four corners**, but we can only build **three edges out of it** because we're missing the edge connecting the last and the first corners. So, any model that relies on a single edge will likely fail in those cases where that particular edge is the missing one. Thus, the model needs to correctly classify at least two edges.

Putting It All Together

In this chapter, we've used different **recurrent neural networks**, plain-vanilla RNNs, GRUs, and LSTMs, to produce a **hidden state representing each sequence** that can be used for **sequence classification**. We used both **fixed-** and **variable-length** sequences, **padding** or **packing** them with the help of a **collate function**, and built models that **ensured the right shape** of the data.

Fixed-Length Dataset

For fixed-length sequences, the data preparation was as usual:

Data Generation & Preparation

```
points, directions = generate_sequences(n=128, seed=13)
train_data = TensorDataset(
    torch.as_tensor(points).float(),
    torch.as_tensor(directions).view(-1, 1).float()
)
train_loader = DataLoader(
    train_data, batch_size=16, shuffle=True
)
```

Variable-Length Dataset

For variable-length sequences, though, we built a **custom dataset** and a **collate function** to **pack the sequences**:

Data Generation

```
var_points, var_directions = generate_sequences(variable_len=True)
```

Data Preparation

```
class CustomDataset(Dataset):
    def __init__(self, x, y):
        self.x = [torch.as_tensor(s).float() for s in x]
        self.y = torch.as_tensor(y).float().view(-1, 1)

    def __getitem__(self, index):
        return (self.x[index], self.y[index])

    def __len__(self):
        return len(self.x)

train_var_data = CustomDataset(var_points, var_directions)
```

Data Preparation

```
def pack_collate(batch):
    X = [item[0] for item in batch]
    y = [item[1] for item in batch]
    X_pack = rnn_utils.pack_sequence(X, enforce_sorted=False)

    return X_pack, torch.as_tensor(y).view(-1, 1)

train_var_loader = DataLoader(train_var_data,
                              batch_size=16,
                              shuffle=True,
                              collate_fn=pack_collate)
```

There Can Be Only ONE ... Model

We've developed many models throughout this chapter, depending both on the **type of recurrent layer** that was used (RNN, GRU, or LSTM) and on the **type of sequence** (packed or not). The model below, though, is able to handle different configurations:

- Its `rnn_layer` argument allows you to use whichever recurrent layer you prefer.
- The `**kwargs` argument allows you to further configure the recurrent layer (using `num_layers` and `bidirectional` arguments, for example).
- The **output dimension** of the recurrent layer is automatically computed to build a **matching linear layer**.
- If the input is a **packed sequence**, it handles the **unpacking and fancy indexing** to retrieve the **actual last hidden state**.

Model Configuration

```
class SquareModelOne(nn.Module):
    def __init__(self, n_features, hidden_dim, n_outputs,
                 rnn_layer=nn.LSTM, **kwargs):
        super(SquareModelOne, self).__init__()
        self.hidden_dim = hidden_dim
        self.n_features = n_features
        self.n_outputs = n_outputs
        self.hidden = None
        self.cell = None
        self.basic_rnn = rnn_layer(self.n_features,
                                   self.hidden_dim,
                                   batch_first=True, **kwargs)
        output_dim = (self.basic_rnn.bidirectional + 1) * \
                     self.hidden_dim
        # Classifier to produce as many logits as outputs
        self.classifier = nn.Linear(output_dim, self.n_outputs)

    def forward(self, X):
        is_packed = isinstance(X, nn.utils.rnn.PackedSequence)
        # X is a PACKED sequence, there is no need to permute

        rnn_out, self.hidden = self.basic_rnn(X)
        if isinstance(self.basic_rnn, nn.LSTM):
```

```
            self.hidden, self.cell = self.hidden

        if is_packed:
            # unpack the output
            batch_first_output, seq_sizes = \
                rnn_utils.pad_packed_sequence(rnn_out,
                                              batch_first=True)
            seq_slice = torch.arange(seq_sizes.size(0))
        else:
            batch_first_output = rnn_out
            seq_sizes = 0 # so it is -1 as the last output
            seq_slice = slice(None, None, None) # same as ':'

        # only last item in sequence (N, 1, H)
        last_output = batch_first_output[seq_slice, seq_sizes-1]

        # classifier will output (N, 1, n_outputs)
        out = self.classifier(last_output)

        # final output is (N, n_outputs)
        return out.view(-1, self.n_outputs)
```

Model Configuration & Training

The model below uses a **bidirectional LSTM** and already achieves a 100% accuracy on the training set. Feel free to experiment with different recurrent layers, the number of layers, single or bidirectional, as well as with switching between fixed- and variable-length sequences.

Model Configuration

```
torch.manual_seed(21)
model = SquareModelOne(n_features=2, hidden_dim=2, n_outputs=1,
                       rnn_layer=nn.LSTM, num_layers=1,
                       bidirectional=True)
loss = nn.BCEWithLogitsLoss()
optimizer = optim.Adam(model.parameters(), lr=0.01)
```

Model Training

```
sbs_one = StepByStep(model, loss, optimizer)
#sbs_one.set_loaders(train_loader)
sbs_one.set_loaders(train_var_loader)
sbs_one.train(100)
```

```
#StepByStep.loader_apply(train_loader, sbs_one.correct)
StepByStep.loader_apply(train_var_loader, sbs_one.correct)
```

Output

```
tensor([[66, 66],
        [62, 62]])
```

Recap

In this chapter, we've learned about **sequential data** and how to use **recurrent neural networks** to perform a classification task. We followed the **journey of a hidden state** through all the transformations happening inside of different recurrent layers: RNN, GRU, and LSTM. We learned the difference between **padding** and **packing** variable-length sequences, and how to **build a data loader for packed sequences**. We also brought back **convolutions**, using the **one-dimensional** version to process sequential data as well. This is what we've covered:

- understanding the importance of **order** in **sequential data**
- generating a synthetic two-dimensional dataset so we can visualize what's happening "*under the hood*" of our models
- learning what a **hidden state** is
- understanding how a hidden state is **modified by a data point** inside an **RNN cell**
- disassembling an RNN cell into its components: **two linear layers** and an **activation function**
- understanding the **reasoning** behind using **hyperbolic tangent** as the activation function of choice in RNNs

- learning that **data points are independently transformed** while the **hidden state is sequentially transformed**
- using an **RNN layer** to automatically handle hidden state inputs and outputs without having to **loop over a sequence**
- discussing the issue with the **shape** of the data and the difference between **typical batch-first (N, L, F)** and **sequence-first (L, N, F)** shapes
- figuring that **stacked RNNs** and **bidirectional RNNs** are simply different ways of composing **two or more simple RNNs** and **concatenating their outputs**
- training a **square model** to classify our sequences into **clockwise** or **counterclockwise** directions
- visualizing the **transformed inputs** and the **decision boundary** separating the **final hidden states**
- visualizing the **journey of a hidden state** through each and every transformation happening inside an RNN layer
- adding **gates** to the RNN cell and turning it into a **gated recurrent unit** cell
- learning that **gates** are simply **vectors of values between zero and one**, one value for **each dimension of the hidden state**
- disassembling a GRU cell into its components to better understand its internal mechanics
- visualizing the **effect of using a gate** on the **hidden state**
- adding **another state** and **more gates** to the RNN cell, making it a **long short-term memory** cell
- disassembling an LSTM cell into its many components to better understand its internal mechanics
- generating **variable-length sequences**
- understanding the **issues with having tensors of different sizes** and using **padding** to make all sequences equal in length
- **packing** sequences as an alternative to padding, and understanding the **way the data is organized in a packed sequence**
- using a **collate function** to make a data loader **yield a mini-batch of your own assembling**
- learning about **1D convolutions** and how they can be used with **sequential data**

- discussing the **shape (N, C, L)** expected by these convolutions
- understanding that **features** are considered **channels** in these convolutions
- learning about **dilated convolutions**
- visualizing how a **convolutional model** learned to classify sequences based on the **edges** of the square

Congratulations! You took your **first step** (quite a *long* one, I might add, so give yourself a pat on the back for it!) toward **building models using sequential data**. You're now familiar with the inner workings of **recurrent layers**, and you learned the **importance of the hidden state** as the **representation of a sequence**. Moreover, you got the **tools** to **put your sequences in shape** (I *had* to make this pun!).

In the next chapter, we'll build on all of this (especially the *hidden state* part) and develop models to **generate sequences**. These models use an **encoder-decoder** architecture, and we can add all sorts of bells and whistles to it, like **attention mechanisms**, **positional encoding**, and much more!

[39] https://github.com/dvgodoy/PyTorchStepByStep/blob/master/Chapter08.ipynb

[40] https://colab.research.google.com/github/dvgodoy/PyTorchStepByStep/blob/master/Chapter08.ipynb

Chapter 9 — Part I

Sequence-to-Sequence

Spoilers

In the first half of this chapter, we will:

- learn about the **encoder-decoder** architecture
- build and train models to predict a **target sequence** from a **source sequence**
- understand the **attention** mechanism and its components ("keys," "values," and "queries")
- build a **multi-headed attention** mechanism

Jupyter Notebook

The Jupyter notebook corresponding to Chapter 9[41] is part of the official ***Deep Learning with PyTorch Step-by-Step*** repository on GitHub. You can also run it directly in **Google Colab**[42].

If you're using a *local installation*, open your terminal or Anaconda prompt and navigate to the `PyTorchStepByStep` folder you cloned from GitHub. Then, *activate* the `pytorchbook` environment and run `jupyter notebook`:

```
$ conda activate pytorchbook

(pytorchbook)$ jupyter notebook
```

If you're using Jupyter's default settings, `http://localhost:8888/notebooks/Chapter09.ipynb` should open Chapter 9's notebook. If not, just click on `Chapter09.ipynb` in your Jupyter's home page.

Imports

For the sake of organization, all libraries needed throughout the code used in any given chapter are imported at its very beginning. For this chapter, we'll need the following imports:

```python
import copy
import numpy as np

import torch
import torch.optim as optim
import torch.nn as nn
import torch.nn.functional as F
from torch.utils.data import DataLoader, Dataset, random_split, \
    TensorDataset

from data_generation.square_sequences import generate_sequences
from stepbystep.v4 import StepByStep
```

Sequence-to-Sequence

Sequence-to-sequence problems are more complex than those we handled in the last chapter. There are **two sequences** now: the **source** and the **target**. We use the former to predict the latter, and they may even have *different lengths*.

A typical example of a sequence-to-sequence problem is **translation**: A sentence goes in (a sequence of words in English), and another sentence comes out (a sequence of words in French). This problem can be tackled using an **encoder-decoder architecture**, first described in the "Sequence to Sequence Learning with Neural Networks"[43] paper by Sutskever, I., et al.

Translating languages is an obviously difficult task, so we're falling back to a much simpler problem to illustrate how the encoder-decoder architecture works.

Data Generation

We'll **keep drawing the same squares** as before, but this time we'll **draw the first two corners** ourselves (the **source sequence**) and ask our model to **predict the next two corners** (the **target sequence**). As with every sequence-related problem, the **order is important**, so it is not enough to get the corners' coordinates right; they should **follow the same direction** (clockwise or counterclockwise).

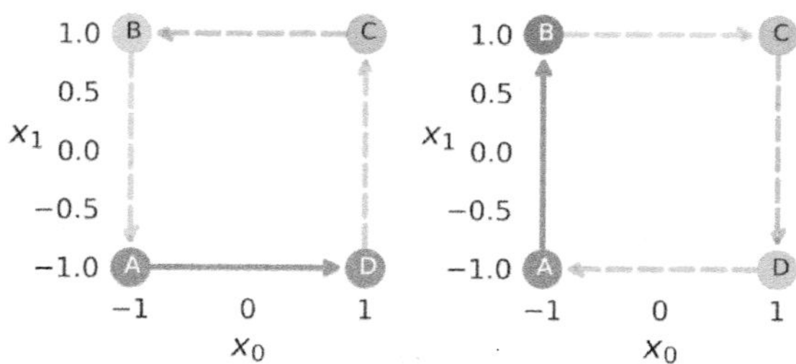

Figure 9.1 - Drawing first two corners, starting at A and moving toward either D or B

Since there are four corners to start from and two directions to follow, there are effectively eight possible sequences (solid colors indicate the corners in the source sequence, semi-transparent colors, the target sequence).

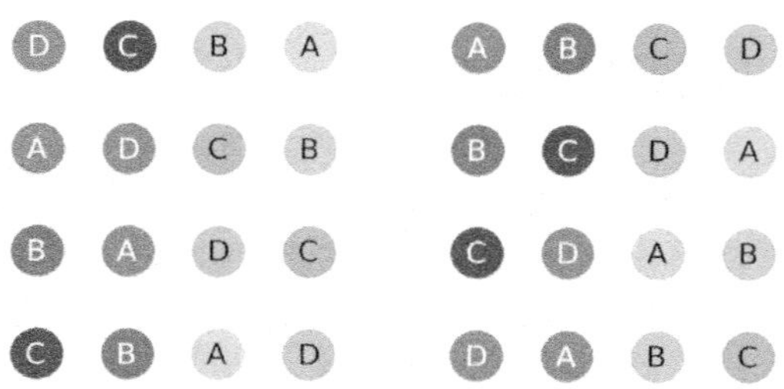

Figure 9.2 - Possible sequences of corners

Since the desired output of our model is a **sequence of coordinates (x_0, x_1)**, we're dealing with a **regression problem** now. Therefore, we'll be using a typical **mean squared error** loss to compare the **predicted and actual coordinates** for the **two points in the target sequence**.

Let's generate 256 random noisy squares:

Data Generation

```
points, directions = generate_sequences(n=256, seed=13)
```

And then let's visualize the first five squares:

```
fig = plot_data(points, directions, n_rows=1)
```

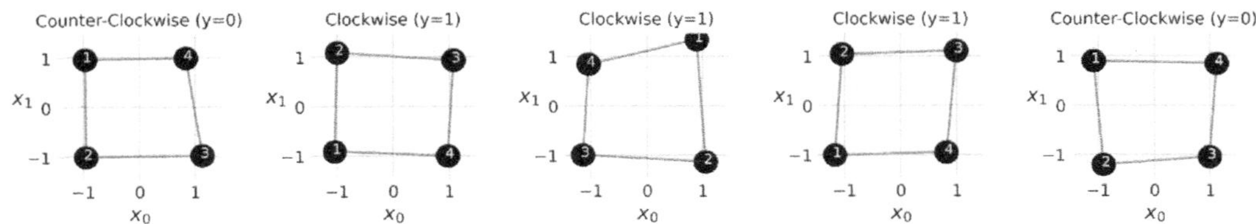

Figure 9.3 - Sequence dataset

The corners show the **order** in which they were drawn. In the first square, the drawing **started at the top-right corner** (corresponding to the *blue* C corner) and followed a **clockwise direction** (corresponding to the *CDAB* sequence). The **source sequence** for that square would include corners ***C*** **and** ***D*** **(1 and 2)**, while the **target sequence** would include corners ***A*** **and** ***B*** **(3 and 4)**, in that order.

In order to **output a sequence** we need a more complex architecture; we need an...

Encoder-Decoder Architecture

The encoder-decoder is a combination of **two models**: the **encoder** and the **decoder**.

Encoder

The **encoder's goal** is to **generate a representation** of the **source sequence**; that is, to **encode it**.

"Wait, we've done that already, right?"

Absolutely! That's what the **recurrent layers** did: They generated a **final hidden state** that was a **representation of the input sequence**. Now you know *why* I insisted *so much* on this idea and repeated it *over and over again* in Chapter 8 :-)

The figure below should look familiar: It is a **typical recurrent neural network** that we're using to **encode the source sequence**.

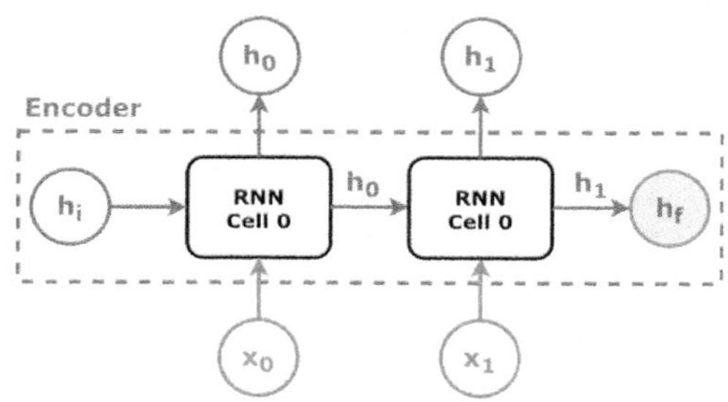

Figure 9.4 - Encoder

The **encoder** model is a slim version of our models from Chapter 8: It simply returns a **sequence of hidden states**.

Encoder

```
class Encoder(nn.Module):
    def __init__(self, n_features, hidden_dim):
        super().__init__()
        self.hidden_dim = hidden_dim
        self.n_features = n_features
        self.hidden = None
        self.basic_rnn = nn.GRU(self.n_features,
                                self.hidden_dim,
                                batch_first=True)

    def forward(self, X):
        rnn_out, self.hidden = self.basic_rnn(X)

        return rnn_out # N, L, F
```

"Don't we need only the ***final hidden state****?"*

That's correct. We'll be using the **final hidden state only** ... for now.

In the "Attention" section, we'll be using **all hidden states**, and that's why we're implementing the encoder like this.

Let's go over a simple example of **encoding**: We start with a sequence of coordinates of a "*perfect*" square and split it into **source and target sequences**:

```
full_seq = (torch.tensor([[-1, -1], [-1, 1], [1, 1], [1, -1]])
            .float()
            .view(1, 4, 2))
source_seq = full_seq[:, :2] # first two corners
target_seq = full_seq[:, 2:] # last two corners
```

Now, let's **encode the source sequence** and take the **final hidden state**:

```
torch.manual_seed(21)
encoder = Encoder(n_features=2, hidden_dim=2)
hidden_seq = encoder(source_seq) # output is N, L, F
hidden_final = hidden_seq[:, -1:]   # takes last hidden state
hidden_final
```

Output

```
tensor([[[ 0.3105, -0.5263]]], grad_fn=<SliceBackward>)
```

Of course, the model is *untrained*, so the final hidden state above is totally *random*. In a **trained model**, however, the final hidden state will **encode information about the source sequence**. In Chapter 8, we used it to **classify the direction** in which the square was drawn, so it is safe to say that the **final hidden state encoded the drawing direction** (clockwise or counterclockwise).

Pretty straightforward, right? Now, let's go over the…

Decoder

The **decoder's goal** is to **generate the target sequence** from **an initial representation**; that is, to **decode it**.

Sounds like a perfect match, doesn't it? **Encode the source sequence**, get its representation (**final hidden state**), and feed it to the **decoder** so it **generates the target sequence**.

"How does the decoder transform a hidden state into a sequence?"

We can use **recurrent layers** for that as well.

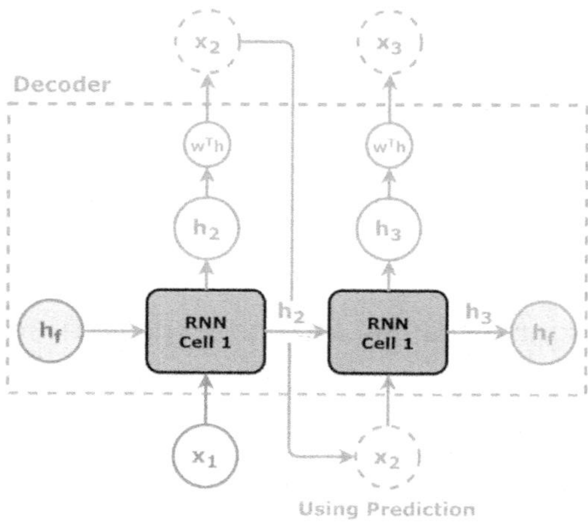

Figure 9.5 - Decoder

Let's analyze the figure above:

- In the **first step**, the **initial hidden state** is the **encoder's final hidden state** (h_f, in blue).
- The first cell will **output** a **new hidden state** (h_2): That's both the **output of that cell** and **one of the inputs of the next cell**, as we've already seen in Chapter 8.
- Before, we'd only run the *final* hidden state through a *linear layer* to produce the logits, but now we'll **run the output of every cell through a linear layer** (w^Th) to **convert each hidden state into predicted coordinates** (x_2).
- The **predicted coordinates** are then used as **one of the inputs of the second step** (x_2).

"*Great, but we're **missing one input in the first step**, right?*"

That's right! The **first cell** takes both an **initial hidden state** (h_f, in blue, the encoder's output) and a **first data point** (x_1, in red).

Let's **pretend** for a moment that the encoder's final hidden state (h_f) **encoded the direction of the drawing**. The decoder receives that information and, starting at its **first data point** (x_1), follows the encoded direction to predict the coordinates of the next corner.

Of course, this is just a gross simplification for the sake of developing intuition. The encoded information is more complex than that.

In our case, the decoder's first data point is actually the **last data point in the source sequence** because the **target sequence** is *not* a new sequence, but the **continuation of the source sequence**.

This is not always the case. In some natural language processing tasks, like translation, where the target sequence *is* a new sequence, the first data point is some "*special*" token that indicates the start of that new sequence.

There is another small, yet **fundamental** difference between the encoder and the decoder: Since the decoder **uses the prediction of one step as input to the next**, we'll have to **manually loop over the generation of the target sequence**.

This also means we need to **keep track of the hidden state** from one step to the next, using the **hidden state of one step as input to the next**.

But, instead of making the hidden state both an input and an output of the `forward()` method, we can easily (and quite elegantly, I might add) handle this by **making the hidden state an attribute** of our decoder model.

The **decoder** model is actually quite similar to the models we developed in Chapter 8:

Decoder

```
class Decoder(nn.Module):
    def __init__(self, n_features, hidden_dim):
        super().__init__()
        self.hidden_dim = hidden_dim
        self.n_features = n_features
        self.hidden = None
        self.basic_rnn = nn.GRU(self.n_features,
                                self.hidden_dim,
                                batch_first=True)
        self.regression = nn.Linear(self.hidden_dim,
                                    self.n_features)

    def init_hidden(self, hidden_seq):
        # We only need the final hidden state
        hidden_final = hidden_seq[:, -1:] # N, 1, H
        # But we need to make it sequence-first
        self.hidden = hidden_final.permute(1, 0, 2) # 1, N, H ①

    def forward(self, X):
        # X is N, 1, F
        batch_first_output, self.hidden = \
                                self.basic_rnn(X, self.hidden) ②

        last_output = batch_first_output[:, -1:]
        out = self.regression(last_output)

        # N, 1, F
        return out.view(-1, 1, self.n_features)              ③
```

① Initializing decoder's hidden state using encoder's **final hidden state**.

② The recurrent layer both **uses** and **updates** the hidden state.

③ The output has the same shape as the input (N, 1, F).

Let's go over the differences:

- Since the **initial hidden state** has to come from the encoder, we need a method to initialize the hidden state and set the corresponding attribute—the encoder's output is *batch-first* though, and the **hidden state** must **always be sequence-first**, so we permute its first two dimensions.

- The **hidden state attribute** is used both as an **input** and as an **output** of the recurrent layer.
- The **shape of the output** must match the **shape of the input**, namely, a **sequence of length one**.
- The `forward()` method will be called **multiple times** as we loop over the generation of the target sequence.

The whole thing is better understood with a hands-on example in code, so it's time to try some **decoding** to **generate a target sequence**:

```
torch.manual_seed(21)
decoder = Decoder(n_features=2, hidden_dim=2)

# Initial hidden state will be encoder's final hidden state
decoder.init_hidden(hidden_seq)
# Initial data point is the last element of source sequence
inputs = source_seq[:, -1:]

target_len = 2
for i in range(target_len):
    print(f'Hidden: {decoder.hidden}')
    out = decoder(inputs)   # Predicts coordinates
    print(f'Output: {out}\n')
    # Predicted coordinates are next step's inputs
    inputs = out
```

Output

```
Hidden: tensor([[[ 0.3105, -0.5263]]], grad_fn=<SliceBackward>)
Output: tensor([[[-0.2339,  0.4702]]], grad_fn=<ViewBackward>)

Hidden: tensor([[[ 0.3913, -0.6853]]], grad_fn=<StackBackward>)
Output: tensor([[[-0.0226,  0.4628]]], grad_fn=<ViewBackward>)
```

We created a **loop** to generate **a target sequence of length two**, using the predictions of one step as inputs to the next. The hidden state, however, was entirely handled by the model itself using its `hidden_state` attribute.

There is **one problem** with the approach above, though—an **untrained model** will make **really bad predictions**, and these predictions will still be used as inputs for subsequent steps. This makes model training **unnecessarily hard** because the **prediction error in one step** is caused by **both the (untrained) model and the prediction error in the previous step**.

"*Can't we use the **actual target sequence** instead?*"

Sure we can! This technique is called **teacher forcing**.

Teacher Forcing

The reasoning is simple: **Ignore the predictions** and use **the real data from the target sequence** instead. In code, we only need to change the **last line**:

```
# Initial hidden state will be encoder's final hidden state
decoder.init_hidden(hidden_seq)
# Initial data point is the last element of source sequence
inputs = source_seq[:, -1:]

target_len = 2
for i in range(target_len):
    print(f'Hidden: {decoder.hidden}')
    out = decoder(inputs) # Predicts coordinates
    print(f'Output: {out}\n')
    # Completely ignores the predictions and uses real data instead
    inputs = target_seq[:, i:i+1]       ①
```

① Inputs to the next step are not predictions anymore.

Output

```
Hidden: tensor([[[ 0.3105, -0.5263]]], grad_fn=<SliceBackward>)
Output: tensor([[[-0.2339,  0.4702]]], grad_fn=<ViewBackward>)

Hidden: tensor([[[ 0.3913, -0.6853]]], grad_fn=<StackBackward>)
Output: tensor([[[0.2265, 0.4529]]], grad_fn=<ViewBackward>)
```

Now, a **bad prediction** can only be traced to the **model** itself, and any bad predictions in previous steps have no effect whatsoever.

*"This is **great** for training time, sure—but what about **testing** time, when the target sequence is unknown?"*

At **testing** time, there is no escape from using only the model's **own predictions from previous steps**.

The problem is, a model trained using **teacher forcing** will minimize the loss given the **correct inputs at every step of the target sequence**. But, since this will **never be the case at testing time**, the model is likely to **perform poorly** when using its **own predictions as inputs**.

"What can we do about it?"

When in doubt, flip a coin. Literally. During training, **sometimes** the model will use **teacher forcing**, and **sometimes** it will use its **own predictions**. So we occasionally help the model by providing an actual input, but we still force it to be robust enough to generate and use its own inputs. In code, we just have to add an **if statement** and **draw a random number**:

```
# Initial hidden state will be encoder's final hidden state
decoder.init_hidden(hidden_seq)
# Initial data point is the last element of source sequence
inputs = source_seq[:, -1:]

teacher_forcing_prob = 0.5
target_len = 2
for i in range(target_len):
    print(f'Hidden: {decoder.hidden}')
    out = decoder(inputs)
    print(f'Output: {out}\n')
    # If it is teacher forcing
    if torch.rand(1) <= teacher_forcing_prob:
        # Takes the actual element
        inputs = target_seq[:, i:i+1]
    else:
        # Otherwise uses the last predicted output
        inputs = out
```

Output

```
Hidden: tensor([[[ 0.3105, -0.5263]]], grad_fn=<SliceBackward>)
Output: tensor([[[-0.2339,  0.4702]]], grad_fn=<ViewBackward>)

Hidden: tensor([[[ 0.3913, -0.6853]]], grad_fn=<StackBackward>)
Output: tensor([[[0.2265, 0.4529]]], grad_fn=<ViewBackward>)
```

You may set `teacher_forcing_prob` to 1.0 or 0.0 to replicate either of the two outputs we generated before.

Now it is time to put the two of them together…

Encoder + Decoder

The figure below illustrates the flow of information from encoder to decoder.

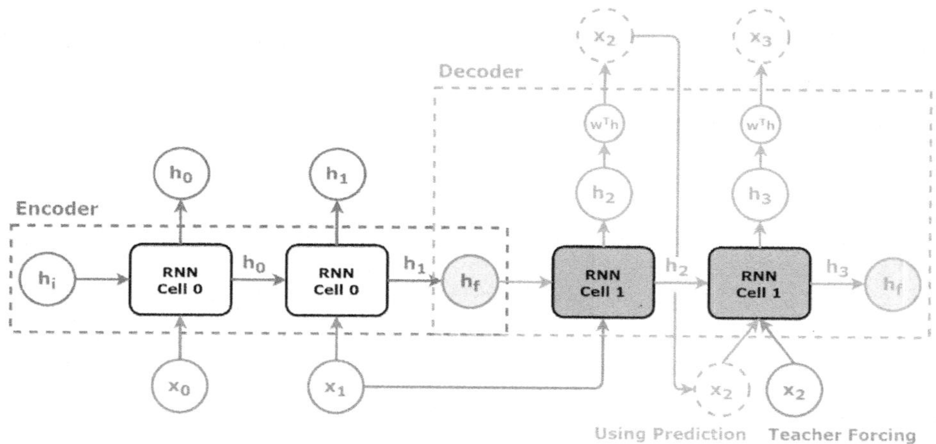

Figure 9.6 - Encoder + decoder

Let's go over it once again:

- The **encoder** receives the **source sequence** (x_0 and x_1, in red) and generates the **representation of the source sequence**, its **final hidden state** (h_f, in blue).
- The **decoder** receives the **hidden state from the encoder** (h_f, in blue), together with the **last known element of the sequence** (x_1, in red), to output a **hidden state** (h_2, in green) that is **converted into the first set of predicted coordinates** (x_2, in green) using a **linear layer** (w^Th, in green).
- In the next iteration of the loop, the model **randomly uses the predicted (x_2, in green) or the actual (x_2, in red) set of coordinates** as one of its inputs to output

the **second set of predicted coordinates** (x_3), thus achieving the **target length**.

- The **final output** of the **encoder + decoder** model is the **full sequence of predicted coordinates**: $[x_2, x_3]$.

We can assemble the bits and pieces we've developed so far into a model that, given the encoder and decoder models, implements a `forward()` method that **splits the input** into the source and target sequences, loops over the **generation of the target sequence**, and implements **teacher forcing** in training mode.

The model below is mostly about handling the **boilerplate** necessary to integrate both encoder and decoder:

Encoder + Decoder

```
class EncoderDecoder(nn.Module):
    def __init__(self, encoder, decoder,
                 input_len, target_len,
                 teacher_forcing_prob=0.5):
        super().__init__()
        self.encoder = encoder
        self.decoder = decoder
        self.input_len = input_len
        self.target_len = target_len
        self.teacher_forcing_prob = teacher_forcing_prob
        self.outputs = None

    def init_outputs(self, batch_size):
        device = next(self.parameters()).device
        # N, L (target), F
        self.outputs = torch.zeros(batch_size,
                                   self.target_len,
                                   self.encoder.n_features).to(device)

    def store_output(self, i, out):
        # Stores the output
        self.outputs[:, i:i+1, :] = out

    def forward(self, X):
        # splits the data in source and target sequences
        # the target seq will be empty in testing mode
        # N, L, F
        source_seq = X[:, :self.input_len, :]
```

```
        target_seq = X[:, self.input_len:, :]
        self.init_outputs(X.shape[0])

        # Encoder expected N, L, F
        hidden_seq = self.encoder(source_seq)
        # Output is N, L, H
        self.decoder.init_hidden(hidden_seq)

        # The last input of the encoder is also
        # the first input of the decoder
        dec_inputs = source_seq[:, -1:, :]

        # Generates as many outputs as the target length
        for i in range(self.target_len):
            # Output of decoder is N, 1, F
            out = self.decoder(dec_inputs)
            self.store_output(i, out)

            prob = self.teacher_forcing_prob
            # In evaluation / test the target sequence is
            # unknown, so we cannot use teacher forcing
            if not self.training:
                prob = 0

            # If it is teacher forcing
            if torch.rand(1) <= prob:
                # Takes the actual element
                dec_inputs = target_seq[:, i:i+1, :]
            else:
                # Otherwise uses the last predicted output
                dec_inputs = out

        return self.outputs
```

The only *real* additions are the `init_outputs()` method, which creates a tensor for storing the generated target sequence, and the `store_output()` method, which actually stores the output produced by the decoder.

Let's create an instance of the model above using the other two we already created:

```
encdec = EncoderDecoder(encoder, decoder,
                        input_len=2, target_len=2,
                        teacher_forcing_prob=0.5)
```

In **training mode**, the model expects the **full sequence** so it can randomly use **teacher forcing**:

```
encdec.train()
encdec(full_seq)
```

Output

```
tensor([[[-0.2339,  0.4702],
         [ 0.2265,  0.4529]]], grad_fn=<CopySlices>)
```

In **evaluation / test mode**, though, it **only needs the source sequence** as input:

```
encdec.eval()
encdec(source_seq)
```

Output

```
tensor([[[-0.2339,  0.4702],
         [-0.0226,  0.4628]]], grad_fn=<CopySlices>)
```

Let's use this knowledge to build our **training and test sets**.

Data Preparation

For the **training set**, we need the **full sequences** as **features** (*X*) to use **teacher forcing**, and the **target sequences** as **labels** (*y*) so we can compute the **mean squared error** loss:

Data Generation — Train

```
points, directions = generate_sequences(n=256, seed=13)
full_train = torch.as_tensor(points).float()
target_train = full_train[:, 2:]
```

For the **test set**, though, we only need **the source sequences** as **features** (*X*) and the **target sequences** as **labels** (*y*):

Data Generation — Test

```
test_points, test_directions = generate_sequences(seed=19)
full_test = torch.as_tensor(test_points).float()
source_test = full_test[:, :2]
target_test = full_test[:, 2:]
```

These are all simple tensors, so we can use `TensorDatasets` and simple data loaders:

Data Preparation

```
train_data = TensorDataset(full_train, target_train)
test_data = TensorDataset(source_test, target_test)
generator = torch.Generator()
train_loader = DataLoader(train_data, batch_size=16,
                          shuffle=True, generator=generator)
test_loader = DataLoader(test_data, batch_size=16)
```

In version 1.7, PyTorch introduced a **modification** to the random sampler in the `DataLoader` that's responsible for **shuffling** the data. In order to **ensure reproducibility**, we need to **assign a** **`Generator`** to the `DataLoader`. Luckily, our `StepByStep` class **already sets a seed to the generator**, if there is one, in its `set_seed()` method, so you don't need to worry about that.

By the way, we **didn't use the directions** to build the datasets this time.

We have everything we need to **train our first sequence-to-sequence model** now!

Model Configuration & Training

The model configuration is very straightforward: We create both encoder and decoder models, use them as arguments to the large `EncoderDecoder` model that handles the boilerplate, and create a loss and an optimizer as usual.

Model Configuration

```
torch.manual_seed(23)
encoder = Encoder(n_features=2, hidden_dim=2)
decoder = Decoder(n_features=2, hidden_dim=2)
model = EncoderDecoder(encoder, decoder,
                       input_len=2, target_len=2,
                       teacher_forcing_prob=0.5)
loss = nn.MSELoss()
optimizer = optim.Adam(model.parameters(), lr=0.01)
```

Next, we use the `StepByStep` class to train the model:

Model Training

```
sbs_seq = StepByStep(model, loss, optimizer)
sbs_seq.set_loaders(train_loader, test_loader)
sbs_seq.train(100)
```

```
fig = sbs_seq.plot_losses()
```

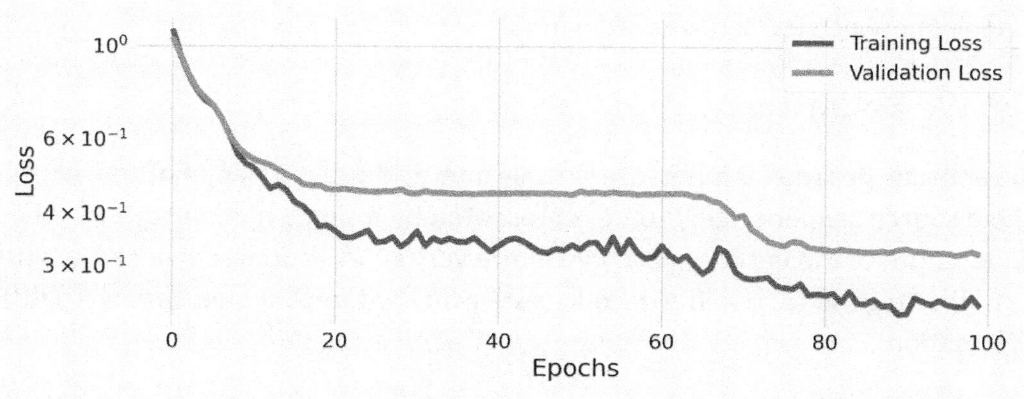

Figure 9.7 - Losses—encoder + decoder

It is hard to tell how badly our model is performing by looking at the loss only, if we're dealing with a "*regression*" problem like this. It is much better to **visualize the predictions**.

Visualizing Predictions

Let's plot the **predicted coordinates** and connect them using **dashed lines**, while using **solid lines** to connect the **actual coordinates**. The first **ten sequences** of the **test set** look like this:

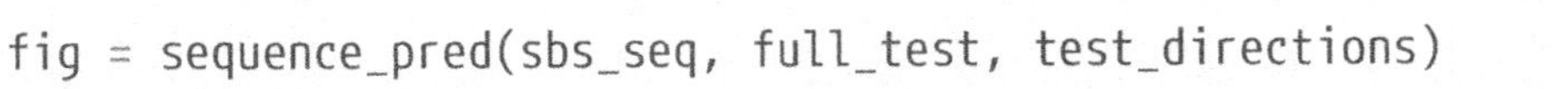

```
fig = sequence_pred(sbs_seq, full_test, test_directions)
```

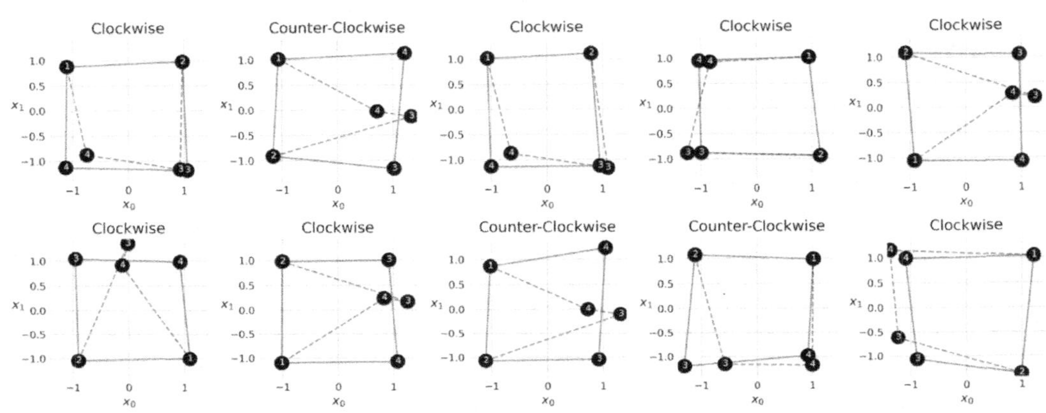

Figure 9.8 - Predictions

The results are, at the same time, very **good** and very **bad**. In **half** of the sequences, the **predicted coordinates** are **quite close** to the actual ones. But, in the other half, the predicted coordinates are **overlapping with each other** and close to the midpoint between the actual coordinates.

Can We Do Better?

The encoder-decoder architecture is really interesting, but it has a **bottleneck**: The whole **source sequence** gets to be **represented by a single hidden state**, the final hidden state of the encoder part. Even for a very short source sequence like ours, it's quite a **big ask** to have the **decoder generate the target sequence with so little information**.

*"Can we make the decoder use **more information**?"*

Sure, we can!

Attention

Here is a (not so) crazy idea: What if the **decoder** could **choose** one (or more) of the **encoder's hidden states** to use instead of being forced to stick with only the final one? That would surely give it more **flexibility** to use the hidden state that's **more useful** at a given step of the **target-sequence generation**.

Let's illustrate it with a simple, non-numerical example: translating from English to French using Google Translate. The original sentence is, "*the European economic zone*," and its French translation is, "*la zone économique européenne*."

Now, let's compare their first words: "*La*," in French, obviously corresponds to "*the*" in English. My question to you is:

*"Could Google (or any translator) have translated "**the**" to "**la**" without any other information?"*

The answer is: **No**. The English language has only *one* definite article—"*the*"—while French (and many other languages) have *many* definite articles. It means that "*the*" **may be translated in many different ways**, and it is only possible to determine the correct (translated) article after finding the *noun* it refers to. The noun, in this case, is *zone*, and it is the **last word** in the English sentence. Coincidentally, its translation is also *zone*, and it is a **singular feminine noun** in French, thus making "*la*" the correct translation of "*the*" in this case.

"So what? What does this have to do with hidden states?"

Well, if we consider the English sentence a **(source) sequence of words**, the French sentence is a **(target) sequence of words.** Assuming we can map each word to a numeric vector, we can use an encoder to encode the words in English, **each word corresponding to a hidden state**.

We know that the decoder's role is to **generate the translated words**, right? Then, if the decoder is allowed to **choose which hidden states from the encoder** it will use to generate each output, it means it can **choose which English words** it will use to generate each translated word.

We have already seen that, in order to translate "*the*" to "*la*," the translator (that would be the decoder) needs to know the corresponding noun too, so it is reasonable to assume that the decoder would choose the *first* and *last* encoded hidden states (corresponding to "*the*" and "*zone*" in the English sentence) to generate the first translated word.

In other words, we can say that the decoder is **paying attention** to different elements in the **source sequence**. That's the famous **attention mechanism** in a nutshell.

Now, try to answer this question:

"Which English word(s) is the decoder paying attention to in order to generate the second French word ("zone")?"

It is reasonable to assume it is paying attention only to the *last* English word; that is, "*zone.*" The remaining English words shouldn't play a role in this particular piece of the translation.

Let's take it one step further and build a matrix with English words (the source sequence) as columns and French words (the target sequence) as rows. The entries in this matrix represent our guesses of **how much attention** the decoder is paying to **each English word** in order to generate **a given French word**.

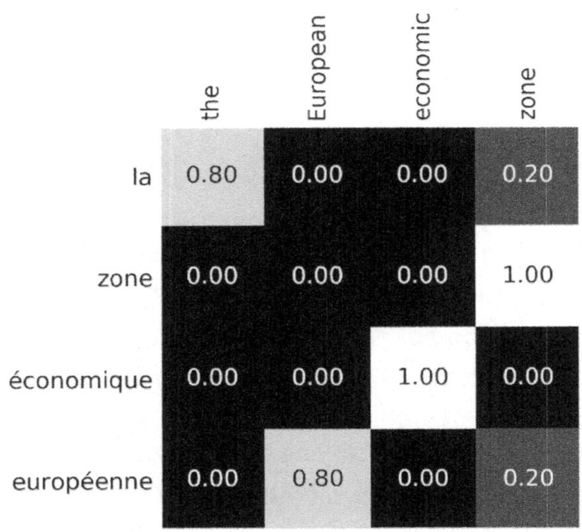

Figure 9.9 - Attention for translation

The numbers above are *completely made-up*, by the way. Since the translated "*la*" is based on "*the*" and "*zone*," I've just guessed that a translator (the decoder) could have assigned 80% of its attention to the definite article and the remaining 20% of its attention to the corresponding noun to determine its gender. These weights, or *alphas*, are the **attention scores**.

The **more relevant** to the decoder a **hidden state from the encoder** is, the **higher** the **score**.

"OK, I get what the attention scores represent, but ***how*** *does the decoder actually use them?"*

If you haven't noticed yet, the **attention scores** actually **add up to one**, so they will be used to compute a **weighted average of the encoder's hidden states.**

We'll work this out in more detail, but, first, it helps to keep it short and simple. So we're translating two words only, from "*the zone*" in English to "*la zone*" in French. Then, we can use the **encoder-decoder** architecture from the previous section.

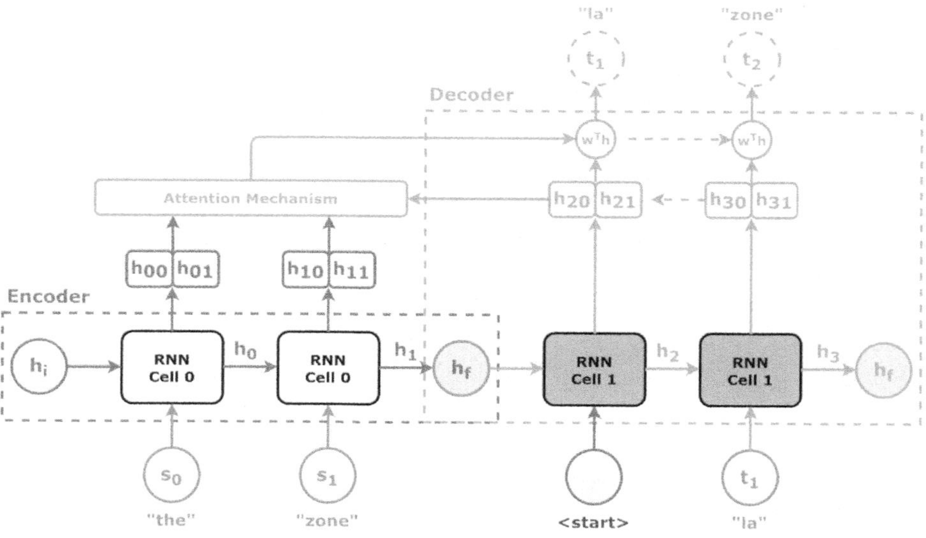

Figure 9.10 - Encoder-Decoder for translation

In the translation example above, the source and target sequences are independent, so the **first input** of the decoder *isn't* the last element of the source sequence anymore, but rather the **special token** that indicates the start of a **new sequence**.

The main difference is, instead of **generating predictions** solely based on its **own**

hidden states, the **decoder** will recruit the **attention mechanism** to help it decide which parts of the source sequence it must pay attention to.

In our made-up example, the attention mechanism informed the decoder it should pay 80% of its attention to the encoder's hidden state corresponding to the word "*the*," and the remaining 20% to the word "*zone*." The diagram below illustrates this.

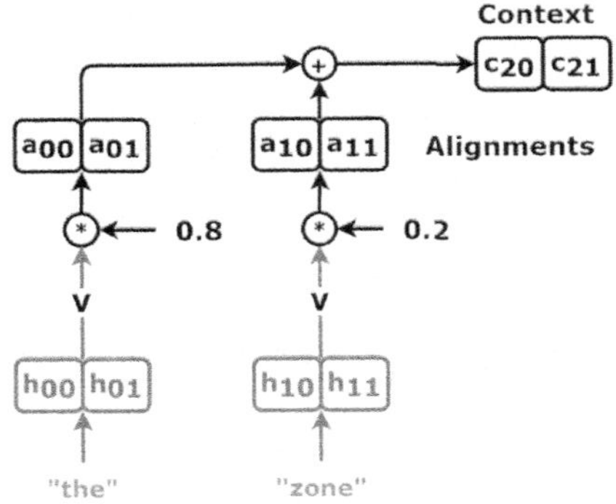

Figure 9.11 - Paying attention to words

"Values"

From now on, we'll be referring to the **encoder's hidden states** (or their affine transformations) as **"values" (V)**. The resulting multiplication of a "value" by its corresponding **attention score** is called an **alignment vector**. And, as you can see in the diagram, the **sum of all alignment vectors** (that is, the weighted average of the hidden states) is called a **context vector**.

$$\text{context vector} = \underbrace{\alpha_0 * h_0}_{\text{alignment vector}_0} + \underbrace{\alpha_1 * h_1}_{\text{alignment vector}_1} = 0.8 * \text{value}_{the} + 0.2 * \text{value}_{zone}$$

Equation 9.1 - Context vector

*"OK, but **where** do the attention scores come from?"*

"Keys" and "Queries"

The attention scores are based on **matching each hidden state of the decoder** (h_2) to **every hidden state of the encoder** (h_0 and h_1). Some of them will be **good matches** (high attention scores) while some others will be **poor matches** (low attention scores).

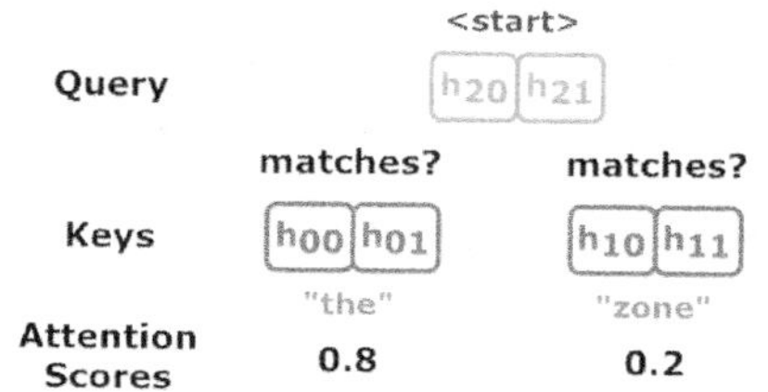

Figure 9.12 - Matching a query to the keys

The **encoder's hidden states** are called **"keys" (K)**, while the **decoder's hidden state** is called a **"query" (Q)**.

*"Wait a minute! I thought the **encoder's hidden states** were called **"values" (V)**."*

You're absolutely right. The **encoder's hidden states** are used **as both "keys" (K) and "values" (V)**. Later on, we'll apply **affine transformations** to the hidden states, one for the "keys," another for the "values," so they will actually have different values.

"Where do these names come from, anyway?"

Well, the general idea is that the **encoder** works like a **key-value store**, as if it were some sort of database, and then the **decoder queries** it. The attention mechanism **looks the query up in its keys** (the matching part) and **returns its values**. Honestly, I don't think this idea helps much, because the mechanism doesn't return a single original value, but rather a weighted average of all of them. But this naming convention is used everywhere, so you need to know it.

"Why is 'the' a better match than 'zone' in this case?"

Fair enough. These are made-up values, and their sole purpose is to illustrate the attention mechanism. If it helps, consider that sentences are more likely to start with "*the*" than "*zone*," so the former is likely a better match to the special `<start>` token.

"OK, I will play along."

Thanks! Even though we haven't actually discussed **how to match** a given "query" (Q) to the "keys" (K), we *can* update our diagram to include them.

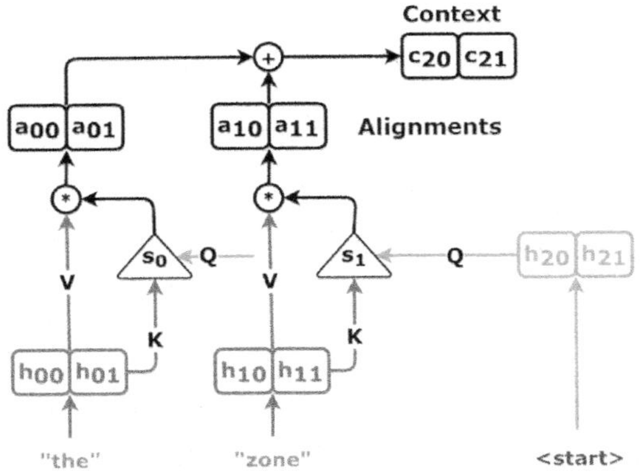

Figure 9.13 - Computing the context vector

The **"query" (Q)** is matched to both **"keys" (K)** to compute the **attention scores (s)** used to compute the **context vector**, which is simply the **weighted average of the "values" (V)**.

Computing the Context Vector

Let's go over a simple example in code using our own sequence-to-sequence problem, and the "*perfect*" square as input:

```
full_seq = (torch.tensor([[-1, -1], [-1, 1], [1, 1], [1, -1]])
            .float()
            .view(1, 4, 2))
source_seq = full_seq[:, :2]
target_seq = full_seq[:, 2:]
```

The **source sequence** is the input of the **encoder**, and the **hidden states** it outputs are going to be both **"values" (V)** and **"keys" (K)**:

```
torch.manual_seed(21)
encoder = Encoder(n_features=2, hidden_dim=2)
hidden_seq = encoder(source_seq)

values = hidden_seq # N, L, H
values
```

Output

```
tensor([[[ 0.0832, -0.0356],
         [ 0.3105, -0.5263]]], grad_fn=<PermuteBackward>)
```

```
keys = hidden_seq # N, L, H
keys
```

Output

```
tensor([[[ 0.0832, -0.0356],
         [ 0.3105, -0.5263]]], grad_fn=<PermuteBackward>)
```

The encoder-decoder dynamics stay exactly the same: We still use the **encoder's final hidden state** as the **decoder's initial hidden state** (even though we're sending the whole sequence to the decoder, it *still* uses the last hidden state only), and we still use the **last element of the source sequence** as **input** to the first step of the **decoder**:

```
torch.manual_seed(21)
decoder = Decoder(n_features=2, hidden_dim=2)
decoder.init_hidden(hidden_seq)

inputs = source_seq[:, -1:]
out = decoder(inputs)
```

The **first "query" (Q)** is the **decoder's hidden state** (remember, hidden states are *always* sequence-first, so we're permuting it to batch-first):

```
query = decoder.hidden.permute(1, 0, 2)  # N, 1, H
query
```

Output

```
tensor([[[ 0.3913, -0.6853]]], grad_fn=<PermuteBackward>)
```

OK, we have the "keys" and a "query," so let's *pretend* we can compute **attention scores (*alphas*)** using them:

```
def calc_alphas(ks, q):
    N, L, H = ks.size()
    alphas = torch.ones(N, 1, L).float() * 1/L
    return alphas

alphas = calc_alphas(keys, query)
alphas
```

Output

```
tensor([[[0.5000, 0.5000]]])
```

We had to make sure *alphas* had the **right shape (N, 1, L)** so that, when multiplied by the **"values"** with **shape (N, L, H)**, it will result in a **weighted sum of the alignment vectors** with **shape (N, 1, H)**. We can use **batch matrix multiplication** (`torch.bmm()`) for that:

$$(N, 1, L) \times (N, L, H) = (N, 1, H)$$

Equation 9.2 - Shapes for batch matrix multiplication

In other words, we can simply **ignore the first dimension**, and PyTorch will go over all the elements in the mini-batch for us:

```
# N, 1, L x N, L, H -> 1, L x L, H -> 1, H
context_vector = torch.bmm(alphas, values)
context_vector
```

Output

```
tensor([[[ 0.1968, -0.2809]]], grad_fn=<BmmBackward0>)
```

*"Why are you spending so much time on **matrix multiplication**, of all things?"*

Although it seems a fairly basic topic, **getting the shapes and dimensions right** is of utmost importance for the correct implementation of an algorithm or technique. Sometimes, using the *wrong* dimensions in an operation *may not raise an explicit error*, but it will **damage the model's ability to learn** nonetheless. For that reason, I believe it is worth it to spend some time going over it in full detail.

Once the **context vector** is ready, we can **concatenate** it to the **"query" (the decoder's hidden state)** and use it as the input for the linear layer that actually generates the predicted coordinates:

```
concatenated = torch.cat([context_vector, query], axis=-1)
concatenated
```

Output

```
tensor([[[ 0.1968, -0.2809,  0.3913, -0.6853]]], grad_fn
=<CatBackward>)
```

The diagram below illustrates the whole thing: encoder, decoder, and attention mechanism.

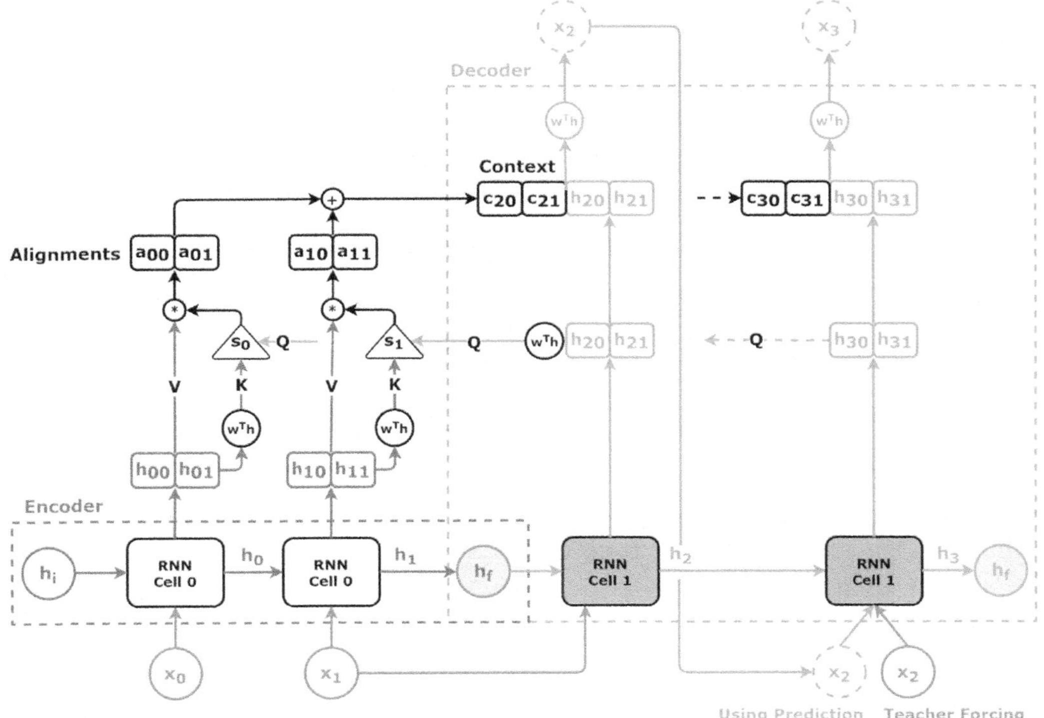

Figure 9.14 - Encoder + decoder + attention

*"The attention mechanism looks different—there are **affine transformations** (w^Th) for both 'keys' and 'queries' now."*

Yes, the **scoring method** will use the **transformed "keys" and "queries"** to compute the **attention scores**, so I've included them in the diagram above. By the way, this is a good moment to *summarize* the information in a table:

	Keys (K)	Queries (Q)	Values (V)
Source	Encoder	Decoder	Encoder
Affine Transformation	Yes	Yes	Not yet
Purpose	Scoring	Scoring	Alignment Vector

*"I guess now it is time to see **how the scoring method** works, right?"*

Absolutely! Let's understand how the **scoring method** transforms a **good match** between a "query" and a "key" into an **attention score**.

Scoring Method

A **"key" (K)** is a hidden state from the encoder. A **"query" (Q)** is a hidden state from the decoder. Both of them are **vectors** with the same number of dimensions; that is, the number of **hidden dimensions** of the underlying recurrent neural networks.

The **scoring method** needs to determine if **two vectors** are a **good match** or not, or, phrased differently, it needs to determine if **two vectors are similar** or not.

*"How do we compute the **similarity** between two vectors?"*

Well, that's actually easy: **Cosine similarity** to the rescue! If two vectors are **pointing in the same direction**, their cosine similarity is a **perfect one**. If they are **orthogonal** (that is, if there is a right angle between them), their cosine similarity is **zero**. If they are pointing in **opposite directions**, their cosine similarity is **minus one**.

Its formula is:

$$\cos\ \theta = \frac{\sum_i q_i k_i}{\sqrt{\sum_j q_j^2}\sqrt{\sum_j k_j^2}}$$

Equation 9.3 - Cosine similarity

Unfortunately, cosine similarity **does not** consider the **norm (size)** of the vectors, only its direction (the sizes of the vectors are in the denominator in the formula above).

*"What if we **scale** the similarity by the **norms** of both vectors?"*

Perfect! Let's do that:

$$\cos\ \theta \sqrt{\sum_j q_j^2}\sqrt{\sum_j k_j^2} = \sum_i q_i k_i$$

Equation 9.4 - Scaled cosine similarity

The two terms next to the cosine are the **norms** of the **"query" (Q)** and **"key" (K)** vectors, and the term on the right is actually the **dot product** between the two vectors:

$$\cos\ \theta\ ||Q||\ ||K|| = Q \cdot K$$

Equation 9.5 - Cosine similarity vs dot product

The **dot product** is equal to the **cosine similarity scaled by the norms of the vectors.** In other words, the dot product is:

- **higher** if both **"key" (K)** and **"query" (Q)** vectors are **aligned** (small angle and **high cosine value**).
- **proportional** to the **norm (size)** of the **"query" vector (Q).**
- **proportional** to the **norm (size)** of the **"key" vector (K).**

The **dot product** is one of the most common ways to compute **alignment (and attention) scores**, but it is *not* the only one. For more information on different mechanisms, and on *attention* in general, please refer to Lilian Weng's amazing blog post[44] on the subject.

To compute the **dot products** all at once, we can use PyTorch's *batch matrix multiplication* (`torch.bmm()`) again. We have to **transpose the "keys" matrix**, though, by **permuting the last two dimensions**:

```
# N, 1, H x N, H, L -> N, 1, L
products = torch.bmm(query, keys.permute(0, 2, 1))
products
```

Output

```
tensor([[[0.0569, 0.4821]]], grad_fn=<BmmBackward0>)
```

*"But these values **do not add up to one**—they cannot be **attention scores**, right?"*

You're absolutely right—these are **alignment scores**.

Attention Scores

To transform alignment scores into **attention scores**, we can use the **softmax** function:

```
alphas = F.softmax(products, dim=-1)
alphas
```

Output

```
tensor([[[0.3953, 0.6047]]], grad_fn=<SoftmaxBackward>)
```

That's more like it—they're adding up to one! The attention scores above mean that the **first hidden state** contributes to **roughly 40%** of the **context vector** while the

second hidden state contributes to the remaining **60%** of the context vector.

We can also **update** our `calc_alphas()` function to **actually compute them**:

```
def calc_alphas(ks, q):
    # N, 1, H x N, H, L -> N, 1, L
    products = torch.bmm(q, ks.permute(0, 2, 1))
    alphas = F.softmax(products, dim=-1)
    return alphas
```

Scaled Dot Product

So far, we've used simple dot products between a "query" and each of the "keys." But, given that the **dot product** between two vectors is the **sum of the elements** after an **element-wise multiplication** of both vectors, guess what happens as the vectors grow to a **larger number of dimensions**? The **variance** gets **larger** as well.

So, we need to (somewhat) **standardize** it by **scaling the dot product** by the **inverse of its standard deviation**:

$$\text{scaled dot product} = \frac{Q \cdot K}{\sqrt{d_k}}$$

Equation 9.6 - Scaled dot product

```
dims = query.size(-1)
scaled_products = products / np.sqrt(dims)
scaled_products
```

Output

```
tensor([[[0.0403, 0.3409]]], grad_fn=<DivBackward0>)
```

Visualizing the Context Vector

Let's start by creating one dummy "query" and three dummy "keys":

```
q = torch.tensor([.55, .95]).view(1, 1, 2) # N, 1, H
k = torch.tensor([[.65, .2],
                  [.85, -.4],
                  [-.95, -.75]]).view(1, 3, 2) # N, L, H
```

Then, let's **visualize** them as vectors, together with their **norms** and the **cosines** of the angles between each "key" and the "query."

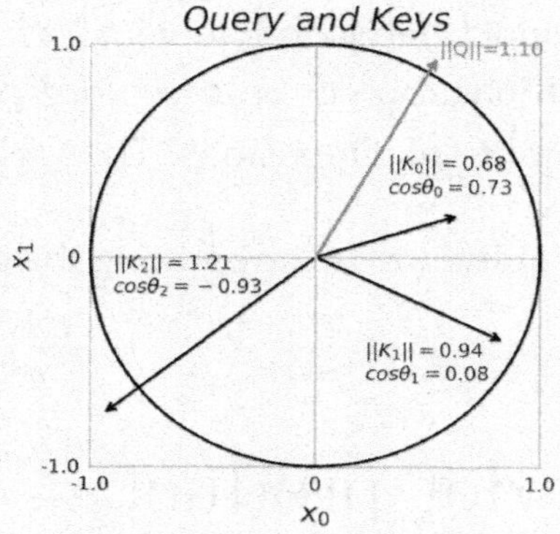

We can use the values in the figure above to compute the **dot product** between each "key" and the "query":

$$
\begin{aligned}
Q \cdot K_0 &= \cos\theta_0 \; ||Q|| \; ||K_0|| = & 0.73* \; 1.10* \; 0.68 = & \; 0.54 \\
Q \cdot K_1 &= \cos\theta_1 \; ||Q|| \; ||K_1|| = & 0.08* \; 1.10* \; 0.94 = & \; 0.08 \\
Q \cdot K_2 &= \cos\theta_2 \; ||Q|| \; ||K_2|| = - & 0.93* \; 1.10* \; 1.21 = - & \; 1.23
\end{aligned}
$$

Equation 9.7 - Dot products

```
# N, 1, H x N, H, L -> N, 1, L
prod = torch.bmm(q, k.permute(0, 2, 1))
prod
```

Output

```
tensor([[[ 0.5475,  0.0875, -1.2350]]])
```

Even though the **first** "key" (K_0) is the **smallest in size**, it is the **most well-aligned** to the "query," and, overall, is the "key" with the **largest dot product**. This means that the **decoder** would **pay the most attention** to this particular key. Makes sense, right?

Applying the **softmax** to these values gives us the following **attention scores**:

```
scores = F.softmax(prod, dim=-1)
scores
```

Output

```
tensor([[[0.5557, 0.3508, 0.0935]]])
```

Unsurprisingly, the first key got the largest weight. Let's use these weights to compute the **context vector**:

$$\text{context vector} = 0.5557 * \begin{bmatrix} 0.65 \\ 0.20 \end{bmatrix} + 0.3508 * \begin{bmatrix} 0.85 \\ -0.40 \end{bmatrix} + 0.0935 * \begin{bmatrix} -0.95 \\ -0.75 \end{bmatrix}$$

Equation 9.8 - Computing the context vector

```
v = k
context = torch.bmm(scores, v)
context
```

Output

```
tensor([[[ 0.5706, -0.0993]]])
```

Better yet, let's **visualize** the context vector.

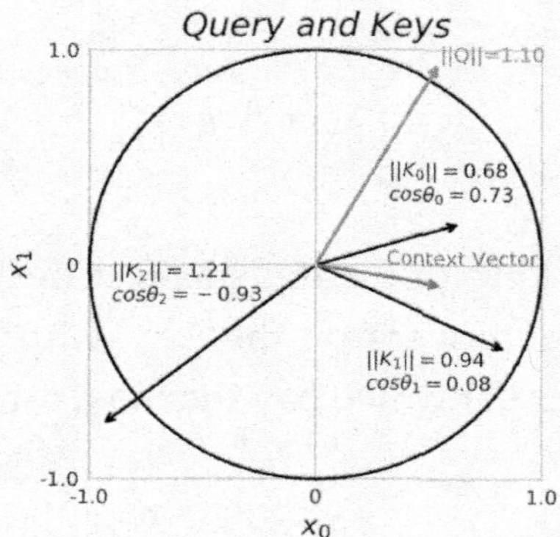

Since the context vector is a **weighted sum of the values** (or keys, since we're not applying any affine transformations yet), it is only logical that its location is somewhere between the other vectors.

"Why do we need to scale the dot product?"

If we don't, the distribution of attention scores will get *too skewed* because the **softmax** function is actually affected by the **scale** of its inputs:

```
dummy_product = torch.tensor([4.0, 1.0])
(F.softmax(dummy_product, dim=-1),
 F.softmax(100*dummy_product, dim=-1))
```

Output

```
(tensor([0.9526, 0.0474]), tensor([1., 0.]))
```

See? As the *scale* of the dot products grows larger, the resulting distribution of the *softmax* gets more and more skewed.

In our case, there isn't much difference because our vectors have **only two dimensions**:

```
alphas = F.softmax(scaled_products, dim=-1)
alphas
```

Output

```
tensor([[[0.4254, 0.5746]]], grad_fn=<SoftmaxBackward>)
```

The computation of the **context vectors** using **scaled dot product** is usually depicted like this:

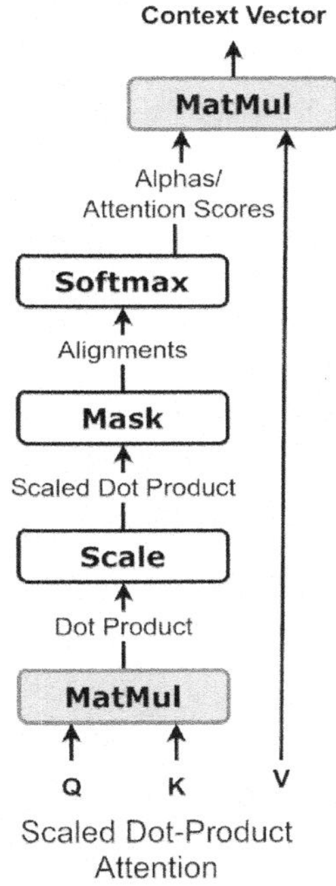

Figure 9.15 - Scaled dot-product attention

If you prefer to see it in code, it looks like this:

```
def calc_alphas(ks, q):
    dims = q.size(-1)
    # N, 1, H x N, H, L -> N, 1, L
    products = torch.bmm(q, ks.permute(0, 2, 1))
    scaled_products = products / np.sqrt(dims)
    alphas = F.softmax(scaled_products, dim=-1)
    return alphas
```

Dot Product's Standard Deviation

You probably noticed that the **square root of the number of dimensions** as the **standard deviation** simply appeared out of thin air. We're not proving it or anything, but we can try to **simulate** a ton of dot products to see what happens, right?

```
n_dims = 10
vector1 = torch.randn(10000, 1, n_dims)
vector2 = torch.randn(10000, 1, n_dims).permute(0, 2, 1)
torch.bmm(vector1, vector2).squeeze().var()
```

Output

```
tensor(9.8681)
```

Even though the values in hidden states coming out of both encoder and decoder are **bounded to (-1, 1) by the hyperbolic tangent**, remember that we're likely performing an **affine transformation** on them to produce both "keys" and "query." This means that the simulation above, where values are drawn from a **normal distribution**, is not as far-fetched as it may seem at first sight.

If you try different values for the number of dimensions, you'll see that, on average, the **variance equals the number of dimensions**. So, the **standard deviation** is given by the **square root of the number of dimensions**:

$$\text{Var}(\text{vector}_1 \cdot \text{vector}_2) = d_{\text{vector}_1} = d_{\text{vector}_1}$$
$$\sigma(\text{vector}_1 \cdot \text{vector}_2) = \sqrt{d_{\text{vector}_1}} = \sqrt{d_{\text{vector}_2}}$$

Equation 9.9 - Standard deviation of the dot product

```
alphas = calc_alphas(keys, query)
# N, 1, L x N, L, H -> 1, L x L, H -> 1, H
context_vector = torch.bmm(alphas, values)
context_vector
```

Output

```
tensor([[[ 0.2138, -0.3175]]], grad_fn=<BmmBackward0>)
```

*"The **mask** is still missing in the code—what is that about?"*

We'll get back to it soon enough in the section after the next one. Hold that thought!

Now we need to organize it all by building a *class* to handle the attention mechanism.

Attention Mechanism

The **complete attention mechanism** is depicted in the figure below.

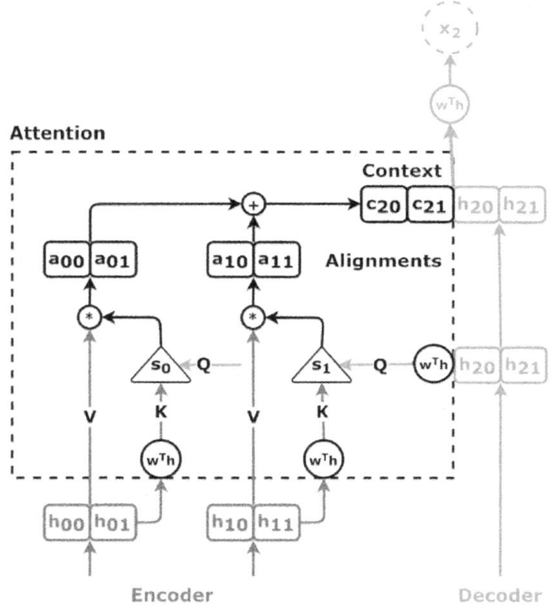

Figure 9.16 - Attention mechanism

For some cool **animations** of the attention mechanism, make sure to check out these great posts: Jay Alammar's "Visualizing a Neural Machine Translation Model"[45] and Raimi Karim's "Attn: Illustrated Attention."[46]

In our sequence-to-sequence problem, both *features* and *hidden states* are *two-*

dimensional. We could have chosen **any number of hidden dimensions**, but using *two hidden dimensions* allowed us to more easily visualize diagrams and plots.

More often than not, this **won't** be the case, and the number of **hidden dimensions** will be **different** than the number of **features** (the **input dimensions**). Currently, this **change in dimensionality** is performed by the **recurrent layers**.

The **self-attention** mechanism (our next topic) **does not** use recurrent layers anymore, so we'll have to tackle this change in dimensionality differently. Luckily, the **affine transformations** we're applying to "keys," "queries," and "values" (soon) can also be used to **change the dimensionality** from the number of *input* to the number of *hidden* dimensions. Therefore, we're including an `input_dim` argument in our `Attention` class to handle this.

The corresponding code, neatly organized into a *model*, looks like this:

```
class Attention(nn.Module):
    def __init__(self, hidden_dim, input_dim=None,
                 proj_values=False):
        super().__init__()
        self.d_k = hidden_dim
        self.input_dim = hidden_dim if input_dim is None \
                         else input_dim
        self.proj_values = proj_values
        # Affine transformations for Q, K, and V
        self.linear_query = nn.Linear(self.input_dim, hidden_dim)
        self.linear_key = nn.Linear(self.input_dim, hidden_dim)
        self.linear_value = nn.Linear(self.input_dim, hidden_dim)
        self.alphas = None

    def init_keys(self, keys):
        self.keys = keys
        self.proj_keys = self.linear_key(self.keys)
        self.values = self.linear_value(self.keys) \
                      if self.proj_values else self.keys

    def score_function(self, query):
        proj_query = self.linear_query(query)
        # scaled dot product
        # N, 1, H x N, H, L -> N, 1, L
        dot_products = torch.bmm(proj_query,
                                 self.proj_keys.permute(0, 2, 1))
        scores =  dot_products / np.sqrt(self.d_k)
        return scores

    def forward(self, query, mask=None):
        # Query is batch-first N, 1, H
        scores = self.score_function(query) # N, 1, L   ①
        if mask is not None:
            scores = scores.masked_fill(mask == 0, -1e9)
        alphas = F.softmax(scores, dim=-1) # N, 1, L    ②
        self.alphas = alphas.detach()

        # N, 1, L x N, L, H -> N, 1, H
        context = torch.bmm(alphas, self.values)        ③
        return context
```

① First step: Alignment scores (scaled dot product)

② Second step: Attention scores (alphas)

③ Third step: Context vector

Let's go over each of the methods:

- In the *constructor* method, there are the following:
  - **three linear layers** corresponding to the **affine transformations** for "keys" and "query" (and for the future transformation of "values" too)
  - one attribute for the number of hidden dimensions (to scale the dot product)
  - a placeholder for the **attention scores** (`alphas`)
- There is an `init_keys()` method to receive a **batch-first sequence of hidden states** from the **encoder**.
  - These are **computed once** at the beginning and will be used **over and over again** with every **new "query"** that is presented to the attention mechanism.
  - Therefore, it is better to **initialize "keys" and "values" once** than to pass them as arguments to the `forward()` method every time.
- The `score_function()` is simply the **scaled dot product**, but using an affine transformation on the "query" this time.
- The `forward()` method takes a **batch-first hidden state** as **"query"** and performs the **three steps** of the **attention mechanism**:
  - Using "keys" and "query" to compute **alignment scores**
  - Using alignment scores to compute **attention scores** (alphas)
  - Using "values" and attention scores to generate the **context vector**

"*There is that unexplained* `mask` *again!*"

I'm on it!

Source Mask

The `mask` can be used to, well, **mask some of the "values"** to **force the attention mechanism to ignore them**.

"Why would I want to force it to do that?"

Padding comes to mind—you likely don't want to pay attention to **stuffed data points** in a sequence, right? Let's try out an example. Pretend we have a source sequence with **one real and one padded data point**, and that it went through an encoder to generate the corresponding "keys":

```
source_seq = torch.tensor([[[-1., 1.], [0., 0.]]])
# pretend there's an encoder here...
keys = torch.tensor([[[-.38, .44], [.85, -.05]]])
query = torch.tensor([[[-1., 1.]]])
```

The **source mask** should be **`False`** for every **padded data point**, and its shape should be **(N, 1, L)**, where **L** is the **length of the source sequence**.

```
source_mask = (source_seq != 0).all(axis=2).unsqueeze(1)
source_mask # N, 1, L
```

Output

```
tensor([[[ True, False]]])
```

The mask will **make the attention score equal to zero** for the **padded data points**. If we use the "keys" we've just made up to initialize an instance of the *attention mechanism* and call it using the **source mask** above, we'll see the following result:

```
torch.manual_seed(11)
attnh = Attention(2)
attnh.init_keys(keys)
context = attnh(query, mask=source_mask)
attnh.alphas
```

Output

```
tensor([[[1., 0.]]])
```

The attention score of the **second data point**, as expected, was **set to zero**, leaving the whole attention on the first data point.

Decoder

We also need to make some **small adjustments** to the **decoder**:

Decoder + Attention

```
class DecoderAttn(nn.Module):
    def __init__(self, n_features, hidden_dim):
        super().__init__()
        self.hidden_dim = hidden_dim
        self.n_features = n_features
        self.hidden = None
        self.basic_rnn = nn.GRU(self.n_features,
                                self.hidden_dim,
                                batch_first=True)
        self.attn = Attention(self.hidden_dim)              ①
        self.regression = nn.Linear(2 * self.hidden_dim,
                                    self.n_features)        ①

    def init_hidden(self, hidden_seq):
        # the output of the encoder is N, L, H
        # and init_keys expects batch-first as well
        self.attn.init_keys(hidden_seq)                     ②
        hidden_final = hidden_seq[:, -1:]
        self.hidden = hidden_final.permute(1, 0, 2) # L, N, H

    def forward(self, X, mask=None):
        # X is N, 1, F
        batch_first_output, self.hidden = \
                                self.basic_rnn(X, self.hidden)
        query = batch_first_output[:, -1:]
        # Attention
        context = self.attn(query, mask=mask)               ③
        concatenated = torch.cat([context, query],
                                 axis=-1)                   ③
        out = self.regression(concatenated)

        # N, 1, F
        return out.view(-1, 1, self.n_features)
```

① Sets attention module and adjusts input dimensions of the regression layer

② Sets the "keys" (and "values") for the attention module

③ Feeds the "query" to the attention mechanism and concatenates it to the context vector

Let's go over a simple example in code, using the updated **decoder** and **attention** classes:

```
full_seq = (torch.tensor([[-1, -1], [-1, 1], [1, 1], [1, -1]])
            .float()
            .view(1, 4, 2))
source_seq = full_seq[:, :2]
target_seq = full_seq[:, 2:]
```

```
torch.manual_seed(21)
encoder = Encoder(n_features=2, hidden_dim=2)
decoder_attn = DecoderAttn(n_features=2, hidden_dim=2)

# Generates hidden states (keys and values)
hidden_seq = encoder(source_seq)
decoder_attn.init_hidden(hidden_seq)

# Target sequence generation
inputs = source_seq[:, -1:]
target_len = 2
for i in range(target_len):
    out = decoder_attn(inputs)
    print(f'Output: {out}')
    inputs = out
```

Output

```
Output: tensor([[[-0.3555, -0.1220]]], grad_fn=<ViewBackward>)
Output: tensor([[[-0.2641, -0.2521]]], grad_fn=<ViewBackward>)
```

The code above does the bare minimum to generate a target sequence using the attention mechanism. To actually **train a model** using **teacher forcing**, we need to put the **two (or three) classes together**…

Encoder + Decoder + Attention

The integration of encoder, decoder, and the attention mechanism, when applied to our sequence-to-sequence problem, is depicted in the figure below (that's the *same figure* from the "Computing the Context Vector" section).

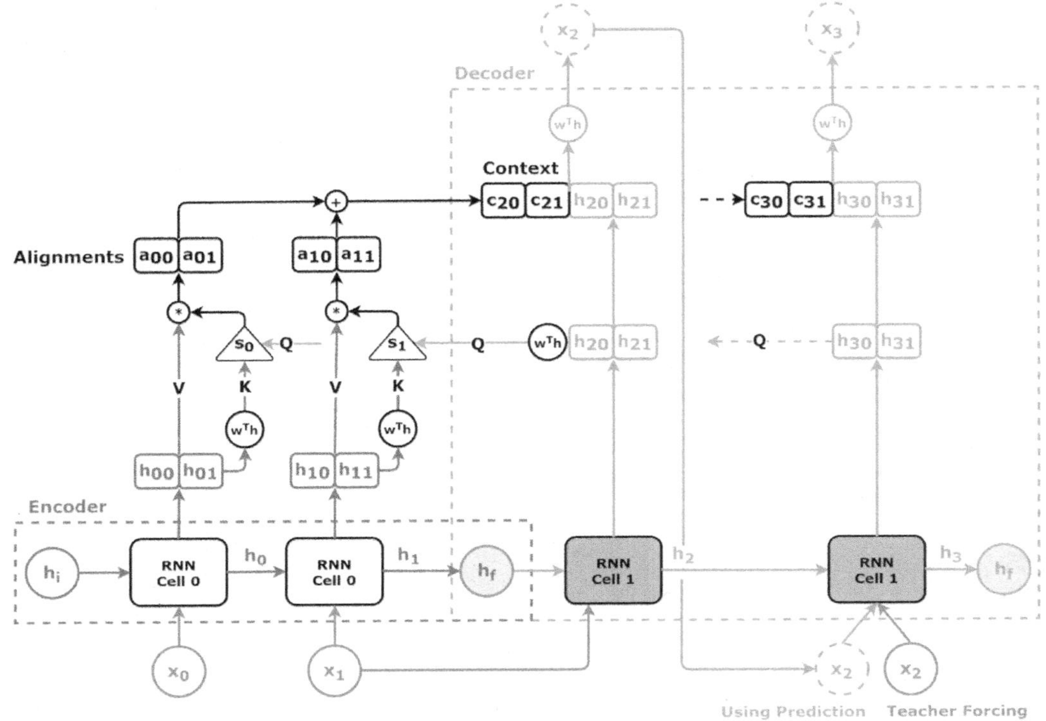

Figure 9.17 - Encoder + decoder + attention

Take time to visualize the flow of information:

- First, the data points in the **source sequence** (in red) feed the **encoder** (in blue) and generate **"keys" (K)** and **"values" (V)** for the **attention mechanism** (in black).
- Next, **each input** of the **decoder** (in green) generates **one "query" (Q) at a time** to produce a **context vector** (in black).
- Finally, the context vector gets **concatenated** to the decoder's current **hidden state** (in green) and transformed to **predicted coordinates** (in green) by the **output layer** (in green).

Our former `EncoderDecoder` class works seamlessly with an instance of `DecoderAttn`:

```
encdec = EncoderDecoder(encoder, decoder_attn,
                        input_len=2, target_len=2,
                        teacher_forcing_prob=0.0)
encdec(full_seq)
```

Output

```
tensor([[[-0.3555, -0.1220],
         [-0.2641, -0.2521]]], grad_fn=<CopySlices>)
```

We *could* use it to train a model already, but we would *miss* something interesting: **visualizing the attention scores**. To visualize them, we need to **store** them first. The easiest way to do so is to create a new class that **inherits** from `EncoderDecoder` and then **override** the `init_outputs()` and `store_outputs()` methods:

Encoder + Decoder + Attention

```
class EncoderDecoderAttn(EncoderDecoder):
    def __init__(self, encoder, decoder, input_len, target_len,
                 teacher_forcing_prob=0.5):
        super().__init__(encoder, decoder, input_len, target_len,
                         teacher_forcing_prob)
        self.alphas = None

    def init_outputs(self, batch_size):
        device = next(self.parameters()).device
        # N, L (target), F
        self.outputs = torch.zeros(batch_size,
                                   self.target_len,
                                   self.encoder.n_features).to(device)
        # N, L (target), L (source)
        self.alphas = torch.zeros(batch_size,
                                  self.target_len,
                                  self.input_len).to(device)

    def store_output(self, i, out):
        # Stores the output
        self.outputs[:, i:i+1, :] = out
        self.alphas[:, i:i+1, :] = self.decoder.attn.alphas
```

The **attention scores** are stored in the `alphas` attribute of the **attention model**, which, in turn, is the **decoder's `attn` attribute**. For each step in the target sequence generation, the corresponding scores are copied to the `alphas` attribute of the `EncoderDecoderAttn` model (line 22).

IMPORTANT: Pay **attention** (pun very much intended!) to the **shape** of the `alphas` attribute: **$(N, L_{target}, L_{source})$**. For each one out of *N* sequences in a mini-batch, there is a **matrix**, where each **"query" (Q)** coming from the **target sequence** (a *row* in this matrix) has as many **attention scores** as there are **"keys" (K)** in the **source sequence** (the *columns* in this matrix).

We'll **visualize** these matrices shortly. Moreover, a proper understanding of *how* attention scores are organized in the `alphas` attribute will make it much easier to understand the next section: "Self-Attention."

Model Configuration & Training

We just have to replace the original classes for both **decoder** and **model** with their **attention** counterparts, and we're good to go:

Model Configuration

```
torch.manual_seed(17)
encoder = Encoder(n_features=2, hidden_dim=2)
decoder_attn = DecoderAttn(n_features=2, hidden_dim=2)
model = EncoderDecoderAttn(encoder, decoder_attn,
                           input_len=2, target_len=2,
                           teacher_forcing_prob=0.5)
loss = nn.MSELoss()
optimizer = optim.Adam(model.parameters(), lr=0.01)
```

Model Training

```
sbs_seq_attn = StepByStep(model, loss, optimizer)
sbs_seq_attn.set_loaders(train_loader, test_loader)
sbs_seq_attn.train(100)
```

```
fig = sbs_seq_attn.plot_losses()
```

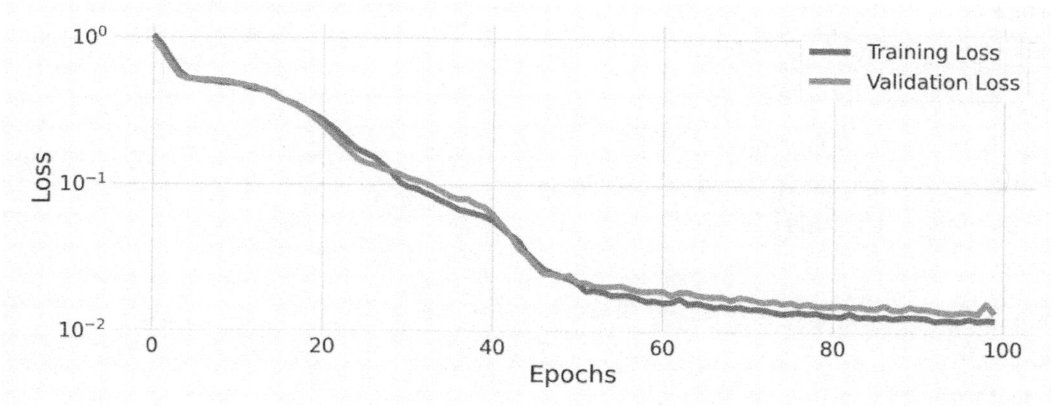

Figure 9.18 - Losses—encoder + decoder + attention

The loss is **one order of magnitude lower** than the previous, *distracted* (without attention?!), model. That looks promising!

Visualizing Predictions

Let's plot the **predicted coordinates** and connect them using **dashed lines**, while using **solid lines** to connect the **actual coordinates**, just like before:

```
fig = sequence_pred(sbs_seq_attn, full_test, test_directions)
```

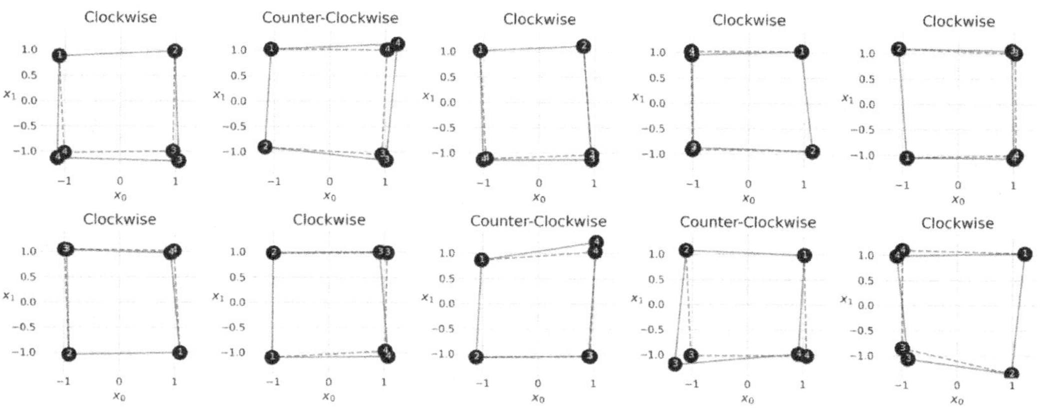

Figure 9.19 - Predicting the last two corners

Much, much better! No overlapping corners, no, sir! The new model is definitely paying attention :-)

Visualizing Attention

Let's look at what the model is paying attention to by checking what's stored in the `alphas` attribute. The scores will be different for each source sequence, so let's try making predictions for the very first one:

```
inputs = full_train[:1, :2]
out = sbs_seq_attn.predict(inputs)
sbs_seq_attn.model.alphas
```

Output

```
tensor([[[0.8196, 0.1804],
         [0.7316, 0.2684]]], device='cuda:0')
```

"How do I interpret these attention scores?"

The **columns** represent the elements in the **source sequence**, and the **rows**, the elements in the **target sequence**:

$$
\begin{array}{c|cc}
 & \text{source} & \\
\text{target} & x_0 & x_1 \\
\hline
x_2 & \alpha_{20} & \alpha_{21} \\
x_3 & \alpha_{30} & \alpha_{31}
\end{array}
\implies
\begin{array}{c|cc}
 & \text{source} & \\
\text{target} & x_0 & x_1 \\
\hline
x_2 & 0.8196 & 0.1804 \\
x_3 & 0.7316 & 0.2684
\end{array}
$$

Equation 9.10 - Attention score matrix

The attention scores we get tell us that the model **mostly paid attention to the first data point** of the **source sequence**. This is *not* going to be the case for every sequence, though. Let's check what the model is paying attention to for the first ten sequences in the training set.

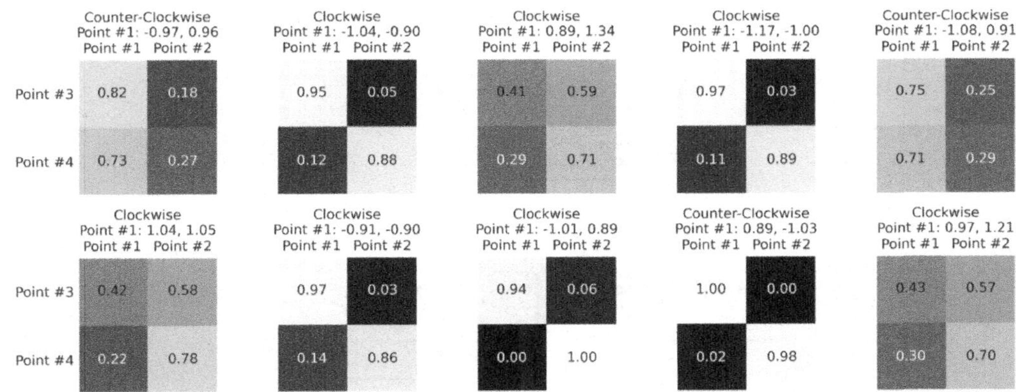

Figure 9.20 - Attention scores

See? For the *second sequence*, it mostly paid attention to either the **first data point** (for predicting point #3) or the **second data point** (for predicting point #4). How *amazing* is that?

Do you know what's even **better than one attention mechanism**?

Multi-Headed Attention

There is no reason to stick with **only one attention mechanism**: We can use **several** attention mechanisms at once, each referred to as an **attention head**.

Each attention head will output **its own context vector**, and they will all get **concatenated together** and **combined** using a **linear layer**. In the end, the **multi-headed attention mechanism** will *still* output a **single context vector**.

Figure 9.21 illustrates the flow of information for **two attention heads**.

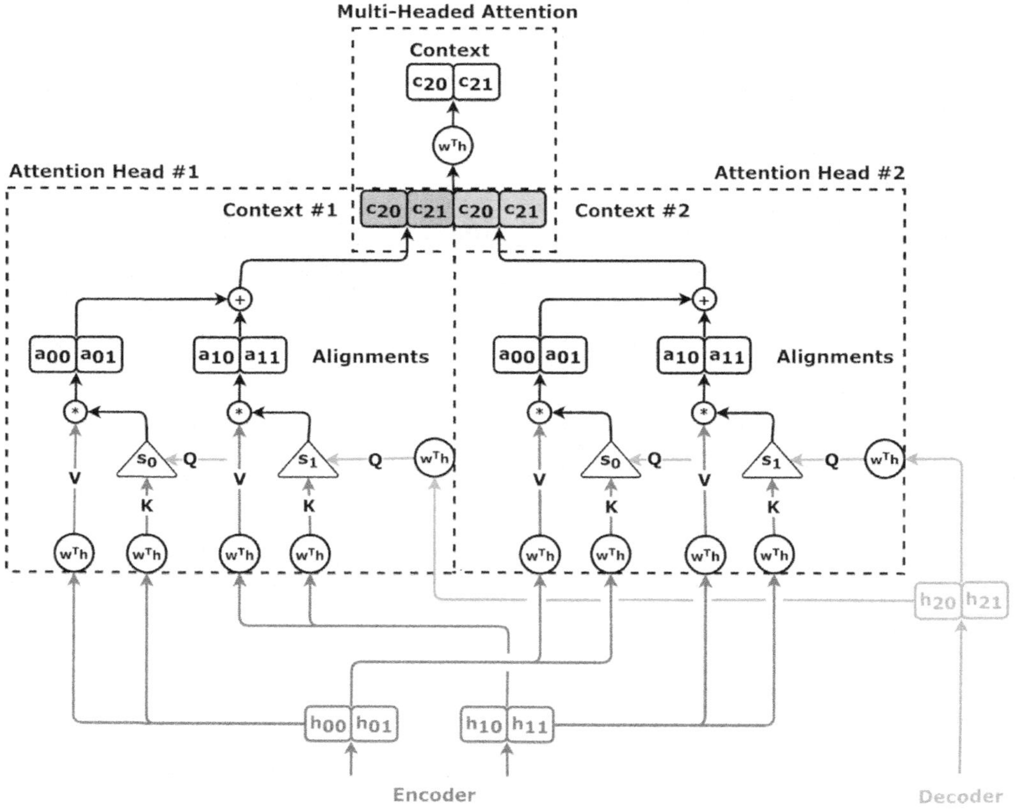

Figure 9.21 - Multi-headed attention mechanism

The **very same** hidden states from both **encoder** ("keys" and "values") and **decoder** ("query") will feed **all attention heads**. At first, you may think that the attention heads will end up being *redundant* (and this may indeed be the case at times), but, thanks to the **affine transformations** of both **"keys" (K)** and **"queries" (Q)**, and **"values" (V)** too, it is more likely that **each attention head** will learn a **distinct pattern**. Cool, right?

"Why are we transforming the 'values' now?"

The *multi-headed attention* mechanism is commonly used together with **self-attention** (the next topic), and, as you'll shortly see, the hidden states will be replaced by the **raw data points**. For that reason, we throw *yet another transformation* into the mix to give the model a chance to **transform the data points** (which has been the role played by the recurrent layer so far).

Wide vs Narrow Attention

This mechanism is known as **wide attention**: Each **attention head** gets the **full hidden state** and produces a **context vector** of the **same size**. This is totally fine if the **number of hidden dimensions** is **small**.

For a **larger number of dimensions**, though, each **attention head** will get a **chunk** of the **affine transformation of the hidden state** to work with. This is a detail of **utmost importance**: It is **not a chunk of the original hidden state**, but of its transformation. For example, say there are **512 dimensions** in the hidden state and we'd like to use **eight attention heads**: Each **attention head** would work with a chunk of **64 dimensions** only. This mechanism is known as **narrow attention**, and we'll get back to it in the next chapter.

"Which one should I use?"

On the one hand, **wide attention** will likely yield better models compared to using **narrow attention** on the same number of dimensions. On the other hand, **narrow attention** makes it possible to use **more dimensions**, which may improve the quality of the model as well. It's hard to tell you which one is best overall, but I can tell you that **state-of-the-art large Transformer models** use **narrow attention**. In our much simpler and smaller model, though, we're sticking with **wide attention**.

The **multi-headed attention mechanism** is usually depicted like this:

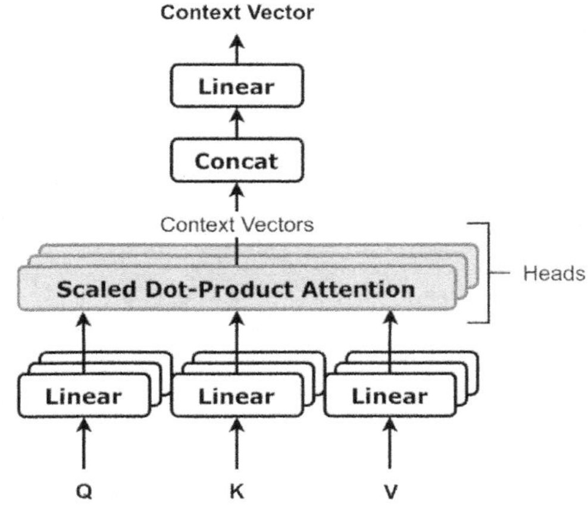

Figure 9.22 - Multi-headed attention mechanism

The code for the multi-headed attention mechanism looks like this:

Multi-Headed Attention Mechanism

```
class MultiHeadAttention(nn.Module):
    def __init__(self, n_heads, d_model,
                 input_dim=None, proj_values=True):
        super().__init__()
        self.linear_out = nn.Linear(n_heads * d_model, d_model)
        self.attn_heads = nn.ModuleList(
            [Attention(d_model,
                       input_dim=input_dim,
                       proj_values=proj_values)
             for _ in range(n_heads)]
        )

    def init_keys(self, key):
        for attn in self.attn_heads:
            attn.init_keys(key)

    @property
    def alphas(self):
        # Shape: n_heads, N, 1, L (source)
        return torch.stack(
            [attn.alphas for attn in self.attn_heads], dim=0
        )

    def output_function(self, contexts):
        # N, 1, n_heads * D
        concatenated = torch.cat(contexts, axis=-1)
        # Linear transf. to go back to original dimension
        out = self.linear_out(concatenated) # N, 1, D
        return out

    def forward(self, query, mask=None):
        contexts = [attn(query, mask=mask)
                    for attn in self.attn_heads]
        out = self.output_function(contexts)
        return out
```

It is pretty much a **list** of **attention mechanisms** with an extra linear layer on top. But it is not *any list*; it is a *special* list—it is an `nn.ModuleList`.

*"What's so **special** about it?"*

Even though PyTorch recursively looks for models (and layers) listed as **attributes** to get a comprehensive list of **all parameters**, it **does not** look for models **inside Python lists**. Therefore, the only way to have a **list of models** (or layers) is to use the appropriate `nn.ModuleList`, which you can still index and loop over just like with any other regular list.

This chapter is *so* long that I've split it into *two parts*, so you can take a break now and let the **attention mechanism** sink in before moving on to its sibling, the **self-attention mechanism**.

TO BE CONTINUED...

[41] https://github.com/dvgodoy/PyTorchStepByStep/blob/master/Chapter09.ipynb

[42] https://colab.research.google.com/github/dvgodoy/PyTorchStepByStep/blob/master/Chapter09.ipynb

[43] https://papers.nips.cc/paper/2014/hash/a14ac55a4f27472c5d894ec1c3c743d2-Abstract.html

[44] https://bit.ly/3aEf81k

[45] http://jalammar.github.io/visualizing-neural-machine-translation-mechanics-of-seq2seq-models-with-attention/

[46] https://towardsdatascience.com/attn-illustrated-attention-5ec4ad276ee3

Chapter 9 — Part II

Sequence-to-Sequence

Spoilers

In the second half of this chapter, we will:

- use **self-attention** mechanisms to replace recurrent layers in both the encoder and the decoder
- understand the importance of the **target mask** to avoid data leakage
- learn how to use **positional encoding**

Self-Attention

Here is a **radical notion**: What if we **replaced the recurrent layer** with an **attention mechanism**?

That's the main proposition of the famous "Attention Is All You Need"[47] paper by Vaswani, A., et al. It introduced the **Transformer** architecture, based on a self-attention mechanism, that was soon going to completely dominate the NLP landscape.

"I pity the fool using recurrent layers."

Mr. T

The recurrent layer in the **encoder** took the **source sequence** in and, *one by one*, generated **hidden states**. But we don't *have to* generate hidden states like that. We can use **another, separate, attention mechanism** to **replace the encoder** (and, wait for it, the decoder too!).

These separate attention mechanisms are called **self-attention** mechanisms since all of their inputs—"keys," "values," and "query"—are **internal** to either an **encoder** or a **decoder**.

The attention mechanism we discussed in the previous section, where "keys" and "values" come from the **encoder**, but the "query" comes from the **decoder**, is going to be referred to as **cross-attention** from now on.

Once again, the **affine transformations** we're applying to "keys," "queries," and "values" may also be used to **change the dimensionality** from the number of *input* dimensions to the number of *hidden* dimensions (this transformation was formerly performed by the recurrent layer).

Let's start with the encoder.

Encoder

The figure below depicts an **encoder** using **self-attention**: The **source sequence** (in red) works as **"keys" (K)**, **"values" (V)**, and **"queries (Q)"** as well. Did you notice I mentioned, "queries," *plural*, instead of "query"?

In the encoder, **each data point** is a **"query"** (the red arrow entering the self-attention mechanism from the side), and thus produces **its own context vector** using **alignment vectors** for **every data point in the source sequence, including itself**. This means it is possible for a data point to generate a context vector that is only paying attention to itself.

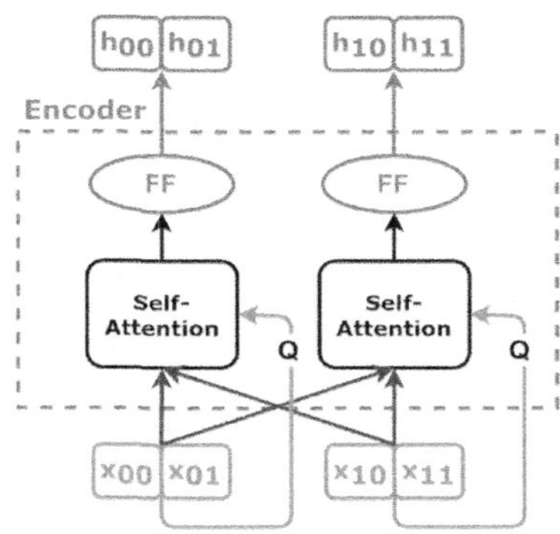

Figure 9.23 - Encoder with self-attention (simplified)

As the diagram above illustrates, each context vector produced by the self-attention mechanism goes through a **feed-forward network** to generate a **"hidden state"** as output. We can dive deeper into the inner workings of the self-attention mechanism.

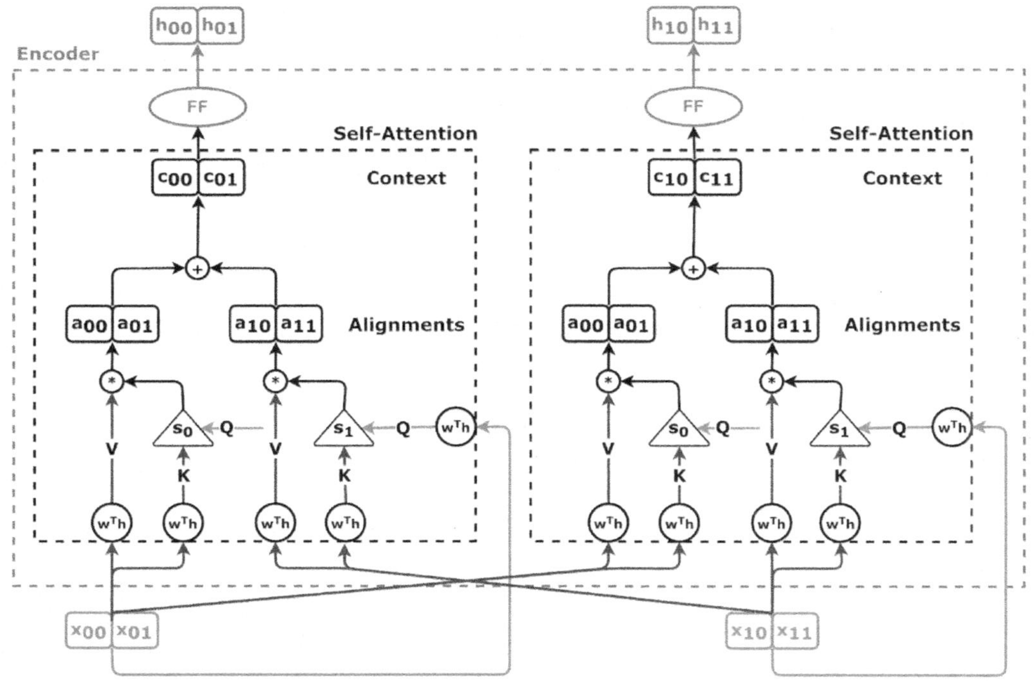

Figure 9.24 - Encoder with self-attention

Let's focus on the self-attention mechanism on the *left*, used to generate the "hidden state" (h_{00}, h_{01}) corresponding to the **first data point** in the source sequence (x_{00}, x_{01}), and see how it works in great detail:

- The transformed coordinates of the first data point are used as **"query" (Q)**.
- This "query" (Q) will be paired, *independently*, with each of the two "keys" (K), one of them being a *different transformation* of the same coordinates (x_{00}, x_{01}), the other being a transformation of the second data point (x_{10}, x_{11}).
- The pairing above will result in **two attention scores** (*alphas*, s_0 and s_1) that, multiplied by their corresponding "values" (V), are added up to become the **context vector**:

$$\alpha_{00}, \alpha_{01} = \text{softmax}(\frac{Q_0 \cdot K_0}{\sqrt{2}}, \frac{Q_0 \cdot K_1}{\sqrt{2}})$$

$$\text{context vector}_0 = \alpha_{00} V_0 + \alpha_{01} V_1$$

Equation 9.11 - Context vector for first input (x_0)

- Next, the context vector goes through the **feed-forward network**, and the first "hidden state" is born!

Next, we shift our focus to the self-attention mechanism on the **right**:

- It is the **second data point**'s turn to be the **"query" (Q)**, being paired with both "keys" (K), generating attention scores and a context vector, resulting in the second "hidden state":

$$\alpha_{10}, \alpha_{11} = \text{softmax}(\frac{Q_1 \cdot K_0}{\sqrt{2}}, \frac{Q_1 \cdot K_1}{\sqrt{2}})$$
$$\text{context vector}_1 = \alpha_{10} V_0 + \alpha_{11} V_1$$

Equation 9.12 - Context vector for second input (x_1)

As you probably already noticed, the **context vector** (and thus the **"hidden state"**) associated with a data point is basically a **function of the corresponding "query" (Q)**, and everything else ("keys" (K), "values" (V), and the parameters of the self-attention mechanism) is held constant for all queries.

Therefore, we can simplify *a bit* our previous diagram and depict **only one self-attention mechanism**, assuming it will be fed a different "query" (Q) every time.

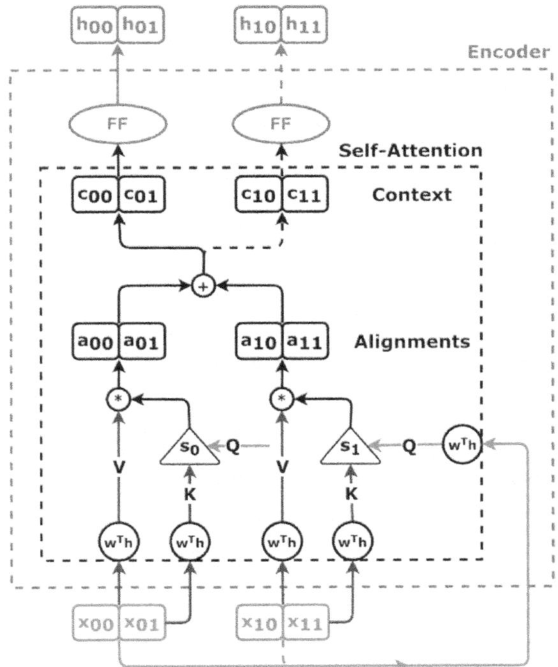

Figure 9.25 - Encoder with self-attention

The **alphas** are the **attention scores**, and they are organized as follows in the `alphas` attribute (as we've already seen in the "Visualizing Attention" section):

$$\begin{array}{c|cc} & \text{source} & \\ \text{target} & x_0 & x_1 \\ \hline h_0 & \alpha_{00} & \alpha_{01} \\ h_1 & \alpha_{10} & \alpha_{11} \end{array}$$

Equation 9.13 - Attention scores

For the **encoder**, the shape of the `alphas` attribute is given by **(N, L_{source}, L_{source})** since it is **looking at itself**.

Even though I've described the process *as if* it were sequential, these operations can be **parallelized** to generate all "hidden states" at once, which is much more efficient than using a recurrent layer that is *sequential* in nature.

We can also use an even more **simplified diagram** of the encoder that abstracts the nitty-gritty details of the self-attention mechanism.

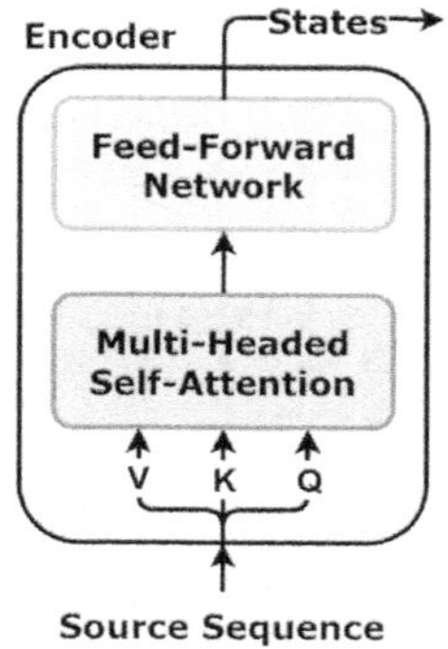

Figure 9.26 - Encoder with self-attention (diagram)

The code for our **encoder** with **self-attention** is actually quite simple since most of the moving parts are inside the attention heads:

Encoder + Self-Attention

```
class EncoderSelfAttn(nn.Module):
    def __init__(self, n_heads, d_model,
                 ff_units, n_features=None):
        super().__init__()
        self.n_heads = n_heads
        self.d_model = d_model
        self.ff_units = ff_units
        self.n_features = n_features
        self.self_attn_heads = \
            MultiHeadAttention(n_heads,
                               d_model,
                               input_dim=n_features)
        self.ffn = nn.Sequential(
            nn.Linear(d_model, ff_units),
            nn.ReLU(),
            nn.Linear(ff_units, d_model),
        )

    def forward(self, query, mask=None):
        self.self_attn_heads.init_keys(query)
        att = self.self_attn_heads(query, mask)
        out = self.ffn(att)
        return out
```

Remember that the **"query"** in the `forward()` method actually gets the **data points** from the **source sequence**. These data points will be **transformed** into different **"keys," "values,"** and **"queries"** inside each of the **attention heads**. The output of the attention heads is a **context vector** (`att`) that goes through a **feed-forward network** to produce a **"hidden state."**

By the way, now that we've gotten rid of the recurrent layer, we'll be talking about **model dimensions** (`d_model`) instead of **hidden dimensions** (`hidden_dim`). You still get to **choose it**, though.

The **mask** argument should receive the **source mask**; that is, the mask we use to **ignore padded data points** in our **source sequence**.

Let's create an encoder and feed it a source sequence:

```
torch.manual_seed(11)
encself = EncoderSelfAttn(n_heads=3, d_model=2,
                          ff_units=10, n_features=2)
query = source_seq
encoder_states = encself(query)
encoder_states
```

Output

```
tensor([[[-0.0498,  0.2193],
         [-0.0642,  0.2258]]], grad_fn=<AddBackward0>)
```

It produced a **sequence of states** that will be the input of the **(cross-)attention** mechanism used by the **decoder**. Business as usual.

Cross-Attention

The **cross-attention** was the first mechanism we discussed: The **decoder** provided a **"query" (Q)**, which served not only as *input* but also got **concatenated to the resulting context vector**. That **won't** be the case anymore! Instead of concatenation, the **context vector** will go through a **feed-forward** network in the **decoder** to generate the **predicted coordinates**.

The figure below illustrates the current state of the architecture: self-attention as encoder, cross-attention on top of it, and the modifications to the decoder.

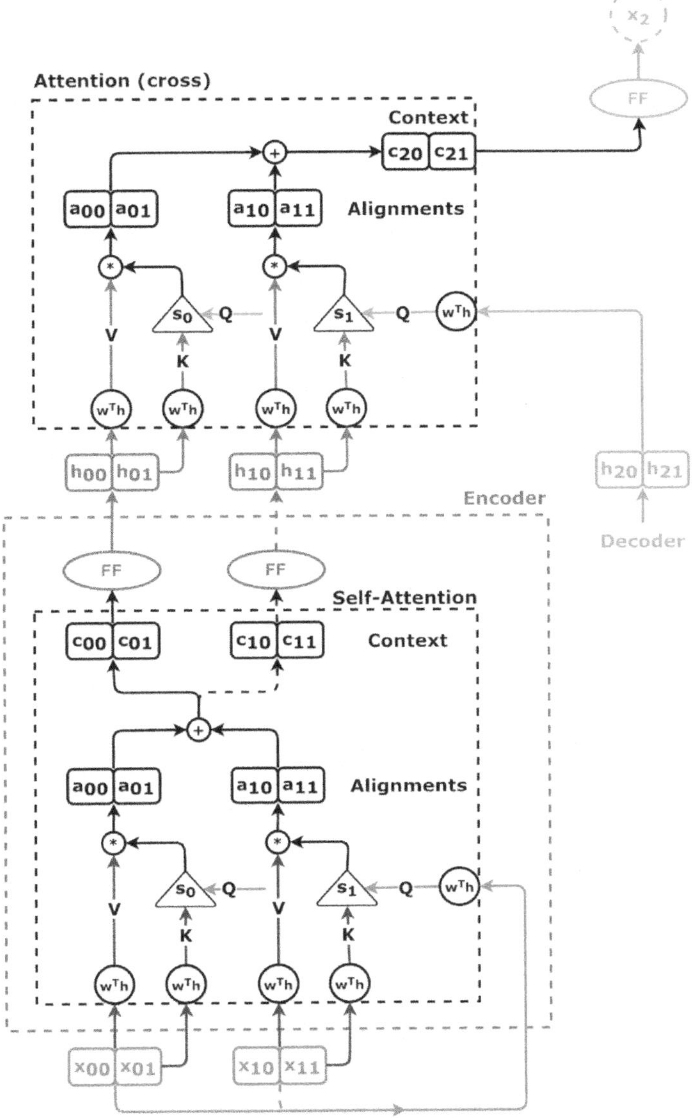

Figure 9.27 - Encoder with self- and cross-attentions

If you're wondering *why* we removed the concatenation part, here comes the answer: We're using **self-attention** as a **decoder** too.

Decoder

There is **one main difference** (in the code) between the **encoder** and the **decoder**—the latter includes a **cross-attention** mechanism, as you can see below:

Decoder + Self-Attention

```
class DecoderSelfAttn(nn.Module):
    def __init__(self, n_heads, d_model,
                 ff_units, n_features=None):
        super().__init__()
        self.n_heads = n_heads
        self.d_model = d_model
        self.ff_units = ff_units
        self.n_features = d_model if n_features is None \
                          else n_features
        self.self_attn_heads = \
            MultiHeadAttention(n_heads, d_model,
                               input_dim=self.n_features)
        self.cross_attn_heads = \                          ①
            MultiHeadAttention(n_heads, d_model)
        self.ffn = nn.Sequential(
            nn.Linear(d_model, ff_units),
            nn.ReLU(),
            nn.Linear(ff_units, self.n_features))

    def init_keys(self, states):                           ①
        self.cross_attn_heads.init_keys(states)

    def forward(self, query, source_mask=None, target_mask=None):
        self.self_attn_heads.init_keys(query)
        att1 = self.self_attn_heads(query, target_mask)
        att2 = self.cross_attn_heads(att1, source_mask)    ①
        out = self.ffn(att2)
        return out
```

① Including **cross-attention**

The figure below depicts the **self-attention** part of a **decoder**.

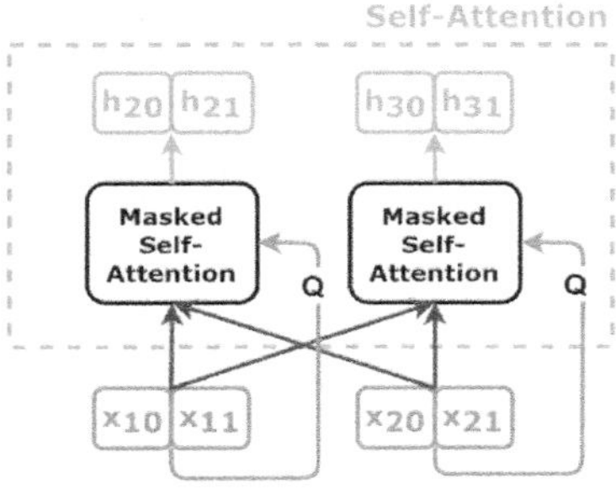

Figure 9.28 - Decoder with self-attention (simplified)

Once again, we can dive deeper into the inner workings of the self-attention mechanism.

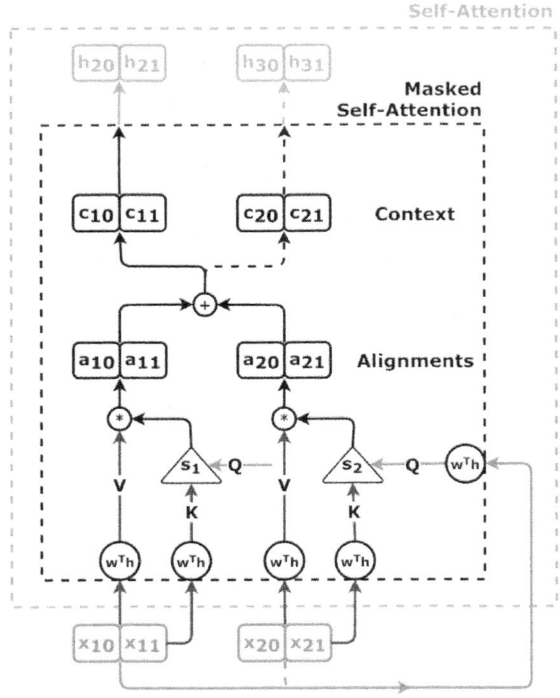

Figure 9.29 - Decoder with self-attention

There is **one small difference in the self-attention** architecture between encoder and decoder: The **feed-forward network** in the decoder sits atop the *cross-attention* mechanism (not depicted in the figure above) instead of the *self-attention* mechanism. The *feed-forward network* also maps the **decoder's output** from the dimensionality of the model (`d_model`) back to the **number of features**, thus yielding **predictions**.

We can also use a **simplified diagram** for the decoder (Figure 9.29, although depicting a *single attention head*, corresponds to the "*Masked Multi-Headed Self-Attention*" box below).

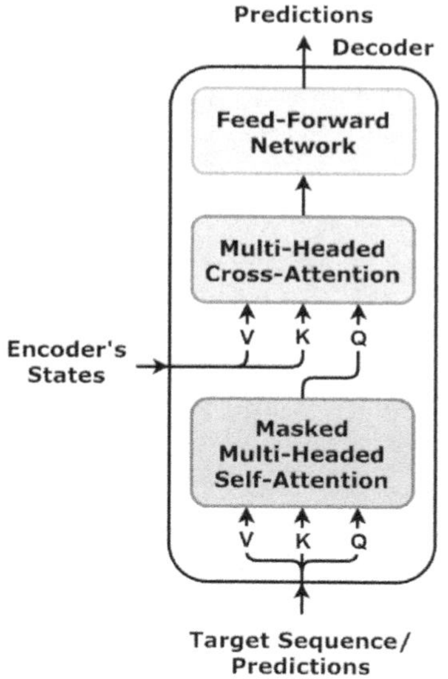

Figure 9.30 - Decoder with self- and cross-attentions (diagram)

The decoder's **first input** (x_{10}, x_{11}) is the **last known element of the source sequence**, as usual. The **source mask** is the same **mask used to ignore padded data points** in the **encoder**.

"*What about the **target mask**?*"

We'll get to that shortly. First, we need to discuss the **subsequent inputs**.

Subsequent Inputs and Teacher Forcing

In our problem, the first two data points are the *source sequence*, while the last two are the *target sequence*. Now, let's define the **shifted target sequence**, which includes the **last known element of the source sequence** and **all elements in the target sequence *but* the last one**.

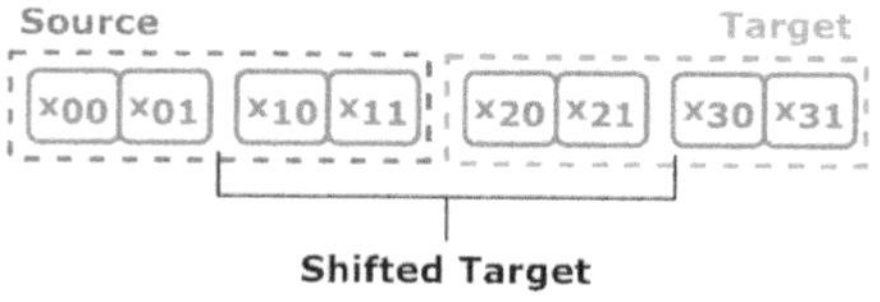

Figure 9.31 - Shifted target sequence

```
shifted_seq = torch.cat([source_seq[:, -1:],
                         target_seq[:, :-1]], dim=1)
```

The *shifted target sequence* was already used (even though we didn't have a name for it) when we discussed *teacher forcing*. There, at every step (after the first one), it randomly chose as the input to the subsequent step either an actual element from that sequence or a prediction. It worked very well with recurrent layers that were *sequential* in nature. But this **isn't** the case anymore.

One of the **advantages** of **self-attention over recurrent layers** is that operations can be **parallelized**. No need to do anything *sequentially* anymore, **teacher forcing included**. This means we're using **the whole shifted target sequence at once** as the **"query"** argument of the **decoder**.

That's very nice and cool, sure, but it raises **one big problem** involving the...

Attention Scores

To understand what the problem is, let's look at the **context vector** that will result in the **first "hidden state"** produced by the **decoder**, which, in turn, will lead to the **first prediction**:

$$\alpha_{21}, \alpha_{22} = \text{softmax}(\frac{Q_1 \cdot K_1}{\sqrt{2}}, \frac{Q_1 \cdot K_2}{\sqrt{2}})$$

$$\text{context vector}_2 = \alpha_{21} V_1 + \alpha_{22} V_2$$

Equation 9.14 - Context vector for the first target

"What's the problem with it?"

The problem is that it is **using a "key" (K_2) and a "value" (V_2)** that are transformations of the **data point it is trying to predict**.

In other words, the model is being allowed to **cheat** by **peeking into the future** because we're giving it **all data points in the target sequence except the very last one**.

If we look at the context vector corresponding to the last prediction, it should be clear that the model simply *cannot* cheat (there's no $\mathbf{K_3}$ or $\mathbf{V_3}$):

$$\alpha_{31}, \alpha_{32} = \text{softmax}(\frac{Q_2 \cdot K_1}{\sqrt{2}}, \frac{Q_2 \cdot K_2}{\sqrt{2}})$$

$$\text{context vector}_3 = \alpha_{31} V_1 + \alpha_{32} V_2$$

Equation 9.15 - Context vector for the second target

We can also check it quickly by looking at the **subscript indices**: As long as the **indices of the "values"** are **lower** than the **index of the context vector**, there is **no cheating**. By the way, it is even *easier* to check what's happening if we use the *alphas* matrix:

	source	
target	x_1	x_2
h_2	α_{21}	α_{22}
h_3	α_{31}	α_{32}

Equation 9.16 - Decoder's attention scores

For the **decoder**, the shape of the `alphas` attribute is given by **(N, $\mathbf{L_{target}}$, $\mathbf{L_{target}}$)** since it is **looking at itself**. Any *alphas* **above the diagonal** are, literally, **cheating codes**. We need to **force** the self-attention mechanism to **ignore them**. If only there was a way to do it...

*"What about those **masks** we discussed earlier?"*

You're absolutely right! They are *perfect* for this case.

Target Mask (Training)

The purpose of the **target mask** is to **zero attention scores for "future" data points**. In our example, that's the *alphas* matrix we're aiming for:

	source	
target	x_1	x_2
h_2	α_{21}	0
h_3	α_{31}	α_{32}

Equation 9.17 - Decoder's (masked) attention scores

Therefore we need a **mask** that **flags every element above the diagonal** as **invalid**, as we did with the *padded data points* in the *source mask*. The **shape** of the **target mask**, though, must **match** the shape of the `alphas` attribute: **(1, L_{target}, L_{target})**.

We can create a function to **generate the mask** for us:

Subsequent Mask

```
def subsequent_mask(size):
    attn_shape = (1, size, size)
    subsequent_mask = (
        1 - torch.triu(torch.ones(attn_shape), diagonal=1)
    ).bool()
    return subsequent_mask
```

```
subsequent_mask(2) # 1, L, L
```

Output

```
tensor([[[ True, False],
         [ True,  True]]])
```

Perfect! The element above the diagonal is indeed set to `False`.

We **must** use this mask while querying the decoder to **prevent it from cheating**. You can choose to use an **additional mask** to "hide" more data from the decoder if you wish, but the **subsequent mask is a necessity** with the self-attention decoder.

Let's see it in practice:

```
torch.manual_seed(13)
decself = DecoderSelfAttn(n_heads=3, d_model=2,
                          ff_units=10, n_features=2)
decself.init_keys(encoder_states)

query = shifted_seq
out = decself(query, target_mask=subsequent_mask(2))

decself.self_attn_heads.alphas
```

Output

```
tensor([[[[1.0000, 0.0000],
          [0.4011, 0.5989]]],


        [[[1.0000, 0.0000],
          [0.4264, 0.5736]]],


        [[[1.0000, 0.0000],
          [0.6304, 0.3696]]]])
```

There we go, no cheating :)

Target Mask (Evaluation/Prediction)

The only difference between training and evaluation, concerning the **target mask**, is that we'll use **larger masks** as we go. The very first mask is actually trivial since there are *no* elements above the diagonal:

$$1^{\text{st}}\ \text{Step}\left\{\begin{array}{c|c} & \text{source} \\ \text{target} & x_1 \\ \hline h_2 & \alpha_{21} \end{array}\right.$$

Equation 9.18 - Decoder's (masked) attention scores for the first target

At evaluation / prediction time we *only* have the source sequence, and, in our example, we use its last element as input for the decoder:

```
inputs = source_seq[:, -1:]
trg_masks = subsequent_mask(1)
out = decself(inputs, trg_masks)
out
```

Output

```
tensor([[[0.4132, 0.3728]]], grad_fn=<AddBackward0>)
```

The mask is not actually masking anything in this case, and we get a prediction for the coordinates of $\mathbf{x}_2$ as expected. Previously, this prediction would have been used as the next input, but things are a *bit* different now.

The **self-attention decoder** expects the **full sequence** as **"query,"** so we **concatenate the prediction** to the **previous "query."**

```
inputs = torch.cat([inputs, out[:, -1:, :]], dim=-2)
inputs
```

Output

```
tensor([[[-1.0000,  1.0000],
         [ 0.4132,  0.3728]]], grad_fn=<CatBackward>)
```

Now there are **two data points** for querying the decoder, so we adjust the mask accordingly:

$$
2^{\text{nd}}\ \text{Step} \left\{ \begin{array}{c|cc} & \text{source} & \\ \text{target} & x_1 & x_2 \\ \hline h_2 & \alpha_{21} & 0 \\ h_3 & \alpha_{31} & \alpha_{32} \end{array} \right.
$$

Equation 9.19 - Decoder's (masked) attention scores for the second target

The **mask** guarantees that the **predicted x_2** (in the first step) **won't change** the **predicted x_2** (in the second step), because predictions are made based on **past data points only**.

```
trg_masks = subsequent_mask(2)
out = decself(inputs, trg_masks)
out
```

Output

```
tensor([[[0.4137, 0.3727],
         [0.4132, 0.3728]]], grad_fn=<AddBackward0>)
```

These are the **predicted coordinates** of both x_2 and x_3. They are very close to each other, but that's just because we're using an *untrained model* to illustrate the mechanics of using target masks for prediction. The **last prediction** is, once again, **concatenated** to the previous "query."

```
inputs = torch.cat([inputs, out[:, -1:, :]], dim=-2)
inputs
```

Output

```
tensor([[[-1.0000,  1.0000],
         [ 0.4132,  0.3728],
         [ 0.4132,  0.3728]]], grad_fn=<CatBackward>)
```

But, since we're *actually* done with the predictions (the desired target sequence has a length of two), we simply *exclude* the first data point in the query (the one coming from the source sequence), and are left with the **predicted target sequence**:

```
inputs[:, 1:]
```

Output

```
tensor([[[0.4132, 0.3728],
         [0.4132, 0.3728]]], grad_fn=<SliceBackward>)
```

Greedy Decoding vs Beam Search

This is called **greedy decoding** because **each prediction** is deemed **final.** "*No backsies*": Once it's done, it's *really* done, and you just move along to the next prediction and never look back. In the context of our sequence-to-sequence problem, a regression, it wouldn't make much sense to do otherwise anyway.

But that **may not** be the case for other types of sequence-to-sequence problems. In machine translation, for example, the decoder outputs **probabilities** for the **next word** in the sentence at each step. The **greedy** approach would simply take the **word with the highest probability** and move on to the next.

However, since **each prediction** is an input to the **next step**, taking the **top word at every step** is **not necessarily the winning approach** (translating from one language to another is not exactly "linear"). It is probably wiser to keep a **handful of candidates** at every step and **try their combinations** to choose the best one: That's called **beam search**. We're not delving into its details here, but you can find more information in Jason Brownlee's "How to Implement a Beam Search Decoder for Natural Language Processing."[48]

Encoder + Decoder + Self-Attention

Let's join the encoder and the decoder together again, each using **self-attention** to compute their corresponding "hidden states," and the decoder using **cross-attention** to make predictions. The full picture looks like this (including the need for *masking* one of the inputs to avoid *cheating*).

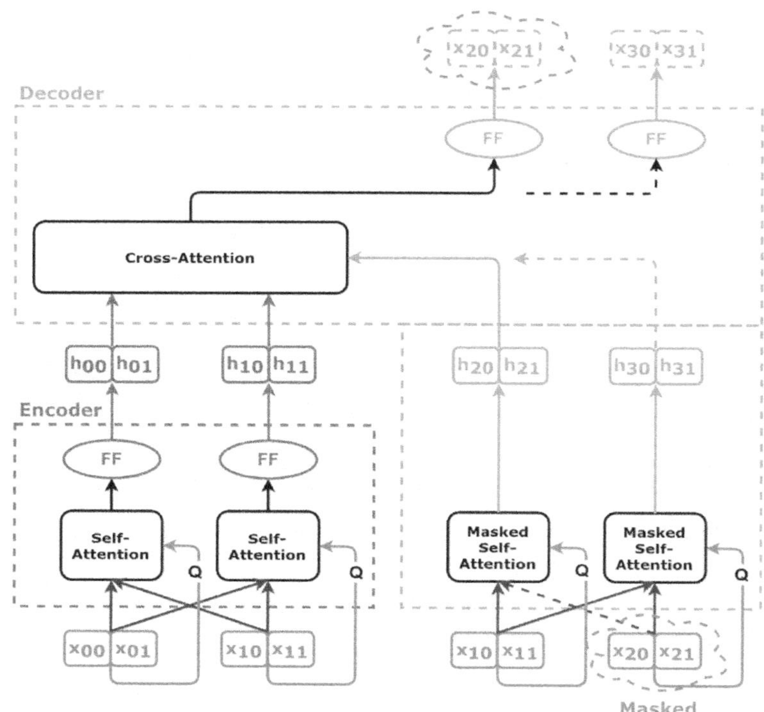

Figure 9.32 - Encoder + decoder + attention (simplified)

For some cool **animations** of the self-attention mechanism, make sure to check out Raimi Karim's "Illustrated: Self-Attention."[49]

But, if you prefer an even more **simplified diagram**, here it is:

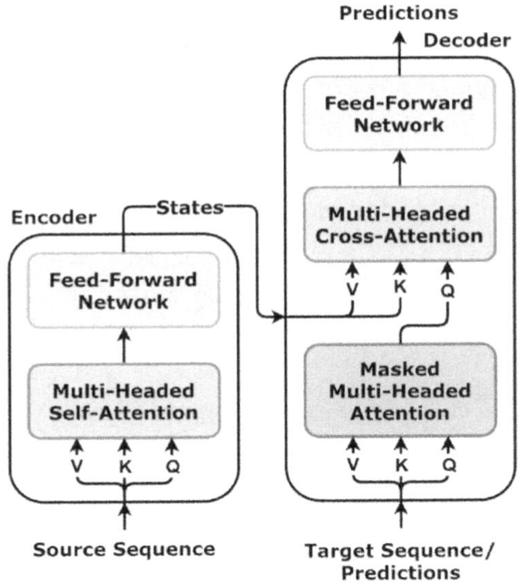

Figure 9.33 - Encoder + decoder + attention (diagram)

The corresponding code for the architecture above looks like this:

Encoder + Decoder + Self-Attention

```
class EncoderDecoderSelfAttn(nn.Module):
    def __init__(self, encoder, decoder, input_len, target_len):
        super().__init__()
        self.encoder = encoder
        self.decoder = decoder
        self.input_len = input_len
        self.target_len = target_len
        self.trg_masks = self.subsequent_mask(self.target_len)

    @staticmethod
    def subsequent_mask(size):
        attn_shape = (1, size, size)
        subsequent_mask = (
            1 - torch.triu(torch.ones(attn_shape), diagonal=1)
        ).bool()
        return subsequent_mask

    def encode(self, source_seq, source_mask):
        # Encodes the source sequence and uses the result
        # to initialize the decoder
```

```
        encoder_states = self.encoder(source_seq, source_mask)
        self.decoder.init_keys(encoder_states)

    def decode(self, shifted_target_seq,
               source_mask=None, target_mask=None):
        # Decodes / generates a sequence using the shifted
        # (masked) target sequence - used in TRAIN mode
        outputs = self.decoder(shifted_target_seq,
                               source_mask=source_mask,
                               target_mask=target_mask)
        return outputs

    def predict(self, source_seq, source_mask):
        # Decodes / generates a sequence using one input
        # at a time - used in EVAL mode
        inputs = source_seq[:, -1:]
        for i in range(self.target_len):
            out = self.decode(inputs,
                              source_mask,
                              self.trg_masks[:, :i+1, :i+1])
            out = torch.cat([inputs, out[:, -1:, :]], dim=-2)
            inputs = out.detach()
        outputs = inputs[:, 1:, :]
        return outputs

    def forward(self, X, source_mask=None):
        # Sends the mask to the same device as the inputs
        self.trg_masks = self.trg_masks.type_as(X).bool()
        # Slices the input to get source sequence
        source_seq = X[:, :self.input_len, :]
        # Encodes source sequence AND initializes decoder
        self.encode(source_seq, source_mask)
        if self.training:
            # Slices the input to get the shifted target seq
            shifted_target_seq = X[:, self.input_len-1:-1, :]
            # Decodes using the mask to prevent cheating
            outputs = self.decode(shifted_target_seq,
                                  source_mask,
                                  self.trg_masks)
        else:
            # Decodes using its own predictions
            outputs = self.predict(source_seq, source_mask)
```

```
        return outputs
```

The encoder-decoder class has *more methods* now to better organize the several steps formerly performed inside the `forward()` method. Let's take a look at them:

- `encode()`: It takes the **source sequence and mask** and **encodes** it into a **sequence of states** that is immediately used to **initialize the "keys" (and "values")** in the **decoder**.
- `decode()`: It takes the **shifted target sequence** and both **source and target masks** to generate a **target sequence**—it is used for **training** only!
- `predict()`: It takes the **source sequence** and the **source mask**, and uses a subset of the **target mask** to **actually predict an unknown target sequence**—it is used for **evaluation / prediction** only!
- `forward()`: It splits the input into the **source** and **shifted target sequences** (if available), **encodes** the source sequence, and calls either `decode()` or `predict()` according to the model's *mode* (`train` or `eval`).

Moreover, the `subsequent_mask()` becomes a *static method*, as the mask is being generated in the constructor and is **sent to the same device as the inputs** using `tensor.type_as()`. The last part is critical: We need to make sure that the *mask is in the same device* as the inputs (and the model, of course).

Model Configuration & Training

Once again, we create both encoder and decoder models and use them as arguments in the large `EncoderDecoderSelfAttn` model that handles the boilerplate, and we're good to go:

Model Configuration

```
torch.manual_seed(23)
encself = EncoderSelfAttn(n_heads=3, d_model=2,
                          ff_units=10, n_features=2)
decself = DecoderSelfAttn(n_heads=3, d_model=2,
                          ff_units=10, n_features=2)
model = EncoderDecoderSelfAttn(encself, decself,
                               input_len=2, target_len=2)
loss = nn.MSELoss()
optimizer = optim.Adam(model.parameters(), lr=0.01)
```

Model Training

```
sbs_seq_selfattn = StepByStep(model, loss, optimizer)
sbs_seq_selfattn.set_loaders(train_loader, test_loader)
sbs_seq_selfattn.train(100)
```

```
fig = sbs_seq_selfattn.plot_losses()
```

Even though we did our best to ensure the **reproducibility** of the results, you may **still** find some differences in the loss curves (and, consequently, in the attention scores as well). PyTorch's documentation about reproducibility[50] states the following:

> "*Completely reproducible results are not guaranteed across PyTorch releases, individual commits, or different platforms. Furthermore, results may not be reproducible between CPU and GPU executions, even when using identical seeds.*"

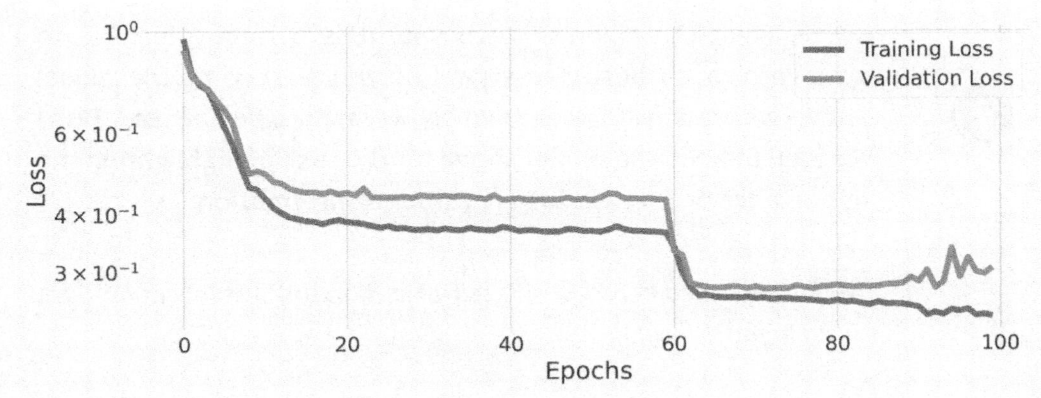

Figure 9.34 - Losses—encoder + decoder + self-attention

The losses are *worse* now—the model using *cross-attention only* was performing better than that. What about the predictions?

Visualizing Predictions

Let's plot the **predicted coordinates** and connect them using **dashed lines**, while using **solid lines** to connect the **actual coordinates**, just like before:

```
fig = sequence_pred(sbs_seq_selfattn, full_test, test_directions)
```

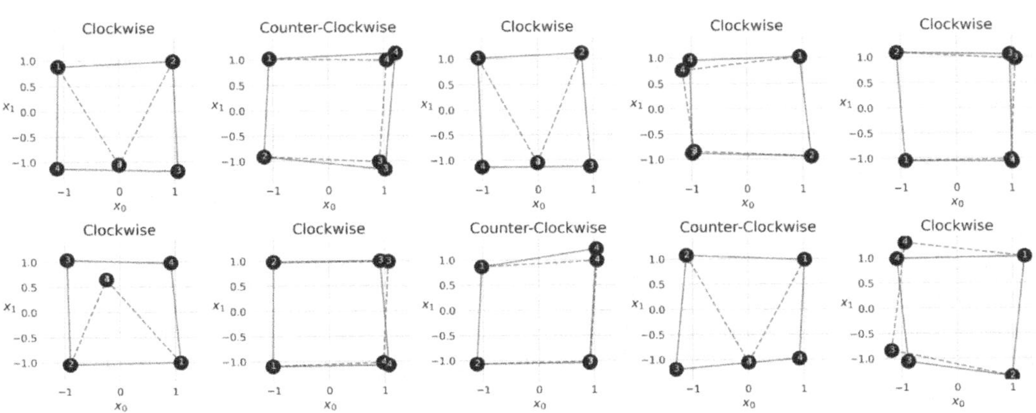

Figure 9.35 - Predictions—encoder + decoder + self-attention

Well, that's a bit *disappointing*; the *triangles* made a comeback!

To be completely honest with you, it is perfectly feasible to achieve a **much better loss** (and no *triangles*) using the model above with a small tweak; namely, trying a *different seed*. But I decided to **keep the model above** for the sake of **highlighting the importance** of our next topic: **positional information**.

"*What happened here? Wasn't **self-attention** the best invention since sliced bread?*"

Self-attention is great, indeed, but it is **missing one fundamental piece of information** that the recurrent layers had: the **order of the data points**. As we know, the **order** is of **utmost importance** in sequence problems, but for the self-attention mechanism there is **no order** to the data points in the **source sequence**.

"*I don't get it—**why** did it lose the order?*"

Sequential No More

Let's compare two **encoders**, one using **recurrent neural networks** (left), the other, **self-attention** (right).

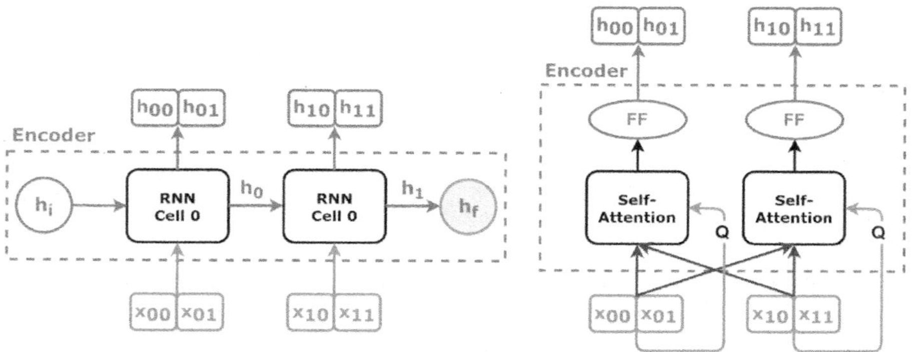

Figure 9.36 - RNN vs self-attention

The recurrent neural network ensured that the **output at each step was fed to the next**, depicted by the $\mathbf{h_0}$ going from one cell to the next. Now, compare it to the encoder using **self-attention**: **Every step is *independent* of the others.** If you *flip* the order of the data points in the source sequence, the encoder will output the "hidden states" in a different order, but it **won't change their values**.

That's exactly what makes it highly *parallelizable*, and it is both a **blessing** and a

curse. On the one hand, it makes computation very efficient; on the other hand, it is **throwing away valuable information**.

"Can we fix it?"

Definitely! Instead of using a model designed to encode the order of the inputs (like the recurrent neural networks), let's **encode the positional information** ourselves and **add it to the inputs**.

Positional Encoding (PE)

We need to find a way to inform the model about the **position** of every **data point** such that it knows the **order of the data points**. In other words, we need to generate a **unique value** for each **position** in the input.

Let's put our simple sequence-to-sequence problem aside for a while and imagine we have a **sequence of four data points** instead. The first idea that comes to mind is to use the **index** of the position itself, right? Let's just use zero, one, two, and three, done! Maybe it wouldn't be *so* bad for a short sequence like this, but what about a sequence of, say, **one thousand** data points? The positional encoding of the last data point would be 999. We *shouldn't* be using *unbounded values* like that as inputs for a neural network.

"What about 'normalizing' the indices?"

Sure, we can try that and divide the indices by the *length* of our sequence (four).

Position	0	1	2	3
Pos/4	0.00	0.25	0.50	0.75

Figure 9.37 - "Normalizing" over the length

Unfortunately, that **didn't** solve the problem—a **longer** sequence will **still generate values larger than one**.

Position	0	1	2	3	4	5	6	7
Pos/4	0.00	0.25	0.50	0.75	1.00	1.25	1.50	1.75

Figure 9.38 - "Normalizing" over a (shorter) length

"What about 'normalizing' each sequence by its own length?"

It solves *that* problem, but it raises **another** one; namely, the **same position** gets **different encoding** values depending on the length of the sequence.

Position	0	1	2	3	4	5	6	7
Pos/4	0.00	0.25	0.50	0.75				
Pos/8	0.00	0.13	0.25	0.38	0.50	0.63	0.75	0.88

Figure 9.39 - "Normalizing" over different lengths

Ideally, the **positional encoding** should remain **constant for a given position**, regardless of the length of the sequence.

*"What if we take the **module** first, and **then** 'normalize' it?"*

Well, that indeed solves the two problems above, but the values **aren't unique anymore**.

Position	0	1	2	3	4	5	6	7
(Pos mod 4)/4	0.00	0.25	0.50	0.75	0.00	0.25	0.50	0.75

Figure 9.40 - "Normalizing" over a module of the length

"OK, I give up! How do we handle this?"

Let's think outside the box for a moment; no one said we must use *only one vector*, right? Let's build **three vectors** instead, using three hypothetical sequence lengths (four, five, and seven).

Position	0	1	2	3	4	5	6	7
(Pos mod 4)/4	0.00	0.25	0.50	0.75	0.00	0.25	0.50	0.75
(Pos mod 5)/5	0.00	0.20	0.40	0.60	0.80	0.00	0.20	0.40
(Pos mod 7)/7	0.00	0.14	0.29	0.43	0.57	0.71	0.86	0.00

Figure 9.41 - Combining results for different modules

The positional encoding above is **unique** up to the 140th position and we can easily extend that by adding more vectors.

"Are we done now? Is this good enough?"

Sorry, but no, not yet. Our solution still has one problem, and it boils down to computing **distances** between two encoded positions. Let's take **position number three** and its two neighbors, positions number two and four. Obviously, the distance between position three and each of its closest neighbors is **one**. Now, let's see what happens if we compute distance using the positional encoding.

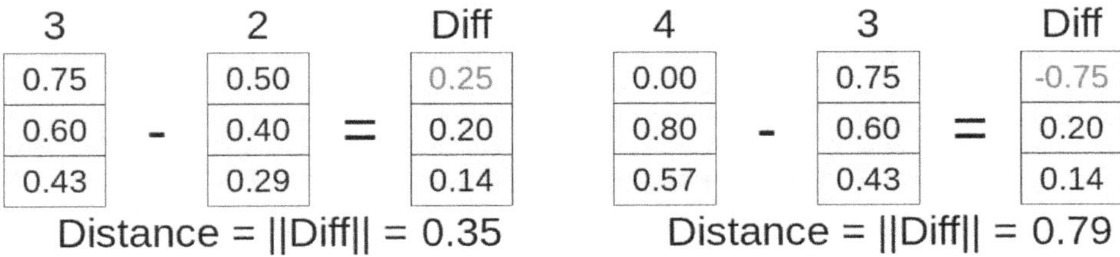

Figure 9.42 - Inconsistent distances

The distance between positions three and two (given by the norm of the difference vector) **is not equal** to the distance between positions three and four. That may seem a bit *too abstract*, but using an encoding with **inconsistent distances** would make it much harder for the model to make sense out of the encoded positions.

This inconsistency arises from the fact that our encoding is **resetting to zero** every time the **module** kicks in. The distance between positions three and four got much larger because, at position four, the first vector goes back to zero. We need some other function that has a **smoother cycle**.

"What if we ***actually*** *use a* ***cycle****, I mean, a* ***circle****?"*

Perfect! First, we take our encodings and **multiply them by 360**.

Position	0	1	2	3	4	5	6	7
Base 4	0	90	180	270	0	90	180	270
Base 5	0	72	144	216	288	0	72	144
Base 7	0	51	103	154	206	257	309	0

Figure 9.43 - From "normalized" module to degrees

Now, each value corresponds to a **number of degrees** that we can use to **move along a circle**. The figure below shows a **red arrow** rotated by the corresponding number of degrees for each position and base in the table above.

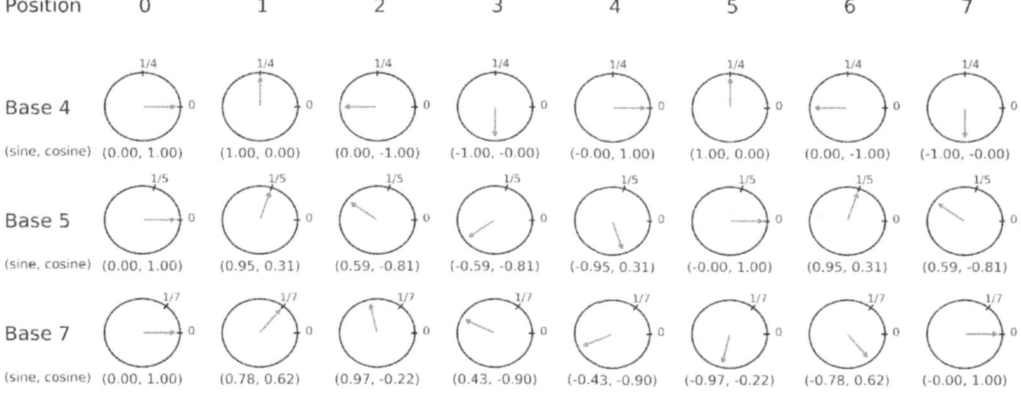

Figure 9.44 - Representing degrees on a circle

Moreover, the circles above show the **sine** and **cosine** values corresponding to the **coordinates** of the tip of each **red arrow** (assuming a circle with a radius of one).

The **sine** and **cosine** values, that is, the **coordinates** of the **red arrow**, are the **actual positional encoding** of a given position.

We can simply read the sine and cosine values, from top to bottom, to build the encodings for each position.

Position	0	1	2	3	4	5	6	7
sine (base 4)	0.00	1.00	0.00	-1.00	0.00	1.00	0.00	-1.00
cosine (base 4)	1.00	0.00	-1.00	0.00	1.00	0.00	-1.00	0.00
sine (base 5)	0.00	0.95	0.59	-0.59	-0.95	0.00	0.95	0.59
cosine (base 5)	1.00	0.31	-0.81	-0.81	0.31	1.00	0.31	-0.81
sine (base 7)	0.00	0.78	0.97	0.43	-0.43	-0.97	-0.78	0.00
cosine (base 7)	1.00	0.62	-0.22	-0.90	-0.90	-0.22	0.62	1.00

Figure 9.45 - Representing degrees using sine and cosine

There were **three vectors**, thus generating **six coordinates or dimensions** (three sines and three cosines).

Next, let's use *these encodings* to calculate the distances, which should be **consistent** now!

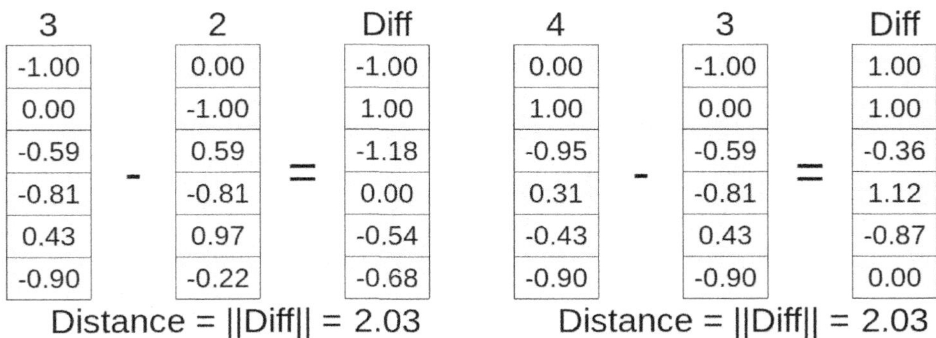

Figure 9.46 - Consistent distances

Awesome, isn't it? The **encoded distance between any two positions *T* steps apart is constant** now. In our encoding, the distance between any two positions **one step** apart will always be 2.03.

"Great! But how do I choose the 'bases' for the encoding?"

It turns out, you don't have to. As the **first vector**, simply move along the circle **as many radians as the index of the position** (one radian is approximately 57.3 degrees). Then, for each **new vector** added to the encoding, move along the circle with **exponentially slower** angular speeds. For example, in the **second vector**, we would move only **one-tenth of a radian** (approximately 5.73 degrees) for each new position. In the **third vector**, we would move only **one-hundredth of a radian**, and so on and so forth. Figure 9.47 depicts the red arrow moving at increasingly slower angular speeds.

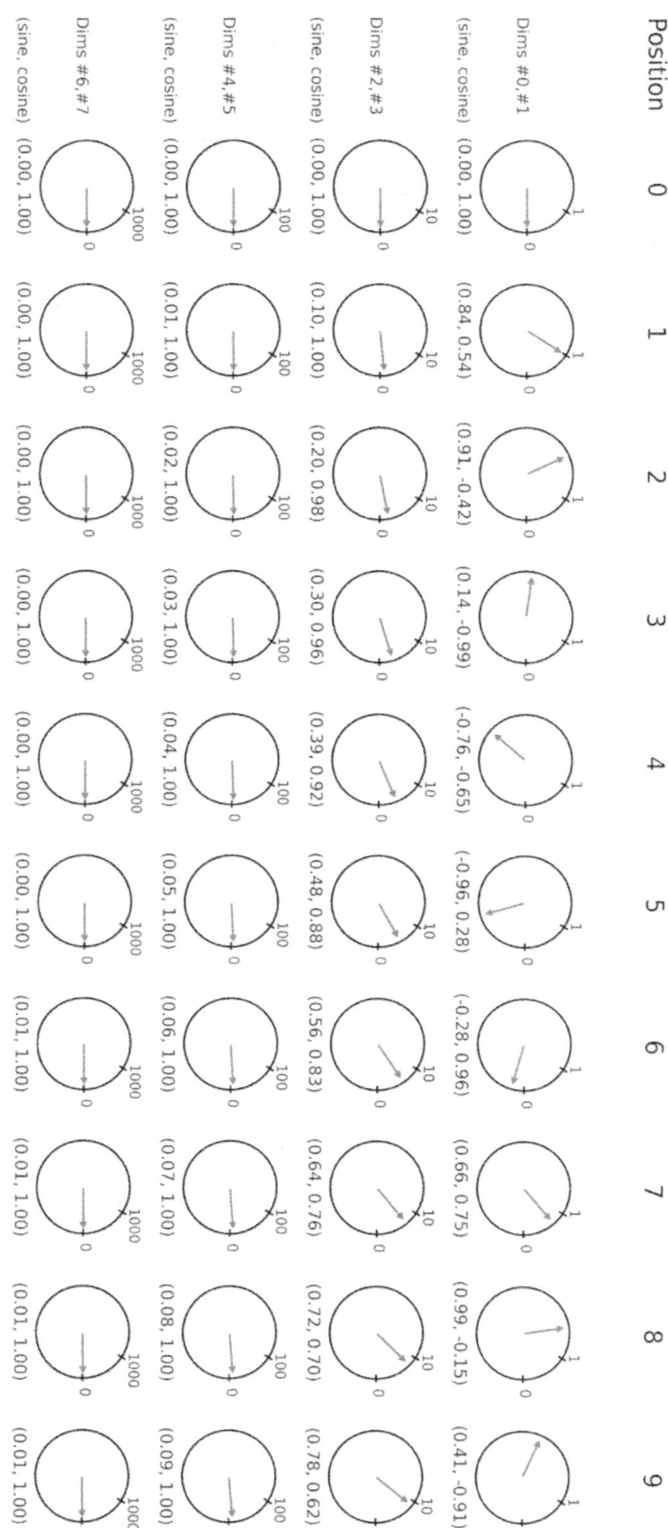

Figure 9.47 - Positional encoding represented as circles

A Note on Encoded Distances

Let's recap what we've already seen:

- The **encoded distance** is defined by the **Euclidean distance** between **two vectors**, or, in other words, it is the **norm (size) of the difference between two encoding vectors.**
- The encoded distance between **positions zero and two (*T*=2)** should be exactly the **same** as the encoded distance between **positions one and three, two and four**, and so on.

In other words, the **encoded distance** between any two positions ***T* steps apart remains constant**. Let's illustrate this by **computing the encoded distances** among the first **five positions** (by the way, we're using the encoding with eight dimensions now):

```
distances = np.zeros((5, 5))
for i, v1 in enumerate(encoding[:5]):
    for j, v2 in enumerate(encoding[:5]):
        distances[i, j] = np.linalg.norm(v1 - v2)
```

The resulting matrix is full of **pretty diagonals**, each **diagonal** containing a **constant value** for the **encoded distance** corresponding to **positions *T* steps apart**.

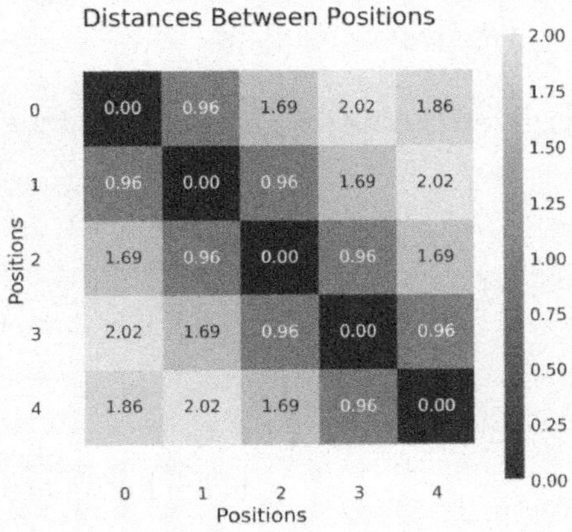

For example, for **positions next to each other (*T*=1)**, our **encoded distance** is **always 0.96**. That's an amazing property of this encoding scheme.

*"Great, but there is something weird—position **four** should have a **larger distance** than position **three** to position zero, right?"*

Not necessarily, no. The distance **does not need to always increase**. It is OK for the distance between positions zero and four (1.86) to be **less than** the distance between positions zero and three (2.02), as long as the **diagonals hold**.

For a more detailed discussion about using *sines* and *cosines* for positional encoding, check Amirhossein Kazemnejad's great post on the subject: "Transformer Architecture: The Positional Encoding."[51]

Since we're using **four different angular speeds**, the **positional encoding** depicted in Figure 9.47 has **eight dimensions.** Notice that the red arrow barely moves in the last two rows.

In practice, we'll **choose the number of dimensions** first, and then compute the corresponding speeds. For example, for encoding with **eight dimensions**, like Figure 9.47, there are **four angular speeds**:

$$\left(\frac{1}{10000^{\frac{0}{8}}}, \frac{1}{10000^{\frac{2}{8}}}, \frac{1}{10000^{\frac{4}{8}}}, \frac{1}{10000^{\frac{6}{8}}}\right) = (1, 0.1, 0.01, 0.001)$$

Equation 9.20 - Angular speeds

The **positional encoding** is given by the two formulas below:

$$\begin{aligned}
\text{PE}_{\text{pos},\ 2d} &= \sin\left(\frac{1}{10000^{\frac{2d}{d_{\text{model}}}}}\text{pos}\right) \\
\text{PE}_{\text{pos},\ 2d+1} &= \cos\left(\frac{1}{10000^{\frac{2d}{d_{\text{model}}}}}\text{pos}\right)
\end{aligned}$$

Equation 9.21 - Positional encoding

Let's see it in code:

```
max_len = 10
d_model = 8
position = torch.arange(0, max_len).float().unsqueeze(1)
angular_speed = torch.exp(
  torch.arange(0, d_model, 2).float() * (-np.log(10000.0) / d_model)
)
encoding = torch.zeros(max_len, d_model)
encoding[:, 0::2] = torch.sin(angular_speed * position)
encoding[:, 1::2] = torch.cos(angular_speed * position)
```

As you can see, each **position** is multiplied by several different **angular speeds**, and the resulting **coordinates** (given by the sine and cosine) compose the **actual encoding**. Now, instead of plotting the circles, we can directly plot **all sine values** (the even dimensions of the encoding) and **all cosine values** (the odd dimensions of the encoding) instead.

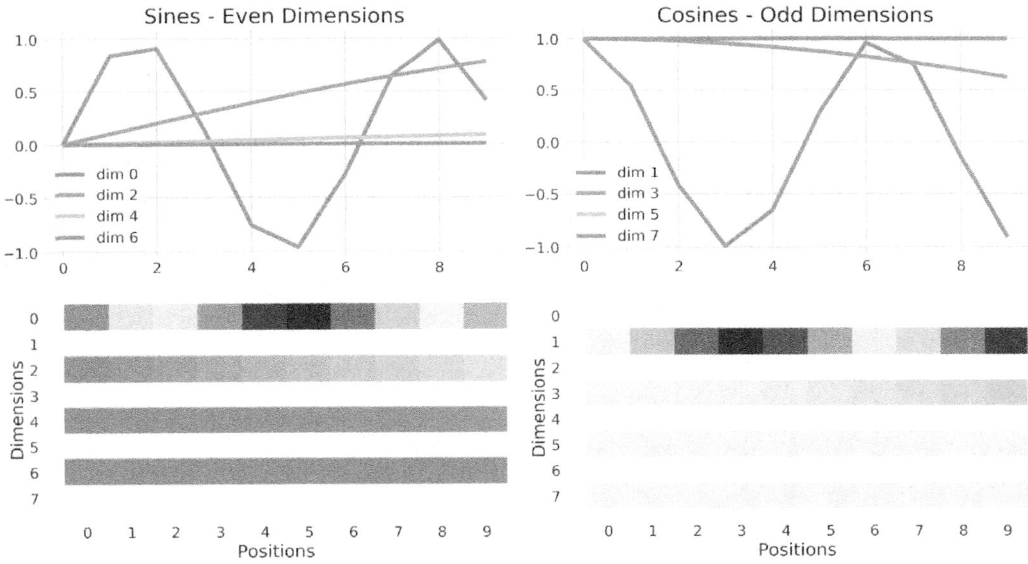

Figure 9.48 - Positional encoding as a heatmap

The plots on the bottom show the **color-coded encoding**, ranging from **minus one (dark blue)** to **zero (green)**, all the way to **one (yellow)**. I chose to plot them with the *positions* on the *horizontal axis* so you can more easily associate them with the corresponding curves on the top. In most blog posts, however, you'll find the *transposed version*; that is, with *dimensions* on the *horizontal axis*.

Let's put both sine and cosine values together and look at the **first four positions**:

```
np.round(encoding[0:4], 4)  # first four positions
```

Output

```
tensor([[ 0.0000,  1.0000,  0.0000,  1.0000,  0.0000,  1.0000,
0.0000,  1.0000],
        [ 0.8415,  0.5403,  0.0998,  0.9950,  0.0100,  1.0000,
0.0010,  1.0000],
        [ 0.9093, -0.4161,  0.1987,  0.9801,  0.0200,  0.9998,
0.0020,  1.0000],
        [ 0.1411, -0.9900,  0.2955,  0.9553,  0.0300,  0.9996,
0.0030,  1.0000]])
```

Each line above represents the **encoding values** for each of its **eight dimensions**. The **first position** will **always** have **alternated zeros and ones** (the sine and cosine of zero, respectively).

Let's put it all together into a class:

Positional Encoding (PE)

```
class PositionalEncoding(nn.Module):
    def __init__(self, max_len, d_model):
        super().__init__()
        self.d_model = d_model
        pe = torch.zeros(max_len, d_model)
        position = torch.arange(0, max_len).float().unsqueeze(1)
        angular_speed = torch.exp(
            torch.arange(0, d_model, 2).float() *
            (-np.log(10000.0) / d_model)
        )
        # even dimensions
        pe[:, 0::2] = torch.sin(position * angular_speed)
        # odd dimensions
        pe[:, 1::2] = torch.cos(position * angular_speed)
        self.register_buffer('pe', pe.unsqueeze(0))

    def forward(self, x):
        # x is N, L, D
        # pe is 1, maxlen, D
        scaled_x = x * np.sqrt(self.d_model)
        encoded = scaled_x + self.pe[:, :x.size(1), :]
        return encoded
```

There are a couple of things about this class I'd like to highlight:

- In the *constructor*, it uses `register_buffer()` to define an **attribute** of the module.
- In the `forward()` method, it is **scaling the input** before adding the positional encoding.

The `register_buffer()` method is used to define an attribute that is **part of the module's state**, yet **is not a parameter**. The positional encoding is a good example: Its values are computed according to the **dimension** and **length** used by the model, and even though these values *are going to be used* during training, they **shouldn't be updated** by gradient descent.

Another example of a *registered buffer* is the `running_mean` attribute of the **batch**

normalization layer. It is used during training, and it is even *modified* during training (unlike positional encoding), but it isn't updated by gradient descent.

Let's create an instance of the positional encoding class and check its `parameters()` and `state_dict()`:

```
posenc = PositionalEncoding(2, 2)
list(posenc.parameters()), posenc.state_dict()
```

Output

```
([], OrderedDict([('pe', tensor([[[0.0000, 1.0000],
                          [0.8415, 0.5403]]]))]))
```

The registered buffer can be accessed just like any other attribute:

```
posenc.pe
```

Output

```
tensor([[[0.0000, 1.0000],
         [0.8415, 0.5403]]])
```

Now, let's see what happens if we **add the positional encoding** to a **source sequence**:

```
source_seq # 1, L, D
```

Output

```
tensor([[[-1., -1.],
         [-1.,  1.]]])
```

```
source_seq + posenc.pe
```

Output

```
tensor([[[-1.0000,  0.0000],
         [-0.1585,  1.5403]]])
```

"What am I looking at?"

It turns out, the *original coordinates* were somewhat **crowded-out** by the addition of the positional encoding (especially the first row). This may happen if the **data points** have values roughly in the **same range** as the **positional encoding**. Unfortunately, this is **fairly common**: Both **standardized inputs** and **word embeddings** (we'll get back to them in Chapter 11) are likely to have **most of their values** inside the [-1, 1] range of the positional encoding.

"How can we handle it then?"

That's what the **scaling** in the `forward()` method is for: It's as if we were "***reversing the standardization***" of the inputs (using a **standard deviation** equal to the **square root of their dimensionality**) to retrieve the hypothetical "*raw*" inputs.

$$\text{standardized } x = \frac{\text{"raw" } x}{\sqrt{d_x}} \implies \text{"raw" } x = \sqrt{d_x} \text{ standardized } x$$

Equation 9.22 - "Reversing" the standardization

By the way, previously, we **scaled** the **dot product** using the **inverse** of the **square root of its dimensionality**, which was its **standard deviation**.

Even though this **is not** the same thing, the analogy might help you **remember** that the **inputs** are also **scaled** by the **square root of their number of dimensions** before the positional encoding gets added to them.

In our example, the **dimensionality is two (coordinates)**, so the inputs are going to be **scaled by the square root of two**:

```
posenc(source_seq)
```

Output

```
tensor([[[-1.4142, -0.4142],
         [-0.5727,  1.9545]]])
```

The results above (after the encoding) illustrate the effect of scaling the inputs: It seems to have lessened the *crowding-out* effect of the positional encoding. For inputs with **many dimensions**, the **effect** will be **much more pronounced**: A 300-dimension embedding will have a scaling factor around 17, for example.

*"Wait, isn't this **bad** for the model?"*

Left unchecked, yes, it could be bad for the model. That's why we'll pull off **yet another normalization** trick: **layer normalization**. We'll discuss it in detail in the next chapter.

For now, *scaling* the coordinates by the *square root of two* isn't going to be an issue, so we can move on and **integrate positional encoding** into our model.

Encoder + Decoder + PE

The new encoder and decoder classes are just **wrapping** their **self-attention** counterparts by assigning the latter to be the `layer` attribute of the former, and **encoding the inputs** prior to calling the corresponding `layer`:

Encoder with Positional Encoding

```
class EncoderPe(nn.Module):
    def __init__(self, n_heads, d_model, ff_units,
                 n_features=None, max_len=100):
        super().__init__()
        pe_dim = d_model if n_features is None else n_features
        self.pe = PositionalEncoding(max_len, pe_dim)
        self.layer = EncoderSelfAttn(n_heads, d_model,
                                     ff_units, n_features)

    def forward(self, query, mask=None):
        query_pe = self.pe(query)
        out = self.layer(query_pe, mask)
        return out
```

```
class DecoderPe(nn.Module):
    def __init__(self, n_heads, d_model, ff_units,
                 n_features=None, max_len=100):
        super().__init__()
        pe_dim = d_model if n_features is None else n_features
        self.pe = PositionalEncoding(max_len, pe_dim)
        self.layer = DecoderSelfAttn(n_heads, d_model,
                                     ff_units, n_features)

    def init_keys(self, states):
        self.layer.init_keys(states)

    def forward(self, query, source_mask=None, target_mask=None):
        query_pe = self.pe(query)
        out = self.layer(query_pe, source_mask, target_mask)
        return out
```

*"Why are we calling the **self-attention encoder (and decoder)** a **layer** now? It's a bit confusing..."*

You're right, it may be a bit confusing, indeed. Unfortunately, *naming conventions* aren't so great in our field. A **layer** is (loosely) used here as a **building block** of a **larger model**. It may look a bit silly; after all, there is **only one layer** (apart from the encoding). Why even bother making it a "*layer*," right?

In the next chapter, we'll use **multiple layers** (of attention mechanisms) to build the famous **Transformer**.

Model Configuration & Training

Since we haven't changed the large encoder-decoder model, we only need to update its arguments (encoder and decoder) to use the new positional encoding-powered classes:

Model Configuration

```
torch.manual_seed(43)
encpe = EncoderPe(n_heads=3, d_model=2, ff_units=10, n_features=2)
decpe = DecoderPe(n_heads=3, d_model=2, ff_units=10, n_features=2)

model = EncoderDecoderSelfAttn(encpe, decpe,
                               input_len=2, target_len=2)
loss = nn.MSELoss()
optimizer = optim.Adam(model.parameters(), lr=0.01)
```

Model Training

```
sbs_seq_selfattnpe = StepByStep(model, loss, optimizer)
sbs_seq_selfattnpe.set_loaders(train_loader, test_loader)
sbs_seq_selfattnpe.train(100)
```

```
fig = sbs_seq_selfattnpe.plot_losses()
```

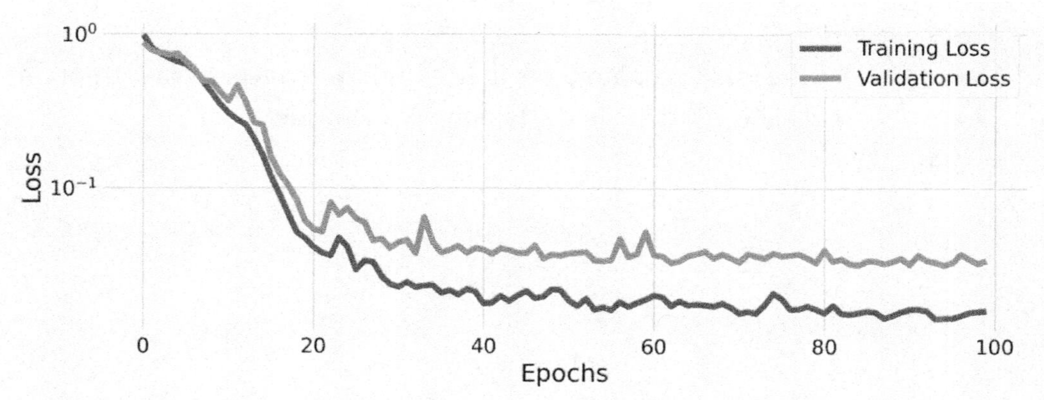

Figure 9.49 - Losses—using positional encoding

Good, the **loss** broke **below 10^{-1}** once again.

Visualizing Predictions

Let's plot the **predicted coordinates** and connect them using **dashed lines**, while using **solid lines** to connect the **actual coordinates**, just like before:

```
fig = sequence_pred(sbs_seq_selfattnpe, full_test, test_directions)
```

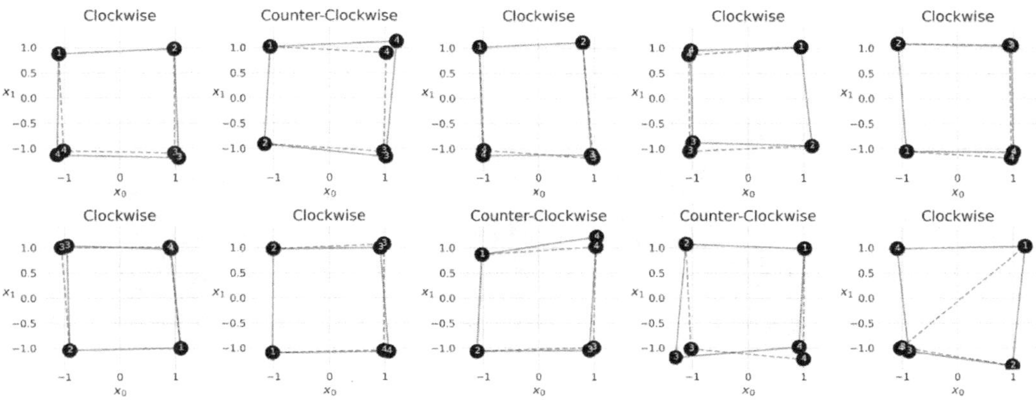

Figure 9.50 - Predicting the last two corners

Awesome, it looks like **positional encoding** is working well indeed—the predicted coordinates are quite close to the actual ones for the most part.

Visualizing Attention

Now, let's check what the model is paying attention to for the first **two sequences** in the training set. Unlike last time, though, there are **three heads** and **three attention mechanisms** to visualize now.

We're starting with the **three heads** of the **self-attention** mechanism of the **encoder**. There are **two data points** in our **source sequence**, so each attention head has a **two-by-two** matrix of attention scores.

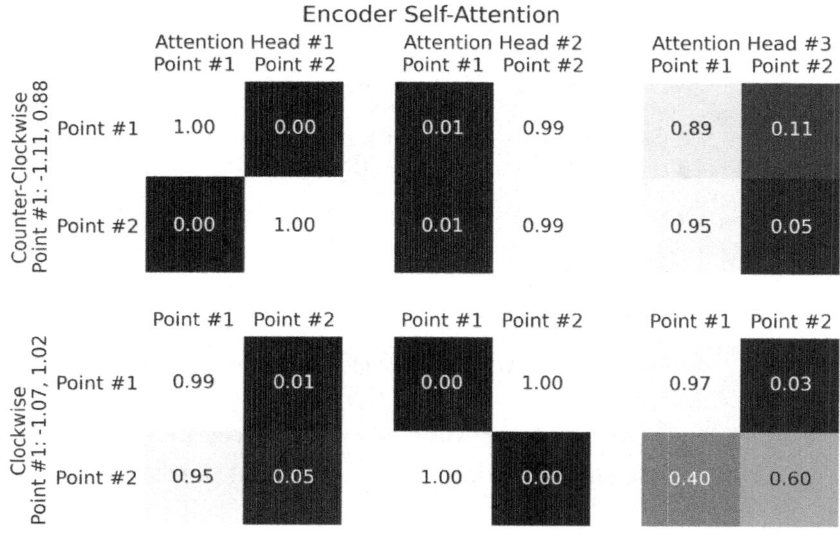

Figure 9.51 - Encoder's self-attention scores for its three heads

It seems that, in **Attention Head #3**, each **data point** is dividing its attention between itself and the other data point. In the **other** attention heads, though, the data points are paying attention to a single data point, either itself or the other one. Of course, these are just two data points used for visualization: The attention scores are *different* for each source sequence.

Next, we're moving on to the **three heads** of the **self-attention** mechanism of the **decoder**. There are **two data points** in our **target sequence** as well, but do not forget that there's a **target mask** to **prevent cheating**.

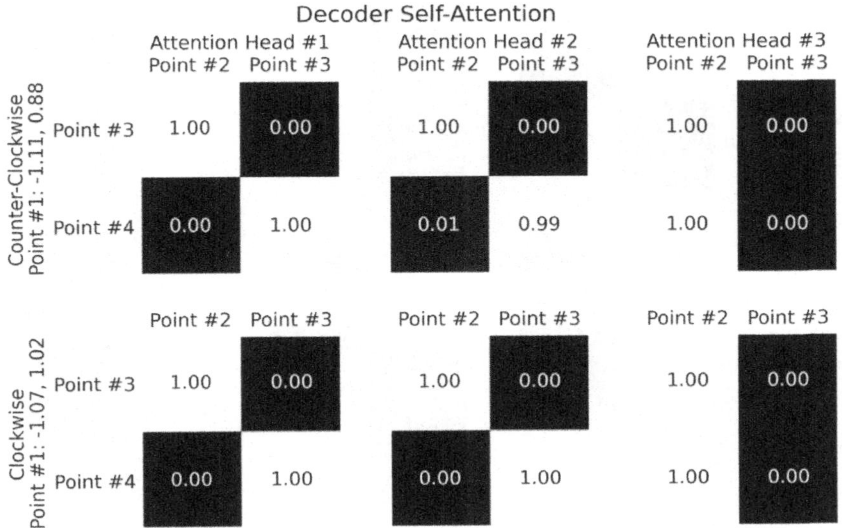

Figure 9.52 - Decoder's self-attention scores for its three heads

The *top-right* value of every matrix is **zero** thanks to the **target mask**: **Point #3** (first row) is not allowed to pay attention to its (supposedly unknown, at training time) **own value** (second column); it can pay attention to **point #2 only** (first column).

On the other hand, **point #4** may pay attention to either one of its predecessors. From the matrices above, it seems to pay attention almost exclusively to one of the two points depending on which head and sequence are being considered.

Then, there is the **cross-attention** mechanism, the first one we discussed.

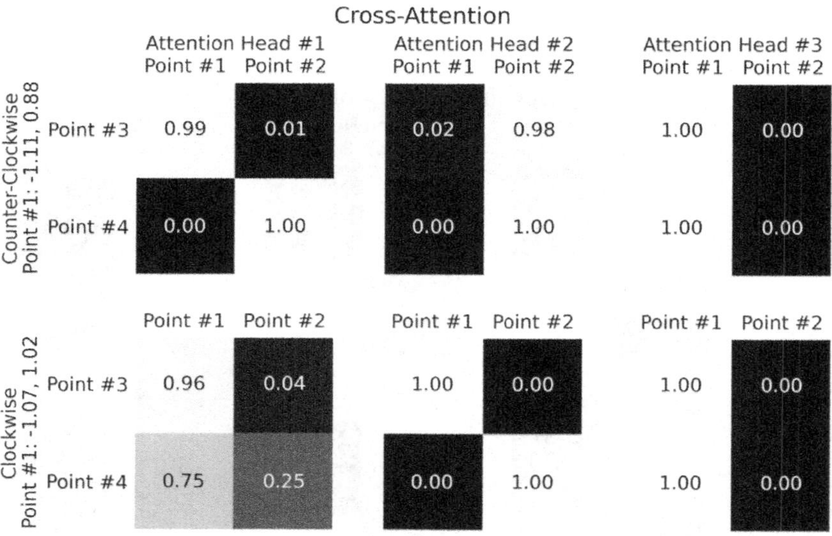

Figure 9.53 - Cross-attention scores for its three heads

There is a lot of variation in the matrices above: In the third head of the first sequence, for example, **points #3 and #4** pay attention to **point #1 only** while the first head pays attention to to alternate points; in the second sequence, though, it's the second head that pays attention to alternate points.

Putting It All Together

In this chapter, we used the same dataset of **colored squares**, but this time we focused on **predicting the coordinates** of the last two corners (**target sequence**) given the coordinates of the first two corners (**source sequence**). In the beginning, we used familiar recurrent neural networks to build an **encoder-decoder architecture**. Then, we progressively built on top of it by using **(cross-)attention**, **self-attention**, and **positional encoding**.

Data Preparation

The training set has the **full sequences** as **features**, while the test set has only the **source sequences** as **features**:

Data Generation & Preparation

```
# Training set
points, directions = generate_sequences(n=256, seed=13)
full_train = torch.as_tensor(points).float()
target_train = full_train[:, 2:]
train_data = TensorDataset(full_train, target_train)
generator = torch.Generator()
train_loader = DataLoader(train_data, batch_size=16,
                          shuffle=True, generator=generator)
# Validation / Test Set
test_points, test_directions = generate_sequences(seed=19)
full_test = torch.as_tensor(test_points).float()
source_test = full_test[:, :2]
target_test = full_test[:, 2:]
test_data = TensorDataset(source_test, target_test)
test_loader = DataLoader(test_data, batch_size=16)
```

Model Assembly

During this chapter, we used the usual **bottom-up** approach for building ever more complex models. Now, we're revisiting the **current stage** of development in a **top-down** approach, starting from the **encoder-decoder architecture**:

Model Configuration

```
class EncoderDecoderSelfAttn(nn.Module):
    def __init__(self, encoder, decoder, input_len, target_len):
        super().__init__()
        self.encoder = encoder
        self.decoder = decoder
        self.input_len = input_len
        self.target_len = target_len
        self.trg_masks = self.subsequent_mask(self.target_len)

    @staticmethod
    def subsequent_mask(size):
        attn_shape = (1, size, size)
        subsequent_mask = (
            1 - torch.triu(torch.ones(attn_shape), diagonal=1)
        ).bool()
        return subsequent_mask
```

```

    def encode(self, source_seq, source_mask):
        # Encodes the source sequence and uses the result
        # to initialize the decoder
        encoder_states = self.encoder(source_seq, source_mask)
        self.decoder.init_keys(encoder_states)

    def decode(self, shifted_target_seq,
               source_mask=None, target_mask=None):
        # Decodes / generates a sequence using the shifted
        # (masked) target sequence - used in TRAIN mode
        outputs = self.decoder(shifted_target_seq,
                               source_mask=source_mask,
                               target_mask=target_mask)
        return outputs

    def predict(self, source_seq, source_mask):
        # Decodes / generates a sequence using one input
        # at a time - used in EVAL mode
        inputs = source_seq[:, -1:]
        for i in range(self.target_len):
            out = self.decode(inputs,
                              source_mask,
                              self.trg_masks[:, :i+1, :i+1])
            out = torch.cat([inputs, out[:, -1:, :]], dim=-2)
            inputs = out.detach()
        outputs = inputs[:, 1:, :]
        return outputs

    def forward(self, X, source_mask=None):
        # Sends the mask to the same device as the inputs
        self.trg_masks = self.trg_masks.type_as(X).bool()
        # Slices the input to get source sequence
        source_seq = X[:, :self.input_len, :]
        # Encodes source sequence AND initializes decoder
        self.encode(source_seq, source_mask)
        if self.training:
            # Slices the input to get the shifted target seq
            shifted_target_seq = X[:, self.input_len-1:-1, :]
            # Decodes using the mask to prevent cheating
            outputs = self.decode(shifted_target_seq,
                                  source_mask,
```

```
                                       self.trg_masks)
        else:
            # Decodes using its own predictions
            outputs = self.predict(source_seq, source_mask)

        return outputs
```

Encoder + Decoder + Positional Encoding

In the **second level**, we'll find both the **encoder** and the **decoder** using **positional encoding** to prepare the inputs before calling the **"layer"** that implements the corresponding **self-attention** mechanism.

In the next chapter, we'll *modify this code* to include **multiple "layers" of self-attention.**

Model Configuration

```
class PositionalEncoding(nn.Module):
    def __init__(self, max_len, d_model):
        super().__init__()
        self.d_model = d_model
        pe = torch.zeros(max_len, d_model)
        position = torch.arange(0, max_len).float().unsqueeze(1)
        angular_speed = torch.exp(
            torch.arange(0, d_model, 2).float() *
            (-np.log(10000.0) / d_model)
        )
        # even dimensions
        pe[:, 0::2] = torch.sin(position * angular_speed)
        # odd dimensions
        pe[:, 1::2] = torch.cos(position * angular_speed)
        self.register_buffer('pe', pe.unsqueeze(0))

    def forward(self, x):
        # x is N, L, D
        # pe is 1, maxlen, D
        scaled_x = x * np.sqrt(self.d_model)
        encoded = scaled_x + self.pe[:, :x.size(1), :]
        return encoded

```

```
class EncoderPe(nn.Module):
    def __init__(self, n_heads, d_model, ff_units,
                 n_features=None, max_len=100):
        super().__init__()
        pe_dim = d_model if n_features is None else n_features
        self.pe = PositionalEncoding(max_len, pe_dim)
        self.layer = EncoderSelfAttn(n_heads, d_model,
                                     ff_units, n_features)

    def forward(self, query, mask=None):
        query_pe = self.pe(query)
        out = self.layer(query_pe, mask)
        return out

class DecoderPe(nn.Module):
    def __init__(self, n_heads, d_model, ff_units,
                 n_features=None, max_len=100):
        super().__init__()
        pe_dim = d_model if n_features is None else n_features
        self.pe = PositionalEncoding(max_len, pe_dim)
        self.layer = DecoderSelfAttn(n_heads, d_model,
                                     ff_units, n_features)

    def init_keys(self, states):
        self.layer.init_keys(states)

    def forward(self, query, source_mask=None, target_mask=None):
        query_pe = self.pe(query)
        out = self.layer(query_pe, source_mask, target_mask)
        return out
```

Self-Attention "Layers"

At first, both classes below were full-fledged encoder and decoder. Now, they've been "*downgraded*" to mere **"layers"** of the soon-to-be-larger **encoder** and **decoder** above. The *encoder layer* has a single self-attention mechanism, and the *decoder* layer has both a self-attention and a cross-attention mechanism.

In the next chapter, we'll **add a lot of bells and whistles** to this part. Wait for it!

```
class EncoderSelfAttn(nn.Module):
    def __init__(self, n_heads, d_model,
                 ff_units, n_features=None):
        super().__init__()
        self.n_heads = n_heads
        self.d_model = d_model
        self.ff_units = ff_units
        self.n_features = n_features
        self.self_attn_heads = \
            MultiHeadAttention(n_heads,
                               d_model,
                               input_dim=n_features)
        self.ffn = nn.Sequential(
            nn.Linear(d_model, ff_units),
            nn.ReLU(),
            nn.Linear(ff_units, d_model),
        )

    def forward(self, query, mask=None):
        self.self_attn_heads.init_keys(query)
        att = self.self_attn_heads(query, mask)
        out = self.ffn(att)
        return out

class DecoderSelfAttn(nn.Module):
    def __init__(self, n_heads, d_model,
                 ff_units, n_features=None):
        super().__init__()
        self.n_heads = n_heads
        self.d_model = d_model
        self.ff_units = ff_units
        self.n_features = d_model if n_features is None \
                          else n_features
        self.self_attn_heads = \
            MultiHeadAttention(n_heads,
                               d_model,
                               input_dim=self.n_features)
        self.cross_attn_heads = \
            MultiHeadAttention(n_heads, d_model)
        self.ffn = nn.Sequential(
            nn.Linear(d_model, ff_units),
```

```
                nn.ReLU(),
                nn.Linear(ff_units, self.n_features),
            )

    def init_keys(self, states):
        self.cross_attn_heads.init_keys(states)

    def forward(self, query, source_mask=None, target_mask=None):
        self.self_attn_heads.init_keys(query)
        att1 = self.self_attn_heads(query, target_mask)
        att2 = self.cross_attn_heads(att1, source_mask)
        out = self.ffn(att2)
        return out
```

Attention Heads

Both self-attention and cross-attention mechanisms are implemented using **wide multi-headed attention**; that is, a straightforward **concatenation** of the results of **several basic attention mechanisms** followed by a **linear projection** to get the **original context vector dimensions** back.

In the next chapter, we'll develop a **narrow multi-headed attention** mechanism.

Model Configuration

```
class MultiHeadAttention(nn.Module):
    def __init__(self, n_heads, d_model,
                 input_dim=None, proj_values=True):
        super().__init__()
        self.linear_out = nn.Linear(n_heads * d_model, d_model)
        self.attn_heads = nn.ModuleList(
            [Attention(d_model,
                       input_dim=input_dim,
                       proj_values=proj_values)
             for _ in range(n_heads)]
        )

    def init_keys(self, key):
        for attn in self.attn_heads:
            attn.init_keys(key)
```

```python

    @property
    def alphas(self):
        # Shape: n_heads, N, 1, L (source)
        return torch.stack(
            [attn.alphas for attn in self.attn_heads], dim=0
        )

    def output_function(self, contexts):
        # N, 1, n_heads * D
        concatenated = torch.cat(contexts, axis=-1)
        out = self.linear_out(concatenated) # N, 1, D
        return out

    def forward(self, query, mask=None):
        contexts = [attn(query, mask=mask)
                    for attn in self.attn_heads]
        out = self.output_function(contexts)
        return out

class Attention(nn.Module):
    def __init__(self, hidden_dim,
                 input_dim=None, proj_values=False):
        super().__init__()
        self.d_k = hidden_dim
        self.input_dim = hidden_dim if input_dim is None \
                         else input_dim
        self.proj_values = proj_values
        self.linear_query = nn.Linear(self.input_dim, hidden_dim)
        self.linear_key = nn.Linear(self.input_dim, hidden_dim)
        self.linear_value = nn.Linear(self.input_dim, hidden_dim)
        self.alphas = None

    def init_keys(self, keys):
        self.keys = keys
        self.proj_keys = self.linear_key(self.keys)
        self.values = self.linear_value(self.keys) \
                      if self.proj_values else self.keys

    def score_function(self, query):
        proj_query = self.linear_query(query)
        # scaled dot product
```

```
        # N, 1, H x N, H, L -> N, 1, L
        dot_products = torch.bmm(proj_query,
                                 self.proj_keys.permute(0, 2, 1))
        scores =  dot_products / np.sqrt(self.d_k)
        return scores

    def forward(self, query, mask=None):
        # Query is batch-first N, 1, H
        scores = self.score_function(query) # N, 1, L
        if mask is not None:
            scores = scores.masked_fill(mask == 0, -1e9)
        alphas = F.softmax(scores, dim=-1) # N, 1, L
        self.alphas = alphas.detach()

        # N, 1, L x N, L, H -> N, 1, H
        context = torch.bmm(alphas, self.values)
        return context
```

Model Configuration & Training

Model Configuration

```
torch.manual_seed(43)
encpe = EncoderPe(n_heads=3, d_model=2, ff_units=10, n_features=2)
decpe = DecoderPe(n_heads=3, d_model=2, ff_units=10, n_features=2)
model = EncoderDecoderSelfAttn(encpe, decpe,
                               input_len=2, target_len=2)
loss = nn.MSELoss()
optimizer = optim.Adam(model.parameters(), lr=0.01)
```

Model Training

```
sbs_seq_selfattnpe = StepByStep(model, loss, optimizer)
sbs_seq_selfattnpe.set_loaders(train_loader, test_loader)
sbs_seq_selfattnpe.train(100)
```

```
sbs_seq_selfattnpe.losses[-1], sbs_seq_selfattnpe.val_losses[-1]
```

Output

```
(0.016193246061448008, 0.034184777294285595)
```

Recap

In this chapter, we've introduced **sequence-to-sequence** problems and the **encoder-decoder architecture**. At first, we used **recurrent neural networks** to **encode a source sequence** so that its representation (hidden state) could be used to **generate the target sequence**. Then, we improved the architecture by using a **(cross-)attention mechanism** that allowed the **decoder** to use the **full sequence of hidden states** produced by the **encoder**. Next, we replaced the recurrent neural networks with **self-attention mechanisms**, which, although more efficient, cause the **loss of information** regarding the **order of the inputs**. Finally, the addition of **positional encoding** allowed us to account for the order of the inputs once again. This is what we've covered:

- generating a synthetic **dataset** of **source** and **target sequences**
- understanding the purpose of the **encoder-decoder architecture**
- using the **encoder** to generate a **representation of the source sequence**
- using **encoder's final hidden state** as the **decoder's initial hidden state**
- using the **decoder** to generate the **target sequence**
- using **teacher forcing** to help the decoder during **training**
- combining both encoder and decoder into a single **encoder-decoder model**
- understanding the **limitations** of using a **single hidden state** to encode the source sequence
- defining the **sequence of (transformed) hidden states** from the **encoder** as **"values" (V)**
- defining the **sequence of (transformed) hidden states** from the **encoder** as **"keys" (K)**
- defining **(transformed) hidden states** produced by the **decoder** as **"queries" (Q)**
- computing **similarities (alignment scores)** between a given **"query"** and **all the "keys"** using **scaled dot-product**
- visualizing the **geometric** interpretation of the **dot-product**

- **scaling the dot-product** according to the **number of dimensions** to keep its **variance constant**
- using **softmax** to transform similarities into **attention scores (alphas)**
- computing a **context vector** as an **average of "values" (V)** weighted by the corresponding **attention scores**
- **concatenating** the **context vector** to the **decoder's hidden state** and running it through a linear layer to get predictions
- building a class for the **attention mechanism**
- ignoring **padded data points** in the source sequence using a **mask**
- visualizing the attention scores
- combining **multiple attention heads** into a **multi-headed (wide) attention mechanism**
- learning the difference between **wide and narrow attention**
- using `nn.ModuleList` to add a **list of layers** as a model attribute
- replacing the recurrent layers with **(self-)attention mechanisms**; after all, **attention is all you need**
- understanding that, in **self-attention** mechanisms, **each data point** will be used to generate a **"value" (V)**, a **"key" (K)**, and a **"query" (Q)**, but they will still have distinct values because of the **different affine transformations**
- building an **encoder** using a **self-attention** mechanism and a simple **feed-forward network**
- realizing that **self-attention scores** are a **square matrix** since **every "hidden state" is a weighted average of all elements** in the input sequence
- reusing the attention mechanism as a **cross-attention mechanism**, such that the decoder still has access to the full sequence from the encoder
- understanding that **self-attention mechanisms leak future data**, thus allowing the **decoder to cheat**
- using a **target mask** to prevent the decoder from paying attention to "future" elements of the sequence
- building a **decoder** using a **(masked) self-attention** mechanism, a **cross-attention** mechanism, and a simple **feed-forward network**
- understanding that **self-attention** mechanisms **cannot** account for the

sequential order of the data

- figuring out that attention is not enough and that we also need **positional encoding** to incorporate sequential order back into the model
- using alternating **sines and cosines** of different frequencies as **positional encoding**
- learning that combining sines and cosines yields interesting properties, such as keeping **constant** the **encoded distance between any two positions** T steps apart
- using `register_buffer()` to add an attribute that should be part of the **module's state without being a parameter**
- visualizing self- and cross-attention scores

Congratulations! That was definitely an *intense* chapter. The **attention mechanism** in its different forms—single-head, multi-headed, **self-attention**, and cross-attention—is very flexible and built on top of fairly simple concepts, but the whole thing is definitely ***not* that easy** to grasp. Maybe you feel a bit *overwhelmed* by the huge amount of information and details involved in it, but don't worry. I guess everyone does feel like that at first; I know I did. It gets better with time!

The good thing is, you have already learned most of the techniques that make up the famous **Transformer** architecture: attention mechanisms, masks, and positional encoding. There are still a few things left to learn about it, like **layer normalization**, and we'll cover them all in the next chapter.

Transform and roll out!

[47] https://arxiv.org/abs/1706.03762

[48] https://machinelearningmastery.com/beam-search-decoder-natural-language-processing/

[49] https://towardsdatascience.com/illustrated-self-attention-2d627e33b20a

[50] https://pytorch.org/docs/stable/notes/randomness.html

[51] https://kazemnejad.com/blog/transformer_architecture_positional_encoding/

Chapter 10
Transform and Roll Out

Spoilers

In this chapter, we will:

- modify the **multi-headed attention** mechanism to use **narrow attention**
- use **layer normalization** to standardize individual data points
- **stack "layers"** together to build **Transformer encoders and decoders**
- add **layer normalization**, **dropout**, and **residual connections** to each "sub-layer" operation
- learn the difference between **norm-last** and **norm-first** "sub-layers"
- train a **Transformer** to predict a target sequence from a source sequence
- build and train a **Vision Transformer** to perform image classification

Jupyter Notebook

The Jupyter notebook corresponding to Chapter 10[52] is part of the official ***Deep Learning with PyTorch Step-by-Step*** repository on GitHub. You can also run it directly in **Google Colab**[53].

If you're using a *local installation*, open your terminal or Anaconda prompt and navigate to the `PyTorchStepByStep` folder you cloned from GitHub. Then, *activate* the `pytorchbook` environment and run `jupyter notebook`:

```
$ conda activate pytorchbook

(pytorchbook)$ jupyter notebook
```

If you're using Jupyter's default settings, `http://localhost:8888/notebooks/Chapter10.ipynb` should open Chapter 10's notebook. If not, just click on `Chapter10.ipynb` in your Jupyter's home page.

Imports

For the sake of organization, all libraries needed throughout the code used in any given chapter are imported at its very beginning. For this chapter, we'll need the following imports:

```
import copy
import numpy as np

import torch
import torch.optim as optim
import torch.nn as nn
import torch.nn.functional as F
from torch.utils.data import DataLoader, Dataset, random_split, \
    TensorDataset
from torchvision.transforms import Compose, Normalize, Pad

from data_generation.square_sequences import generate_sequences
from data_generation.image_classification import generate_dataset
from helpers import index_splitter, make_balanced_sampler
from stepbystep.v4 import StepByStep
# These are the classes we built in Chapter 9
from seq2seq import PositionalEncoding, subsequent_mask, \
    EncoderDecoderSelfAttn
```

Transform and Roll Out

We're actually **quite close** to developing our own version of the famous **Transformer** model. The **encoder-decoder architecture with positional encoding** is missing only a few details to effectively "*transform and roll out*" :-)

"*What's missing?*"

First, we need to revisit the **multi-headed attention** mechanism to make it less computationally expensive by using **narrow attention**. Then, we'll learn about a new kind of normalization: **layer normalization**. Finally, we'll add some more bells and whistles: **dropout**, **residual connections**, and **more "layers"** (like the encoder and decoder "layers" from the last chapter).

Narrow Attention

In the last chapter, we used *full* attention heads to build a **multi-headed attention** and we called it **wide attention**. Although this mechanism works well, it gets prohibitively expensive as the number of dimensions grows. That's when the **narrow attention** comes in: Each **attention head** will get a **chunk** of the **transformed data points (projections)** to work with.

Chunking

This is a detail of **utmost importance**: The attention heads **do not** use **chunks of the original data points**, but rather those of their projections.

"*Why?*"

To understand why, let's take an example of an **affine transformation**, one that generates **"values"** (v_0) from the first data point (x_0).

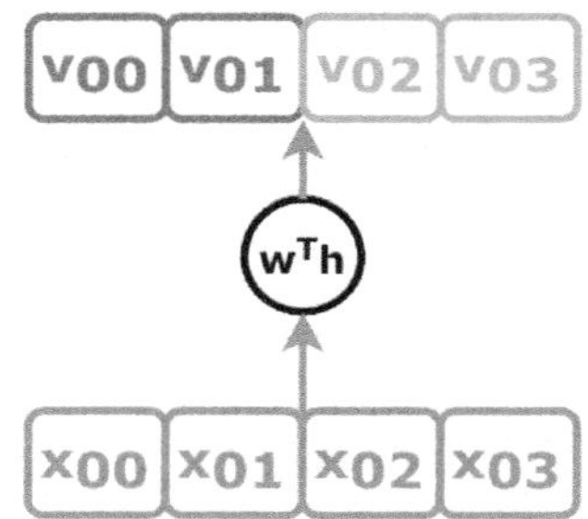

Figure 10.1 - Narrow attention

The transformation above takes a single **data point** of **four dimensions** (features) and turns it into a **"value"** (also with four dimensions) that's going to be used in the **attention mechanism**.

At first sight, it *may* look like we'll get the *same* result whether we *split the inputs into chunks* or we *split the projections into chunks*. But that's definitely **not** the case. So, let's **zoom in** and look at the **individual weights** inside that transformation.

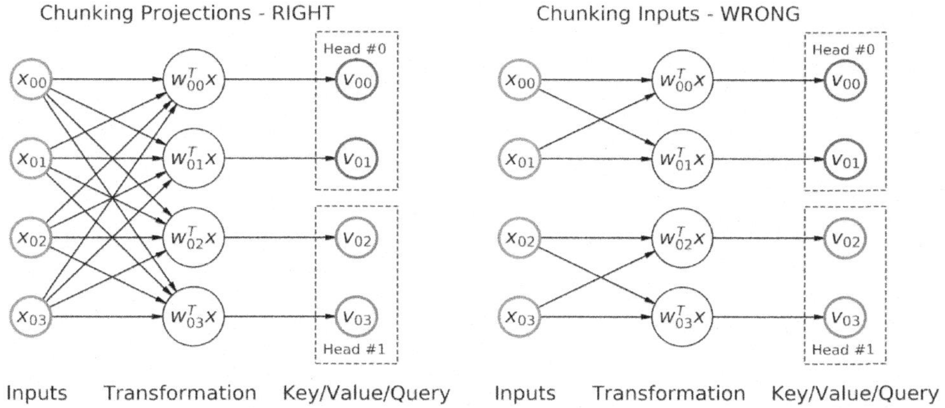

Figure 10.2 - Chunking: the wrong and the right way

On the left, the **correct approach**: It computes the **projections first** and **chunks them later**. It is clear that **each value in the projection** (from $\mathbf{v}_{00}$ to $\mathbf{v}_{03}$) is a **linear combination** of **all features** in the data point.

Since **each head** is working with a **subset of the projected dimensions**, these projected dimensions **may** end up representing **different aspects of the underlying data**. For natural language processing tasks, for example, some attention heads may correspond to linguistic notions of syntax and coherence. A particular head may attend to the **direct objects of verbs**, while another head may attend to **objects of prepositions**, and so on.[54]

Now, compare it to the **wrong approach**, on the right: By **chunking it first**, each value in the projection is a linear combination of **a subset of the features only**.

"Why is it so bad?"

First, it is a *simpler* model (the wrong approach has only *eight weights* while the correct one has *sixteen*), so its learning capacity is limited. Second, since each head can only look at a **subset of the features**, they simply **cannot learn** about **long-range dependencies** in the inputs.

Now, let's use a **source sequence** of **length two** as input, with each data point having **four features** like the chunking example above, to illustrate our new **self-attention** mechanism.

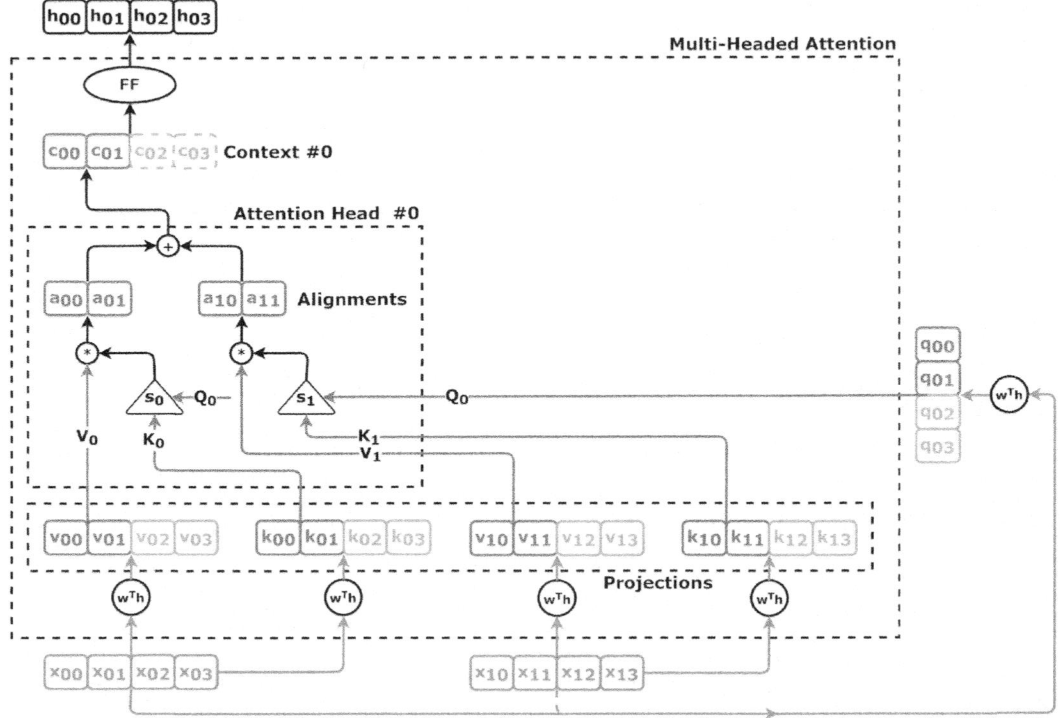

Figure 10.3 - Self-(narrow)attention mechanism

The flow of information goes like this:

- Both **data points** (x_0 and x_1) go through **distinct affine transformations** to generate the corresponding **"values"** (v_0 and v_1) and **"keys"** (k_0 and k_1), which we'll be calling **projections**.
- Both data points also go through **another affine transformation** to generate the corresponding **"queries"** (q_0 and q_1), but we'll be focusing on only the **first query** (q_0) now.
- Each **projection** has the same number of **dimensions** as the **inputs** (four).
- Instead of simply using the projections, as former attention heads did, this attention head uses **only a chunk of the projections** to compute the **context vector**.
- Since projections have four dimensions, let's split them into **two chunks**—blue (left) and green (right)—of **two dimensions each**.
- The **first attention head** uses **only blue chunks** to compute its **context vector**, which, like the projections, has **only two dimensions**.
- The **second attention head** (not depicted in the figure above) uses the **green**

chunks to compute the **other half** of the **context vector**, which, in the end, has the desired dimension.

- Like the former multi-headed attention mechanism, the **context vector** goes through a **feed-forward network** to generate the **"hidden states"** (only the first one is depicted in the figure above).

It *looks* complicated, I know, but it really isn't *that* bad. Maybe it helps to see it in code.

Multi-Headed Attention

The new multi-headed attention class is more than a combination of both the `Attention` and `MultiHeadedAttention` classes from the previous chapter: It implements the *chunking* of the projections and introduces **dropout for attention scores.**

Multi-Headed Attention

```
class MultiHeadedAttention(nn.Module):
    def __init__(self, n_heads, d_model, dropout=0.1):
        super(MultiHeadedAttention, self).__init__()
        self.n_heads = n_heads
        self.d_model = d_model
        self.d_k = int(d_model / n_heads)                       ①
        self.linear_query = nn.Linear(d_model, d_model)
        self.linear_key = nn.Linear(d_model, d_model)
        self.linear_value = nn.Linear(d_model, d_model)
        self.linear_out = nn.Linear(d_model, d_model)
        self.dropout = nn.Dropout(p=dropout)                    ④
        self.alphas = None

    def make_chunks(self, x):                                   ①
        batch_size, seq_len = x.size(0), x.size(1)
        # N, L, D -> N, L, n_heads * d_k
        x = x.view(batch_size, seq_len, self.n_heads, self.d_k)
        # N, n_heads, L, d_k
        x = x.transpose(1, 2)
        return x

    def init_keys(self, key):
        # N, n_heads, L, d_k
        self.proj_key = self.make_chunks(self.linear_key(key)) ①
```

```
        self.proj_value = \
            self.make_chunks(self.linear_value(key))        ①

    def score_function(self, query):
        # Scaled dot product
        proj_query = self.make_chunks(self.linear_query(query))①
        # N, n_heads, L, d_k x N, n_heads, d_k, L ->
        # N, n_heads, L, L
        dot_products = torch.matmul(                        ②
            proj_query, self.proj_key.transpose(-2, -1)
        )
        scores =  dot_products / np.sqrt(self.d_k)
        return scores

    def attn(self, query, mask=None):                       ③
        # Query is batch-first: N, L, D
        # Score function will generate scores for each head
        scores = self.score_function(query) # N, n_heads, L, L
        if mask is not None:
            scores = scores.masked_fill(mask == 0, -1e9)
        alphas = F.softmax(scores, dim=-1) # N, n_heads, L, L

        alphas = self.dropout(alphas)                       ④
        self.alphas = alphas.detach()

        # N, n_heads, L, L x N, n_heads, L, d_k ->
        # N, n_heads, L, d_k
        context = torch.matmul(alphas, self.proj_value)     ②
        return context

    def output_function(self, contexts):
        # N, L, D
        out = self.linear_out(contexts) # N, L, D
        return out

    def forward(self, query, mask=None):
        if mask is not None:
            # N, 1, L, L - every head uses the same mask
            mask = mask.unsqueeze(1)

        # N, n_heads, L, d_k
        context = self.attn(query, mask=mask)
```

```
        # N, L, n_heads, d_k
        context = context.transpose(1, 2).contiguous()          ⑤
        # N, L, n_heads * d_k = N, L, d_model
        context = context.view(query.size(0), -1, self.d_model)⑤
        # N, L, d_model
        out = self.output_function(context)
        return out
```

① Chunking the projections

② Using `torch.matmul()` instead of `torch.bmm()`

③ Former `forward()` method of `Attention` class

④ Dropout for the attention scores

⑤ "Concatenating" the context vectors

Let's go over its methods:

- `make_chunks()`: It takes a tensor of shape (N, L, D) and splits its last dimension in two, resulting in a **(N, L, n_heads, d_k)** shape where **d_k** is the size of the chunk (**d_k = D / n_heads**).
- `init_keys()`: It makes projections for "keys" and "values," and *chunks* them.
- `score_function()`: It *chunks* the projected "queries" and computes the **scaled dot product** (it uses `torch.matmul()` as a replacement for `torch.bmm()` because there is **one extra dimension** due to *chunking*; see the aside below for more details).
- `attn()`: It corresponds to the `forward()` method of the former `Attention` class, and it computes the **attention scores** (*alphas*) and the **chunks of the context vector**.
    - It uses **dropout** on the attention scores for regularization: Dropping an attention score (zeroing it) means that the corresponding **element** in the sequence will be **ignored**.
- `output_function()`: It simply runs the contexts through the feed-forward network since the concatenation of the contexts is going to happen in the `forward()` method now.
- `forward()`: It calls the `attn()` method and **reorganizes the dimensions** of the result to **"concatenate" the chunks** of the **context vector**.

- If a `mask` is provided—(N, 1, L) shape for the source mask (in the encoder) or (N, L, L) shape for the target mask (in the decoder)—it *unsqueezes* a new dimension after the first one to accommodate the **multiple heads** since every head should use the **same mask**.

`torch.bmm()` vs `torch.matmul()`

In the last chapter, we used `torch.bmm()` to perform **batch matrix multiplication**. It was the right tool for the task at hand since we had **two three-dimensional tensors** (for example, computing the context vector using *alphas* and "values"):

$$(N, 1, L) \times (N, L, H) = (N, 1, H)$$

Equation 10.1 - Batch matrix multiplication using `torch.bmm()`

Unfortunately, `torch.bmm()` **cannot** handle tensors with more dimensions than that. Since we have a **four-dimensional tensor** after **chunking**, we need something more powerful: `torch.matmul()`. It is a **more generic** operation that, depending on its inputs, behaves like `torch.dot()`, `torch.mm()`, or `torch.bmm()`.

If we're using `torch.matmul()` to multiply *alphas* and "values" again, while using multiple heads and chunking, it looks like this:

$$(N, n\_heads, L, L) \times (N, n\_heads, L, d_k) = (N, n\_heads, L, d_k)$$

Equation 10.2 - Batch matrix multiplication using `torch.matmul()`

It is quite similar to batch matrix multiplication, but you're free to have as many extra dimensions as you want: It still looks at the **last two dimensions** only.

We can generate some *dummy points* corresponding to a mini-batch of **16 sequences (N)**, each sequence having **two data points (L)**, each data point having **four features (F)**:

```
dummy_points = torch.randn(16, 2, 4) # N, L, F
mha = MultiHeadedAttention(n_heads=2, d_model=4, dropout=0.0)
mha.init_keys(dummy_points)
out = mha(dummy_points) # N, L, D
out.shape
```

Output

```
torch.Size([16, 2, 4])
```

Since we're using the data points as "keys," "values," and "queries," this is a **self-attention** mechanism.

The figure below depicts a multi-headed attention mechanism with its **two heads**, **blue (left)** and **green (right)**, and the **first data point** being used as a **"query"** to generate the first "hidden state" (h_0).

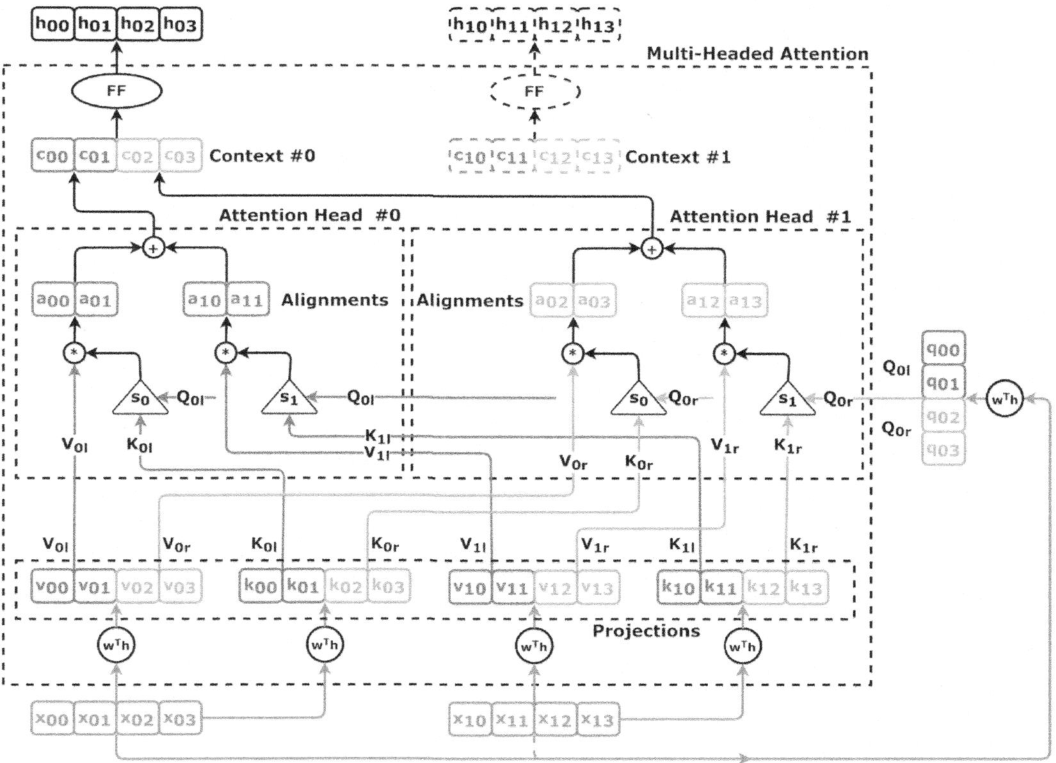

Figure 10.4 - Self-(narrow)attention mechanism (both heads)

To help you out (especially if you're seeing it in black and white), I've **labeled the**

arrows with their corresponding **role (V, K, or Q)** followed by a **subscript** indicating both the **index of the data point** being used **(zero or one)** and **which head** is using it **(left or right)**.

If you find the figure above too confusing, don't sweat it; I've included it for the sake of *completion* since Figure 10.3 depicted only the first head. The important thing to remember here is: "***Multi-headed attention chunks the projections, not the inputs.***"

Let's move on to the next topic...

Stacking Encoders and Decoders

Let's make our encoder-decoder architecture **deeper** by **stacking two encoders** on top of one another, and then do the same with **two decoders**. It looks like this.

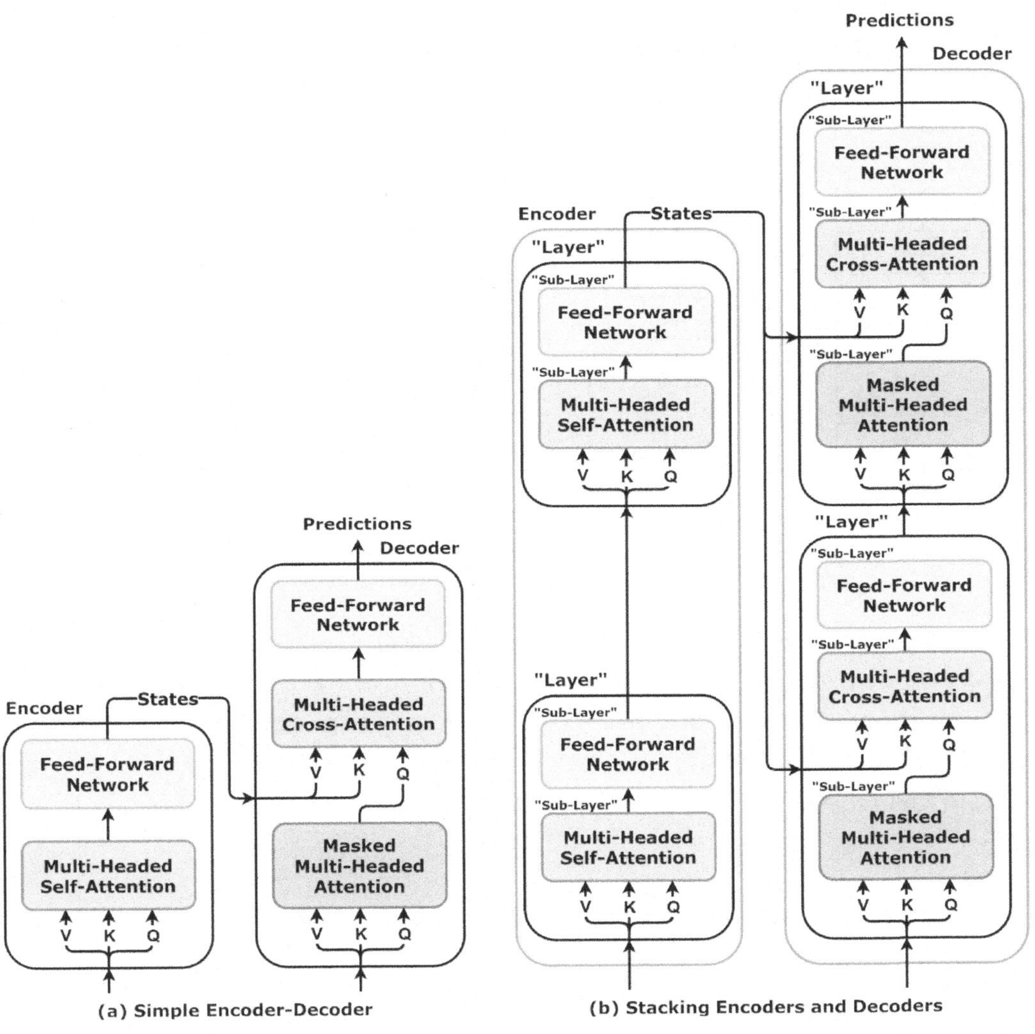

Figure 10.5 - Stacking encoders and decoders

The output of one encoder feeds the next, and the last encoder outputs **states** as usual. These states will feed the **cross-attention** mechanism of **all stacked decoders**. The output of one decoder feeds the next, and the last decoder outputs **predictions** as usual.

The **former encoder** is now a so-called **"layer"**, and a **stack of "layers"** composes the **new, deeper encoder**. The same holds true for the **decoder**. Moreover, **each operation** (multi-headed self- and cross-attention mechanisms, and feed-forward networks) inside a "layer" is now a **"sub-layer."**

The figure above represents an encoder-decoder architecture with **two "layers"** each. But we're *not* stopping there: We're stacking **six "layers"**! It would be *somewhat* hard to draw a diagram for it, so we're simplifying it a bit.

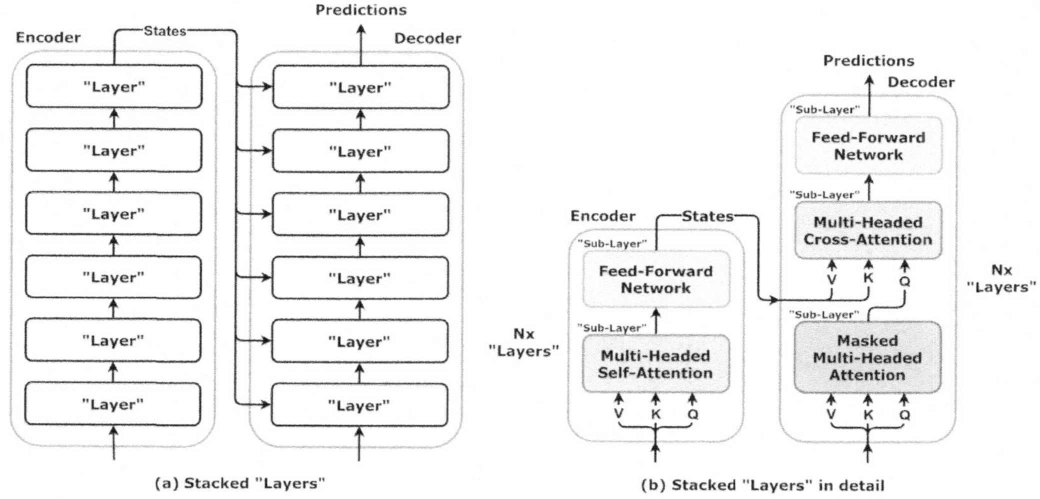

Figure 10.6 - Stacked "layers"

On the one hand, we could simply draw both *stacks of "layers"* and abstract away their inner operations. That's the diagram **(a)** in the figure above. On the other hand, since **all "layers" are identical**, we can **keep representing the inner operations** and just *hint* at the **stack** by adding *"Nx "Layers""* next to it. That's diagram **(b)** in the figure above, and it will be our representation of choice from now on.

By the way, that's exactly how a **Transformer** is built!

"Cool! Is this a Transformer already then?"

Not yet, no. We need to work further on the **"sub-layers"** to **transform** (ahem!) the architecture above into a real **Transformer**.

Wrapping "Sub-Layers"

As our model grows **deeper**, with many **stacked "layers,"** we're going to run into familiar issues, like the vanishing gradients problem. In computer vision models, this issue was successfully addressed by the addition of other components, like **batch normalization** and **residual connections**. Moreover, we know that ...

"... *with great depth comes great complexity* ..."

Peter Parker

...and, along with that, overfitting.

But we *also* know that **dropout** works pretty well as a **regularizer**, so we can throw that in the mix as well.

"*How are we adding normalization, residual connections, and dropout to our model?*"

We'll **wrap each and every "sub-layer"** with them! Cool, right? But that brings up *another* question: **How** to wrap them? It turns out, we can wrap a "sub-layer" in one of two ways: **norm-last** or **norm-first**.

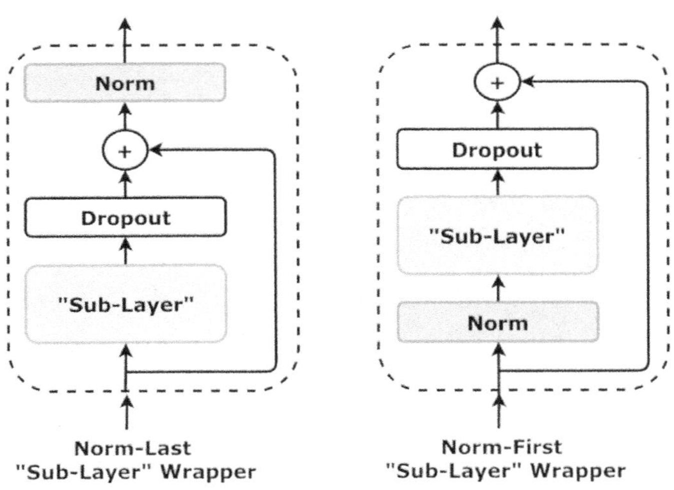

Figure 10.7 - "Sub-Layers"—norm-last vs norm-first

The **norm-last** wrapper follows the "Attention Is All you Need"[55] paper to the letter:

> "*We employ a residual connection around each of the two sub-layers, followed by layer normalization. That is, the output of each sub-layer is* `LayerNorm(x+Sublayer(x))`, *where* `Sublayer(x)` *is the function implemented by the sub-layer itself.*"

The **norm-first** wrapper follows the "sub-layer" implementation described in "The Annotated Transformer,"[56] which **explicitly** places **norm first** as opposed to last for the sake of code simplicity.

Let's turn the diagrams above into equations:

$$
\begin{aligned}
\text{outputs}_{\text{norm-last}} &= \text{norm}(\text{inputs} + \text{dropout}(\text{sublayer}(\text{inputs}))) \\
\text{outputs}_{\text{norm-first}} &= \text{inputs} + \text{dropout}(\text{sublayer}(\text{norm}(\text{inputs})))
\end{aligned}
$$

Equation 10.3 - Outputs—norm-first vs norm-last

The equations are **almost** the same, except for the fact that the **norm-last** wrapper (from "Attention Is All You Need") **normalizes the outputs** and the **norm-first** wrapper (from "The Annotated Transformer") **normalizes the inputs**. That's a **small, yet important, difference**.

"Why?"

If you're using **positional encoding**, you *want* to **normalize your inputs**, so **norm-first** is more convenient.

"What about the outputs?"

We'll **normalize the *final* outputs**; that is, the output of **the last "layer"** (which is the output of its last, not normalized, "sub-layer"). Any intermediate output is simply the input of the subsequent "sub-layer," and each "sub-layer" normalizes its own inputs.

There is *another* important difference that will be discussed in the next section.

From now on, we're **sticking with norm-first**, thus **normalizing the inputs**:

$$
\text{outputs}_{\text{norm-first}} = \text{inputs} + \text{dropout}(\text{sublayer}(\text{norm}(\text{inputs})))
$$

Equation 10.4 - Outputs—norm-first

By **wrapping each and every "sub-layer"** inside both **encoder "layers"** and **decoder "layers,"** we'll arrive at the desired **Transformer architecture**.

Let's start with the…

Transformer Encoder

We'll be representing the encoder using "stacked" layers in detail (like Figure 10.6 (*b*)); that is, showing the internal **wrapped "sub-layers"** (the dashed rectangles).

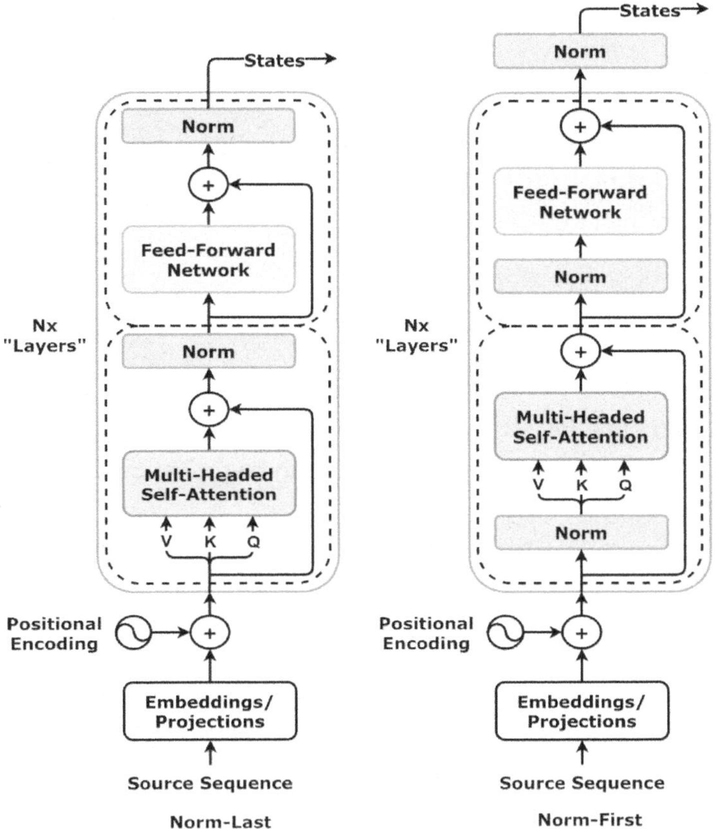

Figure 10.8 - Transformer encoder—norm-last vs norm-first

On the left, the encoder uses a *norm-last wrapper*, and its output (the encoder's **states**) is given by:

$$\text{outputs}_{\text{norm-last}} = \text{norm}(\underbrace{\text{norm}(\text{inputs} + \text{att}(\text{inputs}))}_{\text{Output of SubLayer}_0} + \text{ffn}(\underbrace{\text{norm}(\text{inputs} + \text{att}(\text{inputs}))}_{\text{Output of SubLayer}_0}))$$

Equation 10.5 - Encoder's output: norm-last

On the right, the encoder uses a *norm-first wrapper*, and its output (the encoder's **states**) is given by:

$$\text{outputs}_{\text{norm-first}} = \underbrace{\text{inputs} + \text{att}(\text{norm}(\text{inputs}))}_{\text{Output of SubLayer}_0} + \text{ffn}(\text{norm}(\underbrace{\text{inputs} + \text{att}(\text{norm}(\text{inputs}))}_{\text{Output of SubLayer}_0}))$$

Equation 10.6 - Encoder's output: norm-first

The **norm-first wrapper** allows the **inputs to flow unimpeded** (the inputs aren't normalized) all the way to the top while adding the results of each "sub-layer" along the way (the *last* normalization of *norm-first* happens outside of the "sub-layers," so it's not included in the equation).

"Which one is best?"

There is no straight answer to this question. It actually reminds me of the discussions about placing the batch normalization layer *before* or *after* the activation function. Now, once again, there is no "right" and "wrong," and the order of the different components is not etched in stone.

In PyTorch, the encoder "layer" is implemented as `nn.TransformerEncoderLayer`, and its constructor method expects the following arguments (`d_model`, `nhead`, `dim_feedforward`, and `dropout`) and an optional `activation` function for the feed-forward network, similar to our own `EncoderLayer`. Its `forward()` method, though, has **three arguments**:

- `src`: the **source sequence**; that's the `query` argument in our class

IMPORTANT: PyTorch's **Transformer layers** use **sequence-first** shapes for their inputs (L, N, F), and there is **no batch-first option**.

- `src_key_padding_mask`: the mask for **padded data points**; that's the `mask` argument in our class
- `src_mask`: This mask is used to **purposefully hide some of the inputs** in the source sequence—we're not doing that, so our class doesn't have a corresponding argument—a technique that can be used for training **language models** (more on that in Chapter 11).

Let's see it in code, starting with the "layer," and all its wrapped "sub-layers":

Encoder "Layer"

```
class EncoderLayer(nn.Module):
    def __init__(self, n_heads, d_model, ff_units, dropout=0.1):
        super().__init__()
        self.n_heads = n_heads
        self.d_model = d_model
        self.ff_units = ff_units
        self.self_attn_heads = \
            MultiHeadedAttention(n_heads, d_model, dropout)
        self.ffn = nn.Sequential(
            nn.Linear(d_model, ff_units),
            nn.ReLU(),
            nn.Dropout(dropout),
            nn.Linear(ff_units, d_model),
        )

        self.norm1 = nn.LayerNorm(d_model)  ①
        self.norm2 = nn.LayerNorm(d_model)  ①
        self.drop1 = nn.Dropout(dropout)
        self.drop2 = nn.Dropout(dropout)

    def forward(self, query, mask=None):
        # Sublayer #0
        # Norm
        norm_query = self.norm1(query)
        # Multi-headed Attention
        self.self_attn_heads.init_keys(norm_query)
        states = self.self_attn_heads(norm_query, mask)
        # Add
        att = query + self.drop1(states)

        # Sublayer #1
        # Norm
        norm_att = self.norm2(att)
        # Feed Forward
        out = self.ffn(norm_att)
        # Add
        out = att + self.drop2(out)
        return out
```

① What is that?

Its constructor takes **four arguments**:

- `n_heads`: the number of **attention heads** in the **self-attention mechanism**
- `d_model`: the **number of (projected) features**, that is, the **dimensionality of the model** (remember, this number will be *split* among the attention heads, so it must be a multiple of the number of heads)
- `ff_units`: the number of **units** in the **hidden layer** of the **feed-forward network**
- `dropout`: the **probability** of dropping out inputs

The `forward()` method takes a "query" and a source mask (to ignore padded data points) as usual.

"*What is that* `nn.LayerNorm`*?*"

It is one *teeny-tiny detail* I haven't mentioned before: Transformers do not use *batch normalization*, but rather **layer normalization**.

"*What's the difference?*"

Short answer: Batch normalization *normalizes features*, while **layer normalization normalizes data points**. Long answer: There is a *whole section* on it; we'll get back to it soon enough.

Now we can stack a bunch of "layers" like that to build an **actual encoder** (`EncoderTransf`). Its constructor takes an **instance of an `EncoderLayer`**, the **number of "layers"** we'd like to stack on top of one another, and a **max length** of the source sequence that's going to be used for the positional encoding.

We're using `deepcopy()` to make sure we create *real copies* of the encoder layer, and `nn.ModuleList` to make sure PyTorch can find the "layers" inside the list. Our *default* for the number of "layers" is only one, but the **original Transformer uses six**.

The `forward()` method is quite straightforward (I was actually missing making puns): It adds positional encoding to the "query," loops over the "layers," and normalizes the outputs in the end. The final outputs are, as usual, the **states of the encoder** that will feed the **cross-attention mechanism** of **every "layer"** of the **decoder**.

```
class EncoderTransf(nn.Module):
    def __init__(self, encoder_layer, n_layers=1, max_len=100):
        super().__init__()
        self.d_model = encoder_layer.d_model
        self.pe = PositionalEncoding(max_len, self.d_model)
        self.norm = nn.LayerNorm(self.d_model)
        self.layers = nn.ModuleList([copy.deepcopy(encoder_layer)
                                     for _ in range(n_layers)])

    def forward(self, query, mask=None):
        # Positional Encoding
        x = self.pe(query)
        for layer in self.layers:
            x = layer(x, mask)
        # Norm
        return self.norm(x)
```

In PyTorch, the encoder is implemented as `nn.TransformerEncoder`, and its constructor method expects similar arguments: `encoder_layer`, `num_layers`, and an optional normalization layer to normalize (or not) the outputs.

```
enclayer = nn.TransformerEncoderLayer(
    d_model=6, nhead=3, dim_feedforward=20
)
enctransf = nn.TransformerEncoder(
    enclayer, num_layers=1, norm=nn.LayerNorm
)
```

Therefore, it behaves a bit *differently* than ours, since it **does not** (at the time of writing) implement **positional encoding** for the inputs, and it does not normalize the outputs by default.

Transformer Decoder

We'll be representing the decoder using "stacked" layers in detail (like Figure 10.6 (*b*)); that is, showing the internal **wrapped "sub-layers"** (the dashed rectangles).

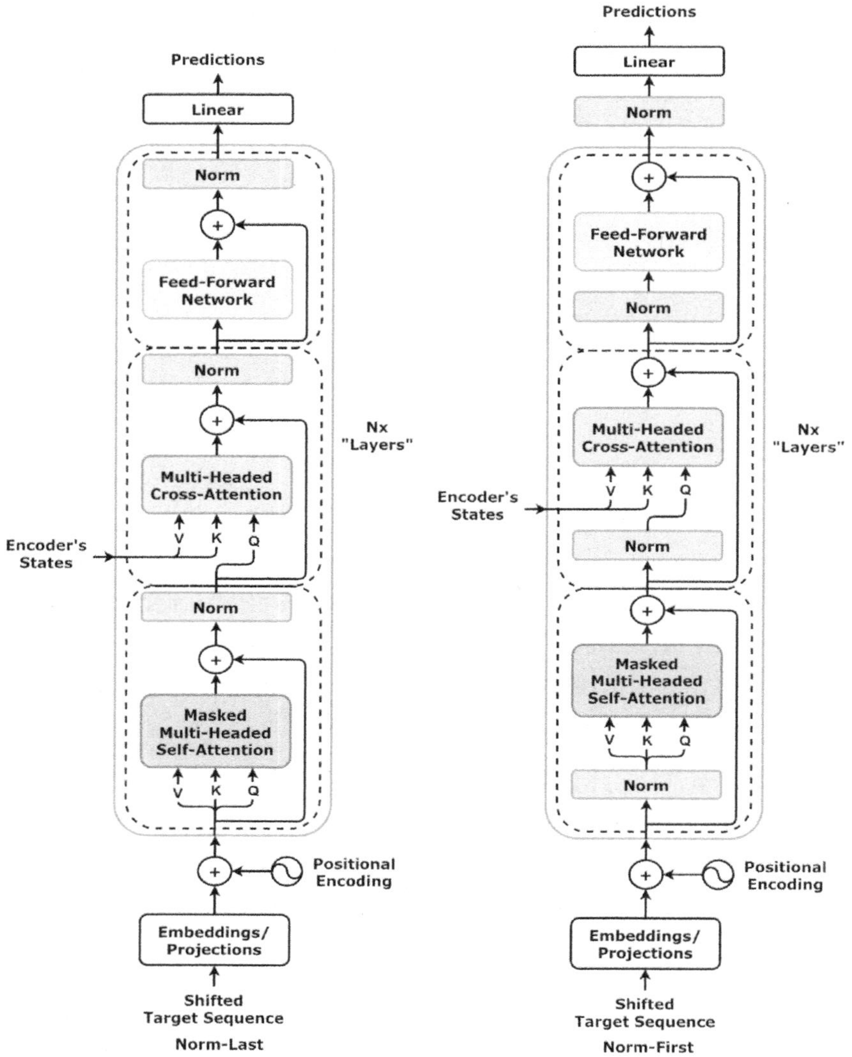

Figure 10.9 - Transformer decoder—norm-last vs norm-first

The **small arrow** on the left represents the **states** produced by the **encoder**, which will be used as inputs for "keys" and "values" of the **(cross-)multi-headed attention** mechanism in **each "layer."**

Moreover, there is **one final linear layer** responsible for projecting the decoder's output back to the original number of dimensions (corner's coordinates, in our case). This linear layer is *not* included in our decoder's class, though: It will be part of the encoder-decoder (or Transformer) class.

Let's see it in code, starting with the "layer" and all its wrapped "sub-layers." By the way, the code below is remarkably similar to that of the `EncoderLayer`, except for the fact that it has a third "sub-layer" (cross-attention) in between the other two.

Decoder "Layer"

```
class DecoderLayer(nn.Module):
    def __init__(self, n_heads, d_model, ff_units, dropout=0.1):
        super().__init__()
        self.n_heads = n_heads
        self.d_model = d_model
        self.ff_units = ff_units
        self.self_attn_heads = \
            MultiHeadedAttention(n_heads, d_model, dropout)
        self.cross_attn_heads = \
            MultiHeadedAttention(n_heads, d_model, dropout)
        self.ffn = nn.Sequential(
            nn.Linear(d_model, ff_units),
            nn.ReLU(),
            nn.Dropout(dropout),
            nn.Linear(ff_units, d_model),
        )

        self.norm1 = nn.LayerNorm(d_model)
        self.norm2 = nn.LayerNorm(d_model)
        self.norm3 = nn.LayerNorm(d_model)
        self.drop1 = nn.Dropout(dropout)
        self.drop2 = nn.Dropout(dropout)
        self.drop3 = nn.Dropout(dropout)

    def init_keys(self, states):
        self.cross_attn_heads.init_keys(states)

    def forward(self, query, source_mask=None, target_mask=None):
        # Sublayer #0
        # Norm
        norm_query = self.norm1(query)
        # Masked Multi-head Attention
        self.self_attn_heads.init_keys(norm_query)
        states = self.self_attn_heads(norm_query, target_mask)
        # Add
```

```python
        att1 = query + self.drop1(states)

        # Sublayer #1
        # Norm
        norm_att1 = self.norm2(att1)
        # Multi-head Attention
        encoder_states = self.cross_attn_heads(norm_att1,
                                               source_mask)
        # Add
        att2 = att1 + self.drop2(encoder_states)

        # Sublayer #2
        # Norm
        norm_att2 = self.norm3(att2)
        # Feed Forward
        out = self.ffn(norm_att2)
        # Add
        out = att2 + self.drop3(out)
        return out
```

The constructor method of the **decoder "layer"** takes the **same arguments** as the **encoder "layer"** does. The `forward()` method takes three arguments: the "query," the **source mask** that's going to be used to ignore padded data points in the source sequence during **cross-attention**, and the **target mask** used to **avoid cheating** by peeking into the future.

In PyTorch, the decoder "layer" is implemented as `nn.TransformerDecoderLayer`, and its constructor method expects the following arguments (`d_model`, `nhead`, `dim_feedforward`, and `dropout`) and an optional `activation` function for the feed-forward network.

Its `forward()` method, though, has **six arguments**. Three of them are equivalent to those arguments in our own `forward()` method:

- `tgt`: the **target sequence**; that's the `query` argument in our class (required)

IMPORTANT: PyTorch's **Transformer layers** use **sequence-first** shapes for their inputs (L, N, F), and there is **no batch-first option**.

- `memory_key_padding_mask`: the mask for **padded data points** in the **source sequence**; that's the `source_mask` argument in our class (optional), and the same as the `src_key_padding_mask` of `nn.TransformerEncoderLayer`
- `tgt_mask`: the mask used to **avoid cheating**; that's the `target_mask` argument in our class (although quite important, this argument is still considered *optional*)

Then, there is the **other required argument**, which corresponds to the `states` argument of the `init_keys()` method in our own class:

- `memory`: the **encoded states** of the **source sequence** as returned by the **encoder**

The remaining two arguments *do not exist* in our own class:

- `memory_mask`: This mask is used to **purposefully hide some of the encoded states** used by the decoder.
- `tgt_key_padding_mask`: This mask is used for **padded data points** in the **target sequence**.

Now we can stack a bunch of "layers" like that to build an **actual decoder**:

Transformer Decoder

```
class DecoderTransf(nn.Module):
    def __init__(self, decoder_layer, n_layers=1, max_len=100):
        super(DecoderTransf, self).__init__()
        self.d_model = decoder_layer.d_model
        self.pe = PositionalEncoding(max_len, self.d_model)
        self.norm = nn.LayerNorm(self.d_model)
        self.layers = nn.ModuleList([copy.deepcopy(decoder_layer)
                                     for _ in range(n_layers)])

    def init_keys(self, states):
        for layer in self.layers:
            layer.init_keys(states)

    def forward(self, query, source_mask=None, target_mask=None):
        # Positional Encoding
        x = self.pe(query)
        for layer in self.layers:
            x = layer(x, source_mask, target_mask)
        # Norm
        return self.norm(x)
```

Its constructor takes an **instance of a `DecoderLayer`**, the **number of "layers"** we'd like to stack on top of one another, and a **max length** of the source sequence that's going to be used for the positional encoding. Once again, we're using `deepcopy()` and `nn.ModuleList` to create multiple "layers".

In PyTorch, the decoder is implemented as `nn.TransformerDecoder`, and its constructor method expects similar arguments: `decoder_layer`, `num_layers`, and an optional normalization layer to normalize (or not) the outputs.

```
declayer = nn.TransformerDecoderLayer(
    d_model=6, nhead=3, dim_feedforward=20
)
dectransf = nn.TransformerDecoder(
    declayer, num_layers=1, norm=nn.LayerNorm
)
```

PyTorch's decoder also behaves a bit *differently* than ours, since it **does not** (at the time of writing) implement **positional encoding** for the inputs, and it does not normalize the outputs by default.

Before putting the **encoder** and the **decoder** together, we still have to make a short pit-stop and address that *teeny-tiny detail…*

Layer Normalization

Layer normalization was introduced by Jimmy Lei Ba, Jamie Ryan Kiros, and Geoffrey E. Hinton in their 2016 paper "Layer Normalization,"[57] but it only got *really* popular after being used in the hugely successful *Transformer* architecture. They say: "*…we transpose batch normalization into layer normalization by computing the mean and variance used for normalization from all of the summed inputs to the neurons in a layer on a* ***single training case***" (the highlight is mine).

Simply put: Layer normalization **standardizes individual data points**, not features.

This is completely different than other typical standardizations where each **feature** is standardized to have **zero mean** and **unit standard deviation** (either in the whole training set using Scikit-learn's `StandardScaler`, or in a mini-batch using *batch norm*). In a tabular dataset, we **standardized the columns**.

Layer normalization, in a tabular dataset, **standardizes the rows.** Each data point will have **the average of its features equal zero,** and the **standard deviation of its features will equal one.**

Let's assume we have a *mini-batch* of three sequences *(N=3)*, each sequence having a *length* of two *(L=2)*, each data point having four *features (D=4)*, and, to illustrate the importance of layer normalization, let's add **positional encoding** to it too:

```
d_model = 4
seq_len = 2
n_points = 3

torch.manual_seed(34)
data = torch.randn(n_points, seq_len, d_model)
pe = PositionalEncoding(seq_len, d_model)
inputs = pe(data)
inputs
```

Output

```
tensor([[[-3.8049,  1.9899, -1.7325,  2.1359],
         [ 1.7854,  0.8155,  0.1116, -1.7420]],

        [[-2.4273,  1.3559,  2.8615,  2.0084],
         [-1.0353, -1.2766, -2.2082, -0.6952]],

        [[-0.8044,  1.9707,  3.3704,  2.0587],
         [ 4.2256,  6.9575,  1.4770,  2.0762]]])
```

It should be straightforward to identify the different dimensions, *N* (three vertical groups), *L* (two rows in each group), and *D* (four columns), in the tensor above. There are **six data points** in total, and their value range is mostly the result of the addition of positional encoding.

Well, **layer normalization standardizes individual data points**, the *rows* in the tensor above, so we need to **compute statistics over the corresponding dimension (D)**. Let's start with the **means**:

$$\overline{X}_{n,l} = \frac{1}{D}\sum_{d=1}^{D} x_{n,l,d}$$

Equation 10.7 - Data points' means over features (D)

```
inputs_mean = inputs.mean(axis=2).unsqueeze(2)
inputs_mean
```

Output

```
tensor([[[-0.3529],
         [ 0.2426]],

        [[ 0.9496],
         [-1.3038]],

        [[ 1.6489],
         [ 3.6841]]])
```

As expected, **six mean values**, one for each data point. The `unsqueeze()` is there to preserve the original dimensionality, thus making the result a tensor of (N, L, 1) shape.

Next, we compute the *biased standard deviations* over the same dimension (D):

$$\sigma_{n,l}(X) = \sqrt{\frac{1}{D}\sum_{d=1}^{D}(x_{n,l,d} - \overline{X}_{n,l})^2}$$

Equation 10.8 - Data points' standard deviations over features (D)

```
inputs_var = inputs.var(axis=2, unbiased=False).unsqueeze(2)
inputs_var
```

Output

```
tensor([[[6.3756],
         [1.6661]],

        [[4.0862],
         [0.3153]],

        [[2.3135],
         [4.6163]]])
```

No surprises here.

The **actual standardization** is then computed using the *mean*, *biased standard deviation*, and a tiny *epsilon* to guarantee numerical stability:

$$\text{standardized } x_{n,l,d} = \frac{x_{n,l,d} - \overline{X}_{n,l}}{\sigma_{n,l}(X) + \epsilon}$$

Equation 10.9 - Layer normalization

```
(inputs - inputs_mean)/torch.sqrt(inputs_var+1e-5)
```

Output

```
tensor([[[-1.3671,  0.9279, -0.5464,  0.9857],
         [ 1.1953,  0.4438, -0.1015, -1.5376]],

        [[-1.6706,  0.2010,  0.9458,  0.5238],
         [ 0.4782,  0.0485, -1.6106,  1.0839]],

        [[-1.6129,  0.2116,  1.1318,  0.2695],
         [ 0.2520,  1.5236, -1.0272, -0.7484]]])
```

The values above are **layer normalized**. It is possible to achieve the very same results by using PyTorch's own `nn.LayerNorm`, of course:

```
layer_norm = nn.LayerNorm(d_model)
normalized = layer_norm(inputs)

normalized[0][0].mean(), normalized[0][0].std(unbiased=False)
```

Output

```
(tensor(-1.4901e-08, grad_fn=<MeanBackward0>),
 tensor(1.0000, grad_fn=<StdBackward0>))
```

Zero mean and unit standard deviation, as expected.

"*Why do they have a* `grad_fn` *attribute?*"

Like *batch normalization*, **layer normalization** can **learn affine transformations**. Yes, plural: Each **feature has its own affine transformation**. Since we're using layer normalization on `d_model`, and its dimensionality is **four**, there will be **four weights** and **four biases** in the `state_dict()`:

```
layer_norm.state_dict()
```

Output

```
OrderedDict([('weight', tensor([1., 1., 1., 1.])),
             ('bias', tensor([0., 0., 0., 0.]))])
```

The weights and biases are used to scale and translate, respectively, the standardized values:

$$\text{layer normed } x_{n,l,d} = b_d + w_d \text{ standardized } x_{n,l,d}$$

Equation 10.10 - Layer normalization (with affine transformation)

In PyTorch's documentation, though, you'll find **gamma** and **beta** instead:

$$\text{layer normed } x_{n,l,d} = \text{standardized } x_{n,l,d} \; \gamma_d + \beta_d$$

Equation 10.11 - Layer Normalization (with affine transformation)

Batch and *layer* normalization look quite similar to one another, but there are some important differences between them that we need to point out.

Batch vs Layer

Although both normalizations **compute statistics**, namely, mean and biased standard deviation, to **standardize** the inputs, **only batch norm** needs to keep track of **running statistics**.

Moreover, since **layer normalization** considers **data points individually**, it **exhibits the same behavior** whether the model is in **training** or in **evaluation** mode.

To illustrate the difference between the two types of normalization, let's generate yet another dummy example (again adding positional encoding to it):

```
torch.manual_seed(23)
dummy_points = torch.randn(4, 1, 256)
dummy_pe = PositionalEncoding(1, 256)
dummy_enc = dummy_pe(dummy_points)
dummy_enc
```

Output

```
tensor([[[-14.4193,  10.0495,  -7.8116, ..., -18.0732,  -3.9566]],

        [[  2.6628,  -3.5462, -23.6461, ..., -18.4375, -37.4197]],

        [[-24.6397,  -1.9127, -16.4244, ..., -26.0550, -14.0706]],

        [[ 13.7988,  21.4612,  10.4125, ..., -17.0188,   3.9237]]])
```

There are *four sequences*, so let's pretend there are **two mini-batches of two sequences each (*N=2*)**. Each sequence has a *length of one* (**L=1** is not *quite* a sequence, I know), and their sole data points have **256 features (*D=256*)**. The figure below illustrates the difference between applying *batch norm* (over features / columns) and **layer norm** (over data points / rows).

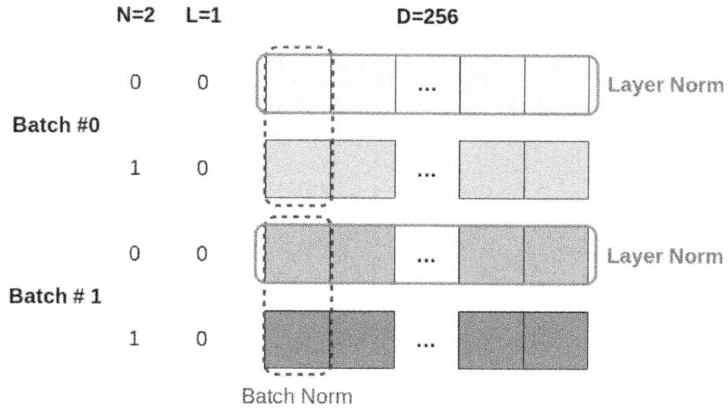

Figure 10.10 - Layer norm vs batch norm

While the size of the mini-batch strongly impacts the running statistics of the batch normalization, and its oscillating statistics may introduce a regularizing effect, **none of this** happens with **layer normalization**!

It steadily delivers data points with zero mean and unit standard deviation regardless of our choice of mini-batch size or anything else. Let's see it in action!

First, we're visualizing the **distribution of the positionally-encoded features** that we generated.

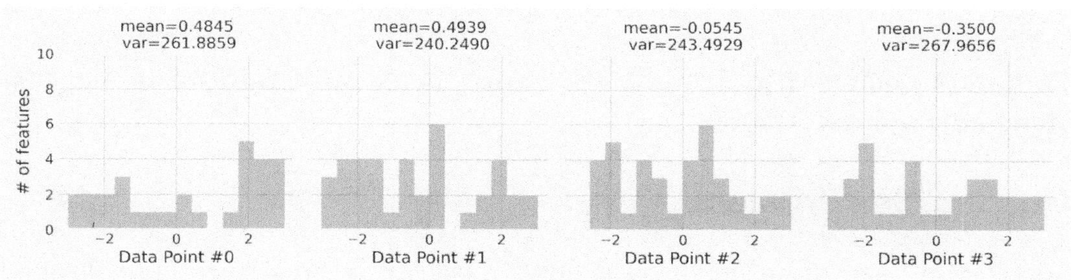

Figure 10.11 - Distribution of feature values

The *actual range* is much larger than that (like -50 to 50), and the *variance* is approximately the same as the dimensionality (256) as a result of the addition of positional encoding. Let's apply **layer normalization** to it:

```
layer_normalizer = nn.LayerNorm(256)
dummy_normed = layer_normalizer(dummy_enc)
dummy_normed
```

Output

```
tensor([[[-0.9210,  0.5911, -0.5127,  ..., -1.1467, -0.2744]],

        [[ 0.1399, -0.2607, -1.5574,  ..., -1.2214, -2.4460]],

        [[-1.5755, -0.1191, -1.0491,  ..., -1.6662, -0.8982]],

        [[ 0.8643,  1.3324,  0.6575,  ..., -1.0183,  0.2611]]],
       grad_fn=<NativeLayerNormBackward>)
```

Then, we're visualizing **both distributions**, original and standardized.

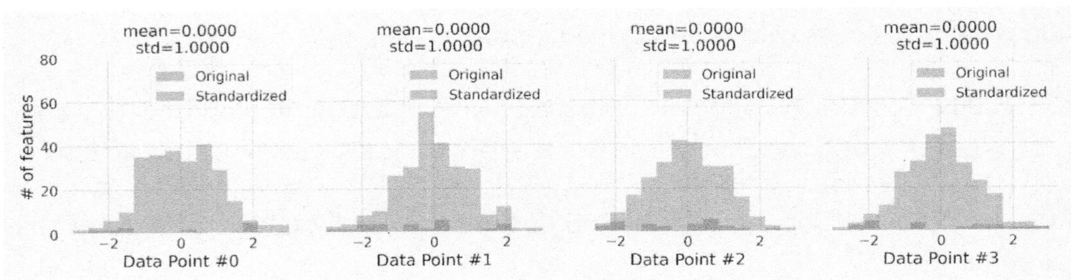

Figure 10.12 - Distribution of layer-normalized feature values

Each **data point** has its **feature values** distributed with **zero mean** and **unit standard deviation**. Beautiful!

Our Seq2Seq Problem

So far, I've been using dummy examples to illustrate how layer normalization works. Let's go back to our **sequence-to-sequence** problem, where the **source sequence** had **two data points**, each data point **representing the coordinates of two corners**. As usual, we're adding **positional encoding** to it:

```
pe = PositionalEncoding(max_len=2, d_model=2)

source_seq = torch.tensor([[[ 1.0349,  0.9661],
                            [ 0.8055, -0.9169]]])
source_seq_enc = pe(source_seq)
source_seq_enc
```

Output

```
tensor([[[ 1.4636,  2.3663],
         [ 1.9806, -0.7564]]])
```

Next, we **normalize it**:

```
norm = nn.LayerNorm(2)
norm(source_seq_enc)
```

Output

```
tensor([[[-1.0000,  1.0000],
         [ 1.0000, -1.0000]]], grad_fn=<NativeLayerNormBackward>)
```

"Wait, what happened here?"

That's what happens when one tries to **normalize two features only**: They become either **minus one** or **one**. Even worse, it will be the *same* for *every data point*. These values won't get us anywhere, that's for sure.

We need to do better, we need…

Projections or Embeddings

Sometimes **projections** and **embeddings** are used interchangeably. Here, though, we're sticking with **embeddings** for **categorical** values and **projections** for **numerical** values.

In Chapter 11, we'll be using **embeddings** to get a **numerical representation** (a vector) for a given **word** or **token**. Since words or tokens are **categorical values**, the **embedding layer** works like a **large lookup table**: It will look up a given word or token in its keys and return the corresponding tensor. But, since we're dealing with **coordinates**, that is, **numerical values**, we are using **projections** instead. A simple linear layer is all that it takes to project our pair of coordinates into a **higher-dimensional** feature space:

```
torch.manual_seed(11)
proj_dim = 6
linear_proj = nn.Linear(2, proj_dim)
pe = PositionalEncoding(2, proj_dim)
source_seq_proj = linear_proj(source_seq)
source_seq_proj_enc = pe(source_seq_proj)
source_seq_proj_enc
```

Output

```
tensor([[[-2.0934,  1.5040,  1.8742,  0.0628,  0.3034,  2.0190],
         [-0.8853,  2.8213,  0.5911,  2.4193, -2.5230,  0.3599]]],
       grad_fn=<AddBackward0>)
```

See? Now each data point in our source sequence has **six features** (the projected dimensions), and they are **positionally-encoded** too. Sure, *this* particular projection is totally random, but that won't be the case once we add the corresponding linear layer to our model. It will learn a meaningful projection that, after being positionally-encoded, will be normalized:

```
norm = nn.LayerNorm(proj_dim)
norm(source_seq_proj_enc)
```

Output

```
tensor([[[-1.9061,  0.6287,  0.8896, -0.3868, -0.2172,  0.9917],
         [-0.7362,  1.2864,  0.0694,  1.0670, -1.6299, -0.0568]]],
       grad_fn=<NativeLayerNormBackward>)
```

Problem solved! Finally, we have **everything** we need to build a full-blown **Transformer**!

In Chapter 9, we used *affine transformations* inside the **attention heads** to map from **input dimensions** to **hidden (or model) dimensions**. Now, this **change in dimensionality** is being performed using **projections** directly on the **input sequences** before they are passed to the encoder and the decoder.

The Transformer

Let's start with the diagram, which is nothing more than an encoder and a decoder side-by-side (we're sticking with **norm-first "sub-layer" wrappers**).

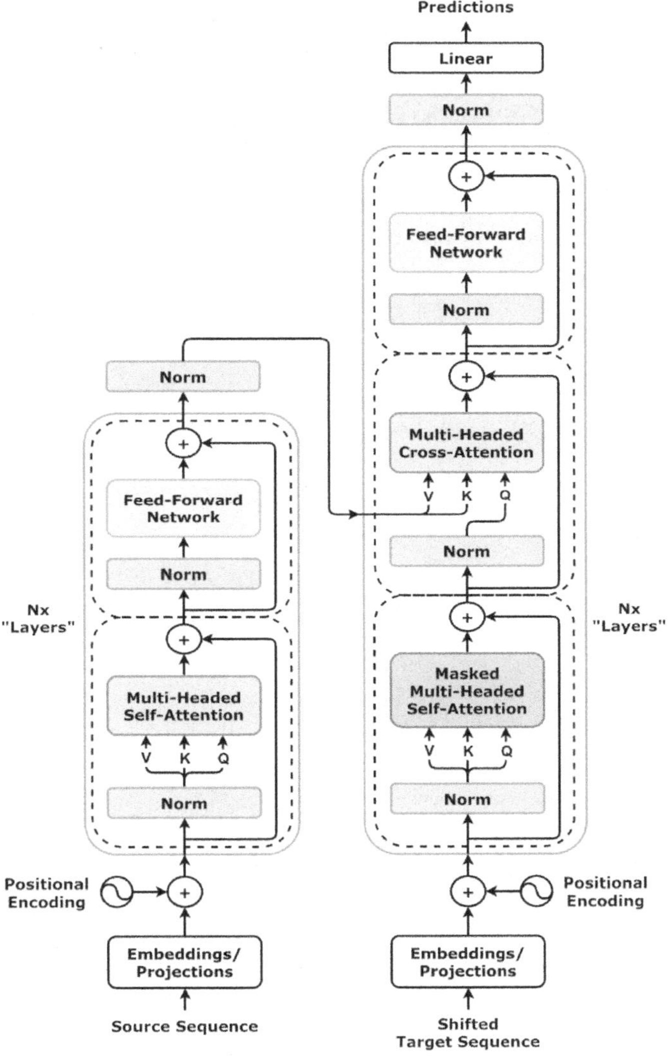

Figure 10.13 - The Transformer (norm-first)

The **Transformer** still is an **encoder-decoder architecture** like the one we developed in the previous chapter, so it should be no surprise that we can actually use our former `EncoderDecoderSelfAttn` class as a *parent class* and add **two extra components** to it:

- A **projection** layer to map our original **features** (`n_features`) to the **dimensionality** of both encoder and decoder (`d_model`).

- A **final linear** layer to map the decoder's outputs back to the original **feature space** (the coordinates we're trying to predict).

We also need to make some **small modifications** to the `encode()` and `decode()` methods to account for the components above:

Transformer Encoder-Decoder

```
class EncoderDecoderTransf(EncoderDecoderSelfAttn):
    def __init__(self, encoder, decoder,
                 input_len, target_len, n_features):
        super(EncoderDecoderTransf, self).__init__(
            encoder, decoder, input_len, target_len
        )
        self.n_features = n_features
        self.proj = nn.Linear(n_features, encoder.d_model)      ①
        self.linear = nn.Linear(encoder.d_model, n_features)    ②

    def encode(self, source_seq, source_mask=None):
        # Projection
        source_proj = self.proj(source_seq)                      ①
        encoder_states = self.encoder(source_proj, source_mask)
        self.decoder.init_keys(encoder_states)

    def decode(self, shifted_target_seq,
               source_mask=None, target_mask=None):
        # Projection
        target_proj = self.proj(shifted_target_seq)              ①
        outputs = self.decoder(target_proj,
                               source_mask=source_mask,
                               target_mask=target_mask)
        # Linear
        outputs = self.linear(outputs)                           ②
        return outputs
```

① Projecting features to model dimensionality

② Final linear transformation from model to feature space

Let's briefly review the model's methods:

- `encode()`: It takes the **source sequence and mask** and **encodes its projection** into a **sequence of states** that is immediately used to **initialize the "keys" (and**

"values") in the **decoder**.

- `decode()`: It takes the **shifted target sequence** and uses **its projection** together with both **source and target masks** to generate a **target sequence** that goes through the **last linear layer** to be transformed back to the **feature space**—it is used for **training** only!

The parent class is reproduced below for your convenience:

Encoder + Decoder + Self-Attention

```
class EncoderDecoderSelfAttn(nn.Module):
    def __init__(self, encoder, decoder, input_len, target_len):
        super().__init__()
        self.encoder = encoder
        self.decoder = decoder
        self.input_len = input_len
        self.target_len = target_len
        self.trg_masks = self.subsequent_mask(self.target_len)

    @staticmethod
    def subsequent_mask(size):
        attn_shape = (1, size, size)
        subsequent_mask = (
            1 - torch.triu(torch.ones(attn_shape), diagonal=1)
        ).bool()
        return subsequent_mask

    def encode(self, source_seq, source_mask):
        # Encodes the source sequence and uses the result
        # to initialize the decoder
        encoder_states = self.encoder(source_seq, source_mask)
        self.decoder.init_keys(encoder_states)

    def decode(self, shifted_target_seq,
               source_mask=None, target_mask=None):
        # Decodes/generates a sequence using the shifted (masked)
        # target sequence - used in TRAIN mode
        outputs = self.decoder(shifted_target_seq,
                               source_mask=source_mask,
                               target_mask=target_mask)
        return outputs

```

```
    def predict(self, source_seq, source_mask):
        # Decodes/generates a sequence using one input
        # at a time - used in EVAL mode
        inputs = source_seq[:, -1:]
        for i in range(self.target_len):
            out = self.decode(inputs,
                              source_mask,
                              self.trg_masks[:, :i+1, :i+1])
            out = torch.cat([inputs, out[:, -1:, :]], dim=-2)
            inputs = out.detach()
        outputs = inputs[:, 1:, :]
        return outputs

    def forward(self, X, source_mask=None):
        # Sends the mask to the same device as the inputs
        self.trg_masks = self.trg_masks.type_as(X).bool()
        # Slices the input to get source sequence
        source_seq = X[:, :self.input_len, :]
        # Encodes source sequence AND initializes decoder
        self.encode(source_seq, source_mask)
        if self.training:
            # Slices the input to get the shifted target seq
            shifted_target_seq = X[:, self.input_len-1:-1, :]
            # Decodes using the mask to prevent cheating
            outputs = self.decode(shifted_target_seq,
                                  source_mask,
                                  self.trg_masks)
        else:
            # Decodes using its own predictions
            outputs = self.predict(source_seq, source_mask)

        return outputs
```

Since the **Transformer** is an **encoder-decoder architecture**, we can use it in a **sequence-to-sequence** problem. Well, we already have one of those, right? Let's reuse Chapter 9's "Data Preparation" code.

Data Preparation

We'll **keep drawing the first two corners of the squares** ourselves, the **source sequence**, and ask our model to **predict the next two corners**, the **target sequence**, as in Chapter 9.

```python
# Generating training data
points, directions = generate_sequences(n=256, seed=13)
full_train = torch.as_tensor(points).float()
target_train = full_train[:, 2:]
# Generating test data
test_points, test_directions = generate_sequences(seed=19)
full_test = torch.as_tensor(test_points).float()
source_test = full_test[:, :2]
target_test = full_test[:, 2:]
# Datasets and data loaders
train_data = TensorDataset(full_train, target_train)
test_data = TensorDataset(source_test, target_test)

generator = torch.Generator()
train_loader = DataLoader(train_data, batch_size=16,
                          shuffle=True, generator=generator)
test_loader = DataLoader(test_data, batch_size=16)
```

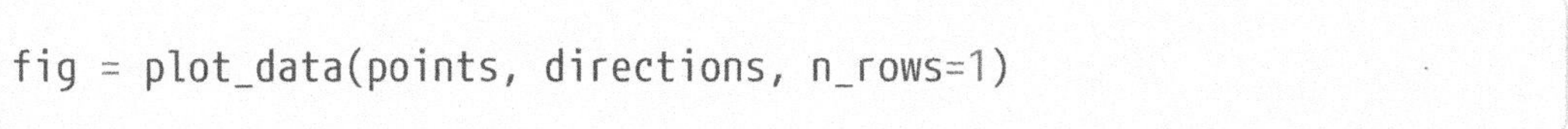

```python
fig = plot_data(points, directions, n_rows=1)
```

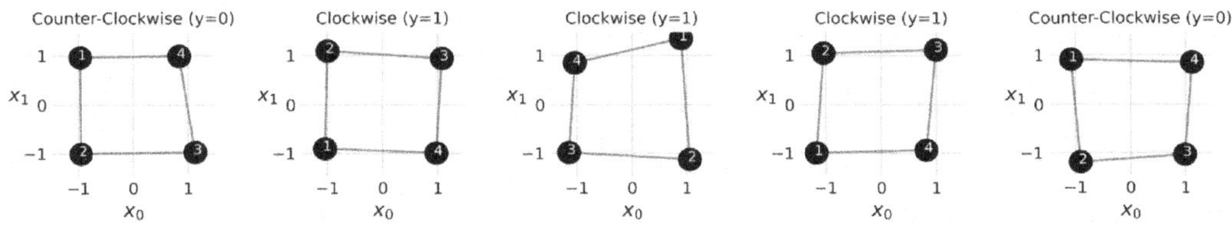

Figure 10.14 - Seq2Seq dataset

The corners show the **order** in which they were drawn. In the first square, the drawing **started at the top-right corner** and followed a **clockwise direction**. The **source sequence** for that square would include corners **on the right edge (1 and 2)**, while the **target sequence** would include corners **on the left edge (3 and 4)**, in that order.

Model Configuration & Training

Let's train our **Transformer**! We start by creating the corresponding "layers" for both encoder and decoder, and use them both as arguments of the `EncoderDecoderTransf` class:

Model Configuration

```
torch.manual_seed(42)
# Layers
enclayer = EncoderLayer(n_heads=3, d_model=6,
                        ff_units=10, dropout=0.1)
declayer = DecoderLayer(n_heads=3, d_model=6,
                        ff_units=10, dropout=0.1)
# Encoder and Decoder
enctransf = EncoderTransf(enclayer, n_layers=2)
dectransf = DecoderTransf(declayer, n_layers=2)
# Transformer
model_transf = EncoderDecoderTransf(
    enctransf, dectransf, input_len=2, target_len=2, n_features=2
)
loss = nn.MSELoss()
optimizer = torch.optim.Adam(model_transf.parameters(), lr=0.01)
```

The original Transformer model was initialized using **Glorot / Xavier uniform** distribution, so we're sticking with it:

Weight Initialization

```
for p in model_transf.parameters():
    if p.dim() > 1:
        nn.init.xavier_uniform_(p)
```

Next, we use the `StepByStep` class to train the model as usual:

Model Training

```
sbs_seq_transf = StepByStep(model_transf, loss, optimizer)
sbs_seq_transf.set_loaders(train_loader, test_loader)
sbs_seq_transf.train(50)
```

```
fig = sbs_seq_transf.plot_losses()
```

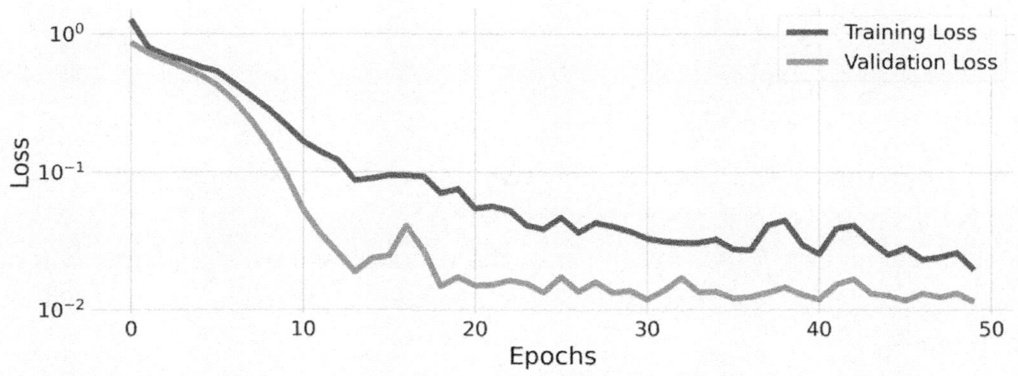

Figure 10.15 - Losses—Transformer model

*"Why is the validation loss **so much better** than the training loss?"*

This phenomenon may happen for a variety of reasons, from having an *easier* validation set to being a "*side effect*" of **regularization** (e.g., dropout) in our current model. The regularization makes it *harder* for the model to learn or, in other words, it yields **higher losses**. In our Transformer model, there are **many dropout layers**, so it gets increasingly more difficult for the model to learn.

Let's observe this effect by using the **same mini-batch** to compute the **loss** using the **trained model** in both **`train`** and **`eval`** modes:

```
torch.manual_seed(11)
x, y = next(iter(train_loader))
device = sbs_seq_transf.device
# Training
model_transf.train()
loss(model_transf(x.to(device)), y.to(device))
```

Output

```
tensor(0.0158, device='cuda:0', grad_fn=<MseLossBackward>)
```

```
# Validation
model_transf.eval()
loss(model_transf(x.to(device)), y.to(device))
```

Output

```
tensor(0.0091, device='cuda:0')
```

See the difference? The loss is roughly **two times** larger in training mode. You can also **set dropout to zero** and retrain the model to verify that both loss curves get much closer to each other (by the way, the overall loss level gets *better* without dropout, but that's just because our sequence-to-sequence problem is actually quite simple).

Visualizing Predictions

Let's plot the **predicted coordinates** and connect them using **dashed lines**, while using **solid lines** to connect the **actual coordinates**, just like before:

```
fig = sequence_pred(sbs_seq_transf, full_test, test_directions)
```

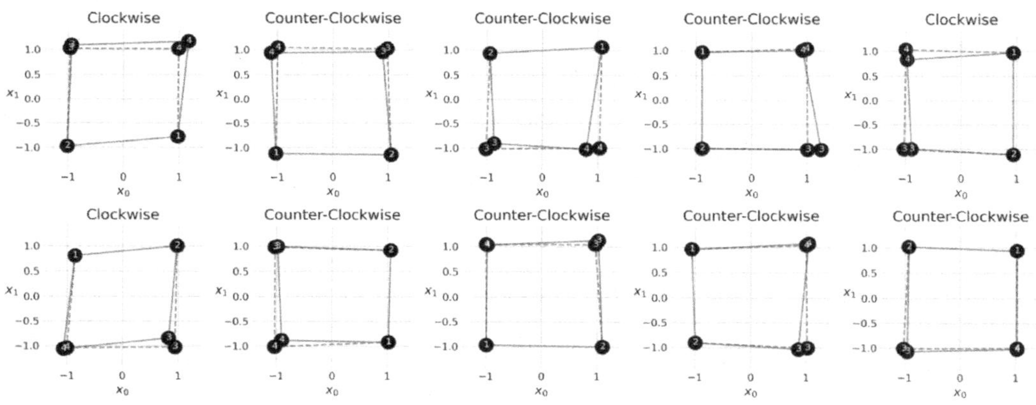

Figure 10.16 - Predictions

Looking good, right?

The PyTorch Transformer

So far we've been using our own classes to build encoder and decoder "layers" and assemble them all into a Transformer. We **don't have to** do it like that, though. PyTorch implements a full-fledged **Transformer** class of its own: `nn.Transformer`.

There are some differences between PyTorch's implementation and our own:

- First, and most important, PyTorch implements **norm-last "sub-layer" wrappers**, normalizing the output of each "sub-layer."

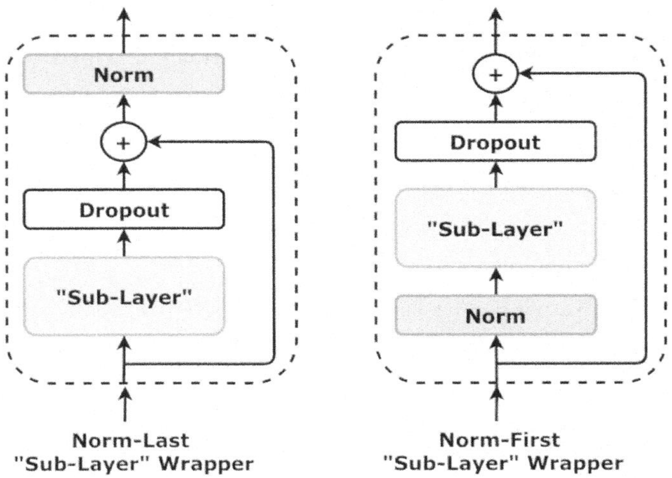

Figure 10.17 - "Sub-Layer"—norm-last vs norm-first

- It **does not** implement **positional encoding**, the **final linear layer**, or the **projection layer**, so we have to handle those ourselves.

Let's take a look at its constructor and `forward()` methods. The constructor expects *many arguments* because PyTorch's Transformer actually **builds both encoder and decoder by itself**:

- `d_model`: the **number of (projected) features**, that is, the **dimensionality of the model** (remember, this number will be *split* among the attention heads, so it must be a multiple of the number of heads; its default value is 512)
- `nhead`: the number of **attention heads** in each **attention mechanism** (default is eight, so each attention head gets 64 out of the 512 dimensions)
- `num_encoder_layers`: the number of "layers" in the encoder (the Transformer uses six layers by default)
- `num_decoder_layers`: the number of "layers" in the decoder (the Transformer uses six layers by default)
- `dim_feedforward`: the number of **units** in the **hidden layer** of the **feed-forward network** (default is 2048)
- `dropout`: the **probability** of dropping out inputs (default is 0.1)
- `activation`: the activation function to be used in the feed-forward network

(ReLU by default)

It is also possible to use a **custom encoder or decoder** by setting the corresponding arguments: `custom_encoder` and `custom_decoder`. But don't forget that the PyTorch Transformer expects **sequence-first** inputs.

The `forward()` method expects both sequences, **source** and **target**, and **all sorts of (optional) masks**.

IMPORTANT: PyTorch's **Transformer** uses **sequence-first** shapes for its inputs (L, N, F), and there is **no batch-first option**.

There are **masks** for **padded data points**:

- `src_key_padding_mask`: the mask for **padded data points** in the **source sequence**
- `memory_key_padding_mask`: It's also a mask for **padded data points** in the **source sequence** and should be, in most cases, the *same* as `src_key_padding_mask`.
- `tgt_key_padding_mask`: This mask is used for **padded data points** in the **target sequence**.

And there are **masks** to **purposefully hide some of the inputs**:

- `src_mask`: It hides inputs in the **source sequence**, this can be used for training **language models** (more on that in Chapter 11).
- `tgt_mask`: That's the mask used to **avoid cheating** (although quite important, this argument is still considered *optional*).
    - The Transformer has a method named `generate_square_subsequent_mask()` that generates the appropriate mask given the size (length) of the sequence.
- `memory_mask`: It hides **encoded states** used by the decoder.

Also, notice that there is no **memory argument** anymore: The encoded states are handled internally by the Transformer and fed directly to the decoder part.

In our own code, we'll be replacing the two former methods, `encode()` and `decode()`, with a single one, `encode_decode()`, that calls the **Transformer** itself and runs its output through the **last linear layer** to transform it into coordinates. Since the Transformer expects and outputs **sequence-first** shapes, there is some back-and-forth **permuting** as well.

```
def encode_decode(self, source, target,
                  source_mask=None, target_mask=None):
    # Projections
    # PyTorch Transformer expects L, N, F
    src = self.preprocess(source).permute(1, 0, 2)
    tgt = self.preprocess(target).permute(1, 0, 2)

    out = self.transf(src, tgt,
                      src_key_padding_mask=source_mask,
                      tgt_mask=target_mask)

    # Linear
    # Back to N, L, D
    out = out.permute(1, 0, 2)
    out = self.linear(out) # N, L, F
    return out
```

By the way, we're keeping the masks to a minimum for the sake of simplicity: Only `src_key_padding_mask` and `tgt_mask` are used.

Moreover, we're implementing a `preprocess()` method that takes an **input sequence** and

- **projects** the original features into the model dimensionality;
- adds **positional encoding** and
- **(layer) normalizes** the result (remember that PyTorch's implementation *does not normalize the inputs*, so we have to do it ourselves).

The full code looks like this:

Transformer

```
class TransformerModel(nn.Module):
    def __init__(self, transformer,
                 input_len, target_len, n_features):
```

```
        super().__init__()
        self.transf = transformer
        self.input_len = input_len
        self.target_len = target_len
        self.trg_masks = \
            self.transf.generate_square_subsequent_mask(
                self.target_len
            )
        self.n_features = n_features
        self.proj = nn.Linear(n_features, self.transf.d_model) ①
        self.linear = nn.Linear(self.transf.d_model,          ②
                                n_features)

        max_len = max(self.input_len, self.target_len)
        self.pe = PositionalEncoding(max_len,
                                     self.transf.d_model)     ③
        self.norm = nn.LayerNorm(self.transf.d_model)         ③

    def preprocess(self, seq):
        seq_proj = self.proj(seq)                             ①
        seq_enc = self.pe(seq_proj)                           ③
        return self.norm(seq_enc)                             ③

    def encode_decode(self, source, target,
                      source_mask=None, target_mask=None):
        # Projections
        # PyTorch Transformer expects L, N, F
        src = self.preprocess(source).permute(1, 0, 2)        ③
        tgt = self.preprocess(target).permute(1, 0, 2)        ③

        out = self.transf(src, tgt,
                          src_key_padding_mask=source_mask,
                          tgt_mask=target_mask)

        # Linear
        # Back to N, L, D
        out = out.permute(1, 0, 2)
        out = self.linear(out) # N, L, F                      ②
        return out

    def predict(self, source_seq, source_mask=None):
        inputs = source_seq[:, -1:]
```

```
        for i in range(self.target_len):
            out = self.encode_decode(
                source_seq, inputs,
                source_mask=source_mask,
                target_mask=self.trg_masks[:i+1, :i+1]
            )
            out = torch.cat([inputs, out[:, -1:, :]], dim=-2)
            inputs = out.detach()
        outputs = out[:, 1:, :]
        return outputs

    def forward(self, X, source_mask=None):
        self.trg_masks = self.trg_masks.type_as(X)
        source_seq = X[:, :self.input_len, :]

        if self.training:
            shifted_target_seq = X[:, self.input_len-1:-1, :]
            outputs = self.encode_decode(
                source_seq, shifted_target_seq,
                source_mask=source_mask,
                target_mask=self.trg_masks
            )
        else:
            outputs = self.predict(source_seq, source_mask)

        return outputs
```

① Projecting features to model dimensionality

② Final linear transformation from model to feature space

③ Adding positional encoding and normalizing inputs

Its constructor takes an instance of the `nn.Transformer` class followed by the typical sequence lengths *and* the number of features (so it can map the predicted sequence back to our feature space; that is, to coordinates). Both `predict()` and `forward()` methods are roughly the same, but they call the `encode_decode()` method now.

Model Configuration & Training

Let's train PyTorch's **Transformer**! We start by creating an instance of it to use as an argument of our `TransformerModel` class, followed by the same initialization scheme as before, and the typical training procedure:

Model Configuration

```
torch.manual_seed(42)
transformer = nn.Transformer(d_model=6,
                             nhead=3,
                             num_encoder_layers=1,
                             num_decoder_layers=1,
                             dim_feedforward=20,
                             dropout=0.1)
model_transformer = TransformerModel(transformer, input_len=2,
                                     target_len=2, n_features=2)
loss = nn.MSELoss()
optimizer = torch.optim.Adam(model_transformer.parameters(),
                             lr=0.01)
```

Weight Initialization

```
for p in model_transformer.parameters():
    if p.dim() > 1:
        nn.init.xavier_uniform_(p)
```

Model Training

```
sbs_seq_transformer = StepByStep(
    model_transformer, loss, optimizer
)
sbs_seq_transformer.set_loaders(train_loader, test_loader)
sbs_seq_transformer.train(50)
```

```
fig = sbs_seq_transformer.plot_losses()
```

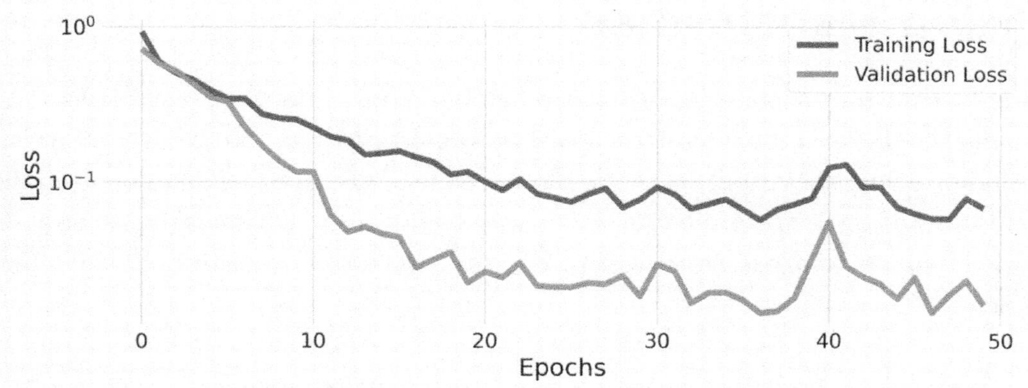

Figure 10.18 - Losses - PyTorch's Transformer

Once again, the validation loss is significantly lower than the training loss. No surprises here since it is roughly the same model.

Visualizing Predictions

Let's plot the **predicted coordinates** and connect them using **dashed lines**, while using **solid lines** to connect the **actual coordinates**, just like before.

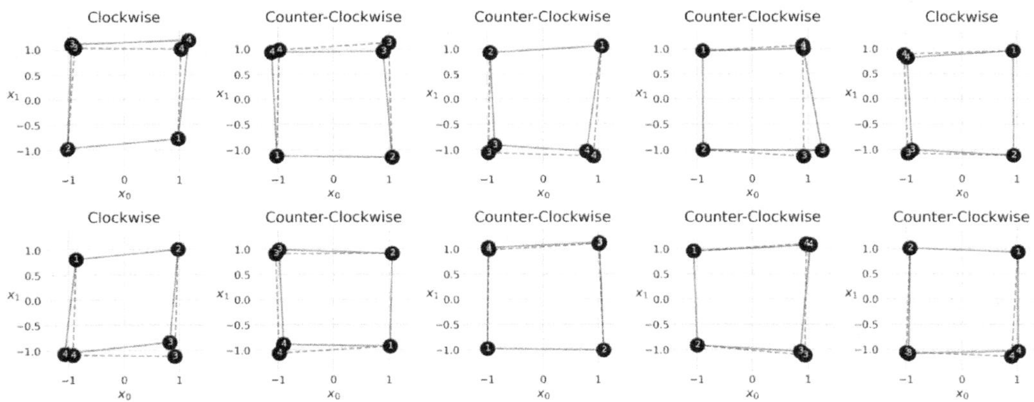

Figure 10.19 - Predictions

Once again, looking good, right?

Vision Transformer

The Transformer architecture is fairly flexible, and, although it was devised to handle NLP tasks in the first place, it is already starting to spread to different areas, including computer vision. Let's take a look at one of the latest developments in the field: the Vision Transformer (ViT). It was introduced by Dosovitskiy, A., et al. in their paper "An Image is Worth 16x16 Words: Transformers for Image Recognition at Scale."[58]

*"Cool, but I thought the Transformer handled **sequences**, not images."*

That's a fair point. The answer is deceptively simple: Let's **break an image** into a **sequence of patches**.

Data Generation & Preparation

First, we need to generate a synthetic dataset of images for a multiclass classification problem. Our images are going to have either a diagonal or a parallel line, and they will be labeled according to the table below:

Line	Label/Class Index
Parallel (Horizontal OR Vertical)	0
Diagonal, Tilted to the Right	1
Diagonal, Tilted to the Left	2

Data Generation

```
images, labels = generate_dataset(img_size=12, n_images=1000,
                                  binary=False, seed=17)
```

Each image, like the example below, is 12x12 pixels in size and has a single channel:

```
img = torch.as_tensor(images[2]).unsqueeze(0).float()/255.
```

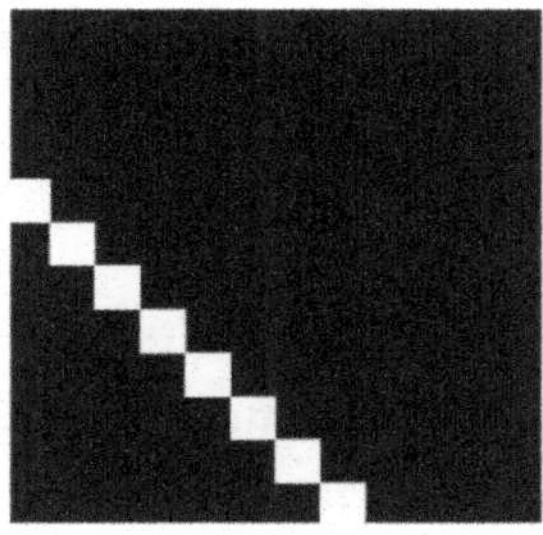

Figure 10.20 - Sample image—label "2"

> *"But this is a **classification problem**, not a sequence-to-sequence one—why are we using a Transformer then?"*

Well, we're *not* using the *full* Transformer architecture, only its **encoder**. In Chapter 8, we used recurrent neural networks to generate a *final hidden state* that we used as the input for classification. Similarly, the **encoder** generates a **sequence of "hidden states"** (the *memory*, in Transformer lingo), and we're using **one "hidden state"** as the input for classification again.

> *"Which one? The last 'hidden state'?"*

No, not the last one, but a **special one**. We'll **prepend a special classifier token** `[CLS]` to our sequence and use its corresponding "hidden state" as input to a classifier. The figure below illustrates the idea.

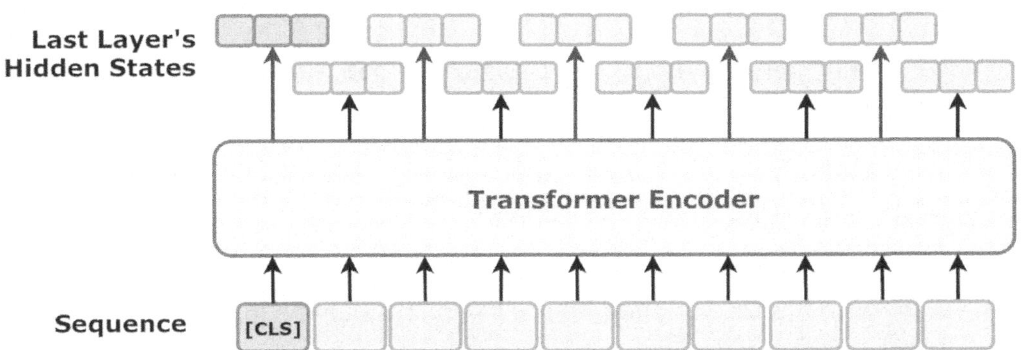

Figure 10.21 - Hidden states and the special classifier token `[CLS]`

But I'm *jumping the gun* here—we'll get back to that in the "Special Classifier Token" section.

WeightedRandomSampler

The **weighted sampler** can be used to tackle **imbalanced datasets** by **adjusting the weights for sampling**: The class with **fewer data points (minority class)** should get **larger weights**, while the class with **more data points (majority class)** should get **smaller weights**. This way, on average, we'll end up with mini-batches containing roughly the same number of data points in each class: a **balanced dataset**.

The **minority class** should have the **largest weight**, so each data point belonging to it gets **overrepresented** to compensate for the imbalance.

The `WeightedRandomSampler` takes many arguments:

- `weights`: A sequence of weights like the one we have just computed.
- `num_samples`: How many samples are going to be drawn from the dataset.
    - A typical value is the **length** of the sequence of weights, as you're likely sampling from the whole training set.
- `replacement`: If `True` (the default value), it draws samples *with* replacement.
    - If `num_samples` equals the length, that is, if the whole training set is used, it makes sense to draw samples **with** replacement to effectively compensate for the imbalance.
    - It only makes sense to set it to `False` **if `num_samples` < length** of the dataset.
- `generator`: Optional, it takes a (pseudo) random number `Generator` that will be used for drawing the samples.
    - To ensure *reproducibility*, we **need** to create and assign a **generator** (which has its own seed) to the sampler, since the **manual seed** we've already set is **not enough**.

We're not delving into more details here, but I've developed the `make_balanced_sampler()` function to handle all the boilerplate code for you:

Helper Function

```
def make_balanced_sampler(y):
    # Computes weights for compensating imbalanced classes
    classes, counts = y.unique(return_counts=True)
    weights = 1.0 / counts.float()
    sample_weights = weights[y.squeeze().long()]
    # Builds sampler with compute weights
    generator = torch.Generator()
    sampler = WeightedRandomSampler(
        weights=sample_weights,
        num_samples=len(sample_weights),
        generator=generator,
        replacement=True
    )
    return sampler
```

Its only argument is the tensor containing the **labels**: The function will compute the weights and build the corresponding weighted sampler on its own.

The *data preparation* step uses a custom dataset to normalize the images, and a helper function (`make_balanced_sampler()`; see the aside for more details) to build a `WeightedRandomSampler` sampler:

Data Preparation

```
class TransformedTensorDataset(Dataset):
    def __init__(self, x, y, transform=None):
        self.x = x
        self.y = y
        self.transform = transform

    def __getitem__(self, index):
        x = self.x[index]
        if self.transform:
            x = self.transform(x)

        return x, self.y[index]
```

```

    def __len__(self):
        return len(self.x)

# Builds tensors from numpy arrays BEFORE split
# Modifies the scale of pixel values from [0, 255] to [0, 1]
x_tensor = torch.as_tensor(images / 255).float()
y_tensor = torch.as_tensor(labels).long()

# Uses index_splitter to generate indices for training and
# validation sets
train_idx, val_idx = index_splitter(len(x_tensor), [80, 20])
# Uses indices to perform the split
x_train_tensor = x_tensor[train_idx]
y_train_tensor = y_tensor[train_idx]
x_val_tensor = x_tensor[val_idx]
y_val_tensor = y_tensor[val_idx]

# We're not doing any data augmentation now
train_composer = Compose([Normalize(mean=(.5,), std=(.5,))])
val_composer = Compose([Normalize(mean=(.5,), std=(.5,))])

# Uses custom dataset to apply composed transforms to each set
train_dataset = TransformedTensorDataset(
    x_train_tensor, y_train_tensor, transform=train_composer)
val_dataset = TransformedTensorDataset(
    x_val_tensor, y_val_tensor, transform=val_composer)

# Builds a weighted random sampler to handle imbalanced classes
sampler = make_balanced_sampler(y_train_tensor)

# Uses sampler in the training set to get a balanced data loader
train_loader = DataLoader(
    dataset=train_dataset, batch_size=16, sampler=sampler)
val_loader = DataLoader(dataset=val_dataset, batch_size=16)
```

Patches

There are different ways of breaking up an image into patches. The most straightforward one is simply **rearranging** the pixels, so let's start with that one.

Rearranging

Tensorflow has a utility function called `tf.image.extract_patches()` that does the job, and we're implementing a simplified version of this function in PyTorch with `tensor.unfold()` (using only a *kernel size* and a *stride*, but no *padding* or anything else):

```
# Adapted from https://discuss.pytorch.org/t/tf-extract-image-
# patches-in-pytorch/43837
def extract_image_patches(x, kernel_size, stride=1):
    # Extract patches
    patches = x.unfold(2, kernel_size, stride)
    patches = patches.unfold(3, kernel_size, stride)
    patches = patches.permute(0, 2, 3, 1, 4, 5).contiguous()

    return patches.view(n, patches.shape[1], patches.shape[2], -1)
```

It works *as if* we were applying a convolution to the image. Each **patch** is actually a *receptive field* (the region the filter is moving over to convolve), but, instead of convolving the region, we're just taking it as it is. The **kernel size** is the **patch size**, and the **number of patches** depends on the **stride**—the smaller the stride, the more patches. If the **stride matches the kernel size**, we're effectively **breaking up** the image into **non-overlapping patches**, so let's do that:

```
kernel_size = 4
patches = extract_image_patches(
    img, kernel_size, stride=kernel_size
)
patches.shape
```

Output

```
torch.Size([1, 3, 3, 16])
```

Since kernel size is four, **each patch has 16 pixels**, and there are **nine patches** in total. Even though each patch is a tensor of 16 elements, if we plot them as if they were four-by-four images instead, it would look like this.

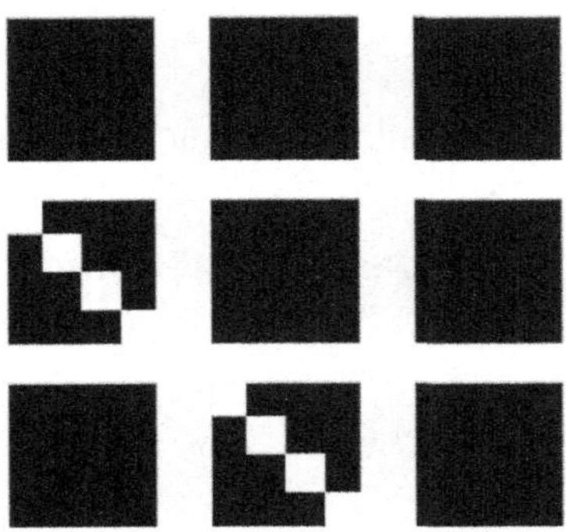

Figure 10.22 - Sample image—split into patches

It is very easy to see how the image was broken up in the figure above. In reality, though, the Transformer needs a **sequence of flattened patches**. Let's reshape them:

```
seq_patches = patches.view(-1, patches.size(-1))
```

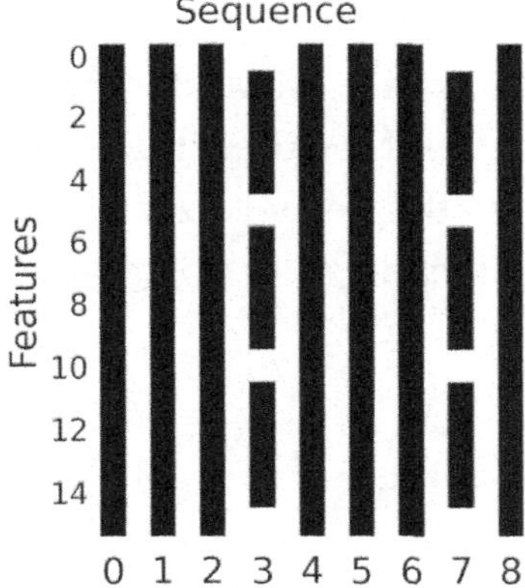

Figure 10.23 - Sample image—split into a sequence of flattened patches

That's more like it: Each image is turned into a **sequence of length nine**, each element in the sequence having **16 features** (pixel values in this case).

Embeddings

If each **patch** is like a *receptive field*, and we even talked about **kernel size** and **stride**, why not go **full convolution** then? That's how the **Visual Transformer (ViT)** actually implemented **patch embeddings**:

Patch Embeddings

```
# Adapted from https://amaarora.github.io/2021/01/18/ViT.html
class PatchEmbed(nn.Module):
    def __init__(self, img_size=224, patch_size=16,
                 in_channels=3, embed_dim=768, dilation=1):
        super().__init__()
        num_patches = (img_size // patch_size) * \
                      (img_size // patch_size)
        self.img_size = img_size
        self.patch_size = patch_size
        self.num_patches = num_patches
        self.proj = nn.Conv2d(in_channels,
                              embed_dim,
                              kernel_size=patch_size,
                              stride=patch_size)

    def forward(self, x):
        x = self.proj(x).flatten(2).transpose(1, 2)
        return x
```

The **patch embedding** is not the original receptive field anymore, but rather the **convolved receptive field**. After convolving the image, given a kernel size and a stride, the **patches get flattened**, so we end up with the same **sequence of nine patches**:

```
torch.manual_seed(13)
patch_embed = PatchEmbed(
    img.size(-1), kernel_size, 1, kernel_size**2
)
embedded = patch_embed(img)
embedded.shape
```

Output

```
torch.Size([1, 9, 16])
```

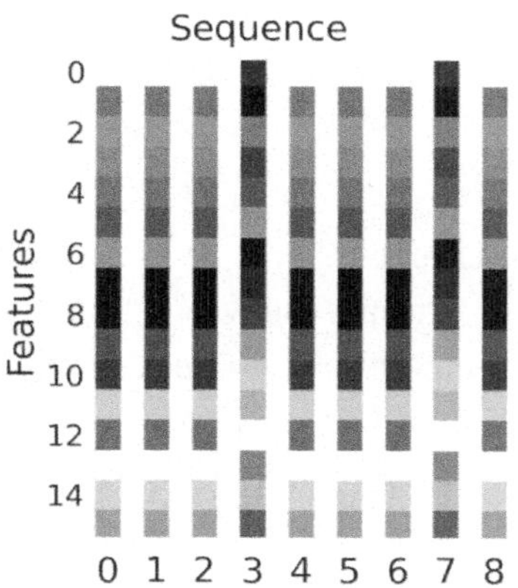

Figure 10.24 - Sample image—split into a sequence of **patch embeddings**

But the patches are **linear projections** of the original **pixel values** now. We're projecting each 16-pixel patch into a 16-dimensional feature space—we're not changing the number of dimensions, but using **different linear combinations of the original dimensions.**

The original image had **144 pixels** and was split into **nine patches** of **16 pixels** each. Each patch **embedding *still* has 16 dimensions**, so, overall, each image is *still* represented by **144 values**. This is by no means a coincidence: The idea behind this choice of values is to **preserve the dimensionality** of the inputs.

Einops

"*There is more than one way to skin a cat,*" as the saying goes, and so there is more than one way to rearrange the pixels into sequences. An alternative approach uses a package called `einops`.[59] It is **very** minimalistic (maybe even a bit too much) and allows you to express complex rearrangements in a couple lines of code. It may take a while to get the hang of how it works, though.

We're not using it here, but, if you're interested, this is the `einops` equivalent of the `extract_image_patches()` function above:

```
# Adapted from https://github.com/lucidrains/vit-pytorch/blob/
# main/vit_pytorch/vit_pytorch.py
# !pip install einops
from einops import rearrange
patches = rearrange(padded_img,
                    'b c (h p1) (w p2) -> b (h w) (p1 p2 c)',
                    p1 = kernel_size, p2 = kernel_size)
```

Special Classifier Token

In Chapter 8, the *final hidden state* represented the *full sequence*. This approach had its shortcomings (the attention mechanism was developed to compensate for them), but it leveraged the fact that **there was an underlying sequential structure** to the data.

This is *not quite the same* for images, though. The **sequence of patches** is a clever way of making the data suitable for the **encoder**, sure, but it does not necessarily reflect a sequential structure; after all, we end up with **two different sequences** depending on which direction we choose to go over the patches: **row-wise** or **column-wise**.

*"Can't we use the **full sequence** of 'hidden states' then? Or maybe **average** them?"*

It is definitely *possible* to use the **average** of the "hidden states" produced by the encoder as input for the classifier.

But it is also common to use a **special classifier token `[CLS]`**, especially in NLP tasks (as we'll see in Chapter 11). The idea is quite simple and elegant: **Add the same token to the beginning of every sequence**. This special token has **an embedding** as well, and it will be **learned** by the model like any other parameter.

The **first "hidden state"** produced by the encoder, the output corresponding to the **added special token**, plays the role of **overall representation** of the image—just like the final hidden state represented the overall sequence in recurrent neural networks.

Remember that the Transformer encoder uses **self-attention** and that **every token** can pay attention **to every other token** in the sequence. Therefore, the **special classifier token** can actually learn **which tokens (patches, in our case)** it needs to pay attention to in order to correctly classify the sequence.

Let's illustrate the addition of the `[CLS]` token by taking two images from our dataset.

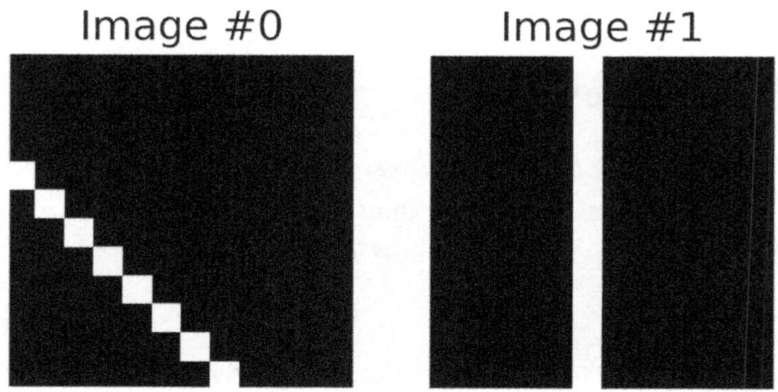

Figure 10.25 - Two images

Next, we get their corresponding **patch embeddings**:

```
embeddeds = patch_embed(imgs)
```

Our images were transformed into **sequences of nine patch embeddings of size 16** each, so they can be represented like this (the features are on the horizontal axis now).

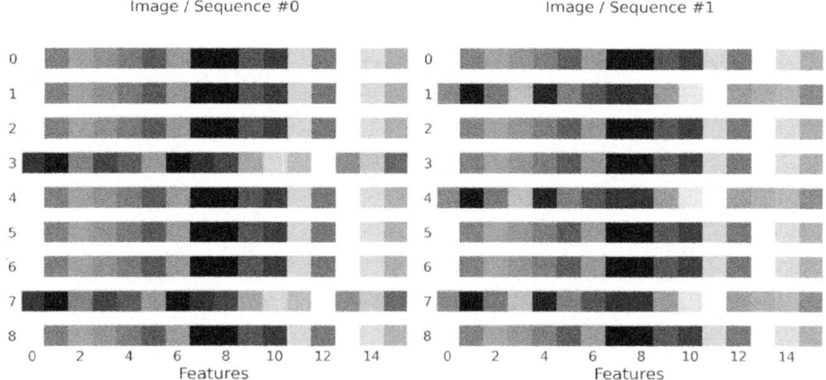

Figure 10.26 - Two patch embeddings

The **patch embeddings** are obviously different for each image, but the **embedding** corresponding to the **special classifier token** that's prepended to the patch embeddings is always the **same**.

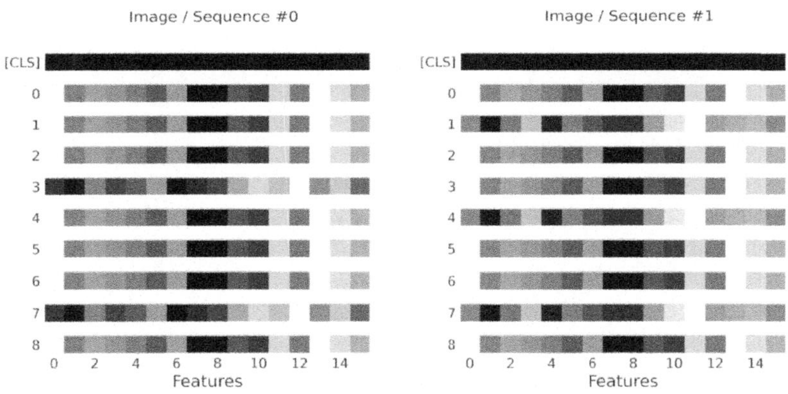

Figure 10.27 - Two patch embeddings + `[CLS]` *embedding*

"How do we do that?"

It's actually simple: We need to define a **parameter** in our model (using `nn.Parameter`) to represent this **special embedding** and **concatenate** it at the beginning of every sequence of embeddings. Let's start by creating the parameter itself (it will be an attribute of our model later):

```
cls_token = nn.Parameter(torch.zeros(1, 1, 16))
cls_token
```

Output

```
Parameter containing:
tensor([[[0., 0., 0., 0., 0., 0., 0., 0., 0., 0., 0., 0., 0., 0.,
0., 0.]]], requires_grad=True)
```

It is just a **vector full of zeros**. That's it. But, since it is a parameter, its values will be updated as the model gets trained. Then, let's fetch a mini-batch of images and get their **patch embeddings**:

```
images, labels = next(iter(train_loader))
images.shape # N, C, H, W
```

Output

```
torch.Size([16, 1, 12, 12])
```

```
embed = patch_embed(images)
embed.shape # N, L, D
```

Output

```
torch.Size([16, 9, 16])
```

There are **16 images**, each represented by a **sequence of nine patches with 16 dimensions each**. The **special embedding** should be the **same** for all 16 images, so we use `tensor.expand()` to **replicate it** along the batch dimension before concatenation:

```
cls_tokens = cls_token.expand(embed.size(0), -1, -1)
embed_cls = torch.cat((cls_tokens, embed), dim=1)
embed_cls.shape # N, L+1, D
```

Output

```
torch.Size([16, 10, 16])
```

Now each **sequence has ten elements**, and we have everything we need to build our model.

The Model

The *main* part of the model is the **Transformer encoder**, which, coincidentally, is implemented by **normalizing the inputs** (norm-first), like our own `EncoderLayer` and `EncoderTransf` classes (and unlike PyTorch's default implementation).

The encoder outputs a sequence of "hidden states" (*memory*), the **first** of which is used as input to a **classifier** ("*MLP Head*"), as briefly discussed in the previous section. So, the model is all about **pre-processing the inputs**, our images, using a series of transformations:

- computing **a sequence of patch embeddings**
- prepending the same **special classifier token `[CLS]` embedding** to every sequence
- adding position embedding (or, in our case, **position encoding** implemented in our **encoder**)

The figure below illustrates the architecture.

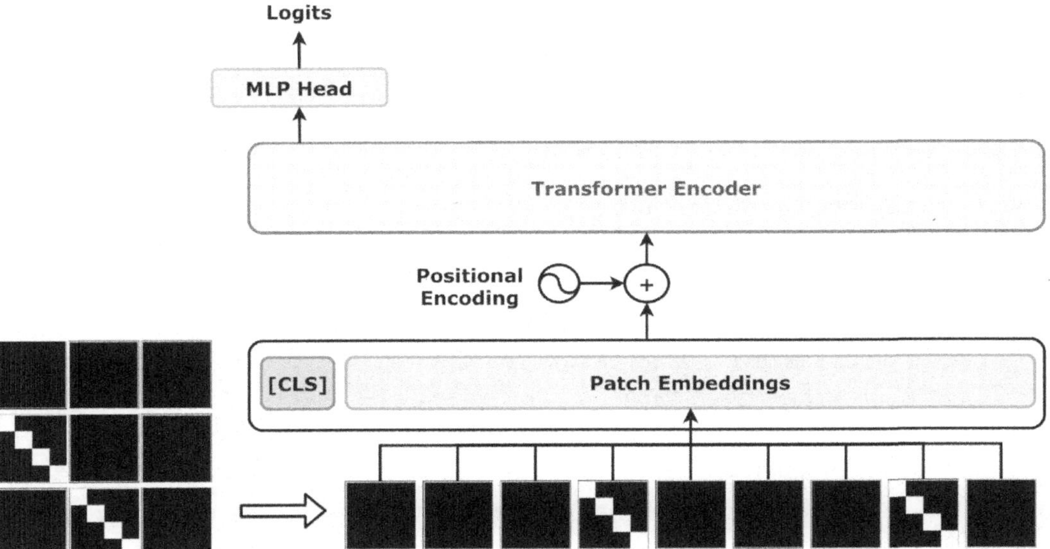

Figure 10.28 - The Vision Transformer (ViT)

Let's see it in code!

```
class ViT(nn.Module):
    def __init__(self, encoder, img_size,
                 in_channels, patch_size, n_outputs):
        super().__init__()
        self.d_model = encoder.d_model
        self.n_outputs = n_outputs
        self.encoder = encoder
        self.mlp = nn.Linear(encoder.d_model, n_outputs)

        self.embed = PatchEmbed(img_size, patch_size,
                                in_channels, encoder.d_model)
        self.cls_token = nn.Parameter(
            torch.zeros(1, 1, encoder.d_model)
        )

    def preprocess(self, X):
        # Patch embeddings
        # N, L, F -> N, L, D
        src = self.embed(X)
        # Special classifier token
        # 1, 1, D -> N, 1, D
        cls_tokens = self.cls_token.expand(X.size(0), -1, -1)
        # Concatenates CLS tokens -> N, 1 + L, D
        src = torch.cat((cls_tokens, src), dim=1)
        return src

    def encode(self, source):
        # Encoder generates "hidden states"
        states = self.encoder(source)
        # Gets state from first token: CLS
        cls_state = states[:, 0]  # N, 1, D
        return cls_state

    def forward(self, X):
        src = self.preprocess(X)
        # Featurizer
        cls_state = self.encode(src)
        # Classifier
        out = self.mlp(cls_state) # N, 1, outputs
        return out
```

It takes an instance of a **Transformer encoder** and a series of image-related arguments (size, number of channels, and patch / kernel size), in addition to the desired **number of outputs** (logits), which corresponds to the number of existing classes.

The `forward()` method takes a mini-batch of images, pre-processes them, encodes them (featurizer), and outputs logits (classifier). It is not *that* different from a typical image classifier; it even uses **convolutions**!

For more details on the *original Vision Transformer*, make sure to check an amazing post[60] by Aman Arora and Dr. Habib Bukhari.

You can also check out Phil Wang's implementation at https://github.com/lucidrains/vit-pytorch.

Model Configuration & Training

Let's train our **Vision Transformer**! You know the drill:

Model Configuration

```
torch.manual_seed(17)
layer = EncoderLayer(n_heads=2, d_model=16, ff_units=20)
encoder = EncoderTransf(layer, n_layers=1)
model_vit = ViT(encoder, img_size=12,
                in_channels=1, patch_size=4, n_outputs=3)
multi_loss_fn = nn.CrossEntropyLoss()
optimizer_vit = optim.Adam(model_vit.parameters(), lr=1e-3)
```

Model Training

```
sbs_vit = StepByStep(model_vit, multi_loss_fn, optimizer_vit)
sbs_vit.set_loaders(train_loader, val_loader)
sbs_vit.train(20)
```

```
fig = sbs_vit.plot_losses()
```

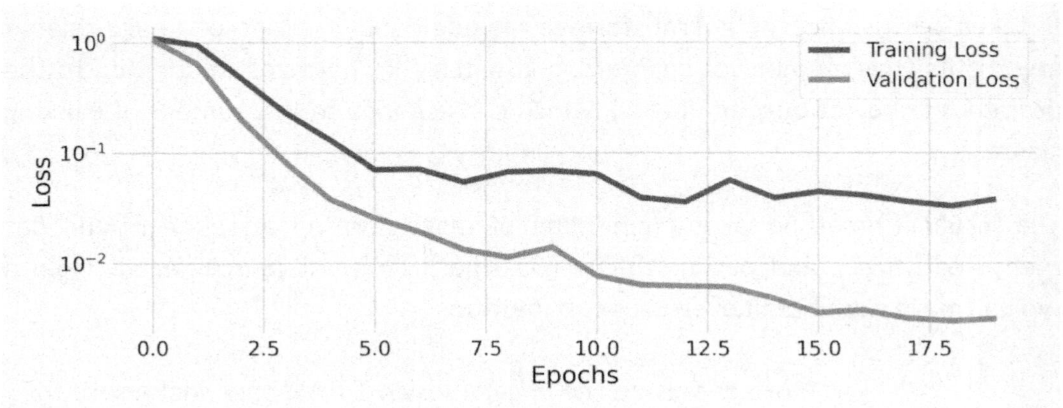

Figure 10.29 - Losses—Vision Transformer

Validation losses are lower than training losses—"*thank you*", dropout!

Once the model is trained, we can check the **embeddings** of our **special classifier token**:

```
model_vit.cls_token
```

Output

```
Parameter containing:
tensor([[[ 0.0557, -0.0345,  0.0126, -0.0300,  0.0335, -0.0422,
0.0479, -0.0248,  0.0128, -0.0605,  0.0061, -0.0178,  0.0921,
-0.0384, 0.0424, -0.0423]]], device='cuda:0', requires_grad=True)
```

Finally, let's see how **accurate** the Vision Transformer is:

```
StepByStep.loader_apply(sbs_vit.val_loader, sbs_vit.correct)
```

Output

```
tensor([[76, 76],
        [65, 65],
        [59, 59]])
```

Nailed it!

Putting It All Together

In this chapter, we used the dataset of **colored squares** to, once again, **predict the coordinates** of the last two corners (**target sequence**) given the coordinates of the first two corners (**source sequence**). We built on top of our self-attention-based encoder-decoder architecture, turning the **former encoder and decoder** classes into "**layers**" and wrapping up its internal operations with "**sub-layers**" to add **layer normalization**, **dropout**, and **residual connections** to each operation.

Data Preparation

The training set has the **full sequences** as **features**, while the test set has only the **source sequences** as **features**:

Data Preparation

```
# Training set
points, directions = generate_sequences(n=256, seed=13)
full_train = torch.as_tensor(points).float()
target_train = full_train[:, 2:]
train_data = TensorDataset(full_train, target_train)
generator = torch.Generator()
train_loader = DataLoader(train_data, batch_size=16,
                          shuffle=True, generator=generator)
# Validation/Test Set
test_points, test_directions = generate_sequences(seed=19)
full_test = torch.as_tensor(test_points).float()
source_test = full_test[:, :2]
target_test = full_test[:, 2:]
test_data = TensorDataset(source_test, target_test)
test_loader = DataLoader(test_data, batch_size=16)
```

Model Assembly

Once again, we used the **bottom-up** approach to increasingly extend our encoder-decoder architecture. Now, we're revisiting the **Transformer** in a **top-down** approach, starting from the **encoder-decoder module (1)**. In its `encode()` and `decode()` methods, it makes a call to an instance of the **encoder (2)**, followed by a call to an instance of the **decoder (3)**. We'll be representing the two called modules (2 and 3) as boxes inside the box corresponding to the caller module (1).

If we follow the complete sequence of calls, this is the resulting diagram for the **Transformer** architecture.

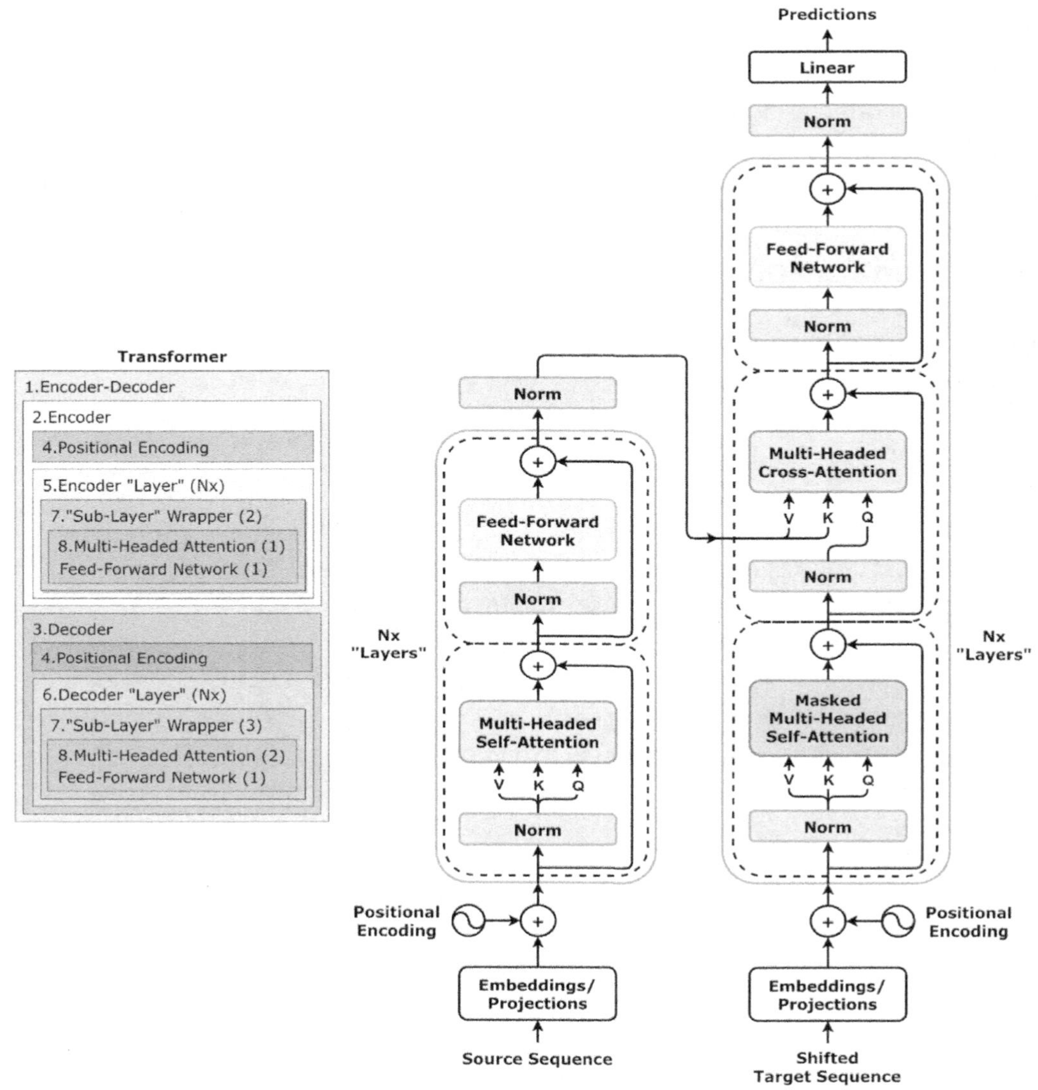

Figure 10.30 - The Transformer

Now, let's revisit the code of the represented modules. They're numbered accordingly, and so are the corresponding calls to them.

1. Encoder-Decoder

The encoder-decoder architecture was actually extended from the one developed in the previous chapter (`EncoderDecoderSelfAttn`), which handled **training** and **prediction** using **greedy decoding**. There are *no changes* here, except for the omission of both `encode()` and `decode()` methods, which are going to be overridden anyway:

Encoder + Decoder + Self-Attention

```
class EncoderDecoderSelfAttn(nn.Module):
    def __init__(self, encoder, decoder, input_len, target_len):
        super().__init__()
        self.encoder = encoder
        self.decoder = decoder
        self.input_len = input_len
        self.target_len = target_len
        self.trg_masks = self.subsequent_mask(self.target_len)

    @staticmethod
    def subsequent_mask(size):
        attn_shape = (1, size, size)
        subsequent_mask = (
            1 - torch.triu(torch.ones(attn_shape), diagonal=1)
        ).bool()
        return subsequent_mask

    def predict(self, source_seq, source_mask):
        # Decodes/generates a sequence using one input
        # at a time - used in EVAL mode
        inputs = source_seq[:, -1:]
        for i in range(self.target_len):
            out = self.decode(inputs,
                              source_mask,
                              self.trg_masks[:, :i+1, :i+1])
            out = torch.cat([inputs, out[:, -1:, :]], dim=-2)
            inputs = out.detach()
        outputs = inputs[:, 1:, :]
        return outputs

    def forward(self, X, source_mask=None):
        # Sends the mask to the same device as the inputs
        self.trg_masks = self.trg_masks.type_as(X).bool()
```

```
        # Slices the input to get source sequence
        source_seq = X[:, :self.input_len, :]
        # Encodes source sequence AND initializes decoder
        self.encode(source_seq, source_mask)
        if self.training:
            # Slices the input to get the shifted target seq
            shifted_target_seq = X[:, self.input_len-1:-1, :]
            # Decodes using the mask to prevent cheating
            outputs = self.decode(shifted_target_seq,
                                  source_mask,
                                  self.trg_masks)
        else:
            # Decodes using its own predictions
            outputs = self.predict(source_seq, source_mask)

        return outputs
```

This is the *actual* encoder-decoder Transformer, which re-implements both `encode()` and `decode()` methods to include the **input projections** and the **last linear layer** of the **decoder**. Notice the **numbered calls** to the **encoder (2)** and **decoder (3)**:

Transformer Encoder-Decoder

```
class EncoderDecoderTransf(EncoderDecoderSelfAttn):
    def __init__(self, encoder, decoder,
                 input_len, target_len, n_features):
        super(EncoderDecoderTransf, self).__init__(
            encoder, decoder, input_len, target_len
        )
        self.n_features = n_features
        self.proj = nn.Linear(n_features, encoder.d_model)
        self.linear = nn.Linear(encoder.d_model, n_features)

    def encode(self, source_seq, source_mask=None):
        # Projection
        source_proj = self.proj(source_seq)
        encoder_states = self.encoder(source_proj, source_mask)①
        self.decoder.init_keys(encoder_states)

    def decode(self, shifted_target_seq,
               source_mask=None, target_mask=None):
        # Projection
        target_proj = self.proj(shifted_target_seq)
        outputs = self.decoder(target_proj,                    ②
                               source_mask=source_mask,
                               target_mask=target_mask)
        # Linear
        outputs = self.linear(outputs)
        return outputs
```

① Calls **Encoder** (2)

② Calls **Decoder** (3)

2. Encoder

The Transformer encoder has a **list** of stacked **encoder "layers" (5)** (remember that our "layers" are *norm-first*). It also adds **positional encoding (4)** to the inputs and **normalizes** the outputs at the end:

Transformer Encoder

```
class EncoderTransf(nn.Module):
    def __init__(self, encoder_layer, n_layers=1, max_len=100):
        super().__init__()
        self.d_model = encoder_layer.d_model
        self.pe = PositionalEncoding(max_len, self.d_model)
        self.norm = nn.LayerNorm(self.d_model)
        self.layers = nn.ModuleList([copy.deepcopy(encoder_layer)
                                     for _ in range(n_layers)])

    def forward(self, query, mask=None):
        # Positional Encoding
        x = self.pe(query)        ①
        for layer in self.layers:
            x = layer(x, mask)    ②
        # Norm
        return self.norm(x)
```

① Calls **Positional Encoding** (4)

② Calls **Encoder "Layer"** (5) multiple times

3. Decoder

The Transformer decoder has a **list** of stacked **decoder "layers" (6)** (remember that our "layers" are *norm-first*). It also adds **positional encoding (4)** to the inputs and **normalizes** the outputs at the end:

Transformer Decoder

```
class DecoderTransf(nn.Module):
    def __init__(self, decoder_layer, n_layers=1, max_len=100):
        super(DecoderTransf, self).__init__()
        self.d_model = decoder_layer.d_model
        self.pe = PositionalEncoding(max_len, self.d_model)
        self.norm = nn.LayerNorm(self.d_model)
        self.layers = nn.ModuleList([copy.deepcopy(decoder_layer)
                                     for _ in range(n_layers)])

    def init_keys(self, states):
        for layer in self.layers:
            layer.init_keys(states)

    def forward(self, query, source_mask=None, target_mask=None):
        # Positional Encoding
        x = self.pe(query)                              ①
        for layer in self.layers:
            x = layer(x, source_mask, target_mask)  ②
        # Norm
        return self.norm(x)
```

① Calls **Positional Encoding** (4)

② Calls **Decoder "Layer"** (6) multiple times

4. Positional Encoding

We haven't changed the positional encoding module; it is here for the sake of completion only:

Positional Encoding

```
class PositionalEncoding(nn.Module):
    def __init__(self, max_len, d_model):
        super().__init__()
        self.d_model = d_model
        pe = torch.zeros(max_len, d_model)
        position = torch.arange(0, max_len).float().unsqueeze(1)
        angular_speed = torch.exp(
            torch.arange(0, d_model, 2).float() *
            (-np.log(10000.0) / d_model)
        )
        # even dimensions
        pe[:, 0::2] = torch.sin(position * angular_speed)
        # odd dimensions
        pe[:, 1::2] = torch.cos(position * angular_speed)
        self.register_buffer('pe', pe.unsqueeze(0))

    def forward(self, x):
        # x is N, L, D
        # pe is 1, maxlen, D
        scaled_x = x * np.sqrt(self.d_model)
        encoded = scaled_x + self.pe[:, :x.size(1), :]
        return encoded
```

5. Encoder "Layer"

The encoder "layer" implements a **list of two "sub-layers" (7)**, which are going to be called with their corresponding operations:

Encoder "Layer"

```
class EncoderLayer(nn.Module):
    def __init__(self, n_heads, d_model, ff_units, dropout=0.1):
        super().__init__()
        self.n_heads = n_heads
        self.d_model = d_model
        self.ff_units = ff_units
        self.self_attn_heads = \
            MultiHeadedAttention(n_heads, d_model, dropout)
        self.ffn = nn.Sequential(
            nn.Linear(d_model, ff_units),
            nn.ReLU(),
            nn.Dropout(dropout),
            nn.Linear(ff_units, d_model),
        )
        self.sublayers = nn.ModuleList(
            [SubLayerWrapper(d_model, dropout) for _ in range(2)]
        )

    def forward(self, query, mask=None):
        # SubLayer 0 - Self-Attention
        att = self.sublayers[0](query,                            ①
                                sublayer=self.self_attn_heads,
                                is_self_attn=True,
                                mask=mask)
        # SubLayer 1 - FFN
        out = self.sublayers[1](att, sublayer=self.ffn)          ①
        return out
```

① Calls **"Sub-Layer" wrapper** (7) twice (self-attention and feed-forward network)

"Wait, I don't remember this SubLayerWrapper *module..."*

Good catch! It is indeed **brand new**! We're defining it shortly (it's number seven, hang in there!).

6. Decoder "Layer"

The decoder "layer" implements a **list** of **three "sub-layers" (7)**, which are going to be called with their corresponding operations:

Decoder "Layer"

```
class DecoderLayer(nn.Module):
    def __init__(self, n_heads, d_model, ff_units, dropout=0.1):
        super().__init__()
        self.n_heads = n_heads
        self.d_model = d_model
        self.ff_units = ff_units
        self.self_attn_heads = \
            MultiHeadedAttention(n_heads, d_model, dropout)
        self.cross_attn_heads = \
            MultiHeadedAttention(n_heads, d_model, dropout)
        self.ffn = nn.Sequential(nn.Linear(d_model, ff_units),
                                 nn.ReLU(),
                                 nn.Dropout(dropout),
                                 nn.Linear(ff_units, d_model))
        self.sublayers = nn.ModuleList(
            [SubLayerWrapper(d_model, dropout) for _ in range(3)]
        )

    def init_keys(self, states):
        self.cross_attn_heads.init_keys(states)

    def forward(self, query, source_mask=None, target_mask=None):
        # SubLayer 0 - Masked Self-Attention
        att1 = self.sublayers[0](query, mask=target_mask,       ①
                                 sublayer=self.self_attn_heads,
                                 is_self_attn=True)
        # SubLayer 1 - Cross-Attention
        att2 = self.sublayers[1](att1, mask=source_mask,        ①
                                 sublayer=self.cross_attn_heads)
        # SubLayer 2 - FFN
        out = self.sublayers[2](att2, sublayer=self.ffn)        ①
        return out
```

① Calls **"Sub-Layer" wrapper** (7) three times (self-attention, cross-attention, and feed-forward network)

7. "Sub-Layer" Wrapper

The **"sub-layer" wrapper** implements the **norm-first** approach to **wrapping "sub-layers."**

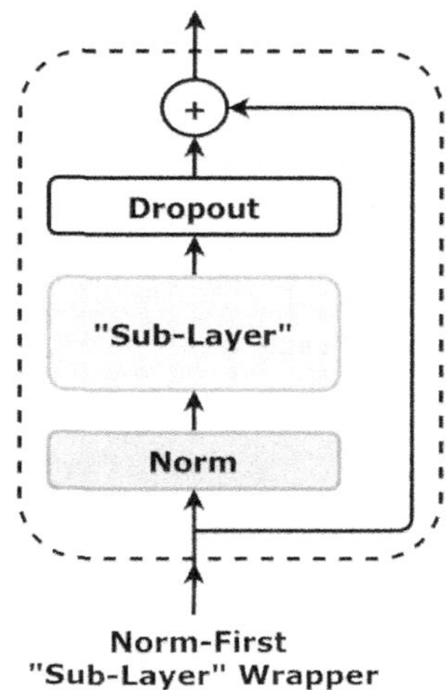

Figure 10.31 - "Sub-Layer" wrapper—norm-first

It normalizes the inputs, calls the "sub-layer" itself (passed as argument), applies dropout, and adds the residual connection at the end:

Sub-Layer Wrapper

```
class SubLayerWrapper(nn.Module):
    def __init__(self, d_model, dropout):
        super().__init__()
        self.norm = nn.LayerNorm(d_model)
        self.drop = nn.Dropout(dropout)

    def forward(self, x, sublayer, is_self_attn=False, **kwargs):
        norm_x = self.norm(x)
        if is_self_attn:
            sublayer.init_keys(norm_x)
        out = x + self.drop(sublayer(norm_x, **kwargs))          ①
        return out
```

① Calls **Multi-Headed Attention** (8) (and the feed-forward network as well, depending on the `sublayer` argument)

To make it more clear how this module was used to replace most of the code in the `forward()` method of the encoder and decoder "layers," here is a *before-after* comparison of the first "sub-layer" (self-attention) of the encoder "layer":

```
# Before
def forward(self, query, mask=None):
    # query and mask go in
    norm_query = self.norm1(query)
    self.self_attn_heads.init_keys(norm_query)
    # the sub-layer is the self-attention
    states = self.self_attn_heads(norm_query, mask)
    att = query + self.drop1(states)
    # att comes out
    ...

# After
def forward(self, query, mask=None):
    # query and mask go in
    # the sub-layer is the self-attention
    # norm, drop, and residual are inside the wrapper
    att = self.sublayers[0](query,
                            sublayer=self.self_attn_heads,
                            is_self_attn=True,
                            mask=mask)
    # att comes out
    ...
```

8. Multi-Headed Attention

The **multi-headed attention** mechanism below replicates the implemented **narrow attention** described at the start of this chapter, **chunking the projections** of "keys" (K), "values" (V), and "queries" (Q) to make the size of the model more manageable:

Multi-Headed Attention

```
class MultiHeadedAttention(nn.Module):
    def __init__(self, n_heads, d_model, dropout=0.1):
        super(MultiHeadedAttention, self).__init__()
        self.n_heads = n_heads
        self.d_model = d_model
        self.d_k = int(d_model / n_heads)
        self.linear_query = nn.Linear(d_model, d_model)
        self.linear_key = nn.Linear(d_model, d_model)
        self.linear_value = nn.Linear(d_model, d_model)
        self.linear_out = nn.Linear(d_model, d_model)
        self.dropout = nn.Dropout(p=dropout)
        self.alphas = None

    def make_chunks(self, x):
        batch_size, seq_len = x.size(0), x.size(1)
        # N, L, D -> N, L, n_heads * d_k
        x = x.view(batch_size, seq_len, self.n_heads, self.d_k)
        # N, n_heads, L, d_k
        x = x.transpose(1, 2)
        return x

    def init_keys(self, key):
        # N, n_heads, L, d_k
        self.proj_key = self.make_chunks(self.linear_key(key))
        self.proj_value = \
            self.make_chunks(self.linear_value(key))

    def score_function(self, query):
        # scaled dot product
        # N, n_heads, L, d_k x # N, n_heads, d_k, L
        # -> N, n_heads, L, L
        proj_query = self.make_chunks(self.linear_query(query))
        dot_products = torch.matmul(
            proj_query, self.proj_key.transpose(-2, -1)
        )
```

```
        scores =  dot_products / np.sqrt(self.d_k)
        return scores

    def attn(self, query, mask=None):
        # Query is batch-first: N, L, D
        # Score function will generate scores for each head
        scores = self.score_function(query) # N, n_heads, L, L
        if mask is not None:
            scores = scores.masked_fill(mask == 0, -1e9)
        alphas = F.softmax(scores, dim=-1) # N, n_heads, L, L
        alphas = self.dropout(alphas)
        self.alphas = alphas.detach()

        # N, n_heads, L, L x N, n_heads, L, d_k
        # -> N, n_heads, L, d_k
        context = torch.matmul(alphas, self.proj_value)
        return context

    def output_function(self, contexts):
        # N, L, D
        out = self.linear_out(contexts) # N, L, D
        return out

    def forward(self, query, mask=None):
        if mask is not None:
            # N, 1, L, L - every head uses the same mask
            mask = mask.unsqueeze(1)

        # N, n_heads, L, d_k
        context = self.attn(query, mask=mask)
        # N, L, n_heads, d_k
        context = context.transpose(1, 2).contiguous()
        # N, L, n_heads * d_k = N, L, d_model
        context = context.view(query.size(0), -1, self.d_model)
        # N, L, d_model
        out = self.output_function(context)
        return out
```

Model Configuration & Training

Model Configuration

```
torch.manual_seed(42)
# Layers
enclayer = EncoderLayer(n_heads=3, d_model=6,
                        ff_units=10, dropout=0.1)
declayer = DecoderLayer(n_heads=3, d_model=6,
                        ff_units=10, dropout=0.1)
# Encoder and Decoder
enctransf = EncoderTransf(enclayer, n_layers=2)
dectransf = DecoderTransf(declayer, n_layers=2)
# Transformer
model_transf = EncoderDecoderTransf(enctransf,
                                    dectransf,
                                    input_len=2,
                                    target_len=2,
                                    n_features=2)
loss = nn.MSELoss()
optimizer = torch.optim.Adam(model_transf.parameters(), lr=0.01)
```

Weight Initialization

```
for p in model_transf.parameters():
    if p.dim() > 1:
        nn.init.xavier_uniform_(p)
```

Model Training

```
sbs_seq_transf = StepByStep(model_transf, loss, optimizer)
sbs_seq_transf.set_loaders(train_loader, test_loader)
sbs_seq_transf.train(50)
```

```
sbs_seq_transf.losses[-1], sbs_seq_transf.val_losses[-1]
```

Output

```
(0.019648547226097435, 0.011462601833045483)
```

Recap

In this chapter, we've extended the **encoder-decoder architecture** and *transformed* it into a **Transformer** (the last pun of the chapter; I couldn't resist it!). First, we modified the **multi-headed attention** mechanism to use **narrow** attention. Then, we introduced **layer normalization** and the need to change the dimensionality of the inputs using either **projections** or **embeddings**. Next, we used our *former encoder and decoder* as **"layers"** that could be **stacked** to form the *new Transformer encoder and decoder*. That made our model much deeper, thus raising the need for **wrapping** the internal operations (self-, cross-attention, and feed-forward network, now called **"sub-layers"**) of each "layer" with a combination of **layer normalization**, **dropout**, and **residual connection**. This is what we've covered:

- using **narrow attention** in the multi-headed attention mechanism
- **chunking the projections** of the inputs to implement narrow attention
- learning that chunking projections allows **different heads** to focus on, literally, **different dimensions** of the inputs
- **standardizing** individual **data points** using **layer normalization**
- using layer normalization to **standardize positionally-encoded inputs**
- changing the **dimensionality** of the inputs using **projections (embeddings)**
- defining an **encoder "layer"** that uses **two "sub-layers"**: a **self-attention** mechanism and a **feed-forward** network
- **stacking** encoder "layers" to build a **Transformer encoder**
- **wrapping "sub-layer" operations** with a combination of **layer normalization**, **dropout**, and **residual connection**
- learning the difference between **norm-last** and **norm-first "sub-layers"**
- understanding that **norm-first "sub-layers"** allow the inputs to **flow unimpeded** all the way to the top through the **residual connections**
- defining a **decoder "layer"** that uses **three "sub-layers"**: a **masked self-attention** mechanism, a **cross-attention** mechanism, and a **feed-forward** network
- **stacking** decoder "layers" to build a **Transformer decoder**
- combining both **encoder and decoder** into a full-blown, norm-first **Transformer** architecture

- **training the Transformer** to tackle our sequence-to-sequence problem
- understanding that the **validation loss** may be much **lower** than the **training loss** due to regularizing effect of **dropout**
- training another model using **PyTorch's (norm-last) Transformer** class
- using the **Vision Transformer** architecture to tackle an **image classification problem**
- splitting an **image** into flattened **patches** by either **rearranging or embedding** them
- adding a **special classifier token** to the embeddings
- using the **encoder's output** corresponding to the special classifier token as **features** for the classifier

Congratulations! You've just assembled and trained your first **Transformer** (and even a cutting-edge **Vision Transformer**!): This is *no small feat*. Now you know what "layers" and "sub-layers" stand for and how they're brought together to build a Transformer. Keep in mind, though, that you may find *slightly different* implementations around. It may be either **norm-first** or **norm-last** or maybe yet another customization. The details may be different, but the overall concept remains: It is all about **stacking attention-based "layers."**

"Hey, what about BERT? Shouldn't we use Transformers to tackle NLP problems?"

I was actually *waiting* for this question: **Yes**, we should, and we will, in the next chapter. As you have seen, it is already *hard enough* to understand the Transformer even when it's used to tackle such a simple sequence-to-sequence problem as ours. Trying to train a model to handle a more complex natural language processing problem would only make it *even harder*.

In the next chapter, we'll start with *some* **NLP concepts and techniques** like tokens, tokenization, word embeddings, and language models, and work our way up to **contextual word embeddings**, **GPT-2**, and **BERT**. We'll be using several Python packages, including the famous **HuggingFace** :-)

[52] https://github.com/dvgodoy/PyTorchStepByStep/blob/master/Chapter10.ipynb

[53] https://colab.research.google.com/github/dvgodoy/PyTorchStepByStep/blob/master/Chapter10.ipynb

[54] https://arxiv.org/abs/1906.04341

[55] https://arxiv.org/abs/1706.03762

[56] http://nlp.seas.harvard.edu/2018/04/03/attention

[57] https://arxiv.org/abs/1607.06450

[58] https://arxiv.org/abs/2010.11929

[59] https://github.com/arogozhnikov/einops

[60] https://amaarora.github.io/2021/01/18/ViT.html

Chapter 11
Down the Yellow Brick Rabbit Hole

Spoilers

In this chapter, we will:

- learn about many useful packages for natural language processing (NLP): NLTK, Gensim, flair, and HuggingFace
- build our own dataset from scratch using **HuggingFace's `Dataset`**
- use different **tokenizers** on our dataset
- learn and load **word embeddings** using **Word2Vec** and **GloVe**
- train many models using **embeddings** in different ways
- use **ELMo** and **BERT** to retrieve **contextual word embeddings**
- use **HuggingFace's `Trainer`** to fine-tune BERT
- fine-tune **GPT-2** and use it in a **pipeline** to **generate text**

Jupyter Notebook

The Jupyter notebook corresponding to Chapter 11[61] is part of the official ***Deep Learning with PyTorch Step-by-Step*** repository on GitHub. You can also run it directly in **Google Colab**[62].

If you're using a *local installation*, open your terminal or Anaconda prompt and navigate to the `PyTorchStepByStep` folder you cloned from GitHub. Then, *activate* the `pytorchbook` environment and run `jupyter notebook`:

```
$ conda activate pytorchbook

(pytorchbook)$ jupyter notebook
```

If you're using Jupyter's default settings, `http://localhost:8888/notebooks/Chapter11.ipynb` should open Chapter 11's notebook. If not, just click on `Chapter11.ipynb` in your Jupyter's home page.

Additional Setup

This is a *special chapter* when it comes to its setup: We won't be using *only* PyTorch but rather a handful of other packages as well, including the *de facto* standard for NLP tasks—HuggingFace.

Before proceeding, make sure you have all of them installed by running the commands below:

```
!pip install gensim==3.8.3
!pip install allennlp==0.9.0
!pip install flair==0.8.0.post1 # uses PyTorch 1.7.1
!pip install torchvision==0.8.2
# HuggingFace
!pip install transformers==4.5.1
!pip install datasets==1.6.0
```

Some packages, like `flair`, may have *strict dependencies* and eventually require the **downgrading** of some other packages in your environment, even PyTorch itself.

The versions above were used to generate the outputs presented in this chapter, but you can use newer versions if you want (except for the `allennlp` package since this specific version is required by `flair` for retrieving ELMo embeddings).

Imports

For the sake of organization, all libraries needed throughout the code used in any given chapter are imported at its very beginning. For this chapter, we'll need the following imports:

```
import os
import json
import errno
import requests
import numpy as np
from copy import deepcopy
from operator import itemgetter
```

```python
import torch
import torch.optim as optim
import torch.nn as nn
import torch.nn.functional as F
from torch.utils.data import DataLoader, Dataset, random_split, \
    TensorDataset

from data_generation.nlp import ALICE_URL, WIZARD_URL, download_text
from stepbystep.v4 import StepByStep
# These are the classes we built in Chapters 9 and 10
from seq2seq import *

import nltk
from nltk.tokenize import sent_tokenize

import gensim
from gensim import corpora, downloader
from gensim.parsing.preprocessing import *
from gensim.utils import simple_preprocess
from gensim.models import Word2Vec

from flair.data import Sentence
from flair.embeddings import ELMoEmbeddings, WordEmbeddings, \
    TransformerWordEmbeddings, TransformerDocumentEmbeddings

from datasets import load_dataset, Split
from transformers import (
    DataCollatorForLanguageModeling,
    BertModel, BertTokenizer, BertForSequenceClassification,
    DistilBertModel, DistilBertTokenizer,
    DistilBertForSequenceClassification,
    AutoModelForSequenceClassification,
    AutoModel, AutoTokenizer, AutoModelForCausalLM,
    Trainer, TrainingArguments, pipeline, TextClassificationPipeline
)
from transformers.pipelines import SUPPORTED_TASKS
```

"Down the Yellow Brick Rabbit Hole"

Where does the phrase in the title come from? On the one hand, if it were "*down the rabbit hole,*" one could guess *Alice's Adventures in Wonderland*. On the other hand, if it were "*the yellow brick road,*" one could guess *The Wonderful Wizard of Oz*. But it is neither (or maybe it is **both**?). What if, instead of trying to guess it ourselves, we **trained a model** to **classify sentences**? This is a book about deep learning, after all :-)

Training models on text data *is* what **natural language processing (NLP)** is all about. The whole field is enormous, and we'll be only *scratching the surface* of it in this chapter. We'll start with the most obvious question: "*how do you convert text data into numerical data?*", we'll end up using a **pre-trained model**—our famous Muppet friend, **BERT**—to **classify sentences**.

Building a Dataset

There are *many* freely available datasets for NLP. The texts are usually already nicely organized into **sentences** that you can easily feed to a pre-trained model like BERT. Isn't it awesome? Well, yeah, but...

"*But what?*"

But the texts you'll find in the real world are *not* nicely organized into sentences. **You** have to organize them yourself.

So, we'll start our NLP journey by following the steps of Alice and Dorothy, from *Alice's Adventures in Wonderland* [63] by Lewis Carroll and *The Wonderful Wizard of Oz* [64] by L. Frank Baum.

Both texts are freely available at the Oxford Text Archive (OTA) [65] under an Attribution-NonCommercial-ShareAlike 3.0 Unported (CC BY-NC-SA 3.0) license.

Figure 11.1 - Left: "Alice and the Baby Pig" illustration by John Tenniel, from Alice's Adventures in Wonderland (1865). Right: "Dorothy meets the Cowardly Lion" illustration by W. W. Denslow, from The Wonderful Wizard of Oz (1900).

The direct links to both texts are alice28-1476.txt[66] (*https://bit.ly/3on4Fyn*, we're naming it `ALICE_URL`) and wizoz10-1740.txt[67] (*https://bit.ly/2ZTTHqR*, we're naming it `WIZARD_URL`). You can download both of them to a local folder using the helper function `download_text()` (included in `data_generation.nlp`):

Data Loading

```
localfolder = 'texts'
download_text(ALICE_URL, localfolder)
download_text(WIZARD_URL, localfolder)
```

If you open these files in a text editor, you'll see that there is a *lot* of information at the beginning (and some at the end) that has been added to the original text of the books for legal reasons. We need to remove these additions to the original texts:

Downloading Books

```
fname1 = os.path.join(localfolder, 'alice28-1476.txt')
with open(fname1, 'r') as f:
    alice = ''.join(f.readlines()[104:3704])
fname2 = os.path.join(localfolder, 'wizoz10-1740.txt')
with open(fname2, 'r') as f:
    wizard = ''.join(f.readlines()[310:5100])
```

The actual texts of the books are contained between lines 105 and 3703 (remember Python's zero-based indexing) and 309 and 5099, respectively. Moreover, we're **joining all the lines** together into a single large string of text for each book because we're going to organize the resulting texts into **sentences**, and in a regular book there are line breaks mid-sentence all over.

We definitely *do not* want to do that manually every time, right? Although it would be more difficult to automatically remove **any** additions to the original text, we *can* **partially** automate the removal of the extra lines by setting the **real start and end** lines of each text in a configuration file (`lines.cfg`):

Configuration File

```
text_cfg = """fname,start,end
alice28-1476.txt,104,3704
wizoz10-1740.txt,310,5100"""
bytes_written = open(
    os.path.join(localfolder, 'lines.cfg'), 'w'
).write(text_cfg)
```

Your local folder (`texts`) should have *three files* now: `alice28-1476.txt`, `lines.cfg`, and `wizoz10-1740.txt`. Now, it is time to perform...

Sentence Tokenization

A **token** is a **piece of a text**, and to **tokenize** a text means to **split it into pieces**; that is, into a **list of tokens**.

"*What kind of pieces are we talking about here?*"

The most common kind of piece is a **word**. So, **tokenizing a text** usually means to **split it into words** using the **white space** as a separator:

```
sentence = "I'm following the white rabbit"
tokens = sentence.split(' ')
tokens
```

Output

```
["I'm", 'following', 'the', 'white', 'rabbit']
```

"What about 'I'm'? Isn't it ***two words****?"*

Yes, and no. Not helpful, right? As usual, it depends—word contractions like that are fairly common, and maybe you *want* to keep them as single tokens. But it is also possible to have the token itself split into its two basic components, "*I*" and "*am*," such that the sentence above has *six tokens* instead of five. For now, we're only interested in **sentence tokenization**, which, as you probably already guessed, means to **split a text into its sentences**.

We'll get back to the topic of **tokenization** at **word** (and **subword**) levels later.

For a *brief* introduction to the topic, check the "Tokenization"[68] section of the *Introduction to Information Retrieval* [69] book by Christopher D. Manning, Prabhakar Raghavan, and Hinrich Schütze, Cambridge University Press (2008).

We're using NLTK's `sent_tokenize()` method to accomplish this instead of trying to devise the splitting rules ourselves (NLTK is the natural language toolKit library and is one of the most traditional tools for handling NLP tasks):

```
import nltk
from nltk.tokenize import sent_tokenize
nltk.download('punkt')
corpus_alice = sent_tokenize(alice)
corpus_wizard = sent_tokenize(wizard)
len(corpus_alice), len(corpus_wizard)
```

Output

```
(1612, 2240)
```

There are 1,612 sentences in *Alice's Adventures in Wonderland* and 2,240 sentences in *The Wonderful Wizard of Oz*.

"*What is this* `punkt`?"

That's the **Punkt Sentence Tokenizer**, and its pre-trained model (for the English language) is included in the NLTK package.

"*And what is a* ***corpus****?*"

A **corpus** is a structured **set of documents**. But there is quite a lot of wiggle room in this definition: One *can* define a *document* as a **sentence**, a **paragraph**, or even a **whole book**. In our case, the document is a **sentence**, so each **book is actually a set of sentences**, and thus each **book** may be considered a **corpus**. The *plural of corpus* is actually **corpora** (yay, Latin!), so we do have a corpora.

Let's check one sentence from the first corpus of text:

```
corpus_alice[2]
```

Output

```
'There was nothing so VERY remarkable in that; nor did Alice\nthink
it so VERY much out of the way to hear the Rabbit say to\nitself,
`Oh dear!'
```

Notice that it **still** includes the **line breaks (\n)** from the original text. The sentence tokenizer *only* handles the sentence splitting; it does *not* clean up the line breaks.

Let's check one sentence from the second corpus of text:

```
corpus_wizard[30]
```

Output

```
'"There\'s a cyclone coming, Em," he called to his wife.'
```

No line breaks here, but notice the **quotation marks (")** in the text.

"*Why do we care about line breaks and quotation marks anyway?*"

Our dataset is going to be a **collection of CSV files**, one file for each book, with each CSV file containing **one sentence per line**.

Therefore, we need to:

- **clean the line breaks** to make sure each sentence is on one line only;
- **define** an appropriate **quote char** to "wrap" the sentence such that the original *commas* and *semicolons* in the original text do not get misinterpreted as *separation chars* of the CSV file; and
- add a **second column** to the CSV file (the first one is the sentence itself) to identify the original *source of the sentence* since we'll be **concatenating**, and **shuffling** the sentences before training a model on our corpora.

The sentence above should end up looking like this:

```
\"There's a cyclone coming, Em," he called to his wife.\,wizoz10
-1740.txt
```

The escape character "\" is a good choice for *quote char* because it is *not present* in any of the books (we would probably have to choose something else if our books of choice were about coding).

The function below does the grunt work of cleaning, splitting, and saving the sentences to a CSV file for us:

Method to Generate CSV of Sentences

```
def sentence_tokenize(source, quote_char='\\', sep_char=',',
                      include_header=True, include_source=True,
                      extensions=('txt'), **kwargs):
    nltk.download('punkt')
    # If source is a folder, goes through all files inside it
    # that match the desired extensions ('txt' by default)
    if os.path.isdir(source):
        filenames = [f for f in os.listdir(source)
                     if os.path.isfile(os.path.join(source, f))
                     and os.path.splitext(f)[1][1:] in extensions]
    elif isinstance(source, str):
        filenames = [source]

```

```
    # If there is a configuration file, builds a dictionary with
    # the corresponding start and end lines of each text file
    config_file = os.path.join(source, 'lines.cfg')
    config = {}
    if os.path.exists(config_file):
        with open(config_file, 'r') as f:
            rows = f.readlines()

        for r in rows[1:]:
            fname, start, end = r.strip().split(',')
            config.update({fname: (int(start), int(end))})

    new_fnames = []
    # For each file of text
    for fname in filenames:
        # If there's a start and end line for that file, use it
        try:
            start, end = config[fname]
        except KeyError:
            start = None
            end = None

        # Opens the file, slices the configures lines (if any)
        # cleans line breaks and uses the sentence tokenizer
        with open(os.path.join(source, fname), 'r') as f:
            contents = (
                ''.join(f.readlines()[slice(start, end, None)])
                .replace('\n', ' ').replace('\r', '')
            )
        corpus = sent_tokenize(contents, **kwargs)

        # Builds a CSV file containing tokenized sentences
        base = os.path.splitext(fname)[0]
        new_fname = f'{base}.sent.csv'
        new_fname = os.path.join(source, new_fname)
        with open(new_fname, 'w') as f:
            # Header of the file
            if include_header:
                if include_source:
                    f.write('sentence,source\n')
                else:
                    f.write('sentence\n')
```

```
            # Writes one line for each sentence
            for sentence in corpus:
                if include_source:
                    f.write(f'{quote_char}{sentence}{quote_char}\
                              {sep_char}{fname}\n')
                else:
                    f.write(f'{quote_char}{sentence}\
                              {quote_char}\n')
        new_fnames.append(new_fname)

    # Returns list of the newly generated CSV files
    return sorted(new_fnames)
```

It takes a `source` **folder** (or a single file) and goes through the files with the right `extensions` (only `.txt` by default), removing lines based on the `lines.cfg` file (if any), applying the **sentence tokenizer** to each file, and generating the corresponding CSV files of sentences using the configured `quote_char` and `sep_char`. It may also use `include_header` and `include_source` in the CSV file.

The CSV files are named after the corresponding text files by dropping the original extension and appending `.sent.csv` to it. Let's see it in action:

Generating Dataset of Sentences

```
new_fnames = sentence_tokenize(localfolder)
new_fnames
```

Output

```
['texts/alice28-1476.sent.csv', 'texts/wizoz10-1740.sent.csv']
```

Each **CSV file** contains the **sentences of a book**, and we'll use both of them to build our own **dataset**.

Sentence Tokenization in spaCy

By the way, NLTK is *not* the only option for sentence tokenization: It is also possible to use spaCy's sentencizer for this task. The snippet below shows an example of a spaCy pipeline:

```
# conda install -c conda-forge spacy
# python -m spacy download en_core_web_sm
import spacy
nlp = spacy.blank("en")
nlp.add_pipe(nlp.create_pipe("sentencizer"))
sentences = []
for doc in nlp.pipe(corpus_alice):
    sentences.extend(sent.text for sent in doc.sents)
len(sentences), sentences[2]
```

Output

```
(1615, 'There was nothing so VERY remarkable in that; nor did
Alice\nthink it so VERY much out of the way to hear the Rabbit
say to\nitself, `Oh dear!')
```

Since spaCy uses a different model for tokenizing sentences, it is no surprise that it found a *slightly different* number of sentences in the text.

HuggingFace's Dataset

We'll be using HuggingFace's datasets instead of regular PyTorch ones.

"Why?"

First, we'll be using HuggingFace's **pre-trained models** (like BERT) later on, so it is only logical to use their implementation of datasets as well. Second, there are many **datasets already available** in their library, so it makes sense to get used to handling text data using their implementation of datasets.

Even though we're using HuggingFace's `Dataset` class to build our own dataset, we're only using a fraction of its capabilities. For a more detailed view of what it has to offer, make sure to check its extensive documentation:

- Quick Tour (*https://bit.ly/3iJzauj*)
- What's in the Dataset Object (*https://bit.ly/2WaeW5k*)
- Loading a Dataset (*https://bit.ly/3zwZzlP*)

And, for a complete list of every dataset available, check the HuggingFace Hub.[70]

Loading a Dataset

We can use HF's (I will abbreviate HuggingFace as HF from now on) `load_dataset()` to load from local files:

Data Preparation

```
from datasets import load_dataset, Split
dataset = load_dataset(path='csv',
                       data_files=new_fnames,
                       quotechar='\\',
                       split=Split.TRAIN)
```

The name of the first argument (`path`) may be a bit misleading—it is actually the **path** to the **dataset processing script**, not the actual files. To load CSV files, we simply use HF's `csv` as in the example above. The list of *actual files* containing the text (sentences, in our case) must be provided in the `data_files` argument. The `split` argument is used to designate which *split* the dataset represents (`Split.TRAIN`, `Split.VALIDATION`, or `Split.TEST`).

Moreover, the CSV script offers more options to control parsing and reading of the CSV files, like `quotechar`, `delimiter`, `column_names`, `skip_rows`, and `quoting`. For more details, please check the documentation on loading CSV files[71].

It is also possible to load data from JSON files, text files, Python dictionaries, and Pandas dataframes.

Attributes

The `Dataset` has many attributes, like `features`, `num_columns`, and `shape`:

```
dataset.features, dataset.num_columns, dataset.shape
```

Output

```
({'sentence': Value(dtype='string', id=None),
  'source': Value(dtype='string', id=None)},
 2,
 (3852, 2))
```

Our dataset has two columns, `sentence` and `source`, and there are 3,852 sentences in it.

It can be indexed like a **list**:

```
dataset[2]
```

Output

```
{'sentence': 'There was nothing so VERY remarkable in that; nor did
Alice think it so VERY much out of the way to hear the Rabbit say to
itself, `Oh dear!',
 'source': 'alice28-1476.txt'}
```

That's the third sentence in our dataset, and it is from *Alice's Adventures in Wonderland*.

And its columns can be accessed as a **dictionary** too:

```
dataset['source'][:3]
```

Output

```
['alice28-1476.txt', 'alice28-1476.txt', 'alice28-1476.txt']
```

The first few sentences all come from *Alice's Adventures in Wonderland* because we haven't *shuffled* the dataset yet.

Methods

The `Dataset` also has many methods, like `unique()`, `map()`, `filter()`, `shuffle()`, and `train_test_split()` (for a comprehensive list of operations, check HF's "Processing data in a Dataset."[72])

We can easily check the unique sources:

```
dataset.unique('source')
```

Output

```
['alice28-1476.txt', 'wizoz10-1740.txt']
```

We can use `map()` to **create new columns** by using a **function** that **returns a dictionary** with the **new column as key**:

Data Preparation

```
def is_alice_label(row):
    is_alice = int(row['source'] == 'alice28-1476.txt')
    return {'labels': is_alice}

dataset = dataset.map(is_alice_label)
```

Each element in the dataset is a `row` corresponding to a dictionary (`{'sentence': ..., 'source': ...}`, in our case), so the function has access to all columns in a given row. Our `is_alice_label()` function tests the `source` column and **creates a `labels` column**. There is **no need** to return the original columns since this is automatically handled by the dataset.

If we retrieve the third sentence from our dataset once again, the new column will already be there:

```
dataset[2]
```

Output

```
{'labels': 1,
 'sentence': 'There was nothing so VERY remarkable in that; nor did
Alice think it so VERY much out of the way to hear the Rabbit say to
itself, `Oh dear!',
 'source': 'alice28-1476.txt'}
```

Now that the labels are in place, we can finally **shuffle the dataset** and **split** it into training and test sets:

Data Preparation

```
shuffled_dataset = dataset.shuffle(seed=42)
split_dataset = shuffled_dataset.train_test_split(test_size=0.2)
split_dataset
```

Output

```
DatasetDict({
    train: Dataset({
        features: ['sentence', 'source'],
        num_rows: 3081
    })
    test: Dataset({
        features: ['sentence', 'source'],
        num_rows: 771
    })
})
```

The *splits* are actually a **dataset dictionary**, so you may want to retrieve the actual datasets from it:

Data Preparation

```
train_dataset = split_dataset['train']
test_dataset = split_dataset['test']
```

Done! We have two—training and test—randomly shuffled datasets.

Word Tokenization

The naïve word tokenization, as we've already seen, simply **splits a sentence into words** using the **white space** as a separator:

```
sentence = "I'm following the white rabbit"
tokens = sentence.split(' ')
tokens
```

Output

```
["I'm", 'following', 'the', 'white', 'rabbit']
```

But, as we've *also* seen, there are issues with the naïve approach (how to handle contractions, for example). Let's try using Gensim,[73] a popular library for topic modeling, which offers some out-of-the-box tools for performing word tokenization:

```
from gensim.parsing.preprocessing import *
preprocess_string(sentence)
```

Output

```
['follow', 'white', 'rabbit']
```

"That doesn't look right ... some words are simply gone!"

Welcome to the world of tokenization :-) It turns out, Gensim's `preprocess_string()` applies **many filters** by default, namely:

- `strip_tags()` (for removing HTML-like tags between brackets)
- `strip_punctuation()`
- `strip_multiple_whitespaces()`
- `strip_numeric()`

The filters above are pretty straightforward, and they are used to remove typical elements from the text. But `preprocess_string()` *also* includes the following filters:

- `strip_short()`: It **discards** any word **less than three characters** long.
- `remove_stopwords()`: It **discards** any word that is considered a **stop word** (like "*the*," "*but*," "*then*," and so on).
- `stem_text()`: It **modifies** words by **stemming** them; that is, reducing them to a **common base form** (from "*following*" to its base "*follow*," for example).

For a brief introduction to **stemming** (and the related **lemmatization**) procedures, please check the "Stemming and lemmatization"[74] section of the *Introduction to Information Retrieval* [75] book by Christopher D. Manning, Prabhakar Raghavan, and Hinrich Schütze, Cambridge University Press (2008).

We **won't** be removing stop words or performing stemming here. Since our goal is to use HF's pre-trained BERT model, we'll also use its corresponding **pre-trained tokenizer**.

So, let's use the *first four filters only* (and make everything lowercase too):

```
filters = [lambda x: x.lower(),
           strip_tags,
           strip_punctuation,
           strip_multiple_whitespaces, strip_numeric]
preprocess_string(sentence, filters=filters)
```

Output

```
['i', 'm', 'following', 'the', 'white', 'rabbit']
```

Another option is to use Gensim's `simple_preprocess()`, which converts the text into a list of lowercase tokens, discarding tokens that are either too short (less than three characters) or too long (more than fifteen characters):

```
from gensim.utils import simple_preprocess
tokens = simple_preprocess(sentence)
tokens
```

Output

```
['following', 'the', 'white', 'rabbit']
```

"Why are we using Gensim? Can't we use NLTK to perform word tokenization?"

Fair enough. NLTK *can* be used to tokenize words as well, but Gensim *cannot* be used to tokenize sentences. Besides, since Gensim has many *other* interesting tools for building vocabularies, bag-of-words (BoW) models, and *Word2Vec* models (we'll get to that soon), it makes sense to introduce it as soon as possible.

Data Augmentation

Let's briefly address the topic of **augmentation** for text data. Although we're not actually including it in our pipeline here, it's worth knowing about some possibilities and techniques regarding data augmentation.

The most basic technique is called **word dropout**, and, as you probably guessed, it simply **randomly replaces words** with some other random word or a special `[UNK]` token (word) that indicates a non-existing word.

It is also possible to replace words with their **synonyms**, so the meaning of the text is preserved. One can use WordNet,[76] a lexical database for the English language, to look up synonyms. Finding synonyms is not so easy, and this approach is limited to the English language.

To circumvent the limitations of the synonyms approach, it is also possible to replace words with **similar words**, numerically speaking. We haven't yet talked about **word embeddings**—numerical representations of words—but they can be used to identify words that **may** have a similar meaning. For now, it suffices to say that there are packages that perform data augmentation on text data using embeddings, like TextAttack.[77]

Let's try augmenting Richard P. Feynman, as an example:

```
# !pip install textattack
from textattack.augmentation import EmbeddingAugmenter
augmenter = EmbeddingAugmenter()
feynman = 'What I cannot create, I do not understand.'
```

```
for i in range(4):
    print(augmenter.augment(feynman))
```

Output

```
['What I cannot create, I do not fathom.']
['What I cannot create, I do not understood.']
['What I notable create, I do not understand.']
['What I significant create, I do not understand.']
```

Some are OK, some are changing the tense, some are simply weird. No one said data augmentation was easy, right?

Vocabulary

The **vocabulary** is a **list of unique words** that appear in the text corpora.

To build our own vocabulary, we need to tokenize our training set first:

```
sentences = train_dataset['sentence']
tokens = [simple_preprocess(sent) for sent in sentences]
tokens[0]
```

Output

```
['and', 'so', 'far', 'as', 'they', 'knew', 'they', 'were', 'quite',
'right']
```

The `tokens` variable is a **list of lists of words**, each (inner) list containing all the words (tokens) in a sentence. These tokens can then be used to build a **vocabulary** using Gensim's `corpora.Dictionary`:

```
from gensim import corpora
dictionary = corpora.Dictionary(tokens)
print(dictionary)
```

Output

```
Dictionary(3704 unique tokens: ['and', 'as', 'far', 'knew', 'quite'
]...)
```

The corpora's dictionary **is not** a typical Python dictionary. It has some specific (and useful) attributes:

```
dictionary.num_docs
```

Output

```
3081
```

The `num_docs` attribute tells us how many *documents* were processed (sentences, in our case), and it corresponds to the length of the (outer) list of tokens.

```
dictionary.num_pos
```

Output

```
50802
```

The `num_pos` attribute tells us how many *tokens* (words) were processed over all documents (sentences).

```
dictionary.token2id
```

Output

```
{'and': 0,
 'as': 1,
 'far': 2,
 'knew': 3,
 'quite': 4,
 ...
```

The `token2id` attribute is a (Python) dictionary containing **the unique words** found in the text corpora, and a **unique ID sequentially assigned** to the words.

The **keys** of the `token2id` dictionary are the actual **vocabulary** of our corpora:

```
vocab = list(dictionary.token2id.keys())
vocab[:5]
```

Output

```
['and', 'as', 'far', 'knew', 'quite']
```

The `cfs` attribute stands for **collection frequencies** and tells us **how many times** a given token appears in the text corpora:

```
dictionary.cfs
```

Output

```
{0: 2024,
 6: 362,
 2: 29,
 1: 473,
 7: 443,
 ...
```

The token corresponding to the **ID zero** ("*and*") appeared 2,024 times across all sentences. But, in **how many distinct documents** (sentences) did it appear? That's what the `dfs` attribute, which stands for **document frequencies**, tells us:

```
dictionary.dfs
```

Output

```
{0: 1306,
 6: 351,
 2: 27,
 1: 338,
 7: 342,
 ...
```

The token corresponding to the **ID zero** ("*and*") appeared in 1,306 sentences.

Finally, if we want to **convert a list of tokens** into a **list of their corresponding indices in the vocabulary**, we can use the `doc2idx()` method:

```
sentence = 'follow the white rabbit'
new_tokens = simple_preprocess(sentence)
ids = dictionary.doc2idx(new_tokens)
print(new_tokens)
print(ids)
```

Output

```
['follow', 'the', 'white', 'rabbit']
[1482, 20, 497, 333]
```

The problem is, however *large* we make the vocabulary, **there will always be a new word that's not in there**.

*"What do we do with words that **aren't** in the vocabulary?"*

If the word **isn't** in the vocabulary, it is an **unknown** word, and it is going to be replaced by the corresponding **special token**: `[UNK]`. This means we need to **add `[UNK]` to the vocabulary**. Luckily, Gensim's `Dictionary` has a `patch_with_special_tokens()` method that makes it very easy to *patch* our vocabulary:

```
special_tokens = {'[PAD]': 0, '[UNK]': 1}
dictionary.patch_with_special_tokens(special_tokens)
```

Besides, since we're at it, let's add **yet another special token: `[PAD]`**. At some point, we'll have to *pad* our sequences (like we did in Chapter 8), so it will be useful to have a token ready for it.

What if, instead of adding more tokens to the vocabulary, we try **removing words** from it? Maybe we'd like to remove *rare words* (**aardvark** always comes to my mind) to get a smaller vocabulary, or maybe we'd like to remove *bad words* (profanity) from it.

Gensim's dictionary has a couple of methods that we can use for this:

- `filter_extremes()`: Keeps the first **keep_n** most frequent words only (it is also possible to **keep** words that appear in **at least no_below documents** or to **remove** words that appear in **more than no_above fraction of documents**).
- `filter_tokens()`: **Removes tokens** from a list of **bad_ids** (`doc2idx()` can be used to get a list of the corresponding IDs of the bad words) or **keeps** only the tokens from a list of **good_ids**.

"What if I want to remove words that appear less than X times in all documents?"

That's not directly supported by Gensim's `Dictionary`, but we can use its `cfs` attribute to find those tokens with low frequency and then filter them out using `filter_tokens()`:

Method to Find Rare Tokens

```
def get_rare_ids(dictionary, min_freq):
    rare_ids = [t[0] for t in dictionary.cfs.items()
                if t[1] < min_freq]
    return rare_ids
```

Once we're happy with the size and scope of a vocabulary, we can **save it to disk** as a plain text file, one token (word) per line. The helper function below takes a **list of sentences**, generates the corresponding **vocabulary**, and saves it to a file named `vocab.txt`:

Method to Build a Vocabulary from a Dataset of Sentences

```
def make_vocab(sentences, folder=None, special_tokens=None,
               vocab_size=None, min_freq=None):
    if folder is not None:
        if not os.path.exists(folder):
            os.mkdir(folder)

    # tokenizes the sentences and creates a Dictionary
    tokens = [simple_preprocess(sent) for sent in sentences]
    dictionary = corpora.Dictionary(tokens)
    # keeps only the most frequent words (vocab size)
    if vocab_size is not None:
        dictionary.filter_extremes(keep_n=vocab_size)
    # removes rare words (in case the vocab size still
    # includes words with low frequency)
    if min_freq is not None:
        rare_tokens = get_rare_ids(dictionary, min_freq)
        dictionary.filter_tokens(bad_ids=rare_tokens)
    # gets the whole list of tokens and frequencies
    items = dictionary.cfs.items()
    # sorts the tokens in descending order
    words = [dictionary[t[0]]
             for t in sorted(dictionary.cfs.items(),
                             key=lambda t: -t[1])]
    # prepends special tokens, if any
    if special_tokens is not None:
        to_add = []
        for special_token in special_tokens:
            if special_token not in words:
                to_add.append(special_token)
        words = to_add + words

    with open(os.path.join(folder, 'vocab.txt'), 'w') as f:
        for word in words:
            f.write(f'{word}\n')
```

We can take the sentences from our training set, add special tokens to the vocabulary, filter out any words appearing only once, and save the vocabulary file to the `our_vocab` folder:

```
make_vocab(train_dataset['sentence'],
           'our_vocab/',
           special_tokens=['[PAD]', '[UNK]'],
           min_freq=2)
```

And now we can use this vocabulary file with a **tokenizer**.

*"But I thought we were **already** using tokenizers … aren't we?"*

Yes, we are. First, we used a sentence tokenizer to split the texts into sentences. Then, we used a word tokenizer to split each sentence into words. But there is **yet another tokenizer**…

HuggingFace's Tokenizer

Since we're using HF's datasets, it is only logical that we use HF's tokenizers as well, right? Besides, in order to use a **pre-trained BERT model**, we need to use the model's **corresponding pre-trained tokenizer**.

"Why?"

Just like pre-trained computer vision models require that the input images are standardized using ImageNet statistics, pre-trained language models like BERT require that the inputs are properly tokenized. The tokenization used in BERT is *different* than the simple word tokenization we've just discussed. We'll get back to that in due time, but let's stick with the simple tokenization for now.

So, before loading a pre-trained tokenizer, let's create our **own tokenizer** using our **own vocabulary**. HuggingFace's tokenizers also expect a **sentence** as input, and they also proceed to perform *some sort* of word tokenization. But, instead of simply returning the tokens themselves, these tokenizers return the **indices in the vocabulary** corresponding to the tokens, and **lots of additional information**. It's like Gensim's `doc2idx()`, but on steroids! Let's see it in action!

We'll be using the `BertTokenizer` class to create a tokenizer based on our own vocabulary:

```
from transformers import BertTokenizer
tokenizer = BertTokenizer('our_vocab/vocab.txt')
```

The purpose of this is to **illustrate how the tokenizer works** using simple word tokenization only! The (pre-trained) tokenizer you'll use for real with a (pre-trained) BERT model **does not need a vocabulary**.

The tokenizer class is very rich and offers a plethora of methods and arguments. We're just using some basic methods that barely scratch the surface. For more details, please refer to HuggingFace's documentation on the `tokenizer` [78] and `BertTokenizer` [79] classes.

Then, let's tokenize a new sentence using its `tokenize()` method:

```
new_sentence = 'follow the white rabbit neo'
new_tokens = tokenizer.tokenize(new_sentence)
new_tokens
```

Output

```
['follow', 'the', 'white', 'rabbit', '[UNK]']
```

Since Neo (from *The Matrix*) **isn't** part of the original *Alice's Adventures in Wonderland*, it couldn't possibly be in our vocabulary, and thus it is treated as an **unknown** word with its corresponding special token.

*"There is nothing new here—wasn't it supposed to return **indices** and more?"*

Wait for it... First, we actually *can* get the **indices** (the token IDs) using the `convert_tokens_to_ids()` method:

```
new_ids = tokenizer.convert_tokens_to_ids(new_tokens)
new_ids
```

Output

```
[1219, 5, 229, 200, 1]
```

"OK, fine, but that doesn't seem very practical."

You're absolutely right. We can use the `encode()` method to perform two steps at once:

```
new_ids = tokenizer.encode(new_sentence)
new_ids
```

Output

```
[3, 1219, 5, 229, 200, 1, 2]
```

There we go, from sentence to token IDs in one call!

*"Nice try! There are **more IDs** than tokens in this output! Something must be wrong..."*

Yes, there are more IDs than tokens. No, there's nothing wrong; it's actually meant to be like that. These extra tokens are **special tokens** too. We *could* look them up in the vocabulary using their indices (three and two), but it's nicer to use the tokenizer's `convert_ids_to_tokens()` method:

```
tokenizer.convert_ids_to_tokens(new_ids)
```

Output

```
['[CLS]', 'follow', 'the', 'white', 'rabbit', '[UNK]', '[SEP]']
```

The tokenizer not only **appended a special separation token (`[SEP]`)** to the output, but also **prepended a special classifier token (`[CLS]`)** to it. We've already added a classifier token to the inputs of a *Vision Transformer* to use its corresponding output in a classification task. We can do the same here to classify text using BERT.

*"What about the **separation token**?"*

This special token is used to, well, **separate** inputs into **two distinct sentences**. Yes, it is possible to feed BERT with two sentences at once, and this kind of input is used for the **next sentence prediction** task. We won't be using that in our example, but we'll get back to it while discussing how BERT is trained.

We can actually *get rid of the special tokens* if we're not using them:

```
tokenizer.encode(new_sentence, add_special_tokens=False)
```

Output

```
[1219, 5, 229, 200, 1]
```

*"OK, but where is the promised **additional information**?"*

That's easy enough—we can simply **call the tokenizer itself** instead of a particular method and it will produce an enriched output:

```
tokenizer(new_sentence,
          add_special_tokens=False,
          return_tensors='pt')
```

Output

```
{'input_ids': tensor([[1219,    5,  229,  200,    1]]),
 'token_type_ids': tensor([[0, 0, 0, 0, 0]]),
 'attention_mask': tensor([[1, 1, 1, 1, 1]])}
```

By default, the outputs are *lists*, but we used the `return_tensors` argument to get PyTorch tensors instead (`pt` stands for PyTorch). There are **three outputs** in the dictionary: `input_ids`, `token_type_ids`, and `attention_mask`.

The first one, `input_ids`, is the familiar list of token IDs. They are the most fundamental input, and sometimes the only one, required by the model.

The second output, `token_type_ids`, works as a **sentence index**, and it only makes sense if the input has **more than one sentence** (and the special separation tokens between them). For example:

```
sentence1 = 'follow the white rabbit neo'
sentence2 = 'no one can be told what the matrix is'
tokenizer(sentence1, sentence2)
```

Output

```
{'input_ids': [3, 1219, 5, 229, 200, 1, 2, 51, 42, 78, 32, 307, 41,
5, 1, 30, 2], 'token_type_ids': [0, 0, 0, 0, 0, 0, 0, 1, 1, 1, 1, 1,
1, 1, 1, 1, 1], 'attention_mask': [1, 1, 1, 1, 1, 1, 1, 1, 1, 1, 1,
1, 1, 1, 1, 1, 1]}
```

Although the tokenizer received **two sentences** as arguments, it considered them a **single input**, thus producing a **single sequence of IDs**. Let's convert the IDs back to tokens and inspect the result:

```
print(
    tokenizer.convert_ids_to_tokens(joined_sentences['input_ids'])
)
```

Output

```
['[CLS]', 'follow', 'the', 'white', 'rabbit', '[UNK]', '[SEP]',
'no', 'one', 'can', 'be', 'told', 'what', 'the', '[UNK]', 'is',
'[SEP]']
```

The two sentences were concatenated together with a special separation token (`[SEP]`) at the end of each one.

The last output, `attention_mask`, works as the **source mask** we used in the **Transformer encoder** and indicates the **padded positions**. In a **batch of sentences**, for example, we may *pad* the sequences to get them all with the same length:

```
separate_sentences = tokenizer([sentence1, sentence2], padding=True)
separate_sentences
```

Output

```
{'input_ids': [[3, 1219, 5, 229, 200, 1, 2, 0, 0, 0, 0], [3, 51, 42,
78, 32, 307, 41, 5, 1, 30, 2]], 'token_type_ids': [[0, 0, 0, 0, 0,
0, 0, 0, 0, 0, 0], [0, 0, 0, 0, 0, 0, 0, 0, 0, 0, 0]],
'attention_mask': [[1, 1, 1, 1, 1, 1, 1, 0, 0, 0, 0], [1, 1, 1, 1,
1, 1, 1, 1, 1, 1, 1]]}
```

The tokenizer received a **list of two sentences**, and it took them as **two independent inputs**, thus producing **two sequences of IDs**. Moreover, since the `padding` argument was `True`, it padded the shortest sequence (five tokens) to match the longest one (nine tokens). Let's convert the IDs back to tokens again:

```
print(
    tokenizer.convert_ids_to_tokens(
        separate_sentences['input_ids'][0]
    )
)
print(separate_sentences['attention_mask'][0])
```

Output

```
['[CLS]', 'follow', 'the', 'white', 'rabbit', '[UNK]', '[SEP]',
'[PAD]', '[PAD]', '[PAD]', '[PAD]']
[1, 1, 1, 1, 1, 1, 1, 0, 0, 0, 0]
```

Each **padded element** in the sequence has a **corresponding zero** in the **attention mask**.

*"Then how can I have a **batch** where **each input** has **two separate sentences**?"*

Excellent question! It's actually easy: Simply use **two batches**, one containing the **first sentence** of each pair, the other containing the **second sentence** of each pair:

```
first_sentences = [sentence1, 'another first sentence']
second_sentences = [sentence2, 'a second sentence here']
batch_of_pairs = tokenizer(first_sentences, second_sentences)
first_input = tokenizer.convert_ids_to_tokens(
                    batch_of_pairs['input_ids'][0]
              )
second_input = tokenizer.convert_ids_to_tokens(
                    batch_of_pairs['input_ids'][1]
              )
print(first_input)
print(second_input)
```

Output

```
['[CLS]', 'follow', 'the', 'white', 'rabbit', '[UNK]', '[SEP]',
'no', 'one', 'can', 'be', 'told', 'what', 'the', '[UNK]', 'is',
'[SEP]']
['[CLS]', 'another', 'first', 'sentence', '[SEP]', '[UNK]',
'second', 'sentence', 'here', '[SEP]']
```

The batch above has only two inputs, and each input has two sentences.

Finally, let's apply our tokenizer to our dataset of sentences, padding them and returning PyTorch tensors:

```
tokenized_dataset = tokenizer(dataset['sentence'],
                              padding=True,
                              return_tensors='pt',
                              max_length=50,
                              truncation=True)
tokenized_dataset['input_ids']
```

Output

```
tensor([[  3,  27,   1,  ...,   0,   0,   0],
        [  3,  24,  10,  ...,   0,   0,   0],
        [  3,  49,  12,  ...,   0,   0,   0],
        ...,
        [  3,   1,   6,  ...,   0,   0,   0],
        [  3,   6, 132,  ...,   0,   0,   0],
        [  3,   1,   1,  ...,   0,   0,   0]])
```

Since our books may have some *really long sentences*, we can use both `max_length` and `truncation` arguments to ensure that sentences longer than 50 tokens get truncated, and those shorter than that, padded.

For more details on **padding** and **truncation**, please check the awesomely named "Everything you always wanted to know about padding and truncation"[80] section of HuggingFace's documentation.

"Are we done? Can we feed the `input_ids` *to BERT and watch the magic happen?"*

Well, yeah, we could—but wouldn't you prefer to **peek behind the curtain** instead? I thought so :-)

Behind the curtain, BERT is actually using **vectors** to represent the **words**. The **token IDs** we'll be sending it are simply the **indices** of an **enormous lookup table**. That lookup table has a very nice name: **Word Embeddings**.

Each **row** of the lookup table corresponds to a different **token**, and each row is represented by a **vector**. The **size of the vectors** is the **dimensionality of the embedding**.

"How do we build these vectors?"

That's the million-dollar question! We can either *build them* or **learn them**.

Before Word Embeddings

Before getting to the *actual* word embeddings, let's start with the **basics** and *build* some simple vectors...

One-Hot Encoding (OHE)

The idea behind OHE is quite simple: Each **unique token** (word) is represented by a **vector full of zeros except for one position**, which corresponds to the **token's index**. As vectors go, it doesn't get any simpler than that.

Let's see it in action using only five tokens—"*and*," "*as*," "*far*," "*knew*," and "*quite*"—and generate **one-hot encoding** representations for them.

Token	0	1	2	3	4
and	1	0	0	0	0
as	0	1	0	0	0
far	0	0	1	0	0
knew	0	0	0	1	0
quite	0	0	0	0	1

Figure 11.2 - One-hot encoding—vocabulary of five words

The figure above would be the OHE representations of these five tokens **if there were only five tokens in total**. But there are 3,704 unique tokens in our text corpora (not counting the added special tokens), so the OHE actually looks like this:

Token	0	1	2	3	4	...	3703
and	1	0	0	0	0	...	0
as	0	1	0	0	0	...	0
far	0	0	1	0	0	...	0
knew	0	0	0	1	0	...	0
quite	0	0	0	0	1	...	0
...	...	...	...	...	...	...	...
ye	0	0	0	0	0	...	1

Figure 11.3 - One-hot encoding—our full vocabulary

That's quite a **large** and **sparse** (that's *fancy* for *way more zeros than non-zeros*) vector, right? And our vocabulary is not even *that* large! If we were to use a typical English vocabulary, we would need vectors of 100,000 dimensions. Clearly, this isn't very practical. Nonetheless, the sparse vectors produced by the one-hot encoding are the basis of a **fairly basic NLP model**: the **bag-of-words (BoW)**.

Bag-of-Words (BoW)

The bag-of-words model is **literally** a bag of words: It simply **sums up the corresponding OHE vectors**, completely disregarding any underlying structure or relationships between the words. The resulting vector has only the **counts** of the words appearing in the text.

We don't have to do the counting manually, though, since Gensim's `Dictionary` has a `doc2bow()` method that does the job for us:

```
sentence = 'the white rabbit is a rabbit'
bow_tokens = simple_preprocess(sentence)
bow_tokens
```

Output

```
['the', 'white', 'rabbit', 'is', 'rabbit']
```

```
bow = dictionary.doc2bow(bow_tokens)
bow
```

Output

```
[(20, 1), (69, 1), (333, 2), (497, 1)]
```

The word "*rabbit*" appears *twice* in the sentence, so its *index* (333) shows the corresponding *count* (2). Also, notice that the fifth word in the original sentence (" *a*") did not qualify as a valid token, because it was filtered out by the `simple_preprocess()` function for being too short.

The BoW model is obviously very **limited** since it represents the **frequencies** of each word in a piece of text and nothing else. Moreover, representing **words** using **one-hot-encoded vectors** also presents severe limitations: Not only do the vectors become more and more **sparse** (that is, have more zeros in them) as the vocabulary grows, but also **every word is orthogonal to all the other words.**

*"What do you mean by one word being **orthogonal** to the others?"*

Remember the **cosine similarity** from Chapter 9? Two vectors are said to be **orthogonal** to each other if there is a **right angle** between them, corresponding to a **similarity of zero**. So, if we use **one-hot-encoded** vectors to represent words, we're basically saying that **no two words are similar to each other**. This is obviously **wrong** (take synonyms, for example).

"How can we get better vectors to represent words then?"

Well, we can try to explore the **structure** and the **relationship** between words in a given sentence. That's the role of...

Language Models

A **language model (LM)** is a model that estimates the **probability of a token** or sequence of tokens. We've been using **token** and **word** somewhat interchangeably, but a token can be a single character or a sub-word too. In other words, a language model will predict the tokens more likely to **fill in a blank**.

Now, pretend you're a language model and fill in the blank in the following sentence.

Nice	to	meet	[BLANK]

Figure 11.4 - What's the next word?

You probably filled the blank in with the word "**you**."

Nice	to	meet	you

Figure 11.5 - Filling in the [BLANK]

What about this sentence?

to	meet	you	[BLANK]

Figure 11.6 - What's the next word?

Maybe you filled this blank in with "**too**," or maybe you chose a different word like "**here**" or "**now**," depending on what you assumed to be preceding the first word.

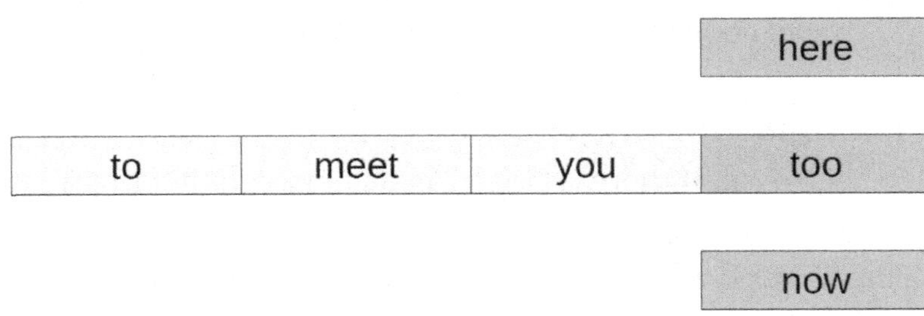

Figure 11.7 - Many options for filling in the [BLANK]

That's easy, right? How did you do it, though? How do you know that "***you***" should follow "*nice to meet*"? You've probably read and said "*nice to meet you*" thousands of times. But have you ever read or said: "*Nice to meet aardvark*"? Me neither!

What about the second sentence? It's not that obvious anymore, but I bet you can still rule out "*to meet you aardvark*" (or at least admit that's *very* unlikely to be the case).

It turns out, we have a language model in our heads too, and it's straightforward to guess which words are good choices to fill in the blanks using **sequences** that are familiar to us.

N-grams

The structure, in the examples above, is composed of **three words** and a **blank**: a **four-gram**. If we were using *two words* and blank, that would be a *trigram*, and, for a given number of words (***n-1***) followed by a blank, an ***n-gram***.

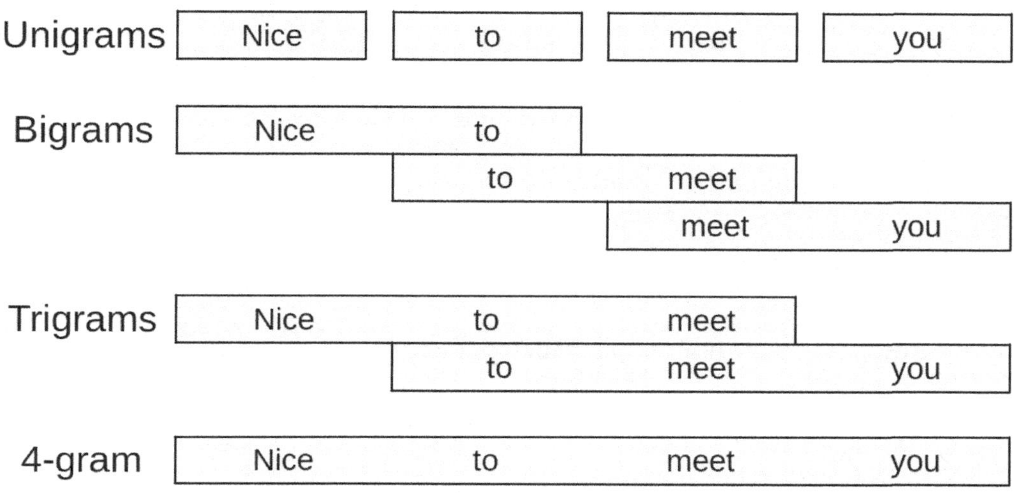

Figure 11.8 - N-grams

N-gram models are based on pure statistics: They fill in the blanks using the **most common sequence** that matches the **words preceding the blank** (that's called the **context**). On the one hand, larger values of ***n*** (longer sequences of words) may yield better predictions; on the other hand, they may yield **no predictions** since a particular sequence of words may have never been observed. In the latter case, one can always fall back to a *shorter n-gram* and try again (that's called a *stupid back-off*, by the way).

For a more detailed explanation of n-gram models, please check the "N-gram Language Models"[81] section of Lena Voita's amazing "NLP Course | For You."[82]

These models are simple, but they are somewhat limited because they can only **look back**.

*"Can we **look ahead** too?"*

Sure, we can!

Continuous Bag-of-Words (CBoW)

In these models, the **context** is given by the **surrounding words**, both **before and after the blank**. That way, it becomes **much easier** to predict the word that best fills in the blank. Let's say we're trying to fill in the following blank:

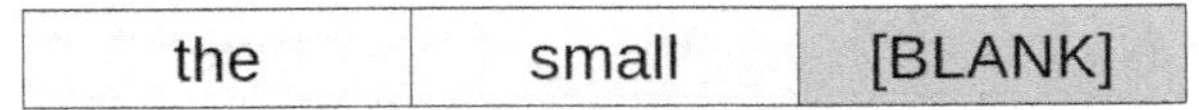

Figure 11.9 - Filling the [BLANK] at the end

That's what a *trigram model* would have to work with. It doesn't look good—the possibilities are endless. Now, consider the same sentence, this time containing the words that **follow the blank**.

Figure 11.10 - Filling the [BLANK] in the center

Well, that's easy: The blank is "***dog***."

"Cool, but what does the bag-of-words have to do with it?"

It is a bag-of-words because it **sums up (or averages) the vectors** of the **context words** ("*the*," "*small*," "*is*," and "*barking*") and uses it to **predict the central word**.

"Why is it continuous? What does it even mean?"

It means the vectors are *not one-hot-encoded* anymore and have **continuous values** instead. The vector of continuous values that represents a given word is a called **word embedding**.

Word Embeddings

"How do we find the values that best represent each word?"

We need to train a model to learn them. This model is called…

Word2Vec

Word2Vec was proposed by Mikolov, T. et al. in their 2013 paper, "Efficient Estimation of Word Representations in Vector Space,"[83] and it included two model architectures: continuous bag-of-words (CBoW) and skip-gram (SG). We're focusing on the former.

In the CBoW architecture, the **target** is the **central word**. In other words, we're dealing with a **multiclass classification problem** where the **number of classes** is given by the **size of the vocabulary** (any word in the vocabulary can be the central word). And we'll be using the **context words**, better yet, their **corresponding embeddings (vectors)**, as **inputs**.

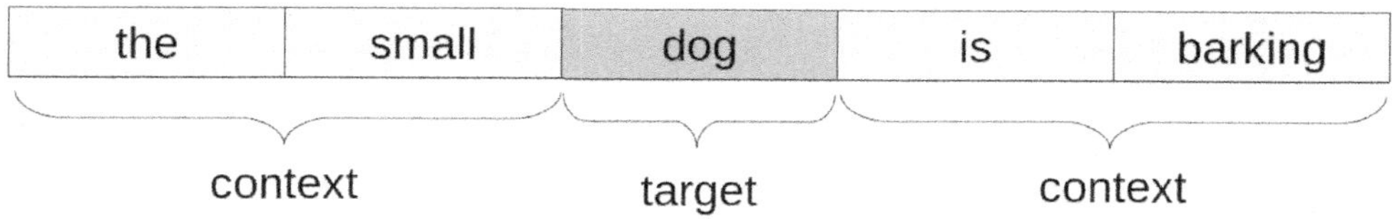

Figure 11.11 - Target and context words

"Wait, how come we're using the embeddings as inputs? That's what we're trying to learn in the first place!"

Exactly! The **embeddings** are also **parameters of the model**, and, as such, they are **randomly initialized** as well. As training progresses, their weights are being updated by gradient descent like any other parameter, and, in the end, we'll have **embeddings** for each word in the vocabulary.

For each pair of context words and corresponding target, the model will **average the embeddings of the context words** and feed the result to a **linear layer** that will compute **one logit for each word in the vocabulary**. That's it! Let's check the corresponding code:

```
class CBOW(nn.Module):
    def __init__(self, vocab_size, embedding_size):
        super().__init__()
        self.embedding = nn.Embedding(vocab_size, embedding_size)
        self.linear = nn.Linear(embedding_size, vocab_size)

    def forward(self, X):
        embeddings = self.embedding(X)
        bow = embeddings.mean(dim=1)
        logits = self.linear(bow)
        return logits
```

That's a fairly simple model, right? If our vocabulary had only five words ("*the*," "*small*," "*is*," "*barking*," and "*dog*"), we could try to represent each word with an **embedding of three dimensions**. Let's create a dummy model to inspect its (randomly initialized) embeddings:

```
torch.manual_seed(42)
dummy_cbow = CBOW(vocab_size=5, embedding_size=3)
dummy_cbow.embedding.state_dict()
```

Output

```
OrderedDict([('weight', tensor([[ 0.3367,  0.1288,  0.2345],
                 [ 0.2303, -1.1229, -0.1863],
                 [ 2.2082, -0.6380,  0.4617],
                 [ 0.2674,  0.5349,  0.8094],
                 [ 1.1103, -1.6898, -0.9890]]))])
```

Token	Dimensions 0	1	2
the	0.3367	0.1288	0.2345
small	0.2303	-1.1229	-0.1863
is	2.2082	-0.6380	0.4617
barking	0.2674	0.5349	0.8094
dog	1.1103	-1.6898	-0.9890

Figure 11.12 - Word embeddings

As depicted in the figure above, PyTorch's `nn.Embedding` layer is a **large lookup table**. It may be *randomly initialized* given the **size of the vocabulary** (`num_embeddings`) and the **number of dimensions** (`embedding_dim`). To actually **retrieve the values**, we need to call the embedding layer with a **list of token indices**, and it will return the corresponding **rows** of the table.

For example, we can retrieve the embeddings for the tokens "*is*" and "*barking*" using their corresponding indices (two and three):

```
# tokens: ['is', 'barking']
dummy_cbow.embedding(torch.as_tensor([2, 3]))
```

Output

```
tensor([[ 2.2082, -0.6380,  0.4617],
        [ 0.2674,  0.5349,  0.8094]], grad_fn=<EmbeddingBackward>)
```

That's why the **main job** of the **tokenizer** is to **transform a sentence into a list of token IDs**. That list is used as an **input to the embedding layer**, and from then on, the tokens are represented by dense vectors.

"How do you choose the number of dimensions?"

It is commonplace to use between 50 and 300 dimensions for word embeddings, but some embeddings may be as large as 3,000 dimensions. That may look like a lot but, compared to one-hot-encoded vectors, it is a bargain! The vocabulary of our tiny dataset would already require more than 3,000 dimensions if it were one-hot-encoded.

In our former example, "***dog***" was the **central word** and the other four words were the **context words**:

```
tiny_vocab = ['the', 'small', 'is', 'barking', 'dog']
context_words = ['the', 'small', 'is', 'barking']
target_words = ['dog']
```

Now, let's pretend that we tokenized the words and got their corresponding indices:

```
batch_context = torch.as_tensor([[0, 1, 2, 3]]).long()
batch_target = torch.as_tensor([4]).long()
```

In its very first training step, the model would **compute the continuous bag-of-words** for the inputs by **averaging the corresponding embeddings**.

Token	Dimensions 0	1	2
the	0.3367	0.1288	0.2345
small	0.2303	-1.1229	-0.1863
is	2.2082	-0.6380	0.4617
barking	0.2674	0.5349	0.8094
CBOW	0.7607	-0.2743	0.3298

Figure 11.13 - Continuous bag-of-words

```
cbow_features = dummy_cbow.embedding(batch_context).mean(dim=1)
cbow_features
```

Output

```
tensor([[ 0.7606, -0.2743,  0.3298]], grad_fn=<MeanBackward1>)
```

The bag-of-words has **three dimensions**, which are the **features** used to **compute the logits** for our multiclass classification problem.

Logits	C	class
0.3542	0	the
0.6937	1	small
-0.2028	2	is
-0.5873	3	barking
0.2099	4	dog

Figure 11.14 - Logits

```
logits = dummy_cbow.linear(cbow_features)
logits
```

Output

```
tensor([[ 0.3542,  0.6937, -0.2028, -0.5873,  0.2099]],
       grad_fn=<AddmmBackward>)
```

The *largest logit* corresponds to the word "***small***" (class index one), so that would be the **predicted central word**: "*The small **small** is barking.*" The prediction is obviously **wrong**, but, then again, that's still a randomly initialized model. Given a large enough dataset of context and target words, we could train the `CBOW` model above using an `nn.CrossEntropyLoss()` to **learn actual word embeddings**.

The Word2Vec model may *also* be trained using the **skip-gram** approach instead of continuous bag-of-words. The skip-gram uses the **central word** to **predict the surrounding words**, thus being a **multi-label multiclass classification problem**. In our simple example, the input would be the central word "*dog*," and the model would try to predict the four context words ("*the*," "*small*," "*is*," and "*barking*") at once.

We're not diving any deeper into the inner workings of the Word2Vec model, but you can check Jay Alammar's "The Illustrated Word2Vec"[84] and Lilian Weng's "Learning Word Embedding,"[85] amazing posts on the subject.

If you're interested in training a Word2Vec model yourself, follow Jason Brownlee's great tutorial: "How to Develop Word Embeddings in Python with Gensim."[86]

So far, it looks like we're learning **word embeddings** just for the sake of getting **more compact (denser)** representations than one-hot encoding can offer for each word. But word embeddings are *more than that.*

What Is an Embedding Anyway?

An embedding is a **representation** of an entity (a word, in our case), and each of its **dimensions** can be seen as an **attribute** or **feature**.

Let's forget about words for a moment and talk about **restaurants** instead. We can rate restaurants over many different **dimensions**, like **food**, **price**, and **service**, for example.

Restaurant	Food	Price	Service
#1	Good	Expensive	Good
#2	Average	Cheap	Bad
#3	Very Good	Expensive	Very Good
#4	Bad	Very Cheap	Average

Figure 11.15 - Reviewing restaurants

Clearly, restaurants #1 and #3 have good food and service but are expensive, and restaurants #2 and #4 are cheap but either the food or the service is bad. It's fair to say that restaurants #1 and #3 are similar to each other, and that they are both very different from restaurants #2 and #4, which, in turn, are somewhat similar to each other as well.

*"What about the **cuisine**? We can't properly compare restaurants without that information!"*

I agree with you, so let's just pretend that all of them are **pizza places** :-)

Although it's fairly obvious to spot the similarities and differences among the restaurants in the table above, it wouldn't be so easy to spot them if there were *dozens of dimensions* to compare. Besides, it would be very hard to **objectively measure the similarity** between any two restaurants using categorical scales like that.

*"What if we use **continuous scales** instead?"*

Perfect! Let's do that and assign values in the range [-1, 1], from very bad (-1) to very good (1), or from very expensive (-1) to very cheap (1).

Restaurant	Food	Price	Service
#1	0.70	-0.40	0.70
#2	0.30	0.70	-0.50
#3	0.90	-0.55	0.80
#4	-0.30	0.80	0.34

Figure 11.16 - Restaurant "embeddings"

These values are like "**restaurant embeddings**" :-)

Well, they're not *quite* embeddings, but at least we can use **cosine similarity** to find out how similar to each other two restaurants are:

```
ratings = torch.as_tensor([[.7, -.4, .7],
                           [.3, .7, -.5],
                           [.9, -.55, .8],
                           [-.3, .8, .34]]).float()
sims = torch.zeros(4, 4)
for i in range(4):
    for j in range(4):
        sims[i, j] = F.cosine_similarity(ratings[i],
                                         ratings[j],
                                         dim=0)
sims
```

Output

```
tensor([[ 1.0000, -0.4318,  0.9976, -0.2974],
        [-0.4318,  1.0000, -0.4270,  0.3581],
        [ 0.9976, -0.4270,  1.0000, -0.3598],
        [-0.2974,  0.3581, -0.3598,  1.0000]])
```

As expected, restaurants #1 and #3 are remarkably similar (0.9976), and restaurants #2 and #4 are somewhat similar (0.3581). Restaurant #1 is quite different from restaurants #2 and #4 (-0.4318 and -0.2974, respectively), and so is restaurant #3 (-0.4270 and -0.3598, respectively).

Although we *can* compute the cosine similarity between two restaurants now, the values in the table above **are not real embeddings**. It was only an example that illustrates well the **concept of embedding dimensions as attributes**.

Unfortunately, the **dimensions** of the **word embeddings** learned by the Word2Vec model **do not have clear-cut meanings** like that.

On the bright side, though, it is possible to do **arithmetic with word embeddings**!

"*Say what?*"

You got that right—**arithmetic**—really! Maybe you've seen this "*equation*" somewhere else already:

KING - MAN + WOMAN = QUEEN

Awesome, right? We'll try this "*equation*" out shortly, hang in there!

Pre-trained Word2Vec

Word2Vec is a simple model but it still requires a sizable amount of text data to learn meaningful embeddings. Luckily for us, someone else had already done the hard work of training these models, and we can use Gensim's `downloader` to choose from a variety of pre-trained word embeddings.

For a detailed list of the available models (embeddings), please check Gensim-data's repository on GitHub: https://github.com/RaRe-Technologies/gensim-data.

"*Why so many embeddings? How are they different from each other?*"

Good question! It turns out, using **different text corpora** to train a Word2Vec model produces **different embeddings**. On the one hand, this shouldn't be a surprise; after all, these are **different datasets** and it's expected that they will produce **different results**. On the other hand, if these datasets all contain **sentences in the same language** (English, for example), how come the embeddings are different?

The embeddings will be influenced by the **kind of language** used in the text: The phrasing and wording used in novels are different from those used in news articles and radically different from those used on Twitter, for example.

"*Choose your word embeddings wisely.*"

Grail Knight

Moreover, not every word embedding is learned using a Word2Vec model architecture. There are *many* different ways of learning word embeddings, one of them being...

Global Vectors (GloVe)

The Global Vectors model was proposed by Pennington, J. et al. in their 2014 paper "GloVe: Global Vectors for Word Representation."[87] It combines the **skip-gram** model with **co-occurrence statistics** at the **global level** (hence the name). We're not diving into its inner workings here, but if you're interested in knowing more about it, check its official website: https://nlp.stanford.edu/projects/glove/.

The pre-trained GloVe embeddings come in many sizes and shapes: Dimensions vary between 25 and 300, and vocabularies vary between 400,000 and 2,200,000 words. Let's use Gensim's `downloader` to retrieve the smallest one: `glove-wiki-gigaword-50`. It was trained on Wikipedia 2014 and Gigawords 5, it contains 400,000 words in its vocabulary, and its embeddings have 50 dimensions.

Downloading Pre-trained Word Embeddings

```
from gensim import downloader
glove = downloader.load('glove-wiki-gigaword-50')
len(glove.vocab)
```

Output

```
400000
```

Let's check the embeddings for "***alice***" (the vocabulary is uncased):

```
glove['alice']
```

Output

```
array([ 0.16386,  0.57795, -0.59197, -0.32446,  0.29762,  0.85151,
       -0.76695, -0.20733,  0.21491, -0.51587, -0.17517,  0.94459,
        0.12705, -0.33031,  0.75951,  0.44449,  0.16553, -0.19235,
        0.06553, -0.12394,  0.61446,  0.89784,  0.17413,  0.41149,
        1.191  , -0.39461, -0.459  ,  0.02216, -0.50843, -0.44464,
        0.68721, -0.7167 ,  0.20835, -0.23437,  0.02604, -0.47993,
        0.31873, -0.29135,  0.50273, -0.55144, -0.06669,  0.43873,
       -0.24293, -1.0247 ,  0.02937,  0.06849,  0.25451, -1.9663 ,
        0.26673,  0.88486], dtype=float32)
```

There we go, 50 dimensions! It's time to try the famous "*equation*": KING - MAN + WOMAN = QUEEN. We're calling the result a "*synthetic queen*":

```
synthetic_queen = glove['king'] - glove['man'] + glove['woman']
```

These are the corresponding embeddings:

```
fig = plot_word_vectors(
    glove, ['king', 'man', 'woman', 'synthetic', 'queen'],
    other={'synthetic': synthetic_queen}
)
```

Figure 11.17 - Synthetic queen

How similar is the "***synthetic queen***" to the **actual "*queen*,"** you ask. It's hard to tell by looking at the vectors above alone, but Gensim's word vectors have a `similar_by_vector()` method that computes **cosine similarity** between a **given vector** and *the whole vocabulary* and returns the **top N most similar words**:

```
glove.similar_by_vector(synthetic_queen, topn=5)
```

Output

```
[('king', 0.8859835863113403),
 ('queen', 0.8609581589698792),
 ('daughter', 0.7684512138366699),
 ('prince', 0.7640699148178101),
 ('throne', 0.7634971141815186)]
```

"*The most similar word to the 'synthetic queen' is ...* ***king****?*"

Yes. It's not *always* the case, but it's fairly common to find out that, after performing

word embedding arithmetic, the word most similar to the result is the **original word** itself. For this reason, it's usual to **exclude the original word** from the similarity results. In this case, the most similar word to the "*synthetic queen*" is, indeed, the actual "*queen.*"

*"OK, cool, but **how** does this arithmetic work?"*

The general idea is that the embeddings learned to **encode abstract dimensions**, like "*gender,*" "*royalty,*" "*genealogy,*" or "*profession.*" None of these abstract dimensions corresponds to a single numerical dimension, though.

In its large 50-dimensional feature space, the model learned to place "*man*" as far apart from "*woman*" as "*king*" is from "*queen*" (roughly approximating the gender difference between the two). Similarly, the model learned to place "*king*" as far apart from "*man*" as "*queen*" is from "*woman*" (roughly approximating the difference of being a royal). The figure below depicts a hypothetical projection in two dimensions for easier visualization:

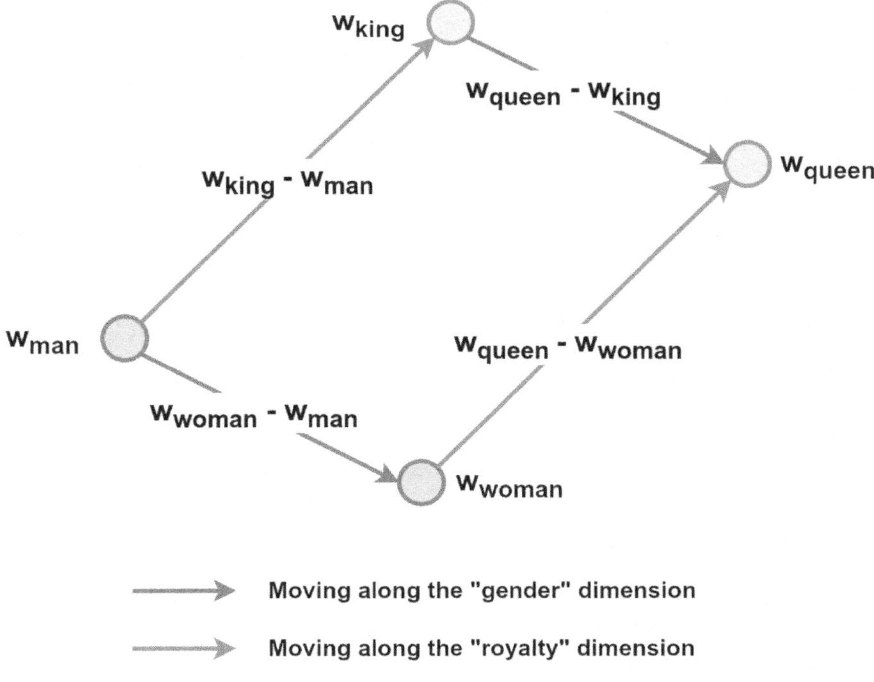

Figure 11.18 - Projection of embeddings

From the figure above, it should be relatively clear that both arrows pointing up (blue) are approximately the same size, thus resulting in the equation below:

$$w_{\text{king}} - w_{\text{man}} \approx w_{\text{queen}} - w_{\text{woman}}$$
$$\implies w_{\text{king}} - w_{\text{man}} + w_{\text{woman}} \approx w_{\text{queen}}$$

Equation 11.1 - Embedding arithmetic

This arithmetic is cool and all, but you won't actually be **using it** much; the whole point was to show you that the **word embeddings** indeed **capture the relationship** between different words. We *can* use them to train *other models*, though.

Using Word Embeddings

It seems easy enough: Get the text corpora tokenized, look the tokens up in the table of pre-trained word embeddings, and then use the embeddings as inputs of another model. But, *what if* the **vocabulary** of your corpora is **not quite properly represented** in the embeddings? Even worse, *what if* the **pre-processing steps** you used resulted in a lot of tokens that **do not exist in the embeddings**?

"Choose your word embeddings wisely."

Grail Knight

Vocabulary Coverage

Once again, the Grail Knight has a point—the chosen word embeddings must provide good **vocabulary coverage**. First and foremost, **most of the usual pre-processing steps do not apply** when you're using pre-trained word embeddings like GloVe: no lemmatization, no stemming, no stop-word removal. These steps would likely end up producing a lot of `[UNK]` tokens.

Second, even without those pre-processing steps, maybe the words used in the given text corpora are simply *not a good match* for a particular pre-trained set of word embeddings.

Let's see how good a match the `glove-wiki-gigaword-50` embeddings are to our own vocabulary. Our vocabulary has 3,706 words (3,704 from our text corpora plus the padding and unknown special tokens):

```
vocab = list(dictionary.token2id.keys())
len(vocab)
```

Output

```
3706
```

Let's see **how many words of our own vocabulary** are **unknown to the embeddings**:

```
unknown_words = sorted(
    list(set(vocab).difference(set(glove.vocab)))
)
print(len(unknown_words))
print(unknown_words[:5])
```

Output

```
44
['[PAD]', '[UNK]', 'arrum', 'barrowful', 'beauti']
```

There are only 44 unknown words: the two special tokens, and some other weird words like "*arrum*" and "*barrowful*." It looks good, right? It means that there are 3,662 matches out of 3,706 words, hinting at 98.81% coverage. But it is actually *better* than that.

If we look at **how often the unknown words** show up in our text corpora, we'll have a precise measure of **how many tokens** will be unknown to the embeddings. To actually get the total count we need to get the IDs of the unknown words first, and then look at their frequencies in the corpora:

```
unknown_ids = [dictionary.token2id[w]
               for w in unknown_words
               if w not in ['[PAD]', '[UNK]']]
unknown_count = np.sum([dictionary.cfs[idx]
                        for idx in unknown_ids])
unknown_count, dictionary.num_pos
```

Output

```
(82, 50802)
```

Only 82 out of 50,802 words in the text corpora cannot be matched to the vocabulary of the word embeddings. That's an impressive 99.84% coverage!

The helper function below can be used to compute the **vocabulary coverage** given a **Gensim's `Dictionary`** and **pre-trained embeddings**:

Method for Vocabulary Coverage

```
def vocab_coverage(gensim_dict, pretrained_wv,
                   special_tokens=('[PAD]', '[UNK]')):
    vocab = list(gensim_dict.token2id.keys())
    unknown_words = sorted(
        list(set(vocab).difference(set(pretrained_wv.vocab)))
    )
    unknown_ids = [gensim_dict.token2id[w]
                   for w in unknown_words
                   if w not in special_tokens]
    unknown_count = np.sum([gensim_dict.cfs[idx]
                            for idx in unknown_ids])
    cov = 1 - unknown_count / gensim_dict.num_pos
    return cov
```

```
vocab_coverage(dictionary, glove)
```

Output

```
0.9983858903192788
```

Tokenizer

Once we're happy with the **vocabulary coverage** of our pre-trained embeddings, we can **save the vocabulary of the embeddings to disk** as a plain-text file, so we can use it with the HF's tokenizer:

Method to Save a Vocabulary from Pre-trained Embeddings

```
def make_vocab_from_wv(wv, folder=None, special_tokens=None):
    if folder is not None:
        if not os.path.exists(folder):
            os.mkdir(folder)

    words = wv.index2word
    if special_tokens is not None:
        to_add = []
        for special_token in special_tokens:
            if special_token not in words:
                to_add.append(special_token)
        words = to_add + words

    with open(os.path.join(folder, 'vocab.txt'), 'w') as f:
        for word in words:
            f.write(f'{word}\n')
```

Saving GloVe's Vocabulary to a File

```
make_vocab_from_wv(glove,
                   'glove_vocab/',
                   special_tokens=['[PAD]', '[UNK]'])
```

We'll be using the `BertTokenizer` class once again to create a tokenizer based on GloVe's vocabulary:

Creating a Tokenizer using GloVe

```
glove_tokenizer = BertTokenizer('glove_vocab/vocab.txt')
```

One more time: The (pre-trained) tokenizer you'll use for real with a (pre-trained) BERT model **does not need a vocabulary**.

Now we can use its **encode()** method to get the indices for the tokens in a sentence:

```
glove_tokenizer.encode('alice followed the white rabbit',
                       add_special_tokens=False)
```

Output

```
[7101, 930, 2, 300, 12427]
```

These are the **indices** we'll use to **retrieve the corresponding word embeddings**. There is **one small detail** we need to take care of first, though…

Special Tokens' Embeddings

Our vocabulary has 400,002 tokens now, but the original pre-trained word embeddings has only 400,000 entries:

```
len(glove_tokenizer.vocab), len(glove.vectors)
```

Output

```
(400002, 400000)
```

The difference is due to the **two special tokens**, `[PAD]` and `[UNK]`, that were **prepended to the vocabulary** when we saved it to disk. Therefore, we need to **prepend their corresponding embeddings** too.

"How would I know the embeddings for these tokens?"

That's actually easy; these embeddings are just 50-dimensional vectors of **zeros**, and we concatenate them to the GloVe's pre-trained embeddings, making sure that the special embeddings come first:

Adding Embeddings for the Special Tokens

```
special_embeddings = np.zeros((2, glove.vector_size))
extended_embeddings = np.concatenate(
    [special_embeddings, glove.vectors], axis=0
)
extended_embeddings.shape
```

Output

```
(400002, 50)
```

Now, if we encode "*alice*" to get its corresponding index, and use that index to retrieve the corresponding values from our *extended embeddings*, they should match the original GloVe embeddings:

```
alice_idx = glove_tokenizer.encode(
    'alice', add_special_tokens=False
)
np.all(full_embeddings[alice_idx] == glove['alice'])
```

Output

```
True
```

OK, it looks like we're set! Let's put these embeddings to good use and *finally* train a model in PyTorch!

Model I — GloVE + Classifier

Data Preparation

It all starts with the *data preparation* step. As we already know, we need to **tokenize** the sentences to get their corresponding **sequences of token IDs**. The sentences (and the labels) can be easily retrieved from HF's dataset, like a dictionary:

Data Preparation

```
train_sentences = train_dataset['sentence']
train_labels = train_dataset['labels']

test_sentences = test_dataset['sentence']
test_labels = test_dataset['labels']
```

Next, we use our `glove_tokenizer()` to tokenize the sentences, making sure that we **pad** and **truncate** them so they all end up with 60 tokens (like we did in the "HuggingFace's Tokenizer" section). We only need the `inputs_ids` to fetch their corresponding embeddings later on:

Data Preparation — Tokenizing

```
train_ids = glove_tokenizer(train_sentences,
                            truncation=True,
                            padding=True,
                            max_length=60,
                            add_special_tokens=False,
                            return_tensors='pt')['input_ids']
train_labels = torch.as_tensor(train_labels).float().view(-1, 1)

test_ids = glove_tokenizer(test_sentences,
                           truncation=True,
                           padding=True,
                           max_length=60,
                           add_special_tokens=False,
                           return_tensors='pt')['input_ids']
test_labels = torch.as_tensor(test_labels).float().view(-1, 1)
```

Both sequences of token IDs and labels are regular PyTorch tensors now, so we can use the familiar `TensorDataset`:

Data Preparation

```
train_tensor_dataset = TensorDataset(train_ids, train_labels)
generator = torch.Generator()
train_loader = DataLoader(
    train_tensor_dataset, batch_size=32,
    shuffle=True, generator=generator
)
test_tensor_dataset = TensorDataset(test_ids, test_labels)
test_loader = DataLoader(test_tensor_dataset, batch_size=32)
```

"Hold on! Why are we going back to `TensorDataset` *instead of using HF's* `Dataset`*?"*

Well, even though HF's `Dataset` was **extremely useful** to load and manipulate all the files from our text corpora, and it will surely work seamlessly with HF's pre-trained models, it's *not ideal* to work with our regular, pure PyTorch training routine.

"Why not?"

It boils down to the fact that, while a `TensorDataset` returns a **typical (features, label) tuple**, the HF's `Dataset` always returns a **dictionary**. So, instead of jumping through hoops to accommodate this difference in their outputs, it's easier to fall back to the familiar `TensorDataset` for now.

We already have **token IDs** and **labels**. But we also have to **load the pre-trained embeddings** that **match the IDs** produced by the tokenizer.

Pre-trained PyTorch Embeddings

The **embedding layer** in PyTorch, `nn.Embedding`, can be either **trained** like any other layer or **loaded** using its `from_pretrained()` method. Let's load the *extended* version of the pre-trained GloVe embeddings:

```
extended_embeddings = torch.as_tensor(extended_embeddings).float()
torch_embeddings = nn.Embedding.from_pretrained(extended_embeddings)
```

By default, the embeddings are **frozen**; that is, they **won't be updated** during model training. You can change this behavior by setting the `freeze` argument to `False`, though.

Then, let's take the first mini-batch of tokenized sentences and their labels:

```
token_ids, labels = next(iter(train_loader))
token_ids
```

Output

```
tensor([[  36,   63,    1,  ...,    0,    0,    0],
        [ 934,   16,   14,  ...,    0,    0,    0],
        [  57,  311,    8,  ...,  140,    3,   83],
        ...,
        [7101,   59, 1536,  ...,    0,    0,    0],
        [  43,   59, 1995,  ...,    0,    0,    0],
        [ 102,   41,  210,  ...,  685,    3,    7]])
```

There are 32 sentences of 60 tokens each. We can use this batch of token IDs to retrieve their corresponding **embeddings**:

```
token_embeddings = torch_embeddings(token_ids)
token_embeddings.shape
```

Output

```
torch.Size([32, 60, 50])
```

Since **each embedding has 50 dimensions**, the resulting tensor has the shape above: 32 sentences, 60 tokens each, 50 dimensions for each token.

Let's make it a bit *simpler* and **average the embeddings** corresponding to **all tokens in a sentence**:

```
token_embeddings.mean(dim=1)
```

Output

```
tensor([[ 0.0665, -0.0071, -0.0534,  ..., -0.0202, -0.1432],
        [ 0.0514,  0.0495,  0.0083,  ...,  0.0162,  0.0687],
        ...,
        [ 0.0516,  0.1091,  0.0917,  ...,  0.0037,  0.0553],
        [ 0.1972,  0.1069, -0.2049,  ..., -0.1026, -0.3731]])
```

Now **each sentence** is represented by an **average embedding of its tokens**. That's a **bag-of-words** or, better yet, a **bag-of-embeddings**. Each tensor is a numerical representation of a sentence, and we can use it as **features** for a classification algorithm.

By the way, for training simple models using bag-of-embeddings as inputs, it is better to use PyTorch's `nn.EmbeddingBag` instead. The outcome is exactly the same as the one above, but it is faster:

```
boe_mean = nn.EmbeddingBag.from_pretrained(
    extended_embeddings, mode='mean'
)
boe_mean(token_ids)
```

Besides, we don't have to take the mean manually anymore, and therefore we can use it in a simple `Sequential` model.

Model Configuration & Training

Let's build a `Sequential` model to classify our sentences according to their source (*Alice's Adventures in Wonderland* or *The Wonderful Wizard of Oz*) using PyTorch's `nn.EmbeddingBag`:

Model Configuration

```
extended_embeddings = torch.as_tensor(
    extended_embeddings
).float()
boe_mean = nn.EmbeddingBag.from_pretrained(
    extended_embeddings, mode='mean'
)
torch.manual_seed(41)
model = nn.Sequential(
    # Embeddings
    boe_mean,
    # Classifier
    nn.Linear(boe_mean.embedding_dim, 128),
    nn.ReLU(),
    nn.Linear(128, 1)
)
loss_fn = nn.BCEWithLogitsLoss()
optimizer = optim.Adam(model.parameters(), lr=0.01)
```

The model is quite simple and straightforward: The bag-of-embeddings generates a **batch of average embeddings** (each sentence is represented by a tensor of `embedding_dim` dimensions), and those embeddings work as **features** for the classifier part of the model.

We can train the model in the usual way:

Model Training

```
sbs_emb = StepByStep(model, loss_fn, optimizer)
sbs_emb.set_loaders(train_loader, test_loader)
sbs_emb.train(20)
```

```
fig = sbs_emb.plot_losses()
```

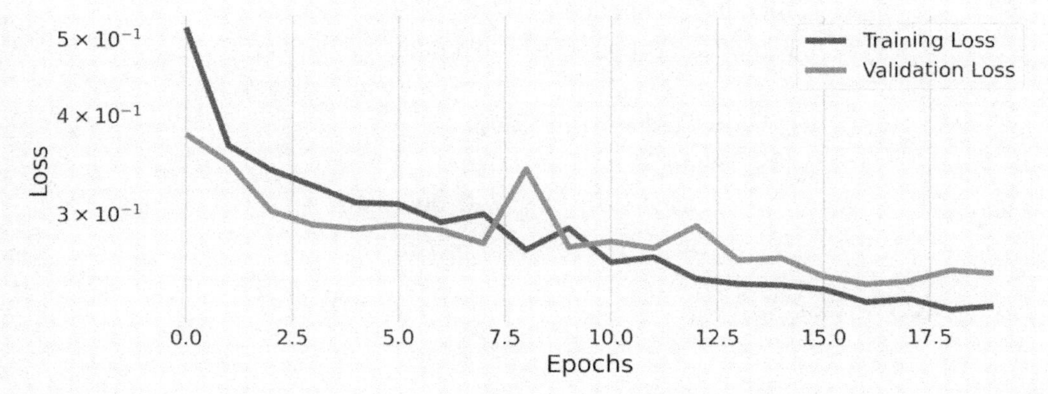

Figure 11.19 - Losses—bag-of-embeddings (BoE)

```
StepByStep.loader_apply(test_loader, sbs_emb.correct)
```

Output

```
tensor([[380, 440],
        [311, 331]])
```

That's 89.62% accuracy on the test set. Not bad, not bad at all!

"OK, but I don't want to use a `Sequential` *model, I want to use a* ***Transformer****!"*

I hear you.

Model II — GloVe + Transformer

We'll use a **Transformer encoder** as a classifier again, just like we did in the "Vision Transformer" section in Chapter 10. The model is pretty much the *same* except that we're using **pre-trained word embeddings** instead of **patch embeddings**:

Model Configuration

```
class TransfClassifier(nn.Module):
    def __init__(self, embedding_layer, encoder, n_outputs):
        super().__init__()
        self.d_model = encoder.d_model
        self.n_outputs = n_outputs
```

```
        self.encoder = encoder
        self.mlp = nn.Linear(self.d_model, n_outputs)

        self.embed = embedding_layer                          ①
        self.cls_token = nn.Parameter(
            torch.zeros(1, 1, self.d_model)
        )

    def preprocess(self, X):
        # N, L -> N, L, D
        src = self.embed(X)
        # Special classifier token
        # 1, 1, D -> N, 1, D
        cls_tokens = self.cls_token.expand(X.size(0), -1, -1)
        # Concatenates CLS tokens -> N, 1 + L, D
        src = torch.cat((cls_tokens, src), dim=1)
        return src

    def encode(self, source, source_mask=None):
        # Encoder generates "hidden states"
        states = self.encoder(source, source_mask)    ②
        # Gets state from first token: CLS
        cls_state = states[:, 0]  # N, 1, D
        return cls_state

    @staticmethod
    def source_mask(X):                                       ②
        cls_mask = torch.ones(X.size(0), 1).type_as(X)
        pad_mask = torch.cat((cls_mask, X > 0), dim=1).bool()
        return pad_mask.unsqueeze(1)

    def forward(self, X):
        src = self.preprocess(X)
        # Featurizer
        cls_state = self.encode(src,
                                self.source_mask(X)) ②
        # Classifier
        out = self.mlp(cls_state) # N, 1, outputs
        return out
```

① The embedding layer is an argument now.

② The encoder receives a source mask to flag the padded (and classification) tokens.

Our model takes an instance of a **Transformer encoder**, a layer of **pre-trained embeddings** (*not* an `nn.EmbeddingBag` anymore!), and the desired **number of outputs** (logits) corresponding to the number of existing classes.

The `forward()` method takes a mini-batch of tokenized sentences, pre-processes them, encodes them (featurizer), and outputs logits (classifier). It really works just like the Vision Transformer from Chapter 10, but now it takes a sequence of words (tokens) instead of image patches.

Let's create an instance of our model and train it in the usual way:

Model Configuration

```
torch.manual_seed(33)
# Loads the pre-trained GloVe embeddings into an embedding layer
torch_embeddings = nn.Embedding.from_pretrained(
    extended_embeddings
)
# Creates a Transformer Encoder
layer = EncoderLayer(n_heads=2,
                     d_model=torch_embeddings.embedding_dim,
                     ff_units=128)
encoder = EncoderTransf(layer, n_layers=1)
# Uses both layers above to build our model
model = TransfClassifier(torch_embeddings, encoder, n_outputs=1)
loss_fn = nn.BCEWithLogitsLoss()
optimizer = optim.Adam(model.parameters(), lr=1e-4)
```

Model Training

```
sbs_transf = StepByStep(model, loss_fn, optimizer)
sbs_transf.set_loaders(train_loader, test_loader)
sbs_transf.train(10)
```

```
fig = sbs_transf.plot_losses()
```

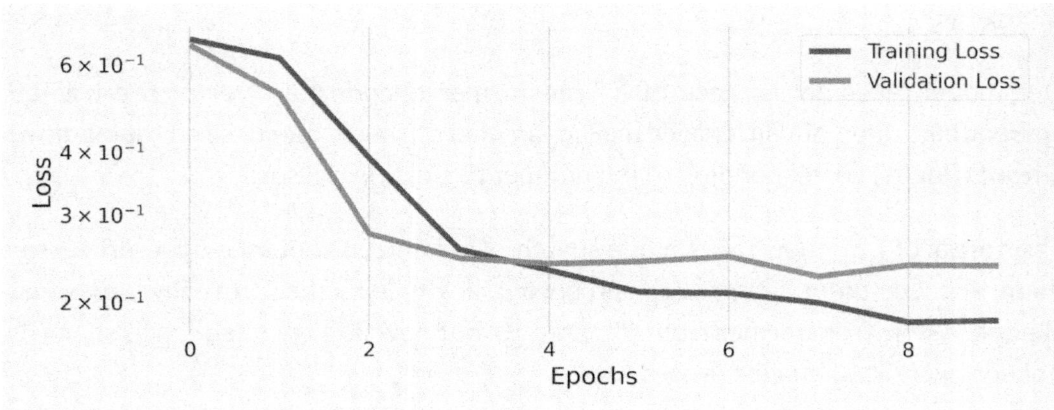

Figure 11.20 - Losses—Transformer + GloVe embeddings

Looks like our model started overfitting really quickly since the validation loss barely improves, if at all, after the third epoch. Let's check its accuracy on the validation (test) set:

```
StepByStep.loader_apply(test_loader, sbs_transf.correct)
```

Output

```
tensor([[410, 440],
        [300, 331]])
```

That's 92.09% accuracy. Well, that's good, but *not so much better* than the simple bag-of-embeddings model as you might expect from a *mighty Transformer*, right?

Let's see what our model is actually **paying attention to**.

Visualizing Attention

Instead of using sentences from the validation (test) set, let's come up with **brand new, totally made-up** sentences of our own:

```
sentences = ['The white rabbit and Alice ran away',
             'The lion met Dorothy on the road']
inputs = glove_tokenizer(sentences, add_special_tokens=False,
                         return_tensors='pt')['input_ids']
inputs
```

Output

```
tensor([[    2,   300, 12427,     7,  7101,  1423,   422],
        [    2,  6659,   811, 11238,    15,     2,   588]],
       device='cuda:0')
```

Yes, both sentences have the same number of tokens, for our convenience. Even though they're made-up sentences, I wonder what our model will say about their source being either *Alice's Adventures in Wonderland* (positive class) or *The Wonderful Wizard of Oz* (negative class):

```
sbs_transf.model.eval()
out = sbs_transf.model(inputs)
# our model outputs logits, so we turn them into probs
torch.sigmoid(out)
```

Output

```
tensor([[0.9888],
        [0.0101]], device='cuda:0', grad_fn=<SigmoidBackward>)
```

The model really thinks that *only the first sentence* comes from *Alice's Adventures in Wonderland*. To really understand *why* that is, we need to dig into its **attention scores**. The code below retrieves the attention scores for the **first (and only)** layer of our Transformer encoder:

```
alphas = (sbs_transf.model
          .encoder
          .layers[0]
          .self_attn_heads
          .alphas)
alphas[:, :, 0, :].squeeze()
```

Output

```
tensor([[[2.6334e-01, 6.9912e-02, 1.6958e-01, 1.6574e-01,
          1.1365e-01, 1.3449e-01, 6.6508e-02, 1.6772e-02],
         [2.7878e-05, 2.5806e-03, 2.9353e-03, 1.3467e-01,
          1.7490e-03, 8.5641e-01, 7.3843e-04, 8.8371e-04]],

        [[6.8102e-02, 1.8080e-02, 1.0238e-01, 6.1889e-02,
          6.2652e-01, 1.0388e-02, 1.6588e-02, 9.6055e-02],
         [2.2783e-04, 2.1089e-02, 3.4972e-01, 2.3252e-02,
          5.2879e-01, 3.5840e-02, 2.5432e-02, 1.5650e-02]]],
        device='cuda:0')
```

"*Why are we* ***slicing the third dimension****? What* ***is*** *the third dimension again?*"

In the multi-headed self-attention mechanism, the **scores** have the following shape: **(N, n_heads, L, L)**. We have **two sentences** (*N=2*), **two attention heads** (*n_heads=2*), and our sequence has **eight tokens** (*L=8*).

"*I'm sorry, but our sequences have* ***seven tokens****, not eight.*"

Yes, that's true. But don't forget about the **special classifier token** that was prepended to the sequence of embeddings. That's also the reason why we're slicing the third dimension: That zero index means **we're looking at the attention scores of the special classifier token**. Since we're using the output corresponding to that token to classify the sentences, it's only logical to check what it's paying attention to, right? Moreover, the **first value in each attention score tensor** above represents **how much attention the special classifier token is paying to itself**.

So, what *is* the model paying attention to then? Let's see!

Figure 11.21 - Attention scores

Clearly, the model learned that "*white rabbit*" and "*Alice*" are **strong signs** that a given sentence belongs to *Alice's Adventures in Wonderland*. Conversely, if there is a "*lion*" or "*Dorothy*" in the sentence, it's likely from *The Wonderful Wizard of Oz*.

Cool, right? Looks like word embeddings are the best invention since sliced bread! That would indeed be the case if only actual languages were *straightforward and organized*—unfortunately, they are nothing like that.

Let me show you two sentences from *Alice's Adventures in Wonderland* (the highlights are mine):

- "*The Hatter was the first to break the silence. `What day of the month is it?' he said, turning to Alice: he had taken his* **watch** *out of his pocket, and was looking at it uneasily, shaking it every now and then, and holding it to his ear.*"
- "*Alice thought this a very curious thing, and she went nearer to* **watch** *them, and just as she came up to them she heard one of them say, `Look out now, Five! Don't go splashing paint over me like that!*"

In the first sentence, the word "*watch*" is a **noun** and it refers to the **object** the Hatter had taken out of his pocket. In the second sentence, "*watch*" is a **verb** and it refers to what Alice is **doing**. Clearly, two **very different meanings for the same word**.

But, if we look the "*watch*" token up in our vocabulary, we'll **always retrieve the same values** from the word embeddings, **regardless of the actual meaning** of the word in a sentence.

Can we do better? Of course!

Contextual Word Embeddings

If a single token is not enough, why not take **the whole sentence**, right? Instead of taking a word by itself, we can take **its context too** in order to compute the vector that best represents a word. That was the whole point of **word embeddings**: finding **numerical representation for words** (or tokens).

"*That's great, but it seems impractical.*"

You're absolutely right! Trying to build a lookup table for every possible combination of word and context is probably not such a great idea—that's why **contextual word embeddings** won't come from a lookup table but from the **outputs of a model** instead.

I want to introduce you to…

ELMo

Born in 2018, ELMo is able to understand that words may have different meanings in different contexts. If you feed it a sentence, it will give you back embeddings for each of the words while taking the full context into account.

Embeddings from **L**anguage **Mo**dels (ELMo, for short) was introduced by Peters, M. et al. in their paper "Deep contextualized word representations"[88] (2018). The model is a **two-layer bidirectional LSTM encoder** using **4,096 dimensions in its cell states** and was trained on a **really large corpus** containing **5.5 billion words**. Moreover, ELMo's representations are **character-based**, so it can easily handle unknown (out-of-vocabulary) words.

You can find more details about its implementation, as well as its **pre-trained weights**, at AllenNLP's ELMo[89] site. You can also check the "ELMo"[90] section of Lilian Weng's great post, "Generalized Language Models."[91]

"*Cool, are we loading a pre-trained model then?*"

Well, we *could*, but ELMo embeddings can be conveniently retrieved using yet another library: flair.[92] `flair` is an NLP framework built on top of PyTorch that offers a **text embedding library** that provides **word embeddings** and **document embeddings** for popular Muppets, oops, models like **ELMo** and **BERT**, as well as classical word embeddings like GloVe.

Let's use the two sentences containing the word "*watch*" to illustrate how to use `flair` to get contextual word embeddings:

```
watch1 = """
The Hatter was the first to break the silence. `What day of the
month is it?' he said, turning to Alice: he had taken his watch out
of his pocket, and was looking at it uneasily, shaking it every now
and then, and holding it to his ear.
"""

watch2 = """
Alice thought this a very curious thing, and she went nearer to
watch them, and just as she came up to them she heard one of them
say, `Look out now, Five!  Don't go splashing paint over me like
that!
"""

sentences = [watch1, watch2]
```

In `flair`, every sentence is a `Sentence` object that's easily created using the corresponding text:

```
from flair.data import Sentence
flair_sentences = [Sentence(s) for s in sentences]
flair_sentences[0]
```

Output

```
Sentence: "The Hatter was the first to break the silence . ` What
day of the month is it ? ' he said , turning to Alice : he had taken
his watch out of his pocket , and was looking at it uneasily ,
shaking it every now and then , and holding it to his ear ."   [
Tokens: 58]
```

Our first sentence has 58 tokens. We can use either the `get_token()` method or the `tokens` attribute to retrieve a given token:

```
flair_sentences[0].get_token(32)
```

Output

```
Token: 32 watch
```

The `get_token()` method assumes indexing starts at **one**, while the `tokens` attribute has the typical **zero-based** indexing:

```
flair_sentences[0].tokens[31]
```

Output

```
Token: 32 watch
```

To learn more about the `Sentence` object in `flair`, please check "Tutorial 1: NLP Base Types."[93]

Then, we can use these `Sentence` objects to retrieve **contextual word embeddings**. But, first, we need to actually **load ELMo** using `ELMoEmbeddings`:

```
from flair.embeddings import ELMoEmbeddings
elmo = ELMoEmbeddings()
```

```
elmo.embed(flair_sentences)
```

Output

```
[Sentence: "The Hatter was the first to break the silence . ` What
day of the month is it ? ' he said , turning to Alice : he had taken
his watch out of his pocket , and was looking at it uneasily ,
shaking it every now and then , and holding it to his ear ."   [
Tokens: 58],
 Sentence: "Alice thought this a very curious thing , and she went
nearer to watch them , and just as she came up to them she heard one
of them say , ` Look out now , Five ! Do n't go splashing paint over
me like that !"   [ Tokens: 48]]
```

There we go! Every token has its own `embedding` attribute now. Let's check the embeddings for the word "*watch*" in both sentences:

```
token_watch1 = flair_sentences[0].tokens[31]
token_watch2 = flair_sentences[1].tokens[13]
token_watch1, token_watch2
```

Output

```
(Token: 32 watch, Token: 14 watch)
```

```
token_watch1.embedding, token_watch2.embedding
```

Output

```
(tensor([-0.5047, -0.4183, ..., -0.2228,  0.7794], device='cuda:0'),
 tensor([-0.5047, -0.4183, ...,  0.8352, -0.5018], device='cuda:0'))
```

ELMo embeddings are **large**: There are **3,072 dimensions**. The first two values of both embeddings are the same but the last two are not. That's a good start—the same word was assigned two different vectors depending on the context it was found in.

If we'd like to find out *how similar* they are to each other, we can use **cosine similarity**:

```
similarity = nn.CosineSimilarity(dim=0, eps=1e-6)
similarity(token_watch1.embedding, token_watch2.embedding)
```

```
tensor(0.5949, device='cuda:0')
```

Even though the first 1,024 values are identical, it turns out that the two words are *not* so similar after all. Contextual word embeddings for the win :-)

To get word embeddings for all tokens in a sentence, we can simply **stack** them up:

Helper Function to Retrieve Embeddings

```
def get_embeddings(embeddings, sentence):
    sent = Sentence(sentence)
    embeddings.embed(sent)
    return torch.stack(
        [token.embedding for token in sent.tokens]
    ).float()
```

```
get_embeddings(elmo, watch1)
```

Output

```
tensor([[-0.3288,  0.2022, -0.5940,  ...,  1.0606,  0.2637],
        [-0.7142,  0.4210, -0.9504,  ..., -0.6684,  1.7245],
        [ 0.2981, -0.0738, -0.1319,  ...,  1.1165,  0.6453],
        ...,
        [ 0.0475,  0.2325, -0.2013,  ..., -0.5294, -0.8543],
        [ 0.1599,  0.6898,  0.2946,  ...,  0.9584,  1.0337],
        [-0.8872, -0.2004, -1.0601,  ..., -0.0841,  0.0618]],
       device='cuda:0')
```

The returned tensor has 58 embeddings of 3,072 dimensions each.

For more details on ELMo embeddings, please check "ELMo Embeddings"[94] and "Tutorial 4: List of All Word Embeddings."[95]

Where do ELMo embeddings come from?

The embeddings from ELMo are a combination of **classical word embeddings** and **hidden states** from the two-layer bidirectional LSTMs. Since both embeddings and hidden states have 512 dimensions each, it follows that, in each direction, there is **one 512-dimension embedding** and **two 512-dimension hidden states** (one for each layer). That's 1,536 dimensions in each direction, and 3,072 dimensions in total.

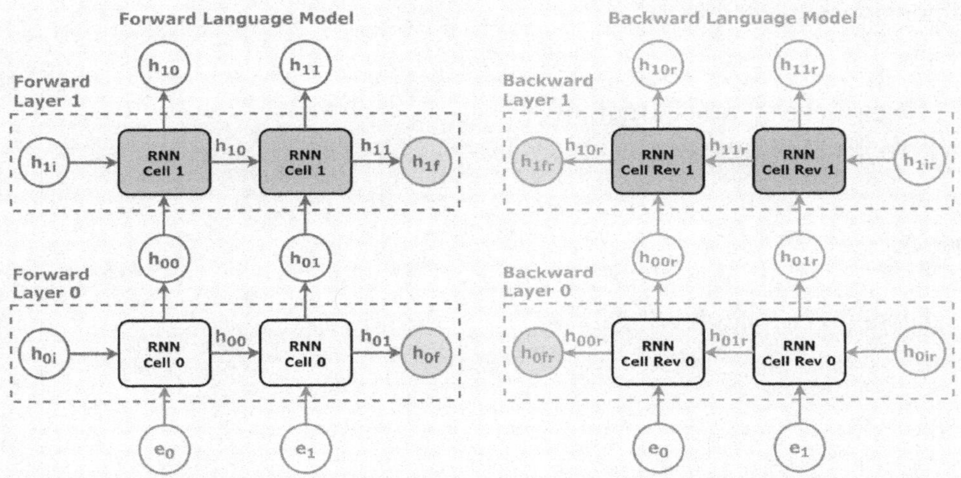

Figure 11.22 - ELMo's two-layer bidirectional LSTMs

The word embeddings are actually duplicated since both LSTMs use the same inputs. From the 3,072 dimensions, the first two chunks of 512 dimensions are actually identical.

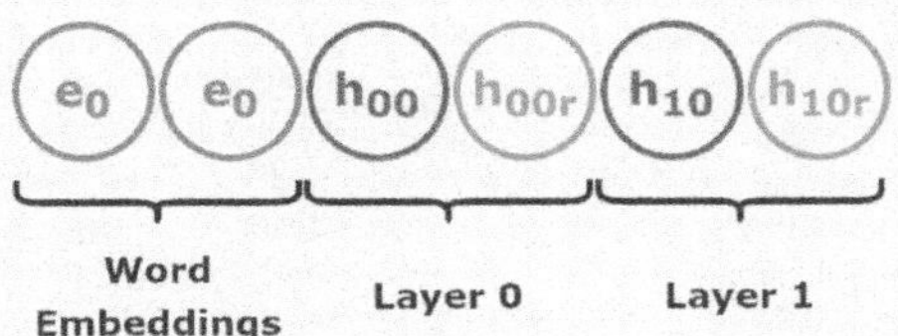

Figure 11.23 - ELMo embeddings

```
token_watch1.embedding[0], token_watch1.embedding[512]
```

Output

```
(tensor(-0.5047, device='cuda:0'), tensor(-0.5047, device
='cuda:0'))
```

Since the *classical word embeddings* are *context-independent*, it also means that both uses of "*watch*" have exactly the same values in their first 1,024 dimensions:

```
(token_watch1.embedding[:1024] ==
 token_watch2.embedding[:1024]).all()
```

Output

```
tensor(True, device='cuda:0')
```

GloVe

GloVe embeddings are not contextual, as you already know, but they can also be easily retrieved using `WordEmbeddings` from `flair`:

```
from flair.embeddings import WordEmbeddings
glove_embedding = WordEmbeddings('glove')
```

Now, let's retrieve the word embeddings for our sentences, but first, and this is **very important**, we need to create **new Sentence objects** for them:

```
new_flair_sentences = [Sentence(s) for s in sentences]
glove_embedding.embed(new_flair_sentences)
```

Output

```
[Sentence: "The Hatter was the first to break the silence . `
What day of the month is it ? ' he said , turning to Alice :
he had taken his watch out of his pocket , and was looking at
it uneasily , shaking it every now and then , and holding it
to his ear ."    [ Tokens: 58],
Sentence: "Alice thought this a very curious thing , and she
went nearer to watch them , and just as she came up to them
she heard one of them say , ` Look out now , Five ! Do n't go
splashing paint over me like that !"    [ Tokens: 48]]
```

Never reuse a Sentence object to retrieve **different word embeddings**! The `embedding` attribute may be **partially overwritten** (depending on the number of dimensions), and you may end up with **mixed embeddings** (e.g., 3,072 dimensions from ELMo, but the first 100 values are overwritten by GloVe embeddings).

Since GloVe is not contextual, the word "*watch*" will have the same embedding regardless of which sentence you retrieve it from:

```
torch.all(new_flair_sentences[0].tokens[31].embedding ==
          new_flair_sentences[1].tokens[13].embedding)
```

Output

```
tensor(True, device='cuda:0')
```

For more details on classical word embeddings, please check "Tutorial 3: Word Embeddings"[96] and "Classic Word Embeddings."[97]

BERT

The general idea, introduced by ELMo, of obtaining **contextual word embeddings using a language model** still holds true for BERT. While ELMo is only a Muppet, **BERT** is both **Muppet and Transformer** (such a bizarre sentence to write!).

BERT, which stands for **B**idirectional **E**ncoder **R**epresentations from **T**ransformers, is a model based on a **Transformer encoder**. We'll *skip* more details about its architecture for now (don't worry, BERT has a full section of its own) and use it to get contextual word embeddings only (just like we did with ELMo).

First, we need to **load BERT** in `flair` using `TransformerWordEmbeddings`:

```
from flair.embeddings import TransformerWordEmbeddings
bert = TransformerWordEmbeddings('bert-base-uncased', layers='-1')
```

By the way, `flair` uses HuggingFace models under the hood, so you can load **any pre-trained model**[98] to generate embeddings for you.

In the example above, we're using the traditional `bert-base-uncased` to generate contextual word embeddings using BERT's **last layer (-1)**.

Next, we can use the same `get_embeddings()` function to get the stacked embeddings for every token in a sentence:

```
embed1 = get_embeddings(bert, watch1)
embed2 = get_embeddings(bert, watch2)
embed2
```

Output

```
tensor([[ 0.6554, -0.3799, -0.2842,  ...,  0.8865,  0.4760],
        [-0.1459, -0.0204, -0.0615,  ...,  0.5052,  0.3324],
        [-0.0436, -0.0401, -0.0135,  ...,  0.5231,  0.9067],
        ...,
        [-0.2582,  0.6933,  0.2688,  ...,  0.0772,  0.2187],
        [-0.1868,  0.6398, -0.8127,  ...,  0.2793,  0.1880],
        [-0.1021,  0.5222, -0.7142,  ...,  0.0600, -0.1419]])
```

Then, let's compare the embeddings for the word "*watch*" in both sentences once again:

```
bert_watch1 = embed1[31]
bert_watch2 = embed2[13]
print(bert_watch1, bert_watch2)
```

Output

```
(tensor([ 8.5760e-01,  3.5888e-01, -3.7825e-01, -8.3564e-01,
          ...,
          2.0768e-01,  1.1880e-01,  4.1445e-01]),
 tensor([-9.8449e-02,  1.4698e+00,  2.8573e-01, -3.9569e-01,
          ...,
          3.1746e-01, -2.8264e-01, -2.1325e-01]))
```

Well, they look *more different* from one another now. But are they, really?

```
similarity = nn.CosineSimilarity(dim=0, eps=1e-6)
similarity(bert_watch1, bert_watch2)
```

Output

```
tensor(0.3504, device='cuda:0')
```

Indeed, they have an even lower similarity now.

For more details on Transformer word embeddings, please check "Transformer Embeddings."[99]

In the "Pre-trained PyTorch Embeddings" section we **averaged (classical) word embeddings** to get a **single vector for each sentence**. We *could* do the same thing using **contextual word embeddings** instead. But we don't have to, because we can use…

Document Embeddings

We can use pre-trained models to generate embeddings for **whole documents** instead of for single words, thus eliminating the need to average word embeddings. In our case, a *document* is a **sentence**:

```
documents = [Sentence(watch1), Sentence(watch2)]
```

To actually get the embeddings, we use `TransformerDocumentEmbeddings` in the same way as in the other examples:

```
from flair.embeddings import TransformerDocumentEmbeddings
bert_doc = TransformerDocumentEmbeddings('bert-base-uncased')
bert_doc.embed(documents)
```

Output

```
[Sentence: "The Hatter was the first to break the silence . ` What
day of the month is it ? ' he said , turning to Alice : he had taken
his watch out of his pocket , and was looking at it uneasily ,
shaking it every now and then , and holding it to his ear ."   [
Tokens: 58],
 Sentence: "Alice thought this a very curious thing , and she went
nearer to watch them , and just as she came up to them she heard one
of them say , ` Look out now , Five ! Do n't go splashing paint over
me like that !"   [ Tokens: 48]]
```

Now, each **document** (a `Sentence` object) will have its **own overall embedding**:

```
documents[0].embedding
```

Output

```
tensor([-6.4245e-02,  3.5365e-01, -2.4962e-01, -5.3912e-01,
        -1.9917e-01, -2.7712e-01,  1.6942e-01,  1.0867e-01,
        ...
         7.4661e-02, -3.4777e-01,  1.5740e-01,  3.4407e-01,
        -5.0272e-01,  1.7432e-01,  7.9398e-01,  7.3562e-01],
       device='cuda:0',
       grad_fn=<CatBackward>)
```

Notice that the individual tokens don't get their own embeddings anymore:

```
documents[0].tokens[31].embedding
```

Output

```
tensor([], device='cuda:0')
```

We can leverage this fact to slightly modify the `get_embeddings()` function so it works with both word and document embeddings:

Helper Function to Retrieve Embeddings

```
def get_embeddings(embeddings, sentence):
    sent = Sentence(sentence)
    embeddings.embed(sent)
    if len(sent.embedding):
        return sent.embedding.float()
    else:
        return torch.stack(
            [token.embedding for token in sent.tokens]
        ).float()
```

```
get_embeddings(bert_doc, watch1)
```

Output

```
tensor([-6.4245e-02,  3.5365e-01, -2.4962e-01, -5.3912e-01,
        -1.9917e-01, -2.7712e-01,  1.6942e-01,  1.0867e-01,
        ...
         7.4661e-02, -3.4777e-01,  1.5740e-01,  3.4407e-01,
        -5.0272e-01,  1.7432e-01,  7.9398e-01,  7.3562e-01],
       device='cuda:0',
       grad_fn=<CatBackward>)
```

For more details on document embeddings, please check "Tutorial 5: Document Embeddings."[100]

We can **revisit the `Sequential` model** from the "Word Embeddings" section and modify it to use **contextual word embeddings** instead. But, first, we need to *change the datasets a bit* as well.

Model III — Pre-processed Embeddings

Data Preparation

Before, the **features** were a sequence of **token IDs**, which were used to **look embeddings up** in the embedding layer and return the corresponding **bag-of-embeddings** (that *was* a document embedding too, although less sophisticated).

Now, we're *outsourcing* these steps to BERT and getting **document embeddings** directly from it. It turns out, using a pre-trained BERT model to retrieve document embeddings is a **pre-processing step** in this setup. Consequently, our model is going to be nothing other than a **simple classifier**.

"Let the pre-processing begin!"

Maximus Decimus Meridius

The idea is to use `get_embeddings()` for each and every sentence in our datasets in order to retrieve their corresponding document embeddings. HuggingFace's dataset allows us to easily do that by using its `map()` method to generate a new column:

Data Preparation

```
train_dataset_doc = train_dataset.map(
    lambda row: {'embeddings': get_embeddings(bert_doc,
                                              row['sentence'])}
)
test_dataset_doc = test_dataset.map(
    lambda row: {'embeddings': get_embeddings(bert_doc,
                                              row['sentence'])}
)
```

Moreover, we need the embeddings to be returned as PyTorch tensors:

Data Preparation

```
train_dataset_doc.set_format(type='torch',
                             columns=['embeddings', 'labels'])
test_dataset_doc.set_format(type='torch',
                            columns=['embeddings', 'labels'])
```

We can easily get the embeddings for all sentences in our dataset now:

```
train_dataset_doc['embeddings']
```

Output

```
tensor([[-0.2932,  0.2595, -0.1252,  ...,  0.2998,  0.1157],
        [ 0.4934,  0.0129, -0.1991,  ...,  0.6320,  0.7036],
        [-0.6256, -0.3536, -0.4682,  ...,  0.2467,  0.6108],
        ...,
        [-0.5786,  0.0274, -0.1081,  ...,  0.0329,  0.9563],
        [ 0.1244,  0.3181,  0.0352,  ...,  0.6648,  0.9231],
        [ 0.2124,  0.6195, -0.2281,  ...,  0.4346,  0.6358]],
       dtype=torch.float64)
```

Next, we build the datasets the usual way:

Data Preparation

```
train_dataset_doc = TensorDataset(
    train_dataset_doc['embeddings'].float(),
    train_dataset_doc['labels'].view(-1, 1).float())
generator = torch.Generator()
train_loader = DataLoader(
    train_dataset_doc, batch_size=32,
    shuffle=True, generator=generator
)
test_dataset_doc = TensorDataset(
    test_dataset_doc['embeddings'].float(),
    test_dataset_doc['labels'].view(-1, 1).float())
test_loader = DataLoader(
    test_dataset_doc, batch_size=32, shuffle=True)
```

Model Configuration & Training

We're using pretty much the **same `Sequential` model** as before, except that it doesn't have an embedding layer anymore, and we're using **only three hidden units** instead of 128:

Model Configuration

```
torch.manual_seed(41)
model = nn.Sequential(
    # Classifier
    nn.Linear(bert_doc.embedding_length, 3),
    nn.ReLU(),
    nn.Linear(3, 1)
)
loss_fn = nn.BCEWithLogitsLoss()
optimizer = optim.Adam(model.parameters(), lr=1e-3)
```

"Isn't that too few? Three?! Really?"

Really! It isn't too few—if you try using 128 like in the previous model, it will *immediately* overfit over a *single epoch*. Given the **embedding length** (768), the model gets **overparameterized** (a situation where there are **many more parameters than data points**), and it ends up **memorizing the training set**.

This is a **simple feed-forward classifier** with a **single hidden layer**. It doesn't get *much* simpler than that!

Model Training

```
sbs_doc_emb = StepByStep(model, loss_fn, optimizer)
sbs_doc_emb.set_loaders(train_loader, test_loader)
sbs_doc_emb.train(20)
```

```
fig = sbs_doc_emb.plot_losses()
```

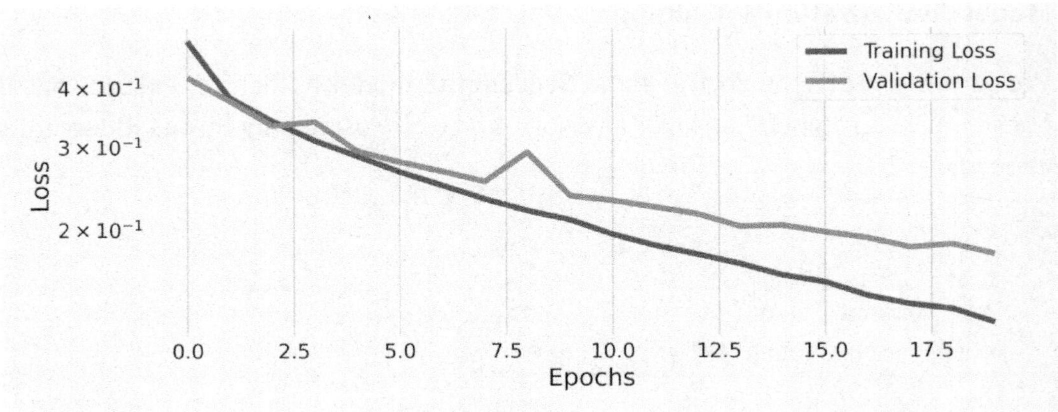

Figure 11.24 - Losses—simple classifier with BERT embeddings

OK, it's still not overfitting, but can it deliver good predictions? You betcha!

```
StepByStep.loader_apply(test_loader, sbs_doc_emb.correct)
```

Output

```
tensor([[424, 440],
        [310, 331]])
```

That's 95.20% accuracy on the validation (test) set! Quite impressive for a model with only *three hidden units*, I might say.

Now, imagine what can be accomplished if we **fine-tune the actual BERT model** instead! Right? Right?

BERT

BERT, which stands for **B**idirectional **E**ncoder **R**epresentations from **T**ransformers, is a model based on a **Transformer encoder**. It was introduced by Devlin, J. et al. in their paper "BERT: Pre-training of Deep Bidirectional Transformers for Language Understanding"[101] (2019).

The original BERT model was trained on two huge corpora: BookCorpus[102] (composed of 800M words in 11,038 unpublished books) and English Wikipedia[103] (2.5B words). It has **twelve "layers"** (the original Transformer had only six), **twelve attention heads**, and **768 hidden dimensions**, totaling **110 million parameters**.

If that's too large for your GPU, though, don't worry: There are **many** different versions of BERT for all tastes and budgets, and you can find them in Google Research's BERT repository: https://github.com/google-research/bert.

You can also check BERT's documentation[104] and model card,[105] available at HuggingFace, for a quick overview of the model and its training procedure.

For a general overview of BERT, please check Jay Alammar's excellent posts on the topic: "The Illustrated BERT, ELMo, and co. (How NLP Cracked Transfer Learning)"[106] and "A Visual Guide to Using BERT for the First Time."[107]

AutoModel

If you want to quickly try *different models* without having to import their corresponding classes, you can use HuggingFace's `AutoModel` instead:

```
from transformers import AutoModel
auto_model = AutoModel.from_pretrained('bert-base-uncased')
print(auto_model.__class__)
```

Output

```
<class 'transformers.modeling_bert.BertModel'>
```

As you can see, it *infers* the correct model class based on the name of the model you're loading, e.g., `bert-base-uncased`.

Let's create our first BERT model by loading the pre-trained weights for `bert-base-uncased`:

```
from transformers import BertModel
bert_model = BertModel.from_pretrained('bert-base-uncased')
```

We can inspect the pre-trained model's configuration:

```
bert_model.config
```

Output

```
BertConfig {
  "architectures": [
    "BertForMaskedLM"
  ],
  "attention_probs_dropout_prob": 0.1,
  "gradient_checkpointing": false,
  "hidden_act": "gelu",
  "hidden_dropout_prob": 0.1,
  "hidden_size": 768,
  "initializer_range": 0.02,
  "intermediate_size": 3072,
  "layer_norm_eps": 1e-12,
  "max_position_embeddings": 512,
  "model_type": "bert",
  "num_attention_heads": 12,
  "num_hidden_layers": 12,
  "pad_token_id": 0,
  "type_vocab_size": 2,
  "vocab_size": 30522
}
```

Some of the items are easily recognizable: `hidden_size` (768), `num_attention_heads` (12), and `num_hidden_layer` (12). Some of the items will be discussed soon: `vocab_size` (30,522) and `max_position_embeddings` (512, the maximum sequence length). There are additional parameters used for training, like dropout probabilities and the architecture used.

Our model needs inputs, and those require…

Tokenization

Tokenization is a **pre-processing step**, and, since we'll be using a **pre-trained BERT model**, we need to use the **same tokenizer** that was used during pre-training. For each pre-trained model available in HuggingFace there is an accompanying pre-trained tokenizer as well.

Let's create our first **real** BERT tokenizer (instead of the fake ones we create to handle our own vocabulary):

```
from transformers import BertTokenizer
bert_tokenizer = BertTokenizer.from_pretrained('bert-base-uncased')
len(bert_tokenizer.vocab)
```

Output

```
30522
```

It seems BERT's vocabulary has **only 30,522 tokens**.

"*Isn't that too few?*"

It *would* be if it weren't for the fact that the **tokens are not (only) words**, but may also be **word pieces**.

"*What is a 'word piece?'*"

It *literally* is a piece of a word. This is better understood with an example: Let's say that a particular word—"*inexplicably*"—is not so frequently used, thus not making it to the vocabulary. Before, we used the *special unknown token* to cover for words that were absent from our vocabulary. But that approach is **less than ideal**: Every time a word is replaced by an `[UNK]` token, some **information gets lost**. We surely can do better than that.

So, what if we **disassemble** an unknown word into **its components (the word pieces)**? Our formerly unknown word, "*inexplicably*," can be disassembled into **five word pieces**: `inexplicably = in + ##ex + ##pl + ##ica + ##bly`.

Every word piece is prefixed with ## to indicate that it does not stand on its own as a word.

Given enough word pieces in a vocabulary, it will be able to **represent every unknown word** using a **concatenation of word pieces**. Problem solved! That's what BERT's pre-trained tokenizer does.

For more details on the **WordPiece** tokenizer, as well as other **sub-word tokenizers** like **Byte-Pair Encoding (BPE)** and **SentencePiece**, please check HuggingFace's "Summary of the Tokenizers"[108] and Cathal Horan's great post "Tokenizers: How machines read"[109] on FloydHub.

Let's tokenize a pair of sentences using BERT's WordPiece tokenizer:

```
sentence1 = 'Alice is inexplicably following the white rabbit'
sentence2 = 'Follow the white rabbit, Neo'
tokens = bert_tokenizer(sentence1, sentence2, return_tensors='pt')
tokens
```

Output

```
{'input_ids': tensor([[  101,  5650,  2003,  1999, 10288, 24759,
5555,  6321,  2206,  1996, 2317, 10442,   102,  3582,  1996,  2317,
10442,  1010,  9253,   102]]),
 'token_type_ids': tensor([[0, 0, 0, 0, 0, 0, 0, 0, 0, 0, 0, 0, 0,
1, 1, 1, 1, 1, 1, 1]]),
 'attention_mask': tensor([[1, 1, 1, 1, 1, 1, 1, 1, 1, 1, 1, 1, 1,
1, 1, 1, 1, 1, 1, 1]])}
```

Notice that, since there are **two sentences**, the `token_type_ids` have two distinct values (zero and one) that work as the **sentence index** corresponding to the sentence each token belongs to. Hold this thought, because we're using this information in the next section.

To actually see the word pieces, it's easier to convert the input IDs back into tokens:

```
print(bert_tokenizer.convert_ids_to_tokens(tokens['input_ids'][0]))
```

Output

```
['[CLS]', 'alice', 'is', 'in', '##ex', '##pl', '##ica', '##bly',
'following', 'the', 'white', 'rabbit', '[SEP]', 'follow', 'the',
'white', 'rabbit', ',', 'neo', '[SEP]']
```

There it is: "*inexplicably*" got disassembled into its word pieces, the separator token `[SEP]` got inserted between the two sentences (and at the end as well), and there is a classifier token `[CLS]` at the start.

AutoTokenizer

If you want to quickly try *different tokenizers* without having to import their corresponding classes, you can use HuggingFace's `AutoTokenizer` instead:

```
from transformers import AutoTokenizer
auto_tokenizer = AutoTokenizer.from_pretrained(
    'bert-base-uncased'
)
print(auto_tokenizer.__class__)
```

Output

```
<class 'transformers.tokenization_bert.BertTokenizer'>
```

As you can see, it *infers* the correct model class based on the name of the model you're loading, e.g., `bert-base-uncased`.

Input Embeddings

Once the sentences are tokenized, we can use their tokens' IDs to look up the corresponding embeddings as usual. These are the **word / token embeddings**. So far, our models used these embeddings (or a bag of them) as their **only input**.

But BERT, being a Transformer encoder, also needs **positional information**. In Chapter 9 we used **positional encoding**, but BERT uses **position embeddings** instead.

"What's the difference between encoding and embedding?"

While the **position encoding** we used in the past had **fixed values** for each position, the **position embeddings** are **learned by the model** (like any other embedding layer). The number of entries in this lookup table is given by the **maximum length of the sequence**.

And there is more! BERT also adds a **third** embedding, namely, **segment embedding**, which is a **position embedding at the sentence level** (since inputs may have either one or two sentences). That's what the **`token_type_ids`** produced by the tokenizer are good for: They work as a *sentence index* for each token.

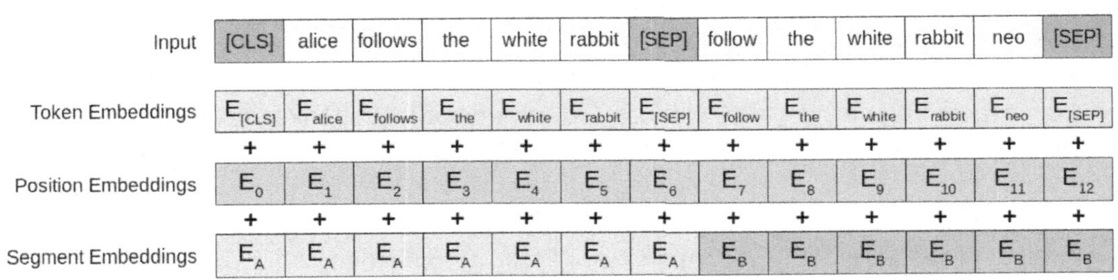

Figure 11.25 - BERT's input embeddings

Talking (or writing) is cheap, though, so let's take a look under BERT's hood:

```
input_embeddings = bert_model.embeddings
```

Output

```
BertEmbeddings(
  (word_embeddings): Embedding(30522, 768, padding_idx=0)
  (position_embeddings): Embedding(512, 768)
  (token_type_embeddings): Embedding(2, 768)
  (LayerNorm): LayerNorm((768,), eps=1e-12, elementwise_affine=True)
  (dropout): Dropout(p=0.1, inplace=False)
)
```

The three embeddings are there: word, position, and segment (named `token_type_embeddings`). Let's go over each of them:

```
token_embeddings = input_embeddings.word_embeddings
token_embeddings
```

Output

```
Embedding(30522, 768, padding_idx=0)
```

The word / token embedding layer has 30,522 entries, the size of BERT's vocabulary, and it has 768 hidden dimensions. As usual, embeddings will be returned by each token ID in the input:

```
input_token_emb = token_embeddings(tokens['input_ids'])
input_token_emb
```

Output

```
tensor([[[ 1.3630e-02, -2.6490e-02, ..., 7.1340e-03,  1.5147e-02],
         ...,
         [-1.4521e-02, -9.9615e-03, ..., 4.6379e-03, -1.5378e-03]]],
       grad_fn=<EmbeddingBackward>)
```

Since each input may have up to 512 tokens, the position embedding layer has exactly that number of entries:

```
position_embeddings = input_embeddings.position_embeddings
position_embeddings
```

Output

```
Embedding(512, 768)
```

Each sequentially numbered position, up to the total length of the input, will return its corresponding embedding:

```
position_ids = torch.arange(512).expand((1, -1))
position_ids
```

Output

```
tensor([[  0,   1,   2,   3,   4,   5,   6,   7,   8,   9,
         ...
         504, 505, 506, 507, 508, 509, 510, 511]])
```

```
seq_length = tokens['input_ids'].size(1)
input_pos_emb = position_embeddings(position_ids[:, :seq_length])
input_pos_emb
```

Output

```
tensor([[[ 1.7505e-02, -2.5631e-02, ...,  1.5441e-02],
         ...,
         [-3.4622e-04, -8.3709e-04, ..., -5.7741e-04]]],
       grad_fn=<EmbeddingBackward>)
```

Then, since there can only be either one or two sentences in the input, the segment embedding layer has **only two entries**:

```
segment_embeddings = input_embeddings.token_type_embeddings
segment_embeddings
```

Output

```
Embedding(2, 768)
```

For these embeddings, BERT will use the `token_type_ids` returned by the tokenizer:

```
input_seg_emb = segment_embeddings(tokens['token_type_ids'])
input_seg_emb
```

Output

```
tensor([[[ 0.0004,  0.0110,  0.0037,  ..., -0.0034, -0.0086],
         [ 0.0004,  0.0110,  0.0037,  ..., -0.0034, -0.0086],
         [ 0.0004,  0.0110,  0.0037,  ..., -0.0034, -0.0086],
         ...,
         [ 0.0011, -0.0030, -0.0032,  ..., -0.0052, -0.0112],
         [ 0.0011, -0.0030, -0.0032,  ..., -0.0052, -0.0112],
         [ 0.0011, -0.0030, -0.0032,  ..., -0.0052, -0.0112]]],
       grad_fn=<EmbeddingBackward>)
```

Since the first tokens, up to and including the first separator, belong to the first sentence, they will all have the **same (first) segment embedding values**. The tokens after the first separator, up to and including the last token, will have the **same (second) segment embedding values**.

Finally, BERT adds up **all three embeddings** (token, position, and segment):

```
input_emb = input_token_emb + input_pos_emb + input_seg_emb
input_emb
```

Output

```
tensor([[[ 0.0316, -0.0411, -0.0564,  ...,  0.0044,  0.0219],
         [-0.0615, -0.0750, -0.0107,  ...,  0.0482, -0.0277],
         [-0.0469, -0.0156, -0.0336,  ...,  0.0135,  0.0109],
         ...,
         [-0.0081, -0.0051, -0.0172,  ..., -0.0103,  0.0083],
         [-0.0425, -0.0756, -0.0414,  ..., -0.0180, -0.0060],
         [-0.0138, -0.0138, -0.0194,  ..., -0.0011, -0.0133]]],
       grad_fn=<AddBackward0>)
```

It will still **layer normalize** the embeddings and apply **dropout** to them, but that's it—these are the **inputs** BERT uses.

Now, let's take a look at its…

Pre-training Tasks

Masked Language Model (MLM)

BERT is said to be an **autoencoding model** because it **is a Transformer encoder** and because it was **trained to "reconstruct" sentences from corrupted inputs** (it does *not* reconstruct the *entire input* but predicts the corrected words instead). That's the **masked language model (MLM)** pre-training task.

In the "Language Model" section we saw that the goal of a language model is to estimate the **probability of a token** or a sequence of tokens or, simply put, to predict the tokens more likely to **fill in a blank**. That looks like a perfect task for a *Transformer decoder*, right?

"*But BERT is an* ***encoder***..."

Well, yeah, but who said the **blank must be at the end**? In the continuous bag-of-words (CBoW) model, the **blank was the word in the center**, and the remaining words were the *context*. In a way, that's what the **MLM task** is doing: It is **randomly choosing words to be masked as blanks** in a sentence. BERT then tries to predict the correct words that fill in the blanks.

Actually, it's a bit more structured than that:

- 80% of the time, it **masks 15% of the tokens** at random: "*Alice followed the [MASK] rabbit.*"
- 10% of the time, it **replaces 15% of the tokens** with some other random word: "*Alice followed the watch rabbit.*"
- The remaining 10% of the time, the **tokens are unchanged**: "*Alice followed the white rabbit.*"

The **target** is the original sentence: "*Alice followed the white rabbit.*" This way, the model effectively learns to reconstruct the original sentence from corrupted inputs (containing missing—masked—or randomly replaced words).

This is the perfect use case (besides *padding*) for the **source mask** argument of the **Transformer encoder**.

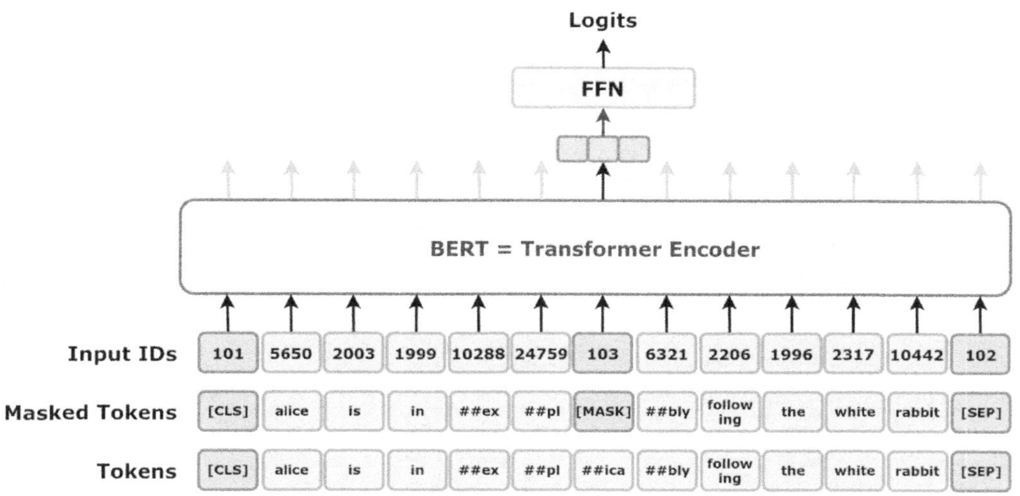

Figure 11.26 - Pre-training task—masked language model (MLM)

Also, notice that BERT **computes logits** for the **randomly masked inputs only**. The remaining inputs are not even considered for computing the loss.

*"OK, but **how** can we randomly replace tokens like that?"*

One alternative, similar to the way we do data augmentation for images, would be to *implement a custom dataset* that performs the replacements on the fly in the `__getitem__()` method. There is a **better alternative**, though: using a **collate function** or, better yet, a **data collator**. There's a data collator that performs the replacement procedure prescribed by BERT: `DataCollatorForLanguageModeling`.

Let's see an example of it in action, starting with an input sentence:

```
sentence = 'Alice is inexplicably following the white rabbit'
tokens = bert_tokenizer(sentence)
tokens['input_ids']
```

Output

```
[101, 5650, 2003, 1999, 10288, 24759, 5555, 6321, 2206, 1996, 2317,
10442, 102]
```

Then, let's create an instance of the data collator and apply it to our mini-batch of one:

```
from transformers import DataCollatorForLanguageModeling
torch.manual_seed(41)
data_collator = DataCollatorForLanguageModeling(
    tokenizer=bert_tokenizer, mlm_probability=0.15
)
mlm_tokens = data_collator([tokens])
mlm_tokens
```

Output

```
{'input_ids': tensor([[  101,  5650,  2003,  1999, 10288, 24759,
103,  6321,  2206,  1996, 2317, 10442,   102]]),
 'labels': tensor([[-100, -100, -100, -100, -100, -100, 5555, -100,
-100, -100, -100, -100, -100]])}
```

If you look closely, you'll see that the **seventh token** (5555 in the original input) was **replaced** by some **other token** (103). Moreover, the **labels** contain the **replaced tokens in their original positions** (and -100 everywhere else to indicate these tokens are irrelevant for computing the loss). It's actually easier to visualize the difference if we convert the IDs back to tokens:

```
print(bert_tokenizer.convert_ids_to_tokens(tokens['input_ids']))
print(bert_tokenizer.convert_ids_to_tokens(
    mlm_tokens['input_ids'][0]
))
```

Output

```
['[CLS]', 'alice', 'is', 'in', '##ex', '##pl', '##ica', '##bly',
'following', 'the', 'white', 'rabbit', '[SEP]']
['[CLS]', 'alice', 'is', 'in', '##ex', '##pl', '[MASK]', '##bly',
'following', 'the', 'white', 'rabbit', '[SEP]']
```

See? The seventh token (`##ica`) got **masked**!

We're **not using collators** in our example, but they can be used together with HuggingFace's `Trainer` (more on that in the "Fine-Tuning with HuggingFace" section) if you're into training some BERT from scratch on the MLM task.

But that's *not* the only thing that BERT is trained to do…

Next Sentence Prediction (NSP)

The second pre-training task is a **binary classification task**: BERT was **trained to predict if a second sentence is actually the next sentence** in the original text or not. The purpose of this task is to give BERT the ability to understand the **relationship between sentences**, which can be useful for some of the tasks BERT can be **fine-tuned** for, like **question answering**.

So, BERT takes **two sentences** as inputs (with the *special separator token* `[SEP]` between them):

- 50% of the time, the **second sentence is indeed the next sentence** (the positive class).
- 50% of the time, the **second sentence is a randomly chosen one** (the negative class).

This task uses the **special classifier token `[CLS]`**, taking the values of the corresponding **final hidden state** as features for a classifier. For example, let's take two sentences and tokenize them:

```
sentence1 = 'alice follows the white rabbit'
sentence2 = 'follow the white rabbit neo'
bert_tokenizer(sentence1, sentence2, return_tensors='pt')
```

Output

```
{'input_ids': tensor([[  101,  5650,  4076,  1996,  2317, 10442,
102,  3582,  1996,  2317, 10442,  9253,   102]]),
 'token_type_ids': tensor([[0, 0, 0, 0, 0, 0, 0, 1, 1, 1, 1, 1,
1]]),
 'attention_mask': tensor([[1, 1, 1, 1, 1, 1, 1, 1, 1, 1, 1, 1,
1]])}
```

If these two sentences were the input of the NSP task, that's what BERT's inputs and outputs would look like.

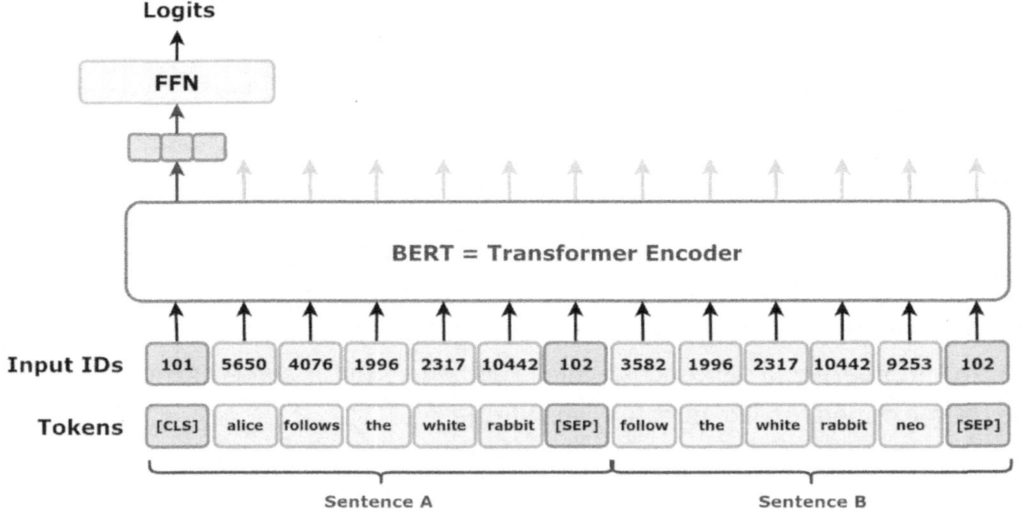

Figure 11.27 - Pre-training task—next sentence prediction (NSP)

The final hidden state is actually *further processed* by a **pooler** (composed of a linear layer and a hyperbolic tangent activation function) before being fed to the classifier (FFN, feed-forward network, in the figure above):

```
bert_model.pooler
```

Output

```
BertPooler(
  (dense): Linear(in_features=768, out_features=768, bias=True)
  (activation): Tanh()
)
```

Outputs

We've seen the many embeddings BERT uses as inputs, but we're more interested in its **outputs**, like the **contextual word embeddings**, right?

By the way, BERT's outputs are always **batch-first**; that is, their shape is **(mini-batch size, sequence length, hidden_dimensions)**.

Let's retrieve the embeddings for the words in the first sentence of our training set:

```
sentence = train_dataset[0]['sentence']
sentence
```

Output

```
'And, so far as they knew, they were quite right.'
```

First, we need to **tokenize** it:

```
tokens = bert_tokenizer(sentence,
                        padding='max_length',
                        max_length=30,
                        truncation=True,
                        return_tensors="pt")
tokens
```

Output

```
{'input_ids': tensor([[ 101, 1998, 1010, 2061, 2521, 2004, 2027,
2354, 1010, 2027, 2020, 3243, 2157, 1012,  102,    0,    0,    0,
0,    0,    0,    0,    0,    0, 0,    0,    0,    0,    0,    0]]),
 'token_type_ids': tensor([[0, 0, 0, 0, 0, 0, 0, 0, 0, 0, 0, 0, 0,
0, 0, 0, 0, 0, 0, 0, 0, 0, 0, 0, 0, 0, 0, 0, 0, 0]]),
 'attention_mask': tensor([[1, 1, 1, 1, 1, 1, 1, 1, 1, 1, 1, 1, 1,
1, 1, 0, 0, 0, 0, 0, 0, 0, 0, 0, 0, 0, 0, 0, 0, 0]])}
```

The tokenizer is **padding** the sentence up to the maximum length (only 30 in this example to more easily visualize the outputs), and this is reflected on the `attention_mask` as well. We'll use both `input_ids` and `attention_mask` as inputs to our BERT model (the `token_type_ids` are irrelevant here because there is only one sentence).

The BERT model may take many other arguments, and we're using three of them to get richer outputs:

```
bert_model.eval()
out = bert_model(input_ids=tokens['input_ids'],
                 attention_mask=tokens['attention_mask'],
                 output_attentions=True,
                 output_hidden_states=True,
                 return_dict=True)
out.keys()
```

Output

```
odict_keys(['last_hidden_state', 'pooler_output', 'hidden_states',
'attentions'])
```

Let's see what's inside each of these four outputs:

- `last_hidden_state` is returned by default and is the most important output of all: It contains the **final hidden states** for each and every token in the input, which can be used as **contextual word embeddings**.

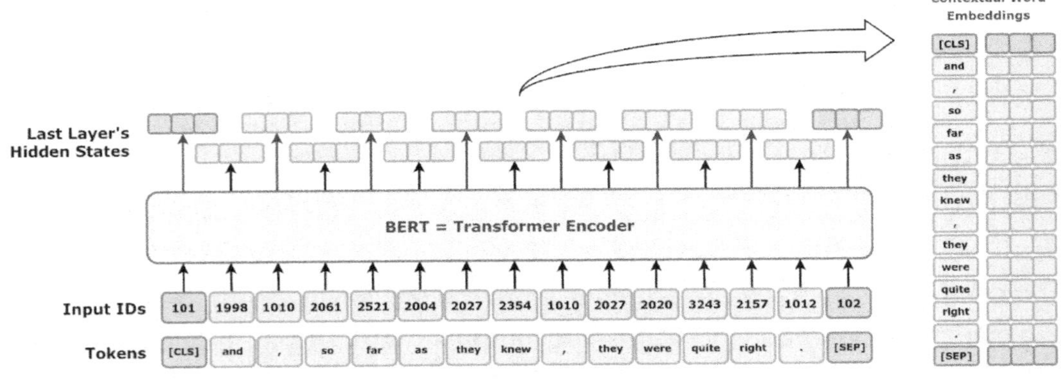

Figure 11.28 - Word embeddings from BERT's last layer

Don't forget that the **first token** is the **special classifier token** `[CLS]` and that there may be padding (`[PAD]`) and separator (`[SEP]`) tokens as well!

```
last_hidden_batch = out['last_hidden_state']
last_hidden_sentence = last_hidden_batch[0]
# Removes hidden states for [PAD] tokens using the mask
mask = tokens['attention_mask'].squeeze().bool()
embeddings = last_hidden_sentence[mask]
# Removes embeddings for the first [CLS] and last [SEP] tokens
embeddings[1:-1]
```

Output

```
tensor([[ 0.0100,  0.8575, -0.5429,  ...,  0.4241, -0.2035],
        [-0.3705,  1.1001,  0.3326,  ...,  0.0656, -0.5644],
        [-0.2947,  0.5797,  0.1997,  ..., -0.3062,  0.6690],
        ...,
        [ 0.0691,  0.7393,  0.0552,  ..., -0.4896, -0.4832],
        [-0.1566,  0.6177,  0.1536,  ...,  0.0904, -0.4917],
        [ 0.7511,  0.3110, -0.3116,  ..., -0.1740, -0.2337]],
       grad_fn=<SliceBackward>)
```

The `flair` library is doing exactly that under its hood! We can use our `get_embeddings()` function to get embeddings for our sentence using the wrapper for BERT from `flair`:

```
get_embeddings(bert_flair, sentence)
```

Output

```
tensor([[ 0.0100,  0.8575, -0.5429,  ...,  0.4241, -0.2035],
        [-0.3705,  1.1001,  0.3326,  ...,  0.0656, -0.5644],
        [-0.2947,  0.5797,  0.1997,  ..., -0.3062,  0.6690],
        ...,
        [ 0.0691,  0.7393,  0.0552,  ..., -0.4896, -0.4832],
        [-0.1566,  0.6177,  0.1536,  ...,  0.0904, -0.4917],
        [ 0.7511,  0.3110, -0.3116,  ..., -0.1740, -0.2337]],
       device='cuda:0')
```

Perfect match!

The **contextual word embeddings** are the **hidden states** produced by the **encoder "layers" of the Transformer**. They can either come from **the last layer only**, like in the example above, or from a concatenation of hidden states produced by several out of the twelve layers in the model.

- `hidden_states` returns hidden states for **every "layer"** in BERT's encoder architecture, including the last one (returned as `last_hidden_state`), and the **input embeddings** as well:

```
print(len(out['hidden_states']))
print(out['hidden_states'][0].shape)
```

Output

```
13
torch.Size([1, 30, 768])
```

The **first** one corresponds to the **input embeddings**:

```
(out['hidden_states'][0] ==
 bert_model.embeddings(tokens['input_ids'])).all()
```

Output

```
tensor(True)
```

And the **last** one is redundant:

```
(out['hidden_states'][-1] == out['last_hidden_state']).all()
```

Output

```
tensor(True)
```

- `pooler_output` is returned by default and, as was already mentioned, it's the output of the **pooler** given the last hidden state as its input:

```
(out['pooler_output'] ==
 bert_model.pooler(out['last_hidden_state'])).all()
```

Output

```
tensor(True)
```

- `attentions` returns the **self-attention scores** for each attention head in each "layer" of BERT's encoder:

```
print(len(out['attentions']))
print(out['attentions'][0].shape)
```

Output

```
12
torch.Size([1, 12, 30, 30])
```

The returned tuple has **twelve elements**, one for each "layer," and each element has a tensor containing the scores for the sentences in the mini-batch (only one in our case). Those scores include each of BERT's **twelve self-attention heads**, with each head indicating **how much attention** each of the **thirty tokens** is paying to all **thirty tokens** in the input. Are you still with me? That's 129,600 attention scores in total! No, I'm not even *trying* to visualize that :-)

Model IV — Classifying Using BERT

We'll use a **Transformer encoder** as a classifier once again (like in "Model II"), but it will be *much easier* now because **BERT will be our encoder**, and it already handles the special classifier token by itself:

```
class BERTClassifier(nn.Module):
    def __init__(self, bert_model, ff_units,
                 n_outputs, dropout=0.3):
        super().__init__()
        self.d_model = bert_model.config.dim
        self.n_outputs = n_outputs
        self.encoder = bert_model
        self.mlp = nn.Sequential(
            nn.Linear(self.d_model, ff_units),
            nn.ReLU(),
            nn.Dropout(dropout),
            nn.Linear(ff_units, n_outputs)
        )

    def encode(self, source, source_mask=None):
        states = self.encoder(
            input_ids=source, attention_mask=source_mask)[0]
        cls_state = states[:, 0]
        return cls_state

    def forward(self, X):
        source_mask = (X > 0)
        # Featurizer
        cls_state = self.encode(X, source_mask)
        # Classifier
        out = self.mlp(cls_state)
        return out
```

Both `encode()` and `forward()` methods are roughly the same as before, but the classifier (`mlp`) has both hidden and dropout layers now.

Our model takes an instance of a **pre-trained BERT model**, the number of units in the hidden layer of the classifier, and the desired **number of outputs** (logits) corresponding to the number of existing classes. The `forward()` method takes a **mini-batch of token IDs**, encodes them using BERT (featurizer), and outputs logits (classifier).

*"Why does the model compute the **source mask** itself instead of using the output from the tokenizer?"*

Good catch! I know that's less than ideal, but our StepByStep class can only take a single mini-batch of inputs, and no additional information like the attention masks. Of course, we *could* modify our class to handle that, but **HuggingFace has its own trainer** (more on that soon!), so there's no point in doing so.

This is actually the *last time* we'll use the StepByStep class since it requires too many adjustments to the inputs to work well with HuggingFace's tokenizers and models.

Data Preparation

To turn the sentences in our datasets into mini-batches of token IDs and labels for a binary classification task, we can create a helper function that takes an **HF's Dataset**, the names of the fields corresponding to the sentences and labels, and a **tokenizer** and **builds a TensorDataset** out of them:

From HF's Dataset *to Tokenized* TensorDataset

```
def tokenize_dataset(hf_dataset, sentence_field,
                     label_field, tokenizer, **kwargs):
    sentences = hf_dataset[sentence_field]
    token_ids = tokenizer(
        sentences, return_tensors='pt', **kwargs
    )['input_ids']
    labels = torch.as_tensor(hf_dataset[label_field])
    dataset = TensorDataset(token_ids, labels)
    return dataset
```

First, we create a **tokenizer** and define the parameters we'll use while tokenizing the sentences:

Data Preparation

```
auto_tokenizer = AutoTokenizer.from_pretrained(
    'distilbert-base-uncased'
)
tokenizer_kwargs = dict(truncation=True,
                        padding=True,
                        max_length=30,
                        add_special_tokens=True)
```

"Which BERT is that? DistilBERT?!"

DistilBERT is a **smaller**, **faster**, **cheaper**, and **lighter** version of BERT, introduced by Sahn, V. et al. in their paper "DistilBERT, a distilled version of BERT: smaller, faster, cheaper and lighter."[110] We're not going into any details about it here, but we're using this version because it's also **friendlier** for fine-tuning in low-end GPUs.

We need to change the labels to **float** as well so they will be compatible with the `nn.BCEWithLogitsLoss()` we'll be using:

Data Preparation

```
train_dataset_float = train_dataset.map(
    lambda row: {'labels': [float(row['labels'])]}
)
test_dataset_float = test_dataset.map(
    lambda row: {'labels': [float(row['labels'])]}
)

train_tensor_dataset = tokenize_dataset(train_dataset_float,
                                        'sentence',
                                        'labels',
                                        auto_tokenizer,
                                        **tokenizer_kwargs)
test_tensor_dataset = tokenize_dataset(test_dataset_float,
                                       'sentence',
                                       'labels',
                                       auto_tokenizer,
                                       **tokenizer_kwargs)
generator = torch.Generator()
train_loader = DataLoader(
    train_tensor_dataset, batch_size=4,
    shuffle=True, generator=generator
)
test_loader = DataLoader(test_tensor_dataset, batch_size=8)
```

*"Batch size **FOUR**?!"*

Yes, four! DistilBERT is still kinda large, so we're using a *very small batch size* such that it will fit a low-end GPU with 6 GB RAM. If you have more powerful hardware at your disposal, by all means, try larger batch sizes :-)

Model Configuration & Training

Let's create an instance of our model using DistilBERT and train it in the usual way:

Model Configuration

```
torch.manual_seed(41)
bert_model = AutoModel.from_pretrained("distilbert-base-uncased")
model = BERTClassifier(bert_model, 128, n_outputs=1)
loss_fn = nn.BCEWithLogitsLoss()
optimizer = optim.Adam(model.parameters(), lr=1e-5)
```

Model Training

```
sbs_bert = StepByStep(model, loss_fn, optimizer)
sbs_bert.set_loaders(train_loader, test_loader)
sbs_bert.train(1)
```

You probably noticed that it **takes quite some time** to train for a single epoch; but, then again, there are more than **66 million parameters** to update:

```
sbs_bert.count_parameters()
```

Output

```
66461441
```

Let's check the accuracy of our model:

```
StepByStep.loader_apply(test_loader, sbs_bert.correct)
```

Output

```
tensor([[424, 440],
        [317, 331]])
```

That's 96.11% accuracy on the validation set—nice! Of course, our dataset is tiny and the model is huge, but still!

Well, you probably don't want to go through all this trouble—adjusting the datasets and writing a model class—to fine-tune a BERT model, right?

Say no more!

Fine-Tuning with HuggingFace

What if I told you that **there is a BERT model for every task**, and you just need to fine-tune it? Cool, isn't it? Then, what if I told you that you can use a **trainer** to do most of the fine-tuning work for you? Amazing, right? The HuggingFace library is **that good**, really!

There are BERT models available for many different tasks:

- Pre-training tasks:
  - Masked language model (`BertForMaskedLM`)
  - Next sentence prediction (`BertForNextSentencePrediction`)
- Typical tasks (also available as `AutoModel`):
  - Sequence classification (`BertForSequenceClassification`)
  - Token classification (`BertForTokenClassification`)
  - Question answering (`BertForQuestionAnswering`)
- BERT (and family) specific:
  - Multiple choice (`BertForMultipleChoice`)

We're sticking with the **sequence classification task** using **DistilBERT** instead of regular BERT so as to make the fine-tuning faster.

Sequence Classification (or Regression)

Let's **load the pre-trained model** using its corresponding class:

Model Configuration

```
from transformers import DistilBertForSequenceClassification
torch.manual_seed(42)
bert_cls = DistilBertForSequenceClassification.from_pretrained(
    'distilbert-base-uncased', num_labels=2
)
```

It comes with a warning:

Output

```
You should probably TRAIN this model on a down-stream task to be
able to use it for predictions and inference.
```

It makes sense!

Since ours is a **binary classification task**, the `num_labels` argument is two, which happens to be the default value. Unfortunately, at the time of writing, the documentation is *not* as explicit as it should be in this case. There is **no mention** of `num_labels` as a possible argument of the model, and it's only referred to in the documentation of the `forward()` method of `DistilBertForSequenceClassification` (highlights are mine):

- **`labels`** (`torch.LongTensor` of shape `(batch_size,)`, optional) – Labels for computing the sequence classification / regression loss. Indices should be in `[0, ..., config.num_labels - 1]`. **If `config.num_labels == 1` a regression loss is computed (Mean-Square loss), If `config.num_labels > 1` a classification loss is computed (Cross-Entropy).**

Some of the returning values of the `forward()` method also include references to the `num_labels` argument:

- **`loss`** (`torch.FloatTensor` of shape `(1,)`, optional, returned when `labels` is provided) – Classification (or regression if `config.num_labels==1`) loss.
- **`logits`** (`torch.FloatTensor` of shape `(batch_size, config.num_labels)`) – Classification (or regression if `config.num_labels==1`) scores (before SoftMax).

That's right! `DistilBertForSequenceClassification` (or any other `ForSequenceClassification` model) **can be used for regression too** as long as you set `num_labels=1` as argument.

If you want to learn more about the **arguments** the pre-trained models may take, please check the documentation on configuration: `PretrainedConfig`.[111]

To learn more about the **outputs** of several pre-trained models, please check the documentation on model outputs.[112]

The `ForSequenceClassification` models add a **single linear layer** (classifier) on **top of the pooled output** from the underlying base model to produce the `logits` output.

More AutoModels

If you want to quickly try *different fine-tuning models* without having to import their corresponding classes, you can use HuggingFace's `AutoModel` corresponding to a fine-tuning task:

```
from transformers import AutoModelForSequenceClassification
auto_cls = AutoModelForSequenceClassification.from_pretrained(
    'distilbert-base-uncased', num_labels=2
)
print(auto_cls.__class__)
```

Output

```
<class 'transformers.modeling_distilbert
.DistilBertForSequenceClassification'>
```

As you can see, it *infers* the correct model class based on the name of the model you're loading, e.g., `distilbert-base-uncased`.

We already have a model, let's look at our dataset...

Tokenized Dataset

The training and test datasets are HF's `Datasets`, and, *finally*, we'll **keep them like that** instead of building `TensorDatasets` out of them. We *still* have to **tokenize** them, though:

Data Preparation

```
auto_tokenizer = AutoTokenizer.from_pretrained(
    'distilbert-base-uncased'
)
def tokenize(row):
    return auto_tokenizer(row['sentence'],
                          truncation=True,
                          padding='max_length',
                          max_length=30)
```

We load a **pre-trained tokenizer** and build a simple function that takes **one row from the dataset** and **tokenizes it**. So far, so good, right?

IMPORTANT: The **pre-trained tokenizer** and **pre-trained model** must have **matching architectures**—in our case, both are pre-trained on `distilbert-base-uncased`.

Next, we use the `map()` method of HF's `Dataset` to **create new columns** by using our **`tokenize()` function**:

Data Preparation

```
tokenized_train_dataset = train_dataset.map(
    tokenize, batched=True
)
tokenized_test_dataset = test_dataset.map(tokenize, batched=True)
```

The `batched` argument **speeds up** the tokenization, but the **tokenizer must return lists** instead of tensors (notice the missing `return_tensors='pt'` in the call to `auto_tokenizer`):

```
print(tokenized_train_dataset[0])
```

Output

```
{'attention_mask': [1, 1, 1, 1, 1, 1, 1, 1, 1, 1, 1, 1, 1, 1, 1, 0,
0, 0, 0, 0, 0, 0, 0, 0, 0, 0, 0, 0, 0, 0],
 'input_ids': [101, 1998, 1010, 2061, 2521, 2004, 2027, 2354, 1010,
2027, 2020, 3243, 2157, 1012, 102, 0, 0, 0, 0, 0, 0, 0, 0, 0, 0, 0,
0, 0, 0, 0],
 'labels': 0,
 'sentence': 'And, so far as they knew, they were quite right.',
 'source': 'wizoz10-1740.txt'}
```

See? Regular Python lists, not PyTorch tensors. It created new columns (`attention_mask` and `input_ids`) and kept the old ones (`labels`, `sentence`, and `source`).

But we don't need *all* these columns for training; we need only the first three. So, let's **tidy it up** by using the `set_format()` method of `Dataset`:

Data Preparation

```
tokenized_train_dataset.set_format(
    type='torch',
    columns=['input_ids', 'attention_mask', 'labels']
)
tokenized_test_dataset.set_format(
    type='torch',
    columns=['input_ids', 'attention_mask', 'labels']
)
```

Not only are we specifying the columns we're actually interested in, but we're also telling it to return PyTorch tensors:

```
tokenized_train_dataset[0]
```

Output

```
{'attention_mask': tensor([1, 1, 1, 1, 1, 1, 1, 1, 1, 1, 1, 1, 1, 1,
1, 0, 0, 0, 0, 0, 0, 0, 0, 0, 0, 0, 0, 0, 0, 0]),
 'input_ids': tensor([ 101, 1998, 1010, 2061, 2521, 2004, 2027,
2354, 1010, 2027, 2020, 3243, 2157, 1012,  102,    0,    0,    0,
0,    0,    0,    0,    0,    0, 0,    0,    0,    0,    0,    0]),
 'labels': tensor(0)}
```

Much better! We're done with our datasets and can move on to the...

Trainer

Even though every pre-trained model on HuggingFace can be fine-tuned in native PyTorch, as we did in the previous section, the library offers an easy-to-use interface for training and evaluation: `Trainer`.

As expected, it takes **a model** and **a training dataset** as required arguments, and that's it:

```
from transformers import Trainer
trainer = Trainer(model=bert_cls,
                  train_dataset=tokenized_train_dataset)
```

We only need to call the `train()` method, and our model will be trained! YES, **this `train()` method** actually **trains the model**! Thank you, HuggingFace :-)

*"Awesome! But ... does it train for **how many epochs**? Which **optimizer** and **learning rate** does it use for training?"*

We can find it all out by looking at its `TrainingArguments`:

```
trainer.args
```

Output

```
TrainingArguments(output_dir=tmp_trainer, overwrite_output_dir=
False, do_train=False, do_eval=None, do_predict=False,
evaluation_strategy=IntervalStrategy.NO, prediction_loss_only=False,
per_device_train_batch_size=8, per_device_eval_batch_size=8,
gradient_accumulation_steps=1, eval_accumulation_steps=None,
learning_rate=5e-05, weight_decay=0.0, adam_beta1=0.9,
adam_beta2=0.999, adam_epsilon=1e-08, max_grad_norm=1.0,
num_train_epochs=3.0, max_steps=-1, lr_scheduler_type=SchedulerType
.LINEAR, warmup_ratio=0.0, warmup_steps=0, logging_dir=runs/Apr21_20
-33-20_MONSTER, logging_strategy=IntervalStrategy.STEPS,
logging_first_step=False, logging_steps=500, save_strategy
=IntervalStrategy.STEPS, save_steps=500, save_total_limit=None,
no_cuda=False, seed=42, fp16=False, fp16_opt_level=O1, fp16_backend
=auto, fp16_full_eval=False, local_rank=-1, tpu_num_cores=None,
tpu_metrics_debug=False, debug=False, dataloader_drop_last=False,
eval_steps=500, dataloader_num_workers=0, past_index=-1, run_name
=tmp_trainer, disable_tqdm=False, remove_unused_columns=True,
label_names=None, load_best_model_at_end=False,
metric_for_best_model=None, greater_is_better=None,
ignore_data_skip=False, sharded_ddp=[], deepspeed=None,
label_smoothing_factor=0.0, adafactor=False, group_by_length=False,
length_column_name=length, report_to=['tensorboard'],
ddp_find_unused_parameters=None, dataloader_pin_memory=True,
skip_memory_metrics=False, _n_gpu=1, mp_parameters=)
```

The `Trainer` creates an instance of `TrainingArguments` by itself, and the values above are the arguments' default values. There is the `learning_rate=5e-05`, and the `num_train_epochs=3.0`, and **many, many others**. The *optimizer* used, even though it's not listed above, is the `AdamW`, a variation of Adam.

We can create an instance of `TrainingArguments` ourselves to get at least a bit of control over the training process. The *only* required argument is the `output_dir`, but we'll specify some other arguments as well:

Training Arguments

```
from transformers import TrainingArguments
training_args = TrainingArguments(
    output_dir='output',
    num_train_epochs=1,
    per_device_train_batch_size=1,
    per_device_eval_batch_size=8,
    evaluation_strategy='steps',
    eval_steps=300,
    logging_steps=300,
    gradient_accumulation_steps=8,
)
```

*"Batch size **ONE**?! You gotta be kidding me!"*

Well, I *would*, if it were not for the **`gradient_accumulation_steps`** argument. That's how we can make the **mini-batch size larger** even if we're using a **low-end GPU** that is capable of handling **only one data point** at a time.

The `Trainer` can **accumulate the gradients** computed at every training step (which is taking only one data point), and, **after eight steps**, it uses the accumulated gradients to **update the parameters**. For all intents and purposes, it is **as if** the mini-batch had **size eight**. Awesome, right?

Moreover, let's set the `logging_steps` to three hundred, so it prints the **training losses** every three hundred mini-batches (and it counts the mini-batches as having size eight due to the gradient accumulation).

*"What about **validation losses**?"*

The `evaluation_strategy` argument allows you to run an evaluation **after every `eval_steps` steps** (if set to `steps` like in the example above) or **after every epoch** (if set to `epoch`).

*"Can I get it to print **accuracy** or other metrics too?"*

Sure, you can! But, first, you need to define a function that takes an instance of `EvalPrediction` (returned by the internal validation loop), **computes the desired metrics**, and **returns a dictionary**:

Method for Computing Accuracy

```
def compute_metrics(eval_pred):
    predictions = eval_pred.predictions
    labels = eval_pred.label_ids
    predictions = np.argmax(predictions, axis=1)
    return {"accuracy": (predictions == labels).mean()}
```

We can use a simple function like the one above to compute accuracy and pass it as the `compute_metrics` argument of the `Trainer` along with the remaining `TrainingArguments` and datasets:

Model Training

```
trainer = Trainer(model=bert_cls,
                  args=training_args,
                  train_dataset=tokenized_train_dataset,
                  eval_dataset=tokenized_test_dataset,
                  compute_metrics=compute_metrics)
```

There we go—we're 100% ready to call the **glorious `train()` method**:

Model Training

```
trainer.train()
```

Output

```
Step Training Loss Validation Loss Accuracy  ...
 300      0.194600        0.159694 0.953307  ...

TrainOutput(global_step=385, training_loss=0.17661244776341822,
metrics={'train_runtime': 80.0324, 'train_samples_per_second':
4.811, 'total_flos': 37119857544000.0, 'epoch': 1.0,
'init_mem_cpu_alloc_delta': 0, 'init_mem_gpu_alloc_delta': 0,
'init_mem_cpu_peaked_delta': 0, 'init_mem_gpu_peaked_delta': 0,
'train_mem_cpu_alloc_delta': 5025792, 'train_mem_gpu_alloc_delta':
806599168, 'train_mem_cpu_peaked_delta': 0,
'train_mem_gpu_peaked_delta': 96468992})
```

It's printing the training and validation losses, and the validation accuracy, every three hundred mini-batches as configured. To check the **final validation figures**, though, we need to call the `evaluate()` method, which, guess what, **actually runs a validation loop**! Thank you, HuggingFace :-)

```
trainer.evaluate()
```

Output

```
{'eval_loss': 0.142591193318367,
 'eval_accuracy': 0.9610894941634242,
 'eval_runtime': 1.6634,
 'eval_samples_per_second': 463.51,
 'epoch': 1.0,
 'eval_mem_cpu_alloc_delta': 0,
 'eval_mem_gpu_alloc_delta': 0,
 'eval_mem_cpu_peaked_delta': 0,
 'eval_mem_gpu_peaked_delta': 8132096}
```

That's 96.11% accuracy on the validation set after one epoch, roughly the same as our own implementation ("Model IV"). Nice!

Once the model is trained, we can **save it to disk** using the `save_model()` method from `Trainer`:

```
trainer.save_model('bert_alice_vs_wizard')
os.listdir('bert_alice_vs_wizard')
```

Output

```
['training_args.bin', 'config.json', 'pytorch_model.bin']
```

It creates a *folder* with the provided name, and it stores the trained model (`pytorch_model.bin`) along with its configuration (`config.json`) and training arguments (`training_args.bin`).

Later on, we can easily **load the trained model** using the `from_pretrained()` method from the corresponding `AutoModel`:

```
loaded_model = (AutoModelForSequenceClassification
                .from_pretrained('bert_alice_vs_wizard'))
loaded_model.device
```

Output

```
device(type='cpu')
```

The model is loaded to the CPU by default, but we can send it to a different device in the usual PyTorch way:

```
device = 'cuda' if torch.cuda.is_available() else 'cpu'
loaded_model.to(device)
loaded_model.device
```

Output

```
device(type='cuda', index=0)
```

Predictions

We can **finally** answer the most important question of all: Where does the sentence in the title, "*Down the Yellow Brick Rabbit Hole*," come from? Let's ask BERT:

```
sentence = 'Down the yellow brick rabbit hole'
tokens = auto_tokenizer(sentence, return_tensors='pt')
tokens
```

Output

```
{'input_ids': tensor([[  101,  2091,  1996,  3756,  5318, 10442,
4920,   102]]),
 'attention_mask': tensor([[1, 1, 1, 1, 1, 1, 1, 1]])}
```

After tokenizing the sentence, we need to make sure the tensors are in the **same device as the model**.

"Do I need to send each tensor to a device, really?"

Not really, no. It turns out, the **output of the tokenizer** isn't *just* a dictionary, but also an instance of `BatchEncoding`, and we can easily call its `to()` method to send the tensors to the same device as the model:

```
print(type(tokens))
tokens.to(loaded_model.device)
```

Output

```
<class 'transformers.tokenization_utils_base.BatchEncoding'>
{'input_ids': tensor([[  101,  2091,  1996,  3756,  5318, 10442,
4920,   102]], device='cuda:0'),
 'attention_mask': tensor([[1, 1, 1, 1, 1, 1, 1, 1]], device
='cuda:0')}
```

That was easy, right?

Let's call the model using these inputs!

Even though the model is loaded in *evaluation mode* by default, it is always a good idea to explicitly **set the model to evaluation mode** using the PyTorch model's `eval()` method during evaluation or test phases:

```
loaded_model.eval()
logits = loaded_model(input_ids=tokens['input_ids'],
                      attention_mask=tokens['attention_mask'])
logits
```

Output

```
SequenceClassifierOutput(loss=None, logits=tensor([[ 2.7745, -
2.5539]], device='cuda:0', grad_fn=<AddmmBackward>), hidden_states
=None, attentions=None)
```

The **largest logit** corresponds to the **predicted class** as usual:

```
logits.logits.argmax(dim=1)
```

Output

```
tensor([0], device='cuda:0')
```

BERT has spoken: The sentence "*Down the Yellow Brick Rabbit Hole*" is more likely coming from *The Wonderful Wizard of Oz* (the negative class of our binary classification task).

Don't you think that's a lot of work to get predictions for a single sentence? I mean, tokenizing, sending it to the device, feeding the inputs to the model, getting the largest logit—that's a lot, right? I think so, too.

Pipelines

Pipelines can handle all these steps for us, we just have to choose the appropriate one. There are *many* different pipelines, one for each task, like the `TextClassificationPipeline` and the `TextGenerationPipeline`. Let's use the former to run our tokenizer and trained model at once:

```
from transformers import TextClassificationPipeline
device_index = (loaded_model.device.index
                if loaded_model.device.type != 'cpu'
                else -1)
classifier = TextClassificationPipeline(model=loaded_model,
                                        tokenizer=auto_tokenizer,
                                        device=device_index)
```

Every pipeline takes at least **two** required arguments: **a model** and **a tokenizer**. We can also send it straight to the same device as our model, but we would need to use the **device index** instead (-1 if it's on a CPU, 0 if it's on the first or only GPU, 1 if it's on the second one, and so on).

Now we can make predictions using **the original sentences**:

```
classifier(['Down the Yellow Brick Rabbit Hole', 'Alice rules!'])
```

Output

```
[{'label': 'LABEL_0', 'score': 0.9951714277267456},
 {'label': 'LABEL_1', 'score': 0.9985325336456299}]
```

The model seems pretty confident that the **first sentence** is from *The Wonderful Wizard of Oz* (negative class) and that the **second sentence** is from *Alice's Adventures in Wonderland* (positive class).

We can make the output a bit more intuitive, though, by **setting proper labels** for each of the classes using the `id2label` attribute of our model's configuration:

```
loaded_model.config.id2label = {0: 'Wizard', 1: 'Alice'}
```

Let's try it again:

```
classifier(['Down the Yellow Brick Rabbit Hole', 'Alice rules!'])
```

Output

```
[{'label': 'Wizard', 'score': 0.9951714277267456},
 {'label': 'Alice', 'score': 0.9985325336456299}]
```

That's much better!

More Pipelines

It's also possible to use pre-trained pipelines for **typical tasks** like **sentiment analysis** without having to fine-tune your own model:

```
from transformers import pipeline
sentiment = pipeline('sentiment-analysis')
```

That's it! The **task defines which pipeline is used**. For sentiment analysis, the pipeline above loads a `TextClassificationPipeline` like ours, but one that's pre-trained to perform that task.

For a complete list of available tasks, please check HuggingFace's `pipeline` [113] documentation.

Let's run the first sentence of our training set through the sentiment analysis pipeline:

```
sentence = train_dataset[0]['sentence']
print(sentence)
print(sentiment(sentence))
```

Output

```
And, so far as they knew, they were quite right.
[{'label': 'POSITIVE', 'score': 0.9998356699943542}]
```

Positive, indeed!

If you're curious about **which model** is being used under the hood, you can check the `SUPPORTED_TASKS` dictionary. For sentiment analysis, it uses the `distilbert-base-uncased-finetuned-sst-2-english` model:

```
from transformers.pipelines import SUPPORTED_TASKS
SUPPORTED_TASKS['sentiment-analysis']
```

Output

```
{'impl': transformers.pipelines.text_classification
.TextClassificationPipeline,
 'tf': None,
 'pt': types.AutoModelForSequenceClassification,
 'default': {'model': {'pt': 'distilbert-base-uncased-finetuned-sst-
2-english',
   'tf': 'distilbert-base-uncased-finetuned-sst-2-english'}}}
```

"*What about **text generation**?*"

```
SUPPORTED_TASKS['text-generation']
```

Output

```
{'impl': transformers.pipelines.text_generation
.TextGenerationPipeline,
 'tf': None,
 'pt': types.AutoModelForCausalLM,
 'default': {'model': {'pt': 'gpt2', 'tf': 'gpt2'}}}
```

That's the **famous GPT-2** model, which we'll discuss briefly in the next, and last, section of this chapter.

GPT-2

The **G**enerative **P**retrained **T**ransformer **2**, introduced by Radford, A. et al. in their paper "Language Models are Unsupervised Multitask Learners"[114] (2018), made headlines with its impressive ability to **generate text** of high quality in a variety of contexts. Just like BERT, it is a **language model**; that is, it is trained to **fill in the blanks** in sentences. But, while BERT was trained to fill in the blanks in the middle of sentences (thus correcting corrupted inputs), **GPT-2** was trained to **fill in blanks at the end of sentences**, effectively **predicting the next word in a given sentence**.

Predicting the **next element in a sequence** is exactly what a **Transformer decoder** does, so it should be no surprise that **GPT-2 is actually a Transformer decoder**.

It was trained on more than 40 GB of Internet text spread over 8 million web pages. Its largest version has **48 "layers"** (the original Transformer had only six), **twelve attention heads**, and **1,600 hidden dimensions**, totaling **1.5 billion parameters**, and it was released in November 2019.[115]

"Don't train this at home!"

On the other end of the scale, the smallest version has *only* twelve "layers," twelve attention heads, and 768 hidden dimensions, totaling 117 million parameters (the smallest GPT-2 is still a bit larger than the original BERT!). This is the version automatically loaded in the `TextGenerationPipeline`.

You can find the models and the corresponding code in Open AI's GPT-2 repository

[116]. For a demo of GPT-2's capabilities, please check AllenNLP's Language Modeling Demo,[117] which uses GPT-2's medium model (345 million parameters).

You can also check GPT-2's documentation[118] and model card,[119] available at HuggingFace, for a quick overview of the model and its training procedure.

For a general overview of GPT-2, see this great post by Jay Alammar: "The Illustrated GPT-2 (Visualizing Transformer Language Models)."[120]

To learn more details about GPT-2's architecture, please check "The Annotated GPT-2"[121] by Aman Arora.

There is also Andrej Karpathy's **minimalistic implementation** of GPT, minGPT (*https://github.com/karpathy/minGPT*) if you feel like trying to train a GPT model from scratch.

Let's load the **GPT-2-based text generation pipeline**:

```
text_generator = pipeline("text-generation")
```

Then, let's use the **first two paragraphs** from *Alice's Adventures in Wonderland* as our base text:

```
base_text = """
Alice was beginning to get very tired of sitting by her sister on
the bank, and of having nothing to do:  once or twice she had peeped
into the book her sister was reading, but it had no pictures or
conversations in it, `and what is the use of a book,'thought Alice
`without pictures or conversation?' So she was considering in her
own mind (as well as she could, for the hot day made her feel very
sleepy and stupid), whether the pleasure of making a daisy-chain
would be worth the trouble of getting up and picking the daisies,
when suddenly a White Rabbit with pink eyes ran close by her.
"""
```

The generator will produce a text of size `max_length`, including the base text, so this value has to be **larger** than the length of the base text. By default, the model in the text generation pipeline has its **`do_sample`** argument set to `True` to generate words using **beam search** instead of greedy decoding:

```
text_generator.model.config.task_specific_params
```

Output

```
{'text-generation': {'do_sample': True, 'max_length': 50}}
```

```
result = text_generator(base_text, max_length=250)
print(result[0]['generated_text'])
```

Output

```
...
Alice stared at the familiar looking man in red, in a white dress,
and smiled shyly.

She saw the cat on the grass and sat down with it gently and
eagerly, with her arms up.

There was a faint, long, dark stench, the cat had its tail held at
the end by a large furry, white fur over it.

Alice glanced at it.

It was a cat, but a White Rabbit was very good at drawing this,
thinking over its many attributes, and making sure that no reds
appeared
```

I've removed the base text from the output above, so that's **generated text** only. Looks decent, right? I tried it several times, and the generated text is usually consistent, even though it *digresses* some times and, on occasion, generates some really weird pieces of text.

"*What is this **beam search**? That sounds oddly familiar.*"

That's true, we briefly discussed **beam search** (and its alternative, greedy decoding) in Chapter 9, and I reproduce it below for your convenience:

> "...**greedy decoding** because **each prediction** is deemed **final**. "*No backsies*": Once it's done, it's *really* done, you just move along to the next prediction and never look back. In the context of our sequence-to-sequence problem, a regression, it wouldn't make much sense to do otherwise anyway.
>
> But that **may not** be the case for other types of sequence-to-sequence problems. In machine translation, for example, the decoder outputs **probabilities** for the **next word** in the sentence at each step. The **greedy** approach would simply take the **word with the highest probability** and move on to the next.
>
> However, since **each prediction** is an input to the **next step**, taking the **top word at every step** is **not necessarily the winning approach** (translating from one language to another is not exactly "linear"). It is probably wiser to keep a **handful of candidates** at every step and **try their combinations** to choose the best one: That's called **beam search**..."

By the way, if you try using *greedy decoding* instead (setting `do_sample=False`), the generated text simply and annoyingly repeats the same text over and over again:

```
'What is the use of a daisy-chain?'
'I don't know,' said Alice, 'but I think it is a good idea.'

'What is the use of a daisy-chain?'
'I don't know,' said Alice, 'but I think it is a good idea.'
```

For more details on the different arguments that can be used for text generation, including a more detailed explanation of both **greedy decoding** and **beam search**, please check HuggingFace's blog post "How to generate text: Using different decoding methods for language generation with Transformers"[122] by Patrick von Platen.

"*Wait a minute! Aren't we* **fine-tuning GPT-2** *so it can write text in a given style?*"

I thought you would never ask... Yes, we are. It's the final example, and we're covering it in the next section.

Putting It All Together

In this chapter, we **built a dataset** using two books and explored many pre-processing steps and techniques: sentence and word tokenization, **word embeddings**, and much more. We used HuggingFace's `Dataset` and **pre-trained tokenizers** extensively for the data preparation step, and leveraged the power of **pre-trained models** like **BERT** to **classify sequences (sentences)** according to their source. We also used HuggingFace's `Trainer` and `pipeline` classes to easily **train models** and **deliver predictions**, respectively..

Data Preparation

In order to capture the *style* of Lewis Carroll's *Alice's Adventures in Wonderland*, we need to use a dataset containing sentences from that book alone, instead of our previous dataset that included *The Wonderful Wizard of Oz* as well.

Data Preparation

```
dataset = load_dataset(path='csv',
                       data_files=['texts/alice28-1476.sent.csv'],
                       quotechar='\\', split=Split.TRAIN)

shuffled_dataset = dataset.shuffle(seed=42)
split_dataset = shuffled_dataset.train_test_split(test_size=0.2,
                                                  seed=42)
train_dataset = split_dataset['train']
test_dataset = split_dataset['test']
```

Next, we **tokenize** the dataset using **GPT-2**'s pre-trained tokenizer. There are *some* differences from BERT, though:

- First, GPT-2 uses **Byte-Pair Encoding (BPE)** instead of WordPiece for tokenization.
- Second, we're **not padding** the sentences, since we're trying to **generate text** and it wouldn't make much sense to **predict the next word after a bunch of padded elements**.
- Third, we're **removing the original columns** (`source` and `sentence`) such that only the output of the tokenizer (`input_ids` and `attention_mask`) remains.

Data Preparation

```
auto_tokenizer = AutoTokenizer.from_pretrained('gpt2')
def tokenize(row):
    return auto_tokenizer(row['sentence'])

tokenized_train_dataset = train_dataset.map(
    tokenize, remove_columns=['source', 'sentence'], batched=True
)
tokenized_test_dataset = test_dataset.map(
    tokenize, remove_columns=['source', 'sentence'], batched=True
)
```

Maybe you've already realized that, without padding, the **sentences have varied lengths**:

```
list(map(len, tokenized_train_dataset[0:6]['input_ids']))
```

Output

```
[9, 28, 20, 9, 34, 29]
```

These are the **first six** sentences, and their lengths range from **nine** to **thirty-four tokens**.

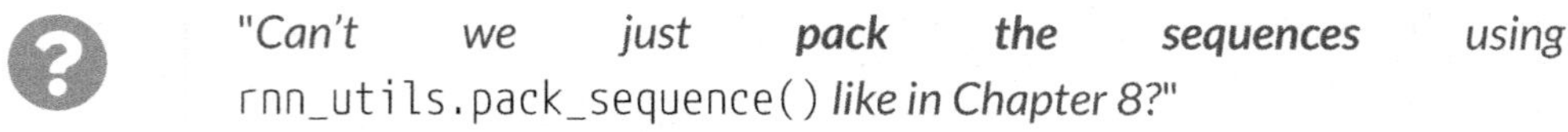

"Can't we just ***pack the sequences*** *using* `rnn_utils.pack_sequence()` *like in Chapter 8?"*

You get the *gist* of it: The general idea is to "*pack*" sequences together, indeed, but in a *different way*!

"Packed" Dataset

The "*packing*" is actually simpler now; it is simply **concatenating** the inputs together and then **chunking them into blocks**.

Block = 128 tokens

Index																
0	63	2437	466	345	760	314	1101	8805	8348	464	2677	3114	7296	6819	379	262
16	2635	25498	11	508	531	287	257	1877	3809	11	4600	7120	25788	1276	3272	12
32	1069	9862	12680	4973	2637	1537	611	314	1101	407	262	976	11	262	1306	1808
48	318	11	5338	287	262	995	716	314	30	464	360	579	1076	6364	4721	465
64	2951	13	63	1026	373	881	21289	272	353	379	1363	4032	1807	3595	14862	11
80	4600	12518	530	2492	470	1464	3957	4025	290	4833	11	290	852	6149	546	416
96	10693	290	33043	13	1870	14862	373	523	881	24776	326	673	4966	572	379	1752
112	287	262	4571	340	6235	84	11	1231	2111	284	4727	262	7457	340	550	925

	# Tokens
Sentence 1	9
Sentence 2	28
Sentence 3	20
Sentence 4	9
Sentence 5	34
Sentence 6	29

Figure 11.29 - Grouping sentences into blocks

The function below was adapted from HuggingFace's language modeling fine-tuning script `run_clm.py`,[123] and it "*packs*" the inputs together:

Method for Grouping Sentences into Blocks

```
# Adapted from https://github.com/huggingface/transformers/blob/
# master/examples/pytorch/language-modeling/run_clm.py
def group_texts(examples, block_size=128):
    # Concatenate all texts.
    concatenated_examples = {k: sum(examples[k], [])
                             for k in examples.keys()}
    total_length = len(
        concatenated_examples[list(examples.keys())[0]]
    )
    # We drop the small remainder, we could add padding
    # if the model supported it instead of this drop, you
    # can customize this part to your needs.
    total_length = (total_length // block_size) * block_size
    # Split by chunks of max_len.
    result = {
        k: [t[i : i + block_size]
            for i in range(0, total_length, block_size)]
        for k, t in concatenated_examples.items()
    }
    result["labels"] = result["input_ids"].copy()
    return result
```

We can apply the function above to our datasets in the usual way and then set their output formats to PyTorch tensors:

Data Preparation

```
lm_train_dataset = tokenized_train_dataset.map(
    group_texts, batched=True
)
lm_test_dataset = tokenized_test_dataset.map(
    group_texts, batched=True
)
lm_train_dataset.set_format(type='torch')
lm_test_dataset.set_format(type='torch')
```

Now, the **first data point** actually contains the **first 128 tokens** of our dataset (the *first five sentences* and *almost all tokens from the sixth*):

```
print(lm_train_dataset[0]['input_ids'])
```

Output

```
tensor([   63,  2437,   466,   345,   760,   314,  1101,  8805,
         8348,   464,  2677,  3114,  7296,  6819,   379,   262,
         2635, 25498,    11,   508,   531,   287,   257,  1877,
         3809,    11,  4600,  7120, 25788,  1276,  3272,    12,
         1069,  9862, 12680,  4973,  2637,  1537,   611,   314,
         1101,   407,   262,   976,    11,   262,  1306,  1808,
          318,    11,  5338,   287,   262,   995,   716,   314,
           30,   464,   360,   579,  1076,  6364,  4721,   465,
         2951,    13,    63,  1026,   373,   881, 21289,   272,
          353,   379,  1363,  4032,  1807,  3595, 14862,    11,
         4600, 12518,   530,  2492,   470,  1464,  3957,  4025,
          290,  4833,    11,   290,   852,  6149,   546,   416,
        10693,   290, 33043,    13,  1870, 14862,   373,   523,
          881, 24776,   326,   673,  4966,   572,   379,  1752,
          287,   262,  4571,   340,  6235,   284,    11,  1231,
         2111,   284,  4727,   262,  7457,   340,   550,   925])
```

Consequently, the **datasets get smaller**, since they do not contain *sentences* anymore but **sequences of 128 tokens** instead:

```
len(lm_train_dataset), len(lm_test_dataset)
```

Output

```
(239, 56)
```

The dataset is ready! We can move on to the…

Model Configuration & Training

GPT-2 is a model for **causal language modeling**, and that's the `AutoModel` we use to load it:

Model Configuration

```
from transformers import AutoModelForCausalLM
model = AutoModelForCausalLM.from_pretrained('gpt2')
print(model.__class__)
```

Output

```
<class 'transformers.modeling_gpt2.GPT2LMHeadModel'>
```

GPT-2's tokenizer **does not** include a **special padding token** by default, but you *may add it* if needed. If you **do add any tokens** to the vocabulary, though, you also need to **let the model know it** using `resize_token_embeddings()`:

```
model.resize_token_embeddings(len(auto_tokenizer))
```

Output

```
Embedding(50257, 768)
```

In our example, it **doesn't make a difference**, but it's a good idea to add the line above to the code anyway to be on the safe side.

The training arguments are roughly the same ones we used to train BERT, but there is an additional one: `prediction_loss_only=True`. Since GPT-2 is a **generative model**, we won't be running any additional metrics during training or validation, and there's no need for anything but the loss.

Model Training

```
training_args = TrainingArguments(
    output_dir='output',
    num_train_epochs=1,
    per_device_train_batch_size=1,
    per_device_eval_batch_size=8,
    evaluation_strategy='steps',
    eval_steps=50,
    logging_steps=50,
    gradient_accumulation_steps=4,
    prediction_loss_only=True,
)

trainer = Trainer(model=model,
                  args=training_args,
                  train_dataset=lm_train_dataset,
                  eval_dataset=lm_test_dataset)
```

After configuring the `Trainer`, we call its `train()` method and then its `evaluate()` method:

Model Training

```
trainer.train()
```

Output

```
Step Training Loss Validation Loss  ...
  50      3.587500        3.327199  ...

TrainOutput(global_step=59, training_loss=3.5507330167091498,
metrics={'train_runtime': 22.6958, 'train_samples_per_second': 2.6,
'total_flos': 22554466320384.0, 'epoch': 0.99,
'init_mem_cpu_alloc_delta': 1316954112, 'init_mem_gpu_alloc_delta':
511148032, 'init_mem_cpu_peaked_delta': 465375232,
'init_mem_gpu_peaked_delta': 0, 'train_mem_cpu_alloc_delta':
13103104, 'train_mem_gpu_alloc_delta': 1499219456,
'train_mem_cpu_peaked_delta': 0, 'train_mem_gpu_peaked_delta':
730768896})
```

```
trainer.evaluate()
```

Output

```
{'eval_loss': 3.320632219314575,
 'eval_runtime': 0.9266,
 'eval_samples_per_second': 60.438,
 'epoch': 0.99,
 'eval_mem_cpu_alloc_delta': 151552,
 'eval_mem_gpu_alloc_delta': 0,
 'eval_mem_cpu_peaked_delta': 0,
 'eval_mem_gpu_peaked_delta': 730768896}
```

There we go: GPT-2 was fine-tuned on *Alice's Adventures in Wonderland* for one epoch.

How good is it at being Lewis Carroll now? Let's check it out!

Generating Text

The GPT-2 model has a `generate()` method with *plenty of options* for generating text (e.g., greedy decoding, beam search, and more). We won't be delving into these details but going the **easy way** instead: assigning our fine-tuned model and pre-trained tokenizer to a **pipeline** and using most of its default values.

```
device_index = (model.device.index
                if model.device.type != 'cpu'
                else -1)
gpt2_gen = pipeline('text-generation',
                    model=model,
                    tokenizer=auto_tokenizer,
                    device=device_index)
```

The only parameter we may have to change is, once again, the `max_length`:

```
result = gpt2_gen(base_text, max_length=250)
print(result[0]['generated_text'])
```

Output

```
Alice was beginning to get very tired of sitting by her sister on
the bank, and of having nothing to do: once or twice she had peeped
into the book her sister was reading, but it had no pictures or
conversations in it, `and what is the use of a book,'thought Alice
`without pictures or conversation?' So she was considering in her
own mind (as well as she could, for the hot day made her feel very
sleepy and stupid), whether the pleasure of making a daisy-chain
would be worth the trouble of getting up and picking the daisies,
when suddenly a White Rabbit with pink eyes ran close by her.

The rabbit was running away quite as quickly as it had jumped to her
feet.She had nothing of the kind, and, as she made it up to Alice,
was beginning to look at the door carefully in one thought.`It's
very curious,'after having been warned,`that I should be talking to
Alice!'`It's not,'she went on, `it wasn't even a cat,' so very very
quietly indeed.'In that instant he began to cry out aloud.Alice
began to sob out, 'I am not to cry out!'`What
```

This time, I've kept the whole thing, the **base** and the **generated text**. I tried it out several times and, in my humble opinion, the output **looks more "*Alice-y*"** now.

What do *you* think?

Recap

In this chapter, we took a *deep dive* into the **natural language processing** world. We built our own dataset from scratch using two books, *Alice's Adventures in Wonderland* and *The Wonderful Wizard of Oz*, and performed **sentence and word tokenization**. Then, we built a **vocabulary** and used it with a **tokenizer** to generate the primary input of our models: **sequences of token IDs**. Next, we created **numerical representations** for our tokens, starting with a basic **one-hot encoding** and working our way to using **word embeddings** to train a model for classifying the source of a sentence. We also learned about the limitations of classical embeddings, and the need for **contextual word embeddings** produced by **language models** like **ELMo** and **BERT**. We got to know our Muppet friend in detail: input embeddings, pre-training tasks, and hidden states (the actual embeddings). We leveraged the HuggingFace library to **fine-tune** a pre-trained model using a **`Trainer`** and to deliver predictions using a **`pipeline`**. Lastly, we used the famous **GPT-2** model to **generate text** that, hopefully, looks like it was written by Lewis Carroll. This is what we've covered:

- using NLTK to perform **sentence tokenization** on our text corpora
- converting each book into a CSV file containing **one sentence per line**
- building a dataset using HuggingFace's **`Dataset`** to load the CSV files
- creating new columns in the dataset using `map()`
- learning about **data augmentation** for **text data**
- using Gensim to perform **word tokenization**
- building a **vocabulary** and using it to **get a token ID** for each word
- adding **special tokens** to the vocabulary, like `[UNK]` and `[PAD]`
- loading our own vocabulary into HuggingFace's **tokenizer**
- understanding the **output** of a tokenizer: `input_ids`, `token_type_ids`, and `attention_mask`
- using the tokenizer to **tokenize two sentences** as a **single input**
- creating **numerical representations** for each token, starting with **one-hot encoding**
- learning about the simplicity and limitations of the **bag-of-words (BoW)** approach

- learning that a **language model** is used to estimate the **probability of a token**, pretty much like **filling in the blanks** in a sentence
- understanding the general idea behind the **Word2Vec** model and its common implementation, the **CBoW (continuous bag-of-words)**
- learning that **word embeddings** are basically a **lookup table** to retrieve the vector corresponding to a given token
- using **pre-trained embeddings** like **GloVe** to perform **embedding arithmetic**
- loading **GloVe embeddings** and using them to **train a simple classifier**
- using a **Transformer encoder** together with **GloVe embeddings** to classify sentences
- understanding the importance of **contextual word embeddings** to distinguish between different meanings for the same word
- using `flair` to retrieve **contextual word embeddings from ELMo**
- getting an overview of **ELMo's architecture** and its **hidden states** (the embeddings)
- using `flair` to **pre-process sentences** into **BERT embeddings** and **train a classifier**
- learning about **WordPiece tokenization** used by BERT
- computing BERT's **input embeddings** using **token**, **position**, and **segment** embeddings
- understanding BERT's pre-training tasks: **masked language model (MLM)** and **next sentence prediction (NSP)**
- exploring the different **outputs** from BERT: **hidden states**, **pooler output**, and **attentions**
- training a classifier using **pre-trained BERT as a layer**
- **fine-tuning BERT** using HuggingFace's models for **sequence classification**
- remembering to **always** use **matching pre-trained model and tokenizer**
- exploring and using the `Trainer` class to **fine-tune large models** using **gradient accumulation**
- combining **tokenizer and model** into a **pipeline** to easily deliver predictions
- loading **pre-trained pipelines** to perform typical tasks, like **sentiment analysis**

- learning about the famous **GPT-2** model and fine-tuning it to **generate text** like Lewis Carroll :-)

Congratulations! You survived an intense *crash course* on (almost) all things NLP, from basic **sentence tokenization** using NLTK all the way up to **sequence classification** using **BERT** and **causal language modeling** using **GPT-2**. You're now equipped to handle **text data** and train or **fine-tune models using HuggingFace**.

In the next chapter, we'll ... oh, wait, there is *no* next chapter. We've actually **finished** our *long* journey!

Thank You!

I really hope you enjoyed reading and learning about all these topics as much as I enjoyed writing (and learning, too!) about them.

If you have any suggestions, or if you find any errors, please don't hesitate to contact me through GitHub (dvgodoy), Twitter (@dvgodoy), or LinkedIn.

I'm looking forward to hearing back from you!

Daniel Voigt Godoy, December 5, 2021

"*You're still here? It's over. Go home!*"

Ferris Bueller

Sorry, but I **had to** end with a silly joke :-)

[61] https://github.com/dvgodoy/PyTorchStepByStep/blob/master/Chapter11.ipynb

[62] https://colab.research.google.com/github/dvgodoy/PyTorchStepByStep/blob/master/Chapter11.ipynb

[63] https://ota.bodleian.ox.ac.uk/repository/xmlui/handle/20.500.12024/1476

[64] https://ota.bodleian.ox.ac.uk/repository/xmlui/handle/20.500.12024/1740

[65] https://ota.bodleian.ox.ac.uk/repository/xmlui/

[66] https://ota.bodleian.ox.ac.uk/repository/xmlui/bitstream/handle/20.500.12024/1476/alice28-1476.txt

[67] https://ota.bodleian.ox.ac.uk/repository/xmlui/bitstream/handle/20.500.12024/1740/wizoz10-1740.txt

[68] https://nlp.stanford.edu/IR-book/html/htmledition/tokenization-1.html

[69] https://nlp.stanford.edu/IR-book/

[70] https://huggingface.co/datasets

[71] https://bit.ly/3umiqP1

[72] https://huggingface.co/docs/datasets/processing.html

[73] https://radimrehurek.com/gensim/

[74] https://nlp.stanford.edu/IR-book/html/htmledition/stemming-and-lemmatization-1.html

[75] https://nlp.stanford.edu/IR-book/

[76] https://wordnet.princeton.edu/

[77] https://github.com/QData/TextAttack

[78] https://huggingface.co/transformers/main_classes/tokenizer.html

[79] https://bit.ly/2Ou06Tj

[80] https://bit.ly/2ObRNvH

[81] https://bit.ly/3ehmLxk

[82] https://lena-voita.github.io/nlp_course.html

[83] https://arxiv.org/abs/1301.3781

[84] https://jalammar.github.io/illustrated-word2vec/

[85] https://lilianweng.github.io/lil-log/2017/10/15/learning-word-embedding.html

[86] https://machinelearningmastery.com/develop-word-embeddings-python-gensim/

[87] https://www.aclweb.org/anthology/D14-1162/

[88] https://arxiv.org/abs/1802.05365

[89] https://allennlp.org/elmo

[90] https://bit.ly/2OIfmNb

[91] https://lilianweng.github.io/lil-log/2019/01/31/generalized-language-models.html

[92] https://github.com/flairNLP/flair

[93] https://github.com/flairNLP/flair/blob/master/resources/docs/TUTORIAL_1_BASICS.md

[94] https://github.com/flairNLP/flair/blob/master/resources/docs/embeddings/ELMO_EMBEDDINGS.md

[95] https://github.com/flairNLP/flair/blob/master/resources/docs/TUTORIAL_4_ELMO_BERT_FLAIR_EMBEDDING.md

[96] https://github.com/flairNLP/flair/blob/master/resources/docs/TUTORIAL_3_WORD_EMBEDDING.md

[97] https://github.com/flairNLP/flair/blob/master/resources/docs/embeddings/CLASSIC_WORD_EMBEDDINGS.md

[98] https://huggingface.co/models

[99] https://github.com/flairNLP/flair/blob/master/resources/docs/embeddings/TRANSFORMER_EMBEDDINGS.md

[100] https://github.com/flairNLP/flair/blob/master/resources/docs/TUTORIAL_5_DOCUMENT_EMBEDDINGS.md

[101] https://arxiv.org/abs/1810.04805

[102] https://yknzhu.wixsite.com/mbweb

[103] https://en.wikipedia.org/wiki/English_Wikipedia

[104] https://huggingface.co/transformers/model_doc/bert.html

[105] https://huggingface.co/bert-base-uncased

[106] https://jalammar.github.io/illustrated-bert/

[107] https://jalammar.github.io/a-visual-guide-to-using-bert-for-the-first-time/

[108] https://huggingface.co/transformers/tokenizer_summary.html

[109] https://blog.floydhub.com/tokenization-nlp/

[110] https://arxiv.org/abs/1910.01108

[111] https://huggingface.co/transformers/main_classes/configuration.html

[112] https://huggingface.co/transformers/main_classes/output.html

[113] https://bit.ly/39E4WoT

[114] https://cdn.openai.com/better-language-models/language_models_are_unsupervised_multitask_learners.pdf

[115] https://openai.com/blog/gpt-2-1-5b-release/

[116] https://github.com/openai/gpt-2

[117] https://demo.allennlp.org/next-token-lm

[118] https://huggingface.co/transformers/model_doc/gpt2.html

[119] https://huggingface.co/gpt2

[120] http://jalammar.github.io/illustrated-gpt2/

[121] https://amaarora.github.io/2020/02/18/annotatedGPT2.html

[122] https://huggingface.co/blog/how-to-generate

[123] https://github.com/huggingface/transformers/blob/master/examples/pytorch/language-modeling/run_clm.py

Index

D

N

O

P

R

S

T

U

V

Made in the USA
Middletown, DE
20 September 2022